THE CHURCH AND THE WORK

IN THREE VOLUMES

VOLUME

I. Assembly Life

II. Rethinking the Work*

III. Church Affairs

*A reprint, with new material added, of this work by the author, and known more popularly by its United States-published title of *The Normal Christian Church Life*.

THE CHURCH AND THE WORK

(In Three Volumes)

ISBN: 978-0935008586

Available from the Publishers at:

11515 Allecingie Parkway
Richmond, Virginia 23235

Printed in the United States of America

THE CHURCH AND THE WORK

I

The Church and the Work

I

Assembly Life

WATCHMAN NEE

Christian Fellowship Publishers, Inc.
New York

THE CHURCH AND THE WORK
(IN THREE VOLUMES)

TRANSLATOR'S PREFACE

In his many years of faithful service to the Lord, Watchman Nee was given much light and experience in matters concerning the church and the Work. From time to time he shared with his younger colleagues in the Work what God had shown him. Since what was shared proved to be of such great value and help to the younger brethren, his spoken ministry was subsequently compiled and published in successive stages. The first volume to appear on this particular subject of the church and the Work was entitled *Assembly Life*, which consisted of notes of a series of Bible studies the author conducted in Shanghai from February 19 to 26, 1934. It will be of interest to note that this particular Bible study series was held almost immediately after the Third Victory Conference had taken place in January 1934, at which the messages on *God's Plan and the Overcomers** were given. And hence these assembly life messages served as a supplement, or more exactly a complement, to the spiritual truths and principles released at that conference. Consequently, the emphasis of this first volume in the present trilogy is more on the practical outworking of the spiritual truths revealed, particularly as it has to do with assembly life.

These Bible studies proved to be not only timely but also needful. For it is necessary to realize that in the previous

*Watchman Nee, *God's Plan and the Overcomers* (New York: Christian Fellowship Publishers, 1977), translated from the Chinese as a synopsis of these messages, the original manuscript of the full text (containing over 100,000 words) having been destroyed during political upheavals in China.—*Translator*

decade—commencing with the years 1926-27 when the work by Watchman Nee and a few others of kindred spirit began in Shanghai—God had raised up many brothers and sisters in different localities with the same vision as theirs; and there was therefore the need for clarification and instruction on the various aspects of assembly life.

After this first volume of the present trilogy was published and its contents carried into practice, many more assemblies were raised up and many more workers were, in the sovereignty of God, joined to the Work. As a result, in 1937 Watchman Nee convened two separate conferences in Shanghai and Hankow. The talks given there were directed towards his younger colleagues. "At these two conferences," wrote the author later, "we sought in the first place to examine the teaching of God's word concerning His churches and His Work, and in the second place to review our past missions in the light of our findings."* Within a year afterwards the talks which Watchman Nee had delivered at these two conferences on the churches and the Work were published in Chinese at Shanghai in January 1938 under the title, *Rethinking the Work.* Later while in England on a visit during the years 1938-39, the author translated the volume into English at London where it was published in April 1939 under the title *Concerning Our Missions*** and which forms the second volume of the present trilogy on the church and the Work.

After the publication in Shanghai of *Rethinking the Work,* the Work in China expanded into the interior as a result of war (the Sino-Japanese conflict which erupted in mid-1937). Moreover, the workers became separated from one another due to

---

*See his "Introduction" to *Rethinking the Work* (January 1938), in Volume Two of this present trilogy.—*Translator*

**Long afterwards, *Concerning Our Missions* has come to be more popularly known and read under the title of *The Normal Christian Church Life,* first published in the United States by the International Students Press (Washington, D.C.) in 1962.—*Translator*

the division of the country into Occupied and Free China. With the conclusion of the war in 1945, a new situation arose which required a further reconsideration of the Work. This new situation centered around the need for better coordination in the Work as well as the need for additional workers. Once again fresh light was sought and given in the Scriptures. Training sessions were held at Kuling Mountain outside Foochow during the years of 1948 and 1949. At the first of these sessions on August 19, 1948, a talk was given by the author on the principles of "the church is local" and "the Work is regional," which according to their respective emphasis later came to be known as "the Antioch principle" and "the Jerusalem principle."* At these same sessions a further series of lectures was also delivered by him on the general topic of our behavior in the house of God. And thus the third volume of this present trilogy constitutes a compilation of these talks and is entitled *Church Affairs*.

Hence it can perhaps be seen why it has been thought valuable to add this third volume to the second even as the second has been added to the first. These three are not contradictory but are rather complementary, for through the years more light was given in the Scriptures and more experience was added to the practice. The first volume treats principally the basic subject of assembly life; the second volume deals preeminently with the topic of the church; while the third volume, although admittedly engaged in a general discussion of church affairs that relate to believers' behavior in God's house, is nonetheless primarily concerned with the matter of the Work, since such affairs are viewed from the standpoint of the Work itself.

In presenting these three volumes as a trilogy on the church and the Work, it might be useful to make a few remarks. *First of all*, it should be understood by the reader from the very

*This talk serves as the opening chapter of Volume Three of this present trilogy.—*Translator*

outset that the contents of this trilogy is limited to the subject matter dealt with, that is to say, it is limited to the subject of the church and the Work. As the author himself pointed out when writing his Preface to the English translation of Volume Two of this present trilogy, he would have preferred to have had those books translated "which better represent" his ministry, for from today's vantage point, the ministry of the author in its totality is of a much fuller and more spiritual nature than is that which is to be found in these three volumes now before the reader. Nevertheless, the technical side of Christianity cannot be neglected, because spiritual reality has its practical outworking. As Watchman Nee wrote in his introduction to *Rethinking the Work* (1938): "It is death to have a wine-skin without wine, but it is loss to have wine without a wine-skin. We must have the wine-skin after we have the wine. Paul wrote the Ephesian epistle, but he could also write the Corinthian epistle; and Corinthians presents us with Ephesian truths in practical expression."

Second, in spite of the special character of this trilogy, which focuses on the practical aspect of the local church and the Work, it was far from Watchman Nee's intention that these volumes should ever be followed as a manual. To the contrary, his real aim was to show the practicality of all spiritual truths.* Methods are mentioned as illustrations, not as mandatory procedures. Spiritual truths must be applied spiritually; that is to say, they need to be crystallized into forms given by the Holy Spirit at each particular time and in each set of circumstances. Hence principles never change, but practices will frequently need adjustments.

Third, the various contents of the volumes in this trilogy are presented according to the time sequence in which they

---

*See, for example, the author's very clear remarks on this entire point in both his "Preface" (1939) and "Introduction" (1938) to *Concerning Our Missions*, which the reader can find in Volume Two of this present trilogy under the original title, of course, of *Rethinking the Work*.—*Translator*

were first presented. And thus they give us a more complete developmental understanding of the Scriptural concept of the churches and the Work as Watchman Nee gradually came to see it. There is, however, more than mere historical value to be gained from these volumes. The principles herein laid down are as relevant to our day as they were in the years in which they were first presented, even though the application of these truths is always to be flexible.

Fourth and finally, even though in these volumes Watchman Nee uses the terms "apostles," "elders," and "deacons," it was clearly his understanding that it is the function, and *not* the title, of these offices which is essential. A New Testament church is not realized by simply having elders and deacons appointed, nor is the New Testament Work truly recognized by merely calling workers apostles. The reality, not the appearance, is what God is recovering today.

This trilogy on the church and the Work is now being released to the English-speaking world with the prayer that it may serve as a reference for all who diligently study God's word and honestly desire to keep it.

Volume One

ASSEMBLY LIFE

TRANSLATOR'S PREFACE

The purpose of God is to establish Christ—and not just the personal Christ but also the corporate Christ, which is the Church: "as the body is one, and hath many members, and all the members of the body, being many, are one body; so also is the Christ" (1 Cor. 12.12 Darby). The work of the Holy Spirit in these past two thousand years has been centered on building this body of Christ. We will fail God in seeing His purpose and fail the Holy Spirit in cooperating with His work if we are not "holding fast the Head, from whom all the body, being supplied and knit together through the joints and bands, increaseth with the increase of God" (Col. 2.19). The body of Christ is not only most spiritual but also most practical. It is an earthly testimony as well as a heavenly body. All its spiritual principles must be and can be practiced in a local assembly. Here in these pages, therefore, we shall find that Watchman Nee shares with us the practical aspects of the assembly life. He touches on such practical matters as authority in the church, ministry in the church, church fellowship, church meetings, and the boundary of a local assembly.

It is important for the reader to remember that this volume emphasizes only the practical side of the Church, and hence concentrates on the life of the local assembly. There is another side of the Church—that of the spiritual principles inherent in the Church universal—which is *not* the subject of this book. To maintain the right balance and to obtain the whole concept of the Church, both the principle and the practice, both the universal and the local, must be received and kept. For it must never be forgotten that a new wine-skin is for containing the new wine; and therefore the first without the second is meaningless.

May the Head of the Church find himself expressed corporately among His people.

CONTENTS

Being a sequence of messages given by the author during a series of Bible studies he conducted in Shanghai, China, from February 19th to 26th, 1934.

Scripture quotations are from the American Standard Version of the Bible (1901), unless otherwise indicated.

Introduction

The purpose of this special series of meetings is for us to search the word of God together on the particular subject of assembly life. At the outset we will not read all the passages in the Scriptures which touch upon this topic; we will only refer to them as we proceed in our Bible study.

During the Victory Conference recently concluded* and which preceded this special series of Bible study meetings, we touched on the will of God which He had planned before the foundation of the world. God's purpose is for men to have His life, and to be like His Son. His purpose is to establish Christ—yet not just the personal Christ but also the corporate Christ. And this corporate Christ is the Church. Thus, we have been made aware of the significance of the Church in the eyes of God today. Unfortunately, carnal believers currently pay no attention to God's emphasis, and even spiritual believers are failing to set their priority straight. They often replace the Church of God with their many works.

To substitute the Church of God with some work is what Satan tempts people to do today. But we know God's purpose from the beginning to the end is to obtain a corporate Christ—

*An outline synopsis (96 pages) of the series of messages given at this conference by the author can be found in Watchman Nee, *God's Plan and the Overcomers* (New York: Christian Fellowship Publishers, 1977), translated from the Chinese.—*Translator*

the Church—so that Christ himself may be the Head and the believers may be the members of the body. Yet how Satan is determined to destroy this plan! And that is why he deceives men into putting in place of the Church this or that work.

What do we mean when we say this? Well, today some greatly emphasize evangelism. They are substituting the work of evangelism for the Church. We know many are most able to preach the gospel and win souls, and no one can deny that evangelism is a good work. But to so make it a substitute for the Church that people will not think of the Church can turn out to be a deception of Satan. I believe what I say here ought to be emphasized because we need to see that the ultimate reason God wants the gospel preached is to prepare individual living stones for the corporate Christ, and it would therefore be wrong to substitute the Church with evangelism.

Some believers form missions, encouraging people to preach the gospel abroad. They are zealous in giving contributions and in sending people out. Yet why is it that today many of them only know missions but not the Church? This is because from eternity God's eyes have been upon the Church whereas in this age men's eyes have been upon missions; they have forgotten the Church.

"God never establishes missions; He only establishes the Church," said Mr. Gordon. Yet today people create mission boards, set up evangelistic organizations, establish schools and hospitals, open orphanages and "endeavor" societies to help the needy ones. Are these undertakings good? They are all good. But if these are erected as substitutes for the Church, God will not be satisfied. Can we not see the cunning hand of the enemy in all this? Satan cleverly entices people to substitute the Church—which God has prepared in His eternal will to establish—with the work He will use. How we need to have our eyes opened so that we may focus our attention on the Church, since God's aim is the life of the Church—which is the life of the body of Christ.

Many Christians may declare that they have not formed missions, endeavor societies, Sunday schools, hospitals, schools, and so forth. That may be true; but let me ask this: What have you been doing? A great many of you think that as long as you are zealous, victorious and holy, you are fine. Allow me to speak frankly that these achievements are not what God is after, for they are not His ultimate aim. I do not say zeal, victory and holiness are not important. All these *are* important. But God's ultimate aim does not lie in them. God wants a corporate Church, a spiritual home. He does not want isolated, individual stones or bricks. He desires a body, not just a member. He wants Christ to have the preeminence in the Church, to be her Head. Although stones and bricks are definitely needed, they do not answer to God's ultimate purpose.

During the years you have been a Christian, how often have you thought of what God really seeks? Have you ever thought of the Church? Or is it that what you ponder about is how to pray, how to overcome sin, how to lead sinners to Christ, or how to study the Bible well? Do you consider these matters or the Church? Since what God aims at is having the Church, then whatever falls short of it falls short of His aim. I do not say that these various matters mentioned are not significant and good. I only say that whatever comes short of the Church does not fulfill God's purpose. It is well to have Sunday schools, orphanages, "endeavor" societies, and gospel preaching. Nevertheless, such activities and establishments cannot be compared to the Church of God and must never be a substitution for it. God desires and greatly loves the Church. The Lord Jesus even died for the Church. And the Holy Spirit has been outpoured for the Church.

Throughout the New Testament we can find this very principle, that everything is for the Church: "Christ also loved the church, and gave himself up for it" (Eph. 5.25). He has risen from the dead and is now far above all rule and authority and power and dominion. He is to be "head over all things to the church" (Eph. 1.22). Indeed, the Lord is building the Church upon this rock. The work of the Holy Spirit in these past two thousand years has been to establish the Church. God saves sinners and gives them victory in order to build the Church. He bestows apostles, prophets, evangelists, pastors and teachers upon the Church for its edification. It is also declared that Christ is to sanctify the Church, "having cleansed it by the washing of water with the word, that he might present the church to himself a glorious church, not having spot or wrinkle or any such thing; but that it should be holy and without blemish" (Eph. 5.26,27). All this too is for the Church. The final goal of God is to have the New Jerusalem, which is a type or figure of the Church. The entire Bible, in fact, is centered upon this ultimate end.

Hence let me say emphatically that if today our aim, work and living are not for the Church—so as to accomplish this that the Lord desires—then we are a great failure. May the Lord have mercy on us, delivering us from our petty ideas so that we may enter into His thought and into that which God has revealed in the Bible.

As we have said, then, God's aim is the Church. What He purposes to obtain is the New Jerusalem. And today He puts this purpose before men. He takes the Church, which New Jerusalem represents, and puts it as a unit in each city. Before New Jerusalem descends from heaven, God wants to have a miniature New Jerusalem in each city. This is to say that He wants to have a church in each city to manifest His eternal purpose. From start to finish, the greatest work of God is to build up the body of Christ. He would therefore like to establish a local assembly in each city. This serves as a miniature of the great Church of God—a diminutive manifestation of New Jerusalem—since the horizon of God's purpose is too vast a thing to be grasped in its totality. And hence in every city there is a miniature. God gathers together all who are saved in the city and makes them a local assembly. Thus is the will of God manifested.

Perhaps it would be helpful to explain it in this way: Suppose you are going abroad by way of an ocean liner. You ask the clerk of the steamship company where your room is, for the ship is so huge that it looks like a city to you. The clerk can help you by showing you in his office a model built after the likeness of the big ship; except that of course it is a miniature. Going to the ship's model he will open up deck after deck to you and show you how you may find your way to your room. So that when you at last board the ocean liner, you are able to find your assigned room with ease. Now in like manner, the New Jerusalem of God's eternal purpose is so immense that He must set in each city a local assembly as a representative model of His will. And thus the various things concerning this small model of the great Church of God—such as things in regard to meeting, for example—can be examined by us without too much difficulty.

After so many years of working in China to preach the gospel, few people have come to notice what God himself emphasizes and is after. The Roman Catholic Church, for instance, came to China over three hundred years ago. And if we count from the time of the arrival of the Nestorian Church, it can be said that Christianity has been in our land for over a thousand years. Yet it would appear that few people have ever given attention to this miniature expression of God's eternal purpose. We instead stress personal victory and works. We fail to see how to express God's will concerning the church in a locality. May God be gracious to us that we may understand that personal victory and works and these other things mentioned are nothing in themselves. They are indeed related to the local assembly, but they can never take the place of the church, since God establishes the local assembly as the center. All these other things flow into and are joined to this center. Consequently, our concern today should not merely be about victory, evangelism, or prayers answered; it should go a step further to include asking ourselves how we can be coordinated with other brothers and sisters.

Fukien is famous for its masonry work. Masons in that province are able to cut irregular stones and put them together beautifully. Unlike the stone walls on Kuling Mountain which are merely composed of stones piled together, these stones in Fukien are carefully hewed and fitted compactly together. The question in these skilled workers' minds is not whether a stone is big or small, nice looking or ugly; rather, it is how does this or that stone fit with the other stones? Can these stones be built into a house? Today many Christians are truly nice looking and smooth, but they cannot be put together because they are either this or that in such a way that they cannot be fitted in with other Christians. We know that every saved person is a living stone. The issue, however, is not centered upon whether he can overcome or whether the other has power; instead, it is focused on whether this living stone or that living stone can fit in with other stones so as to leave no gaps.

When we as living stones come together on the Lord's Day morning to listen to messages delivered, and come in the evening to break bread, can we be viewed as stones that are being fitted together? Or when we seek to be good brothers and sisters, is such seeking for the purpose of helping a meeting—that is to say, of helping the church? What we are now about to embark upon in our studies together is to take the broader view of the Church about which we have been speaking and to extend it into a consideration of those smaller, more practical matters as are raised by just such questions as these which have been asked.

The larger principles pertaining to the Church we have already touched upon at some length—both in the conference only recently concluded and in our preliminary remarks just now. From this point onwards, however, our emphasis will be to focus attention not so much on the spiritual principles of the Church but on its practices—how in various ways we can be good brothers and sisters in assembly life. In this connection, then, we shall be studying such aspects as the authority and the ministry of the church, how to meet, how to maintain unity, and so forth. Yet it needs to be pointed out that although we shall now be dealing primarily with the outward matters of the Church, we must recognize the fact that these outward things do nevertheless still contain spiritual elements in them all. And this we should constantly keep in mind as we go through these studies together.

1 Authority in the Church

In order to understand authority in the Church, we must first know what authority is; otherwise, we will never come to grips with it.

What is authority? There is nothing in the universe more difficult to explain than this. The Bible speaks of two matters difficult to interpret: glory and authority. What is holiness, righteousness, gentleness or patience? Many seem to have little difficulty in understanding these matters. But what can the glory of God and the authority of God mean? Few can really comprehend and expound these two things. The first is related to God himself; the second is related to His government. God himself is glorious, and His government is maintained by His authority.

God's authority is that law or principle by which He organizes the universe. He rules His creation with authority. How, in the first place, did God create the heavens and the earth? By authority. How did He restore the world? Again, by authority. It is most amazing that when on the first day he made the light, He did not as it were collect massive amounts of electricity and make light. Not at all. He simply gave the command, Let there be light, and there was light. Similarly on the second day, He said, Let there be a firmament, and there was a firmament. He gives his command in word and does everything by means of authority. Word here represents command, which in turn represents authority. It is not by power nor by method. Do you now see that God uses only authority? By it He created the universe, and by it He also rules the universe. Both the beginning of the universe and its continuity ever since subsist through the authority of God.

In the beginning—after the universe was created—we know that God set up cherubim or archangels to rule all things. God himself has the preeminence over all things, and He ruled the first world through His cherubim. At a certain point, however, sin came in. Now sin is lawlessness, and lawlessness is basically the overturning of God's authority. And the fall of one of God's cherubs (Lucifer) who becomes Satan was due to this very thing of lawlessness, because as the Bible explains, he wanted to exalt himself to be equal with God. Thereafter, sin entered the world as well, and again it was due to lawlessness, because as we are told in Genesis, Eve did not submit herself to Adam. In the absence of any command from her husband, she ate the fruit of the tree of the knowledge of good and evil.

Although the world is now full of sins, authority is still the principle of God's government in relation to the world. We may easily notice the authority that has been established by God in many areas of earthly life: wives are to be subject to their husbands, servants are to be subject to their masters, employees to their employers, students to their teachers, citizens to various governmental or administrative officials, subordinates to their chiefs—the latter classes in all these relationships are authorities that have been set up by God. For He wants men to be submissive to authority. These authorities are not only appointed by God, they also represent God. It is clearly stated in the Letter to the Romans: "There is no power but of God; and the powers that be are ordained of God" (13.1). No Christian student should boycott a class, no Christian laborer should strike, no Christian son or daughter should be unfilial, no Christian people should rise up in insurrection. For if they do these things, they are not merely overthrowing the people directly over them whom they oppose, they are also overturning the very authority of God. What God uses to create and to sustain the universe is His authority. Both Lucifer and Adam tried to subvert that authority, and thus both had sinned; for whoever in God's created order does not recognize authority or submit to it is guilty of lawlessness, and lawlessness, as we have seen, is sin.

Many believers have never perceived this marvelous thing called authority. To be a good Christian one must know what authority is, because it represents God. By tracing authority to its highest source, you will eventually see God. This is why a Christian should not only submit to the chief executive and the other officials of his country but also to the police on the street. You cannot despise a policeman because he may earn so little a month. He has authority, and he represents not only the government but also God, for there is no authority in the world except it be of God. Oh, do let us see that the Bible is very strict on this point. Paul, Peter and Jude are all in agreement with this word found in the book of Acts: "Thou shalt not speak evil of a ruler of thy people" (23.5). In our conversation, therefore, we should be careful not to vilify the leaders of our government.

In the book of Jude it is recorded that when the angel Michael contended with the devil about the body of Moses, Michael did not bring against Satan a railing judgment, but said, "The Lord rebuke thee" (v.9). This is because at one time Michael had been a subordinate angel to Lucifer (Satan) the archangel. Hence he simply said, "The Lord rebuke thee." He did not speak on his own; he only appealed to the higher authority of God. Michael knew what authority was, and thus he dared not reprimand the devil by himself.

When our Lord was on earth, He was completely under authority. While young, He was in subjection to His parents' authority. He kept all their rules. Though He is the Creator, He accepted all the limitations in being a man. He did indeed say to His mother, "Knew ye not that I must be in my Father's house?" (Luke 2.49) Yet had you or I uttered these words, we would not have returned home with our parents to continue being subject to them. But how different was the Lord. He obediently went down with them. And when much later He stepped into public ministry, He was in subjection to the authority of the government of the day. Even when He was unfairly judged, He still was subject to its authority. He did not revile those in authority. He allowed them to inflict their worst on Him. Never has the world seen a person so submissive to authority as He was.

Once Paul stood before the Jewish council to be judged. He was truly willing to be in subjection to authority. When the high priest commanded those who stood by him to strike him on the mouth, Paul, not knowing it was the high priest, said to him, "God shall smite thee, thou whited wall"! (Acts 23.3) But when he was told he should not revile the high priest, Paul quickly apologized. From the Scriptures we may readily discern how very important this matter of authority is.

The biblical word which is coupled with that of authority is "submission," with the Bible therefore speaking of authority on the one hand and submission on the other. Authority and submission are interrelated. If a person is submissive, he is in subjection to God's authority. Otherwise, he is one who will try to overturn the authority of God.

In the Church God established His authority, to which we all must be in subjection. We need to submit to authority in our home, in society, and in the world. God has ordained that we submit to such authority. Let us lay hold of this principle. All who think of overthrowing authority are in reality those who think of overturning God. Do not imagine that we may be in subjection to God while at the same time we are disobedient to our parents or are rebellious against husbands or masters or school principals or whoever else is in authority. Never can this be. If we do not submit to these authorities whom God has ordained on earth, how can we obey God? By the same token, if we are not in subjection to the authority in the church, we are being disobedient to God.

What I am concerned about is that many brothers and sisters come here to meet with different motives in their hearts. Some come probably for the sake of exercising mutual love and care. That is good. Let it be known, however, that we are not without authority in our midst. We do have authority here in our midst, and we must learn to submit to it. How frequently Christians harbor a wrong concept within them which says that to come out of a sect is to be free to do anything, that hereafter everybody is equal and nobody can reprove the other. To them it is a free-for-all situation; everyone can be lawless. Let me say, though, that it is a great mistake if anyone should have left the oppressive control of a sect (as true as that may have been) so that he might do anything he pleases elsewhere. Please understand that, due to the authority which is found here, you will perhaps experience even more restraint.

People leave sects out of three different motivations—(1) They are disappointed in the sect. A person, for example, may have expected to become a pastor there but was unable to arrive at his aspiration. So he leaves after he has quarreled with someone in the sect. (2) They seek freedom. Some have left their sect because they were under man's control and restriction. They wanted to be free-lance evangelists who would not receive any salary nor accept any control. They wished to move according to their pleasure. Yet let us see that there is no such thing as a free-style evangelist before God. Instead, believers have the life of "the body." Believers have to accept the restriction of the church; they do not have absolute freedom. And (3) they see the body of Christ. They began to realize on the one hand that division and party is of the flesh, and so they left the sect in order to come out of human restriction and to work according to the leading of the Holy Spirit. On the other hand, they also began to see the body of Christ. They commenced to realize that whatever they do must be restricted by the brethren. They were willing to learn to be members in the body. (Unfortunately, many who have come out of large sects have not seen the body of Christ, and have themselves then become a small sect. They failed to see how they must accept restraint from the brothers and sisters.)

From God's standpoint, only the third class of people above have the right motive. For the purpose of God is for His people to obtain body life and to abstain from independent action. God sets authority in the Church and He wishes to manifest His authority there. Accordingly, each member needs to learn to submit to God's authority and to accept the restraint of other members. Every brother or sister must see negatively the error of sectarianism and see positively the body of Christ, in which there is no independent action.

What Is Authority in the Church?

How is divine authority in the Church delegated? The authorities which God sets in the Church are the elders and the apostles. God appoints the first in a local assembly, He appoints the second in the midst of many assemblies. The authority of an apostle is over various assemblies, whereas the authority of an elder is in the local assembly. In order to manifest His authority in the Church, God sets up elders in local assemblies to represent His authority. Hence the other name used in Scripture for elder is "bishop," which carries within its meaning the sense of authority in his "overseership." The Bible instructs us to submit to the elders because they have authority. And because all authorities initiated by God are representative in character, so the authority of the elders is also representative—to manifest the authority of God. Irrespective of how well the elders represent divine authority, a Christian must nonetheless learn to submit to them because all authorities are of God.

At the inauguration of any gathering of believers in a locality, there are no elders. But gradually some people who commence to function like elders will begin to be manifested within the group. As was mentioned already, elder and bishop are different names for the same office. The term elder points to the person, while bishop points to the service. Furthermore, the elders in the Bible are always plural and never singular in number. For things are less likely to go wrong when the spirits of two, three, or more persons are receiving the same guidance. Individualism is never a biblical principle; it can easily lead to error.

How God Appoints Elders

How does God appoint elders? In a gathering, there will be a few brothers who appear to be more advanced spiritually than the rest. They seem to have a better testimony, and they do desire to perform the work of an eldership. They begin to function as elders would. Accordingly, an apostle will make them elders to serve the local brethren. The church at Ephesus can serve as a good example of this. At first there were only saved believers in Ephesus because elders had not yet been appointed. But on the second visit of the relevant apostle (in this case, Paul), we find elders are there. The first apostolic trip which Paul took out from Antioch was for the purpose of preaching the gospel and saving souls. Later on, he established elders in each city previously visited (Acts 14.23). Before an assembly is established, the saints are weak, and therefore they need support. But when individuals are raised up to take the responsibility of elders, the apostle concerned will appoint them.

In other instances, however, the apostles were unable to go

to places to appoint elders, and so they sent special envoys to perform the task. Timothy, Titus and others were such persons sent by the apostles. They went to different cities and appointed elders to take local responsibility in the church according to the order of the apostles.

Since the appointment of elders is for the purpose of representing the authority of God, these elders should understand that Christ is the Head and that He desires to express His will in the Church. They need to seek the mind of the Lord in order to manifest His authority in the assembly. For God uses these men to make decisions on matters as to whether to proceed or to stop. All the other brethren in the assembly need to learn to submit to them. Naturally we do not expect anyone to control us, but these elders do not lord it over us; they simply represent God's delegated authority, to which we submit ourselves.

What God has ordained from eternity are both authority and submission. Yet many believers do not like to submit to authority. The world today is full of lawlessness, and I am afraid "the mystery of lawlessness" (2 Thess. 2.7) has already infiltrated the Church. How greatly children criticize their parents without fear, how often wives dominate their husbands, how much students attack their principals and teachers, and how laborers freely strike against their companies! Such things are rampant in our time. Even as the Scriptures predict, now is the time when "the lawless one shall be revealed" (2 Thess. 2.8). If we Christians are not careful, we too will be following after the Antichrist instead of Christ himself. How can we ever expect others to submit to authority if we ourselves do not submit to it? If God should be pleased to place some in the position of authority, we others should learn to submit to them: "Obey them that have the rule over you, and submit to them: for they watch in behalf of your souls, as they that shall give account" (Heb. 13.17). In the light of this, we need to submit to the elders.

The Title and the Appointment of Elders

To briefly sum up, then, (1) elders are bishops, (2) elders are plural in number, and (3) elders are appointed by apostles or those specially sent by them. Today we know that the question of apostles (as to whether they exist) is unresolved. How, then, will the elders be chosen? From a study of God's word, we would agree to the following deduction: Since the question of apostles is still unsettled, there is no way to appoint elders officially. We cannot give the title of elder to anyone. If we were to do so, we would have to ask where the apostle is who can appoint the elders. Having said this, however, we do not mean to say that there are not men today who can *function* as elders. Though there may not be the *title* of elders today, there nevertheless are men in every place who are like elders and who do the work of the eldership. They act as informal or unofficial elders. Yet the question still remains, How are they raised up? Who asks them to act as elders informally? We must answer that they are appointed by the informal apostles.

Though this question of apostles remains controversial, there is nonetheless a class of people today who are performing the works of apostles—such works as preaching the gospel and establishing churches. They confess that they fall short of the holiness, power, victory and labor of the apostles because they can only do a small portion—perhaps one thousandth—of the works of the early apostles. Yet God uses these people in our day to labor in various places just as He used the apostles in the earlier days. Formerly it was these apostles who established churches everywhere, but now it is these informal apostles who do such work. We admit they are far inferior to the early apostles, that they are not worthy to be called apostles; nevertheless, we cannot but acknowledge them as doing part of the apostolic work. These men are those whom God uses in today's ruinous state of the Church as apostles.

God uses these servants to save sinners and to gather

believers together. They are therefore the most qualified persons to help those believers whom they lead and to know who among them should receive honor and act as elders. We who labor in apostolic work are only helping the brethren to submit to these local men. We must be careful lest we fall into the traditional concept of apostolic succession or the special teaching that bishops have apostolic authority. Suppose, for example, that brother Chu is laboring in Potung and that he has led people to Christ. If he asks brother Wang to come to appoint elders, the latter will not know whom to appoint, for only brother Chu knows the local condition. He has led them and nourished them. He knows their spiritual state because he cares for their souls. He alone can help the brethren there to submit to those few among them who function as elders.

We cannot but submit to authority. May God give us humility. If we are not to act as elders, then we are to submit to people who are as elders. We need to learn to be submissive people. If our flesh has been deeply judged, we will view submission to be something easy, beautiful and sweet. But wherever the flesh is *not* judged, the church will never be built there. If the brethren have their flesh dealt with, there will be no problem in submission. Hence those who do the work of apostles ought to assist the brethren to see who should act as elders and how they should submit to these men.

Qualifications of Elders

The qualifications of elders is clearly described in the Scriptures. The elders must be able to rule their families as well as their own selves. They must know how to deal with outsiders. They must have firm assurance of God's truth and be apt to teach the truth. Let us briefly describe the various qualifications as follows:

(1) *Self-controlled.* Why must elders be self-controlled? Because how can one rule over the church if he is unable to

control his temper? To rule over one's own heart and spirit is harder to do than anything else. He who is not in subjection to the authority of Christ cannot make others submit to Christ. Paul's letters of I Timothy and Titus speak of elders being temperate and not brawlers. These traits all point to the matter of self-control.

Furthermore, an elder must be the husband of one wife. All who have concubines cannot be elders, because this would indicate that there is lack of self-control.

(2) *Rule over one's house well.* He who does not know how to rule his own house is unfit to rule the church. How can he manage the brethren if he cannot manage his own children? Eldership is a position, not a gift. To be an evangelist is to have a gift, but to be an elder speaks of having a position in the church. For this reason, an elder needs to be experienced and capable of ruling. And his house is his test. If he is unable to be a good husband and good father for his wife and children to submit to him, he cannot be an elder in the church. God uses an elder's own wife and children to test him first as to whether or not he is able to deal with brothers and sisters.

Then, too, God uses a person's work such as in a business firm, at school, or at a hospital to test that one. If he is able to manage a business or to run a school, he may have the potential for governing the church. Should he be totally unable in these matters, then how can he rule the church of God?

(3) *Good testimony.* An elder must have a good testimony from those that are without the church. Because he must represent the church, sometimes he will have to contact the world. If he does not have a good testimony before the world, the entire church will be despised. A person who has a bad name in the world may not necessarily be bad, for the greedy, selfish, unclean Adamic world almost always speaks evilly of people; rarely does it speak well of anyone, especially of the Christian. But if that man has a good name in the world, then there must indeed be some good about him. Hence, a good tes-

timony is what is an acceptable qualification; a bad name cannot be acceptable.

(4) *Holding firmly the truth of God.* An elder manages church affairs, not the affairs of a business firm. Managing the latter does not require the bearing of a testimony, a faithfulness to truth, or an ability to teach the Bible. An elder, though, must be apt to teach the brothers and sisters. He is the doorkeeper of the church. If all the brothers want to preach, what has to be done? The elders will need to discern who should and who should not speak. Those who are flippant and without a good testimony should not speak. The elders can either encourage or discourage brothers. And thus the elders need a firm grasp of truth so that they may correctly decide; if not, they will fail to discern and will thus consider every brother to be good in speaking.

Furthermore, elders must be able to discern and decide in other matters. They must know what teaching is false and not allow it to enter the church, and what truth they must accept into the church. In this way, the brethren will not become confused.

The Responsibility of the Elders

(1) *Elders are bishops.* The Bible calls the elders bishops. The work of a bishop is to oversee from above, he having special insight in seeing beforehand any danger in the assembly, both individually and corporately. With there being so many brothers and sisters in the church, it is inevitable that there will be sins, strifes, dishonesty, debts, or other such infamous deeds among them. These matters await the attention of the responsible brothers who act as elders. For the leaven must not be permitted to come into the assembly. It is therefore the duty of these informal elders to deal with such confusions. They will visit these brothers and sisters who have created problems and try to deal with these situations. When such dealings occur, the

brethren should learn to submit to the decisions of the elders, for they have the authority of the Lord.

The authority advocated by the Roman Catholic Church is too excessive. Its failure lies in having the appearance but not the reality of authority. To have the right authority, its authority figures must be joined to the source of authority which is God himself.

(2) *The elders decide and express the views of the church.* Concerning the views of the church, the elders are the ones to publicly express them. It is not left to the individual brethren to freely express their opinions as being those of the church. Otherwise, this will overturn the authority of the elders. All public declarations, reports and doctrinal views must be decided and/or promulgated by the elders. A believer may speak only for himself, but the elders speak for the entire assembly. Because they themselves are subject to the Head, they are able to speak on behalf of the church.

(3) *The elders oversee the sisters meetings.* The Bible calls for only the brothers to be elders, and not the sisters as well. The place which God assigned to the sisters is not one of ruling, but one of being ruled. God does not permit women to rule the church. In the Bible there are mentioned deaconesses as well as deacons, but there is no woman elder. This would indicate that in the management of church affairs, God sets man as head of the women. Sisters should therefore learn to be submissive by God's grace. They may serve as they are given gifts; but they should leave decisions to those who are responsible as elders.

Sisters, for example, may bear witness to other sisters who want to be baptized or to break the bread, but the final decision is left to the elders. Being gifted by God, sisters may indeed receive honor from the brethren. Yet from the Scriptures we see that authority is more important than gift, that truth is more essential than ability.

As another example, if the sisters want to have a sisters meeting of the church at a certain time, they may express their thought and desire to the responsible brothers, who will consider whether such request is proper and give their consent accordingly. And thus the sisters move in unity instead of moving independently. Their meeting will then be reckoned as one of the church meetings.

Why must the sisters go through such a procedure? Because they are usually more emotional, hence more easily deceived. The elders have the responsibility of protecting the sisters. Every matter which pertains to the church should be decided by one of the responsible brothers. And as the sisters are under the proper covering, they are protected and so are kept from many problems.

In all corporate, not private, matters the elders should take responsibility. This includes the sisters.

(4) *The elders take care of all matters concerning meetings and preaching.* Those who serve as elders must restrain any wrongdoing in the church. In a church meeting, for instance, some brothers—who do not have the gift of teaching, yet love to teach as if addicted to it—might stand up and say things which ought not be said. (Strangely enough, the more gifted that people are, the less they like to speak, because they want to be hidden. I wish more of them would be less reserved and speak more.) Those who act as elders must therefore restrain whatever is improperly done. If there is any inappropriate prayer or speaking or report from any of the brethren, the elders should explain to them after the meeting so that it will not be repeated. If not, the same act will recur and the weak brethren will be offended or harmed.

Please note that there is no strict organization among us. We will receive all believers who are in the denominations. Our door is wide open. All in the denominations who are saved can come and break bread with us. However, if said people, after breaking bread with us, should purposely draw away some brothers and sisters to their homes to listen to some divisive teachings, such action should be reported immediately to the elders so that division may be prevented. Today we are not without personal liberty, but we can enjoy the limited freedom of the assembly only under the authority and arrangement of God. How often a little leaven may be introduced and soon a party is formed to the detriment of the whole lump. Brethren must therefore take note of these things and learn to submit to authority lest they do something unapproved.

(5) *The elders decide on matters pertaining to the Lord's Day meetings and on the writing of commendatory letters.* The elders should decide whether the meeting on the Lord's Day should be in the morning or in the afternoon. Regarding letters of commendation, it is not for just any brother to write as he pleases. Naturally, anyone can introduce people to the brethren at other localities, but only the elders can write on behalf of the church. This ought to help us to see that the elders are responsible for the whole assembly. They are to oversee all things in the church. The elders must learn to exercise authority and to do things well, while the brethren must learn how to submit.

(6) *Elders are to set examples.* After elders are recognized, they deserve the respect of the brethren. At the same time, they themselves should take up responsibility with fear and trembling. They ought to see themselves as really being without any authority. The Bible lays the two sides of this truth together in a marvelous way. From the viewpoint of the brethren, the elders represent God's authority, and therefore they must submit. From the viewpoint of the elders, they deem themselves to be without authority. Now upon hearing about the authority of the elders, will we not be fearful lest they misuse their divinely delegated authority? What if they try to lord it over us? But God in His word speaks to the elders on this wise: "The elders therefore among you I exhort . . . Tend the flock of God which is among you, exercising the oversight . . .; neither as lording it over the charge allotted to you, but making yourselves ensamples to the flock" (1 Peter 5.1-3). By this we see

that the elders do not have any authority in themselves; they only have the authority of God. Only when they are in Christ, fully understanding God's mind and accordingly expressing it, do they really have authority. They are not to lord it over the flock, but need to be careful of themselves that they submit to God's authority and thus be examples to the flock. Only in this way will brothers and sisters see their authority. On the one hand, the brethren should submit to the authority of Christ which the elders represent. On the other hand, the elders must see that they have no authority in their own selves; they are simply to be examples (see 1 Timothy, Titus, and Acts 20 for more details on the authority of the elders.)

(7) *Accusation against an Elder.* 1 Timothy tells us this: "Against an elder receive not an accusation, except at the mouth of two or three witnesses" (5.19). In this matter, we must notice two things. First, there must be a written accusation. A spoken accusation is not to be accepted because people can so easily change their words and hence there not be sufficient evidence. Second, there must be two or three witnesses. To rely on but one person's witness is not trustworthy. The Bible requires two or three as a minimum number of witnesses. In view of this, workers or special envoys of the workers must take special care in dealing with such matters as accusations against an elder. Once again, let me call your attention to this fact, that since there are no official apostles nor official elders today, people who function in the work of the apostles or elders are responsible for undertaking such discipline as may be required in such a situation.

Elders in Relation to Elders of Other Assemblies

God's gift is not restricted by environment; but position *is* limited to environment. God's giftings in such areas of ministry as evangelism, pastoring or teaching may be exercised anywhere. For these are God's gifts to the whole Church; that is to say, they are for all the local assemblies (see Eph. 4.11,12). Hence one who is doing the work of an apostle should not take care of one assembly and serve as a pastor in the denomination today. The Bible does not give any warrant to having such a position. If one is a teacher, he can teach in whatever place to which he may go. If he cannot preach in one place, he will not be able to preach in another. This is not a matter of knowledge but of God's ordained gift. If the gift is there, notwithstanding the knowledge, people will be helped. What is gift? Gift is the ability which God grants to the body of Christ on the ground of Christ being the Head. Such ability suffers no change. Let me illustrate: A mason can lay bricks whether he is in Shanghai or in Nanking. A tailor can make dresses in Shanghai as well as in Peking. Environment will not change a gift.

Eldership, however, is different. It belongs only to locality. He who is an elder in Shanghai may not be an elder in Nanking, and an elder in Nanking is not an elder in Shanghai. This is because the spiritual condition, background, environment, custom and educational level of each local assembly is different. One who can be an elder in Shanghai may not be an elder in Kiangpei. An elder in the country may not be an elder in the city. It entirely depends on locality. Hence giftings in Scripture are for the whole Church whereas eldership in the Bible is marked for local assemblies. He who is gifted should not stay in only one place but should go to different places to share his gift. An elder, on the other hand, should remain in one place with respect to fulfilling his responsibility.

Let me use the illustration of a mason again. One may be a foreman among the masons in Shanghai. But if he goes to Nanking, his profession will still be masonry, yet he may not be a foreman. Masonry is his ability, and such ability remains in him whenever he goes to Nanking. In like manner, the office and the gift in the Church are two different things. Office or position is for the local assembly, but gift is not for the local assembly alone. What error can easily be committed when an elder in one assembly offers an opinion upon his going to another locality. This is something he should not do unless asked.

Do not conclude that because something is done in a certain way in one assembly it therefore should be done in the same way in another assembly. No, the environmental factors such as education, custom and so forth are different, and hence things cannot necessarily be done in the same way in both places. But gift is not so since it can be exercised in one place just as well as in another place.

Questions

(1) Suppose we announce unofficial elders; will not people consider us as being denominational? How should we answer them?

Let me first explain what we leave behind when we leave the denominations. If we do not know what we have left behind, it is true, we too may become a denomination. According to my understanding, when we leave the denominations, we leave behind two things: (a) various divisions such as are caused by the use of different names for the denominations; and (b) the pastoral system found in denominations. What is the pastoral system? It is bringing the intermediary priestly system of Judaism into Christianity. Unfortunately both Catholics and Protestants have adopted this.

Among the so-called Christian countries, the Roman Catholic Church has adopted the teaching of Judaism. In Judaism, there was this special class of priests who served as an intermediary. For the Jews to approach God they had to go through the hands of the priests because they could not contact God directly. This was clearly shown in the instance of Micah recorded in the book of Judges. Micah of Ephraim made an ephod, but he would need a Levite to be priest in his house (see

Judges 17). What is Judaism? In Judaism, men could not worship God directly but needed an intermediary—the priests—between themselves and God. So too is the Roman Catholic Church today. God is on one side and men are on the other. The latter cannot communicate directly but only through the mediation of the "fathers" who are priests. It requires priests to disperse the communion, to preach, and to pray. And such a system brings people back to the Old Testament practice.

The Protestants are divided into national churches and private churches. The Anglicans can be used as an illustration of a national church. In the Anglican Church (Church of England), there are the laity and the sacerdotal class. People in the sacerdotal class are also called priests, just as in Judaism and in the Roman Catholic Church. They too have brought in Judaism: God is above, the people are below, and in between is the sacerdotal class called the priests. In their approach to God, the laity must go through the priests, and hence the latter monopolize all spiritual things.

With respect to private churches in Protestantism—such as the Presbyterian, the Methodist, and so forth—they also have an intermediary class. God is above, the church members are below, and in between are the ministers or pastors. The pastors have become the intermediaries who do all spiritual things for the believers. It is the duty of the minister or pastor to distribute communion, to baptize people, and to preach sermons. They manage everything for their church members; they become the medium between God and men. So that from Judaism up through Roman Catholicism to the present-day variety of denominations in Protestantism, the same system requiring an intermediary class prevails.

What, though, does the New Testament say about this? "Ye are . . . a royal priesthood," says Peter (1 Peter 2.9). "He made us to be a kingdom, to be priests unto his God and Father," says John (Rev. 1.6). We therefore do not need anyone to be a substitute for us believers by standing as mediator between ourselves and God, because we *all* are priests who can approach Him directly: "Having therefore, brethren, boldness to enter into the holy place by the blood of Jesus, by the way which he dedicated for us, a new and living way" (Heb. 10.19,20a). It is not through the intermediary characteristic found in Judaism, Catholicism or Protestantism that we draw near to God. Neither are we like the high priest of old who once every year entered the tabernacle or temple's holiest place of all to meet Jehovah God. No, we today come to Him daily through the Lord Jesus' blood. All of us are priests, and we may communicate with God boldly at any time.

Hence, what is Christianity under the New Testament? It abrogates the aforementioned intermediary class system. Every believer is directly responsible for himself towards God. Do not make the workers in our midst the intermediary in local churches. There is no such thing among us. We all may go to God. The workers have no special position in the church. For God maintains a direct relationship with the individual believers in the church.

Someone may ask us, Why do you oppose "pastors"? I say in response that I do not oppose "pastors"; I only object to the "pastoral system." If anyone has the gift of a pastor, we treasure him very much. Yet whether a person has a pastoral gift or not, we must not make anyone into a special priest and introduce a disguised form of priestly system into our midst. Even those with a pastoral gift we will not treat as intermediaries.

I am afraid that, for some brethren, leaving the denominations means throwing away all controls. They think they can thereafter be free to the extent of being lawless—that they may do anything they like. If so, then I would call *that* leaving the *church*, not leaving the denomination. They are not leaving the denominations; they are casting aside authority. To leave a denomination is to leave division and the intermediary pastoral system; it is not to make us isolated, individual believers. In our midst we have God's ordained authority. When we submit to our brothers, we submit to God's authority.

It is recorded in Luke concerning our Lord, "Knew ye not that I must be in my Father's house?" (2.49) He must indeed be occupied with His Father's business; even so, at age twelve He went back from Jerusalem with His earthly parents and was subject to them. This is the submission of our Lord. Had we been our Lord we probably would have done differently. We would probably have contended that we must be about the Father's business and therefore have refused to return. Such would have shown our insubmission. To be occupied with the Father's business includes to be mindful of the Father's authority, and this includes God's authority upon the parents. So that when we submit to them, we are submitting to authority.

Let us never dream that by leaving a denomination we can be lawless and out from under any control whatsoever. To be like this would be worse than those who remain in the denominations, because though the latter may not have God's *ordained* authority, they at least have man's authority, whereas we would be insubordinate to the authority of God. The Bible endorses no sect, yet it calls for elders. When we break away from the sects and the denominations which the Bible does not endorse, we do not for that reason also break away from the eldership authority; for the Bible *does* teach and endorse the practice of eldership. We are not to discard eldership simply because it is found in something (denominationalism) which we feel it necessary to break away from. After all, there are brethren in the denominations, too; but can we, again for that reason, break fellowship with them as well? We cannot.

(2) Are elders appointed by God?

"To all the flock, in which the Holy Spirit hath made you overseers" (Acts 20.28 mg.). It is said explicitly that the elders are appointed by the Holy Spirit. What the apostles do in making men elders is but expressing the mind of the Holy Spirit.

(3) How about the supply of the elders? Is the way of supplying the elders the same as that of supplying the workers?

There is no difference. The Bible never makes workers who receive no salary a privileged class for receiving supply. Though beyond a certain point Peter fished no more, Paul still made tents. There is no difference nor class distinction between workers with a secular profession and workers without such profession. Elders who are gifted and who give so much of their time to manage church affairs that they are unable to take a secular job should receive double honor. If an elder is not as busy, it is well for him on the one hand to have a job to support himself and on the other hand to manage church affairs.

This is not only true with elders, it also applies to workers. A gifted person may work on a job as well as work for the Lord so long as his job does not interfere with his work for the Lord. I myself hope I may serve the Lord on the one hand and on the other hand hold down a secular job. I say this not because I am so poor that I am starving. To live by faith is not something extraordinary in holiness. Some people may deem it most spiritual and supernatural. Today believers give too much credit to those who live by faith. It is due to the general declension of faith among Christians.

Actually, living by faith is nothing to be surprised at, for in the early church, this was quite common. As a matter of fact, every believer should have such faith. Everyone who has a job lives by faith. I frequently think that brothers in business have greater faith than I do. Otherwise, how dare they open a shop and purchase with much money many goods in advance. For how do they know there will be any customers?

We know that, in the Bible, elders are viewed as brothers.

Among brethren there may be differences in gift and position, but there is no such distinction as being with or without a profession. Making any distinction in the matter of supply is a carry-over from the denominations. People forget that Paul *did* make tents. If, in a denomination, a minister should both pastor a church and take a job as well, he would be misunderstood. Let us, however, not have such a concept.

The Roman Catholic Church states that after a person is ordained, he is thereafter holy. There is an indelible aura about him that separates him from the common people. They forget that the apostle Paul always carried on the work of a tentmaker. We workers today may not have a secular job when we are busy, but when we have time there is no reason why we cannot hold down a job too.

(4) Is it all right for an evangelist to open a school?

It is by all means acceptable for a person to open a school or a store. Paul himself might have opened a tent shop, but it was not for all the believers in Ephesus to jointly open it.

It is wrong for the entire church to open a school, hospital, or bakery, but it is all right for some of the brethren to jointly undertake such an endeavor.

(5) Am I correct in saying that in the entire Bible the word "pastor" is mentioned only once, in Ephesians chapter 4?

The word "pastor" in relation to the church is indeed only mentioned in Ephesians 4.11. To be able to pastor is a gift which God gives by way of men to the Church for its building up. Elders are set apart by the apostles for the oversight of a local assembly. But the apostles cannot set apart a gift. They never appoint prophets, evangelists, pastors and teachers, because these are gifts given by God. For example: Suppose I am owner of a company. I can appoint a foreman and assistant foremen because these are positions. But I cannot appoint a person to be a mason if he does not know how to build with bricks. Similarly, the apostles can only set apart offices such as that of elders, but they cannot set apart prophets, evangelists, pastors or teachers because these as gifts are wholly in God's hand to give and to appoint.

No one can strive or quarrel over gift. If you see someone excel in preaching, you may want to preach too. Yet unless God permits, you will never make it. For it is said in 1 Corinthians 12.11 that "all these worketh the one and the same Spirit, dividing to each one severally even as he will." Gifts are not appointed by men, nor obtained through men's will. They are given to each person by the Holy Spirit according to His pleasure. For instance, the ability to pastor is a spiritual gift which God gives to the Church by the Holy Spirit. And if we see anyone with this pastoral gift, we treasure that one very much. Yet we cannot ordain him as a pastor, just as we cannot ordain a person to be a mason. We should not make a pastor a priest who serves as an intermediary between God and men. We do not reject "pastors" in the Scriptures; we only oppose the "pastoral system." Let us be careful lest we bring in any human invention practiced in the denominations.

(6) Can believers vote for elders?

No. Elders are appointed by apostles, by those who nowadays do the work of the apostles. In the Bible men never resorted to the practice of voting except in the one place recorded in Acts when the early church chose the seven men (Acts 6.3-6). Even then, these men were prayed for, and had hands laid on them, by the apostles.

(7) Among the numerous pastors ordained in the denominations, is there not one single true pastor?

According to human ordination, none so ordained becomes a pastor; but according to gift, some of those ordained may indeed have the gift of pastoring. We ought to see, however, that no one becomes a pastor through human examination, seminary study, men's ordination, or men's invitation. A true pastor is one gifted by God with the ability of pastoring.

(8) How does the gift of pastoring build up the church?

The Greek word translated "pastor" is only used in Scripture once, in Ephesians 4. The remaining instances of this same Greek word are translated as "shepherd." Hence the meaning of this word is that of feeding or watching over. When God gives a man a pastor's gift, he is given the ability to lead the believers in feeding them, in helping them to grow, in teaching them the Bible, and in praying with them.

The evangelist will lead people to salvation, that is to say, he will bring people in. The teacher is able to release the truth so that all may understand the truth of the Scriptures. The pastor can help them grow. He may not be able to preach, but he certainly knows how to feed the believers.

(9) Can women receive the pastor's gift?

God's *gifting* makes no distinction with respect to sex. The daughters of Philip the evangelist, for example, had the gift of prophesying. A woman may have the *gift* of pastoring.

(10) Can sisters witness, and preach the gospel to unbelieving men?

The Bible neither absolutely forbids nor encourages this. We do not have any distinctive example in the Bible. According to my personal opinion, sisters who exceed their position of being covered may be deemed excessive in this regard. By head covering, I do not mean the physical covering on their heads, though this is also important. I mean the hidden, submissive attitude and posture of heart which God gives to them. Even the brothers must have their heads covered before God, for the brothers are covered by Christ. Christ is the head of all men, and man is the head of woman. Therefore, women must be doubly covered. She is covered on the one hand by Christ and on the other hand by man. The physical covering upon her head expresses a sister's submission to the authority of the brothers, that she does nothing independently. Many things done by sisters are truly precious. It is best if they are covered by the brothers. Therefore, it is not good for sisters to do pioneer works alone.

The words of a sister were once quoted in a Western newspaper. She said how she at one time had done everything by herself. But while she was returning to her own country because of sickness, she began to realize how wrong she had been. Whereupon she confessed her fault before God.

Many think that since there was the case of Deborah in Israel, why can there not be Deborahs today? We need to remember that not all the women of Israel were Deborahs and that Deborah herself had Barak as a covering to her head. All godly women desire to have their heads covered. They honor what God has ordained and they respect the order and position which God has appointed for them. It is rather hard for me to say these things because I am not a sister. Yet if I were a sister, I would feel very much freer to say these things. Sisters should stand on the position of head covering. This does not mean they should not serve. It simply means that God has set the brothers as "protectors" of the sisters. The brothers should be more exposed. And whether it be for glory or shame, such will then fall on the brothers. Yet this is not because the brothers covet the glory of the sisters, it only serves as a means of protecting the sisters and to keep the order of God.

According to her very nature a sister would prefer to stand in an unexposed position; for Paul says, "Doth not even nature itself teach you?" (1 Cor. 11.14) What kind of home is it if the wife stands in her husband's position and acts as head over her man? Now the same applies to the church. In Proverbs it speaks of a worthy woman who works diligently that her husband may be known at the city gates (31.10-31).

How precious it is to submit to authority—such as servants to that of masters, children to that of parents, wives to husbands, people to officials, and women to men. God stresses authority, whereas Satan emphasizes power. It is already a sign of the fall if we only ask, Am I able?, instead of asking first, Should I? I hope all the sisters will stand in the place of submitting to God's authority. This question of authority is truly most important. Unfortunately, however, it seems to have little import in the lives of brothers and sisters.

According to the light of the Scriptures, sisters should be silent in church meetings with respect to teaching God's word. But they certainly can witness and preach the gospel to men if they stand in the place of their heads being covered.

(11) Can a person have two kinds of gift simultaneously?

Indeed, he can. Sometimes people have even more than two gifts.

(12) Was Peter the first pastor?

We may probably say so.

(13) Why do we mention elders at this time? Will we not be misunderstood as being a sect (or denomination) because of having elders?

Actually we had mentioned this matter of elders several years ago, but at that time we did not see persons being raised up as elders. It was a transitional period for us then. For the Bible says "not [to elevate] a novice" to eldership (1 Tim. 3.6). A novice is one who is green and inexperienced. So that we are definitely told that a novice, one who is a green hand, cannot be an elder. The time is now come, however, for us to deal in our midst with this matter of eldership.

(14) Is it correct to say that among ourselves we have people who are like elders but who do not have the title of elders, just as we do not have the official title of apostles?

True. But to answer more fully, I need first to explain the matter of church ground. Should people ask, Who are you? Are you the church in Shanghai?, how would you reply? You should say we are not the church in Shanghai. If you are asked, Are you the church at Hardoon Road?, you should also answer, no. We do not acknowledge ourselves as the church in Shanghai because aside from us there are many other saved people in the city who are in the denominational churches and who do not meet with us. Neither do we consider ourselves as the church at Hardoon Road, for there are perhaps other saved souls living along Hardoon Road who do not meet with us. In order to be called the church in Shanghai, all the believers in Shanghai must be included; otherwise, it cannot be recognized as the church in Shanghai.

People will then ask, If you are not the church, what are you? We confess that we are *not* the church, but we are those who assemble on the *ground* of the church. Let me illustrate it in this way. The temple in the Old Testament was magnificently built. It was later burned, and not one stone remained upon another. Suppose one day in Jerusalem some people came and set up a tent on the foundation of the razed temple. If they were asked who they were, they would reply: "We are not the temple; we are a tent set on the foundation of the burned down temple." In like manner do we ourselves meet today. Should we be asked who we are, our answer is, "We are not the church in Shanghai, we are but a number of brothers and sisters in Shanghai who assemble on the ground of the church to maintain the testimony of the church." The temple is now destroyed, it has been destroyed with fire. We are but a tent. All whose eyes are open should know the ruin of the Church today, how it has fallen in outward appearance.

Therefore, we cannot—nay, we dare not—call ourselves the church in Shanghai. We only desire to stand in the light of the church and assemble on the ground of the church. We are not the church in Shanghai, but we do meet on the ground of the church in Shanghai. We stand on the same ground as does the church in Shanghai, yet we are not the church at all. Though we are not the temple, we are nonetheless a miniature of the temple in order to manifest this temple life. Hence the elders and deacons in our midst are non-official in character. The reason we have elders and deacons is because though we are a small tent, we are nonetheless set upon the temple ground, and therefore we must follow the pattern of the temple.

Long after the temple was destroyed by the Babylonians, people such as Zerubbabel and Ezra returned to rebuild it. Those old men who had seen the glory of the first temple knew that this rebuilt one was far inferior to the former one. Yet in spite of this fact, people such as Zerubbabel, Ezra, and Nehemiah still offered sacrifices according to the former ordinance.

The temple mentioned in John chapter 2 was not the original one but was the rebuilt one. Still the Lord Jesus drove out the sheep and the cattle from it, saying: "Make not my Father's house a house of merchandise" (v.16). This statement our Lord declared by standing on the ground of the temple. Even though this temple was not the original one, yet the ground, as well as the principle, of the temple was nonetheless there. In spite of the falling outwardly, the ground remains. And hence it is possible to maintain the principle of God's service in a small way.

The nation of Israel was composed of twelve tribes; nevertheless God chose Jerusalem to put His name there. Thrice a year the men of Israel must travel to Jerusalem to offer sacrifices and to worship God. During the time when Rehoboam was king, the nation was divided into Judah and Israel. Judah had two tribes who still worshiped God in Jerusalem. Israel had ten tribes with Jeroboam as their king. According to God's command, the people must go to Jerusalem three times annually to worship Him. Jeroboam was afraid if his people went to Jerusalem three times a year their hearts might return to the king of Judah and rebel against him. Accordingly, he selected what people deemed to be a good location—even Bethel—and made a golden calf, set up an altar, and ordered his people to worship there instead of going to Jerusalem. At that time a young prophet was sent to reprimand him by prophesying against the altar and giving a sign. When Jeroboam heard the word of the prophet, he stretched out his hand, saying: "Lay hold on him" (1 Kings 13.4). But his hand dried up and he could not draw it back. Jeroboam let the prophet go. This shows that though the nation was *divided outwardly*, the *principle of serving God together in Jerusalem must still not be lost*. The Bethel that was set up by man could never replace the Jerusalem of God. Outward law could not substitute for God's decision. The break in politics could not alter the principle of God. Consequently, outward destruction, defeat and ruin cannot change the principle ordained by God.

During the time of the dividing of the Promised Land, nine and a half tribes of the children of Israel were allocated God's Promised Land on the west side of the Jordan River, but two and a half tribes chose instead to stay in the territory on the east side of the Jordan. After the allocation was completed under the hand of Joshua, the two and a half tribes built a great altar by the bank of the river Jordan. When the congregation of the children of Israel heard about it, they went up to fight against the two and a half tribes because the latter had built "an altar besides the altar of Jehovah our God" (Joshua 22.19). It was not only sinful to rebel against Jehovah, it was sinful to offer any burnt-offering, meal offering or peace-offering on any altar besides the altar of God.

How did the two and a half tribes answer? They said they had no desire to establish a new center of worship, and that furthermore, what they had built was not to be a new altar of offering but to serve as a witness that they had a portion in the Land. The altar in front of the tabernacle of God alone was the place of worship (see Joshua 22). These two and a half tribes represent the spiritually defeated ones, but even they could not alter the principle which God had ordained. Therefore, even after the nation was divided and was no longer one as in the time of David, the children of Israel must still worship in Jerusalem.

Today in spite of the division and failure and outward ruin of the church in Shanghai as well as in many other places, we must still stand on the ground of the church to worship God. And hence it is by this principle that we have our elders. We now have elders in our midst, but they are not official as in the denominations.

(15) Will God withdraw His gifts?

Gifts are given by God. They will not be withdrawn. We can have three different attitudes towards God's gifts: (a) we can misuse the gifts as did the Corinthian believers; (b) we can bury a gift as did the servant spoken of in Matthew 25; or (c) God can withhold a gift due to our unbelief.

(16) May we ask for gifts?

We may, for it is clearly stated in 1 Corinthians 14.1: "Desire earnestly spiritual gifts."

(17) What is meant by misusing gifts?

God does not withdraw gifts, but at the judgment seat of Christ He will ask us how we exercised our gifts. To misuse a gift is to use it according to man or for his own glory, just as the Corinthian believers did. God does not withdraw His gifts, "for the gifts and the calling of God are not repented of" (Rom. 11.29). For example, a sister may take it upon herself to teach in the church and as a result men are helped. We will ask, If sisters are supposed to be silent in the assembly, why, then, are men helped? For although this is the exercising of a gift, it is nevertheless a misusing of a gift. Let us see that these men are helped only because it is in fact the gift of God. Or as another example, sometimes an evangelist may go to where God has not sent him, and yet some people still get saved. Although people are helped, this too is a misuse of gift. Still another example is that of those who bury their gifts. These are mostly the people with but one talent. They consider their gift too insignificant, and therefore they tend to not use it. But additionally, a gift is sometimes stopped or ceases to operate because the believer does not appropriate it by faith.

(18) Can a person know his gift?

Sometimes one knows, yet sometimes he does not know but other people know. They know by the fruit of his labor. The Corinthian believers knew they were gifted. How pitiful, some reflect, that Moses did not know his face shone. Thank God that Moses did not know. If he *had* known, his face might not have shone. Let us let other people decide what our gift is.

(19) If the misuse and the burying of gift will incur God's judgment, would it not be better not to ask for a gift lest we be judged?

The more gifting a believer receives, the more opportunity for him to serve. For those believers who have not been dealt with by God, it may appear better not to ask for gifts lest they be judged. But for those who know God, they should ask for more gifts for the sake of the church and not for themselves. We long that God will raise up many gifts.

(20) How do we know we have misused a gift?

In the parable of the talents in Matthew 25.14-30, there are three different kinds of gifts: one of five talents, one of two talents, and one of one talent. These gifts are distributed to three different classes of servants. They all are charged to trade with them. Gift is capital. After the servants receive the gifts to trade with, they may do business resulting in either profit or loss. If they make a profit, the owner will not suffer; if they incur loss, the owner will suffer. A brother with the gift of evangelism will save souls. But if his work is done not in accordance with God's will but to glorify self, to meet needs, or to mind the things of men, he will lose spiritual power though not the power of the gift.

Today many servants of the Lord are leading meetings everywhere—saving, reviving and helping many people. Among them are the truly gifted of God, yet we may also notice that though they have gifts, some do not stand on the ground God wants them to take. We may wonder why they can still save, revive, and help people. This actually is the misusing of gifts. They can save souls and revive believers because they have God's gifts. It is His gift that saves, revives or helps. Such misuse of a gift is highly dangerous. For God will not say anything or do anything today. But wait until we all come to the judgment seat of Christ and then we shall all render our accounts. The reckoning on that day will be based on the gifts given to us today.

Never infer that as long as our work is well done, is prosperous or is well received by men, everything must be right. We need to guard against the misuse of gifts. Frequently a believer preaches for the sake of fame and praise of men, and his conscience knows this is wrong. Once a brother returned from preaching the gospel in a certain place. I asked him about the work he had done this time. His answer was: "I went and I returned. A few people were saved. But I still do not know if it was God's will for me to go." This is the misuse of gift. Today God entrusts this gift to you and me; He will reckon with us at the judgment seat. Nevertheless, let us keep a daily account with God lest in consideration of the many years we have, we may use our gifts carelessly.

Gift is a kind of spiritual ability, power or knowledge which God gives to man to help him work. For example, I may have good penmanship. Notwithstanding my fellowship with God being good or bad, I can still write well. I can write well *in* God's will, and I can write well *outside* God's will. Likewise is it with a gift. To exercise gifts in the will of God will help people; to exercise gifts outside the will of God will also help people. The difference is in spiritual value. Since this sin of misusing gifts will not be reckoned with until we stand before the judgment seat of Christ, it behooves us to be careful lest we work to gain glory and praise for ourselves. This will be misusing our gift.

(21) Does every believer have a gift?

Yes, he has at least one talent. There is no servant without a gift. 1 Corinthians 12 says that "to each one is given the manifestation of the Spirit to profit withal. For to one is given . . . and to another . . ." (vv.7,8). Hence everyone has a gift. All who are born again have gifts, though not all have the same gift. Respecting the gifts which build up the whole body, there are only five kinds mentioned in Ephesians 4. Regarding the gifts which help the growth of local assemblies, there are the many kinds mentioned in 1 Corinthians 12 and Romans 12. Not all believers have the gifts of Ephesians 4, but all may have one of the gifts of Romans 12 and 1 Corinthians 12.

(22) How do we know we are not misusing gifts?

In order not to misuse the gifts, we must accept the cross of Christ. For this cross—the cross which cuts off the flesh—is the foundation. The reason why there are problems in local assemblies is because brothers and sisters are not willing to accept the cross of Christ. All which comes out of the resurrection of Christ is for the body of Christ. The difficulties in the church stem from those things which people dig out from the tomb. If we are willing to accept the cross of Christ, and let it do a deeper work in us so as to take away our own ambition, we then will not misuse our gifts. It is just as we have mentioned before concerning elders. Who is unfit to be an elder? He who hopes to be an elder when he hears about elders. Who is fit to be an elder? He who considers himself unfit when he hears about elders. All who aspire to rule are unfit to rule; no authority can be placed in his hands. Only those who do not think of ruling may rule.

(23) Why, then, does 1 Timothy 3.1 (mg.) say that "if a man seeketh the office of an overseer, he desireth a good work"?

This statement was uttered out of a fear of people shrinking back. Today there are too many Peters who refuse to have their feet washed. The drawing back of the flesh is as fleshly as the boasting of the flesh. Here we have another evidence of the two sides of truth. 1 Timothy 3 also says: "not a novice, lest being puffed up he fall into the condemnation of the devil" (v.6). The Lord discourages these people to aspire for eldership lest they become proud and fall into the trap of the devil. But those who consider themselves useless and their flesh as weak tend to shrink back. So the Lord encourages them by saying that "if a man seeketh the office of an overseer, he desireth a good work." To those who *want* to be elders, God pronounces them to be unfit; but to those who are fit and yet draw back, He says to them to go ahead.

May brethren see the two sides of the flesh. It either boasts or shrinks back. Never take the boasting of the flesh as courage, nor the withdrawing of the flesh as humility. If we look at our strong point, we will incline to be proud; if we look at our weakness and failure, we will tend to shrink back and do nothing. Let us not confuse boasting with courage and withdrawing with humility. What is humility? It is not looking at the good as well as the bad in oneself. Hence true humility is not looking at self at all. Courage is being strong in the Lord. It comes by looking at Him. So that Ephesians 6.10 says for us to "be strong in the Lord, and in the strength of his might." He who measures himself and claims to be adequate is boasting. Such, though, is no strength at all.

It is therefore possible for us to look to the Lord on the one hand and not look at ourselves on the other, to be strong on the one hand and to be humble on the other. And such is victory. The defeat of many people is due to the fault of seeing either the power of the flesh or the weakness of the flesh, thus leading to either boasting or withdrawing. We can apply this principle not only to the matter of elders and deacons but also to our daily affairs.

(24) What does the passage in Ephesians 4 which speaks of apostles, prophets, evangelists, pastors, and teachers refer to—people, things, or titles?

Ephesians 4 points to people, whereas 1 Corinthians 12 points to things. The first passage states that God gives to the Church these five classes of people—some apostles, some prophets, some evangelists, and some pastors and teachers. The second passage declares that the gifts which God gives enable some to prophesy, some to speak in tongues, and so on. Paul, for instance, was God's gift to the Church: he was an apostle. But he had many gifts bestowed upon him, such as prophesying, speaking in tongues, healings, and so forth. The gifts which the Holy Spirit manifested in Paul have profited people of all ages. His work continues even today.

(25) How do we deal with brothers who are lawless in the meeting?

In case a person disturbs the meetings persistently and yet he has not committed any sin that warrants his being excommunicated, he should be strictly dealt with according to the teaching of Romans 16.17: "Now I beseech you, brethren, mark them that are causing the divisions and occasions of stumbling, contrary to the doctrine which ye learned; and turn away from them." Take note of him and turn away from him (that is to say, do not maintain fellowship with him). No church affair should be put into the hand of such people.

(26) If an elder has a problem, how do you deal with it?

The elders in the Bible are plural in number. If one elder has problems, the other elders can deal with him.

(27) If the elders are not officially appointed, any accusation against them would have to be unofficial too. Is that correct?

That is correct.

The Deacons

Deacons in the Scriptures are the brethren who serve people. In the church there must not only be responsible brothers like elders but also servants such as deacons. The church needs people who make the decisions and who supervise the brethren. It also needs people who specialize in serving people, and to take care of many mundane matters. Those who decide on things and supervise the church are the elders, while those who execute things as ordered and who help people are the deacons. God needs elders to be watchmen; He also needs deacons to do things and run errands for the believers. For example, the handling of funds belonging to the meeting is the work of the deacons, while the decision over the use of these funds belongs to the elders. What is decided by the elders is to be communicated to the brethren through the deacons. The elders are like foremen, and the deacons are like laborers. The deacons make no decision of their own; they simply carry out the orders of the elders. The deacons assist the elders in church affairs. We hope there will be brothers and sisters raised up in our midst to be deacons and deaconesses.

Questions

(1) Are deacons chosen by vote?

No. The selection of deacons during the time of the early apostles was not done by majority vote. Those deacons were already under the scrutiny of the apostles; they were manifested naturally. The biblical way of choosing deacons was for them to be naturally manifested. People who were fit to be deacons were chosen by the church and recognized by the apostles. This is the way we should follow.

(2) Why, then, was the apostle Matthias chosen by casting lots (Acts 1.20-26)?

This is because the Holy Spirit had not yet come. The disciples did not know which one should fill the vacancy left by Judas. Accordingly, they selected two men and cast lots to decide the one who would fill the apostolic office.

(3) Did not the disciples choose the seven deacons as recorded in Acts 6?

Acts 6 does not state explicitly that those seven men were deacons. It only shows us that the work they did was like the work of deacons. We can only call them deacons by the work which they did. Later on, we find in Acts that Philip was one of the seven, but again it does not plainly say he was one of the seven deacons. So that though the fact of their being deacons is mentioned in the Scriptures, there is no clear statement that the deacons were elected. I think the appointment of deacons should take place in the same way as the appointment of elders. They should be appointed by the apostles or those sent by the apostles. If there is a gap in the Bible that does not clearly show us what to do in a particular matter, we need to be very careful in pursuing such.

(4) When should the elders and the deacons be appointed?

As early as possible.

(5) If there are only three brothers in a local assembly, who will be elders and who will be deacons?

These brothers have to act as both elders and deacons. In the entire Bible, only the Letter to the Philippians gives a complete picture of church order: "Paul and Timothy, servants of Christ Jesus, to all the saints in Christ Jesus that are at Philippi, with the overseers and deacons" (Phil. 1.1 mg.). By this we know that a local church is composed of the saints, the elders, and the deacons.

(6) Why does 1 Timothy say: "And let these also first be proved; then let them serve as deacons, if they be blameless" (3.10)?

Deacons are active workers. They usually are younger people. They must be tested lest they do things according to their flesh and blood. Send them out on errands a few times before deciding if they are fit to be deacons.

(7) If in a locality a few brothers start to meet, should there be deacons first or elders first?

Because there needs first to be people bearing responsibility before there can be the breaking of bread, the elders should come first and then the deacons. This is the teaching in Acts. Antioch is a good example. At the establishing of a local church, people should be taught to submit to elders as well as to one another. If not, in a church of five brethren there will be five parties. Though they may break the bread and remember the Lord, they do not discern the body. They do not see themselves as the body of Christ. Each of them instead thinks only of his own self and is his own head. Hence we must learn to submit to elders and to one another.

2 The Practice of Fellowship

The Church Is One

The Bible teaches that the Church is one. The Church which Paul belonged to is the same Church to which we all belong. Our Church is the Church also of the apostle John, Martin Luther, Calvin and all the other regenerated people throughout Church history. The Church of the Bible has no distinction as to time, geography, or race. In the eyes of God, from the beginning to the end, past and present, at home and abroad, there is only one Church, not two or more Churches. The Bible recognizes the body of Christ, which is one and one only. There can never be two bodies of Christ because there is but one Head. Though the members are many, the body is one. Hence all the saved people, ancient and modern, at home and abroad, form one Church, one body.

Why, then, are there "the churches" in various places? Since the Letter to the Ephesians speaks of one body, one Spirit, one hope, one Lord, one faith, one baptism and one God (Eph. 4.4-6), why do the Scriptures mention the churches? Is there any contradiction in the Bible? For it speaks of one body on the one hand and the churches on the other. This tells us of the different aspects of the Church. Actually, there is only one Church, for the body of Christ is one. But in different localities, there may be as many as three to five thousand believers gathered together or as little as two or three (Matt. 18.20). In any city or village where a group of believers is gathered together, those believers there are the church in that city or village. The Scriptures most emphatically employ the phrase "the church in (or at)" such and such a place. The word "in" shows us that the Church is one, even though its various members are scattered and sojourn in many, many localities. The Bible treats all the believers who sojourn in a given locality as constituting the local church, a miniature representative of the one and only Church.

One thing is exceedingly precious: "We, who are many, are one bread" (1 Cor. 10.17). The "we" here includes all the believers. There is only one loaf. Hence do not imagine that there is one loaf in Shanghai and another loaf in Peking, and so forth. From the physical viewpoint, there may be tens of thousands of loaves throughout the world; from the spiritual viewpoint, however, there is but one bread loaf before God. Why is there but one loaf? Because being in the flesh we are restricted by time and space. If it were possible, all the believers in the entire world would break one loaf of bread together. But we know that that is not possible. Even so, though all the believers in all the different places throughout the world break the bread respectively, before God there is but one bread loaf being broken. The bread which the hands of the brethren in Shanghai touch is the same bread which the brethren in Peking and the brethren in Hanchow touch. The bread which is broken everywhere represents the one body of Christ. For God has only one Church in the world. And this Church is spread out throughout every city and every village world-wide. And the churches which are thus spread out are called the churches in these cities and villages. For the sake of convenience, these churches in the many cities and villages of the world are called "the churches of God" (2 Thess. 1.4; 1 Cor. 11.16; cf. also 1 Thess. 2.14). In actuality, the churches of God are the Church of God. The Lord calls us to break bread lest we forget the churches at various places. We are not to be an independent church, but to be joined with others as one

Church. This is why we use one bread loaf to aid us in recognizing that though there are many believers—past and present, at home and abroad—and many local churches, there is nevertheless but one loaf of bread.

The bread which we believers world-wide break may amount to tens of thousands of loaves, yet the body of Christ which the bread represents is only one. The Lord that the bread speaks of is also one. So that all the miniature local churches stand for the entire body of Christ. A local assembly may have only fifty people gathered together, but what it represents is the entire body of believers, both past and present, at home and abroad. The bread which any local assembly breaks, however small that assembly may be, represents Peter, Paul, Martin Luther, Wesley, and you and me. Wherever the local assembly is, it is a representation of the body of Christ. Therefore no church may take independent action. In all its actions it must take the entire body into consideration. In the meeting, you should not see just the few brothers and sisters who sit by you; instead you should see the entire body of Christ. What you do is not only related to the brothers and sisters immediately around you but it is also related to the whole body of Christ. Because we are one body, what you as a member do is what the body of Christ does. One member may affect the whole body.

The Chinese who live in the South Seas are mainly Fukien and Kwangtung* in origin. In many cities and villages in the South Seas there are Overseas Chinese Fraternities. Though the number of the members of these fraternities varies, wherever the fraternities are in power, the Chinese which they represent are in power; and wherever these fraternities are under oppression, the Chinese they represent also come under oppression. Now just as these fraternities represent China throughout the South Seas, so we in the place where we sojourn

---

*Two southern mainland Chinese provinces.—*Translator*

represent the Church. From this we can readily perceive the relationship the action of each local assembly has to that of the entire body of Christ, as well as the mutual relationship that obtains among these local assemblies themselves. Though you may be only a miniature church in a single locality, God will nonetheless use this miniature church to manifest the universal Church. So that the small local assembly here is to represent the all-inclusive body of Christ. For this reason it cannot but maintain relationship with other local assemblies as well as with brothers and sisters in other places.

Being Received to Break Bread

If a brother is being received by you to break bread with you, you do not receive him just to your particular assembly. The fact of the matter is you receive him into the churches of God, into the House of God. When we receive a person in Shanghai, we think of the assemblies in Hanchow and Peking. If they will not receive him, we should not receive him either because we receive on their behalf. We cannot take independent action. We must discern the body of Christ. If what we do personally cannot represent the assembly where we are, then we should not do it. Unless a matter is decided unanimously by the entire church, it should not be done, for it will not be the action of the body but an independent move instead. The Bible advocates only body action, not independent action.

Why do we inquire diligently when a brother asks to be received at the table? Because we receive him not only for the brethren in Shanghai but also for the brethren in Hanchow, Peking and other places. If he travels to other places later on, he will be received by the brethren at other places on the basis of a letter of recommendation from the local assembly in Shanghai because they believe in what the brethren in Shanghai have done. Hence, for the sake of the brethren at other localities, we must be careful in receiving anyone to the Lord's table.

Must Recognize Gifts

If a person is being recognized by the brethren in other assemblies as being a pastor, teacher, or evangelist, he should be able to shepherd, teach, or preach the gospel in Shanghai too. The brethren in Shanghai should recognize his gift, because a person will not lose his gift through changing places geographically. Let a local assembly, therefore, recognize the gifted person already recognized by other assemblies. For office may change through the change of locality, but gift will remain the same despite the geographical change. Office is restricted to locality, but gift is not so restricted. For this reason, a local assembly must exercise great care in discerning whether a person is gifted, since it is done not only for its own locality but also for the brethren in other localities. We must truly think of the whole Church of God.

Co-Workers

Concerning this matter of co-workers, let me illustrate it first with one incident. A worker at a certain place had the desire to invite another brother to come and work with him. He asked whether it was a good idea to invite that brother. I told him that he had really no need to ask me, for he ought to know himself. Suppose he introduced that brother to Peking or Shanghai or Nanking; would the brethren receive him? He answered probably not. So I said that that being the case, he could not invite that brother either. For if he were to acknowledge that brother as a fellow-worker, he would actually be bringing in that brother to work with all those who worked with him. He would be receiving that brother not only for himself and for the few who met in his local assembly but also for the entire body of Christ—even for the apostle Paul and others like him if they were still living today on earth. He would be receiving that brother into the Work on behalf of Paul and Peter and others. He would be adding one more co-worker to them. In essence, he would be taking an independent action. But all independent actions must be rejected because they have no place in the body of Christ. Therefore, each and every assembly should exercise caution and refrain from taking any independent action but learn to follow God in coordinating each action with other assemblies.

Must Meet Where Church Ground Is

Suppose a person from here has fellowship with a brother in Peking while on a visit there. When this brother from Peking comes to Shanghai, he should have fellowship with us too. If he comes to Shanghai and has no fellowship with us, something is wrong.

Brother Yu had fellowship with a few brothers from the West on Kuling Mountain. They met together often. But when he came to Shanghai, it happened that two of the brethren from the West also came to Shanghai. They stayed here for several months, yet they never came to break bread with us. When I asked brother Yu about this, I was told that they were too busy to come. I knew, however, that they had other reasons for not coming to the meeting. This shows independent action, not body action. If they could fellowship with brother Yu in Kuling, why could they not have fellowship with the people in Shanghai with whom brother Yu fellowships? It was not right for them to have fellowship with brother Yu and not to have fellowship with the brethren in Shanghai who regularly had fellowship with brother Yu. For when they chose to fellowship with brother Yu, they chose to fellowship with all who have any fellowship with brother Yu. They should not choose an individual meeting to have fellowship with; they should choose to have fellowship with all meetings that have fellowship with one another.

For example, today you come to break bread in our meeting here in Shanghai. You come because you consider this to be a better place to hear good messages. And so you have fellowship with the brethren who meet here. Later on, you go to Peking. There is also a meeting there that has fellowship with us here. But it is rather weak and has only a little over ten people meeting together. But in addition, there is in Peking a well known preacher who speaks well and yet he has no fellowship with us. When you arrive in Peking, you deliberate within your heart whether you should meet with those weak brethren or go to hear the famous preacher. If you go to the place where the famous preacher is, you are taking independent action. Since you are in fellowship with us here, you will be in fellowship with the brethren there with whom we have fellowship. You cannot choose where to meet. This is the principle of body fellowship. You cannot move independently.

We frequently think we may choose the place to meet according to our pleasure. If so, then we do not realize we do not have that option, but must choose the place where God wants us to be. For in the meeting we receive the greatest blessing, bear the greatest responsibility, and also accept the greatest restriction. Wherever we go, we go to where the church ground is. Do not speculate about how denominations bind people, for our fellowship binds people more strongly than does sectarianism. Yet what *they* have is legal organization; what *we* have is body organism. I suspect that nothing in the world binds people together more strongly than the principle of the body. None of the members of our physical body can freely move for a single day. Even a small finger cannot be free for a day. Our bonding is the bonding of the body, therefore there is no independency.

May we truly see the body of Christ and how we may not

take independent action. After believing in the Lord, we are not only saved through faith, we must also take our place as brethren. We are not only Christians, we are brethren to one another. This is brotherly love.

Each Is Responsible

Practically speaking, we would like to ask the question —What is the responsibility of the brethren? Each brother or sister must not only bear the responsibility of the local meeting but also consider all the brothers and sisters who are in Christian fellowship throughout the earth. To be truly Scriptural, we must look beyond China and see all the brethren throughout the world. For we participate with them in the fellowship of God and of His Son. Today we have a drawback, which is, that those who meet in Shanghai see only the brethren in the Shanghai meeting. Those who meet in Peking see only the brethren in the Peking meeting. Believers lack a world vision and love. This is a great deficiency. Just as many people only see their sins and how through faith in Christ they have received forgiveness without then connecting it in the slightest to the notion of brotherly fellowship, so there are many who only consider the local brethren who are seen without giving any thought to the brethren in other places who are not seen. Neither of these is the will of God.

The salvation work of God is to obtain living stones for the building of the spiritual house. If stones are scattered, they cannot be a spiritual house. But as we together break the bread, we manifest the entire body of Christ. Hence, each of us who breaks bread is responsible to the entire body of Christ; that is to say, each is responsible towards all who are in fellowship everywhere. Each time we receive a brother to break bread with us, we ought to show him that in breaking bread he must discern not only the Lord's body (His personal body broken for us on the cross), but also discern the body of *Christ* (His corporate body, the Church). It is sinful not to discern the body.

All the brethren who break bread ought to know what are the Scriptural conditions for anyone to break bread; namely, (1) he or she must be a saved person; and (2) he or she must be a person who has not committed the sins mentioned in 1 Corinthians 5. Besides these two conditions, we also should inform them of the responsibility they bear. They are to be responsible not only to the local church gathering but also to gatherings elsewhere. Should they fail to see their responsibility, we must not refuse to receive them, but we should nonetheless exhort them to consider very carefully such relationship. For in the breaking of bread, we remember the Lord, but we also take up the responsibility of fellowship towards the Church.

Now this that I have been enunciating is not a new practice. It has existed since the beginning of the Christian era. Whenever a brother arrives at a certain place, he should seek out other brethren for fellowship. No one should go to another area for four or five months without ever trying to find a meeting place. Before he leaves his home area, a person should first ask the responsible brothers to give him a letter of recommendation, and then inquire if there is any meeting where he can have fellowship. And if it so happens that there are two or three meetings in the new place to choose from, let him select the meeting which stands on church ground. By so doing, the brethren there will derive benefit from him and he will derive benefit from them. And let him always keep in mind that he is as much responsible to the church in the place to which he goes as he was to that of the place he leaves. He ought to behave in the new place as a brother.

If we all keep the fellowship of the saints according to the teaching of the Scriptures, how precious such fellowship will be. Our responsibility is towards the entire body of Christ, not simply towards the local assembly where we are. We should be interested in and concerned with the affairs of all the brothers and sisters throughout the world. May God bring us back to this original position.

Responsibility between Assemblies

The Bible tells us that what God ordains for one assembly He also ordains for another. If the decision of two assemblies is different, something must be wrong. Either the decision of the one assembly is wrong or the decision of the other assembly is wrong. 1 Corinthians gives the clearest instruction on the management of church affairs. We are told that this letter was written "unto the church of God which is at Corinth, . . . with all that call upon the name of our Lord Jesus Christ in *every place*" (1 Cor. 1.2). In other words, all the churches operate according to the same principle. This letter, for instance, speaks about the head covering of the sisters. Paul concludes his instruction by saying: "if any man seemeth to be contentious, we have no such custom, neither the *churches of God*" (11.16). The apostle does not allow the action of one assembly to be different from that of the other. Thus, we realize we cannot be independent. One assembly must consider the other assemblies. Whenever we do anything, we should think about its relationship to other assemblies. It is not possible for a sister not to cover her head in Peking yet cover her head in Shanghai. The practice of all the churches of God is the same. Again, "as in *all the churches of the saints*, let the women keep silence in the churches: for it is not permitted unto them to speak" (14.33b,34). That the women are not to teach in the church is a practice kept by all the churches of the saints.

Since the assemblies in various localities have been established at different times, the conditions of these assemblies will also vary. Some may be clear on church truth; some others may not be very clear. What must we do then? We should be humble enough to learn from the other assemblies. "Ye became imitators of us, and of the Lord," observes the apostle elsewhere in his writings, "having received the word in much affliction, with joy of the Holy Spirit" (1 Thess. 1.6); and again: "ye, brethren, became imitators of the churches of God which are in Judea in Christ Jesus" (1 Thess. 2.14). Here we are told that the church at Thessalonica imitated the churches in Judea. Why did the church at Thessalonica imitate them? Because the gospel was first preached to the Jews in Judea and hence the churches there were more spiritually advanced. No assembly may act independently. It is not just the individual believers who ought not act independently, even an assembly of believers should not act independently.

Independent Assembly

If someone plans to set up an assembly which will have no fellowship with other assemblies, that group does not stand on the ground of the church. For let us see that there was no church mentioned in the Bible which did not care for the other churches. It is not the will of God that we care only for the churches in China and cut off all relationships with the churches abroad. For before God, there is no distinction between Chinese and foreign churches. The Church of God is found throughout the world. Unless it is impossible to find any assembly standing on church ground in other countries, we ourselves will lose the ground of the body if we limit our fellowship to China.

What a Sect Is

I am fearful lest unlawful believers should rise up in our midst who lust after fame and the authority of the elders. If they cannot achieve their objective here, they will go to virgin soil—say, a village or an island—to preach the gospel and to win souls in order to gather some saved ones together, begin to break bread, and appoint elders and deacons. And they may do everything according to the Scriptures, yet ultimately they will have no communication with us. They will hold tight to their own locality. They will reckon that they can ignore us and go their separate way. Yet will they realize that in so doing they shall be going the sectarian way by not gathering on the ground of the church? Those who may conduct themselves in such a manner are as the sects mentioned in the Bible because their fellowship will be limited to a few hundred people. Even though all the meetings, the breaking of bread, and the appointment of elders and deacons may be according to the Scriptural procedure, their fellowship will still be limited to but one locality, and therefore they will be sectarian.

If the fellowship of an assembly is limited to merely its own locality and not also to the wider realm of the body of Christ which includes all believers everywhere, then that assembly is a sect. Furthermore, if the fellowship of any assembly includes only believers in several localities and still not the entire body of Christ both past and present and at home and abroad, it also is a sect. And finally, if a number of lawless people should go out from us here and set up another meeting whose fellowship is limited only to that meeting, that too is a sect.

Suppose the brethren in Chefoo endorse the policy of exclusivism. They labor well and do everything according to the Scriptures; yet they refuse to have fellowship with anybody else. They are a sectarian group from which you must be delivered. Each sect has its special mark. If any group should take the limits of its locality to be the limits of its fellowship, it is a sect. We must not only see whether what people do is according to the Scriptures or not, we must also inquire as to whether they consider themselves to be a sect or not. Any meeting which does not belong to the body of Christ is to be rejected. If we wish to serve God well, we must learn not to violate His command and learn to accept the unity of the brethren. We cannot limit ourselves to merely one locality but should try in spiritual things to be one with assemblies in other localities. This does not suggest that the standard of our conduct is set by majority vote; rather, it is by the unanimous decision of the brethren. Oneness and one accord is the work of the Holy Spirit, while majority vote is man-made.

The principle of the Open Brethren* is for each local assembly to take care of its own affairs and to have nothing to do with matters belonging to other assemblies. And hence, people excommunicated from the assembly in Nanking could break bread in the assembly in Shanghai. The Open Brethren even claim that they have never quarreled with other assemblies. According to their practice, of course, they cannot quarrel —since Shanghai will take care of Shanghai only and Nanking will take care of Nanking only. Each assembly can live in peace since each of them lives separately. The fact of the matter is, however, that these Open Brethren do have their quarrels. If in a meeting of an Open Brethren assembly some people differ in doctrine, they can go out and form another assembly. Open Brethren can even have several separate assemblies in one locality, and with no fellowship being conducted among them. And yet they claim that they do not quarrel with anybody! Each Open Brethren believer can run to the kind of assembly which pleases him. I ask, Is there any difference between this way and the denominational way? In truth, I can see no difference except in the size of the assemblies. Actually, neither the Open Brethren way nor the way of the denominations is the teaching and practice shown in the Scriptures.

Taking Same Action

Suppose the assembly in Shanghai excommunicates a brother, and yet the assembly in Nanking receives him. The assembly in Shanghai cannot for this reason excommunicate

---

*Referring to a wing of the Plymouth Brethren.—*Translator*

the assembly in Nanking. It may, however, raise a question with the assembly in Nanking. For whoever is excommunicated from one assembly is excommunicated from all assemblies; and whoever is received by one assembly is received by all the assemblies of God. Such a relationship will manifest the reality of the body of Christ.

Nonetheless, there is the other side of the truth which we must not overlook. The government of each assembly is locally independent. Shanghai cannot overturn, or interfere with, the decision of Nanking; and vice versa. Yet in making decisions, either Shanghai or Nanking needs to remember how its decision will affect other assemblies. Extra care needs to be taken. Even though no assembly may interfere with the government of another, each assembly must seek to know the will of God with singleness of purpose and to not act rashly because it is locally governed. It may ask the help of another assembly in order to reach a decision which will be in accordance with the Lord's will as well as with the Lord's word. The heart of the matter is whether the flesh has been dealt with or whether it is spiritual. If the answer is positive, an assembly will consider other assemblies.

Suppose the assembly in Nanking has received an unsaved person inadvertently and later recommends him to the assembly in Shanghai. On the day the letter of commendation arrives in Shanghai, that person becomes a brother in Shanghai, and therefore he is no longer under the government of the assembly in Nanking. It is now up to the assembly in Shanghai to deal with the case. There is no need for the assembly in Shanghai to consult with the assembly in Nanking. However, if a brother is wrongly excommunicated by the assembly in Shanghai and he later goes to Nanking where the brethren there discover the error, those in Nanking cannot receive this excommunicated brother at once but should first write to Shanghai and inquire about the case. Whether he will be received or not depends on how the assembly in Shanghai responds.

This whole matter rests on our flesh being put on the cross. Even the relationship of assembly is based on this principle. If we are wrong, we should submit to our brethren. If we insist on carrying out *our* opinion, we will soon become a sect. Sometimes a brother may deem himself infallible; then he himself is a sect. Hence, we must judge the flesh with severity, putting it to death that we may live in the Holy Spirit while we manage church affairs. Otherwise, if the flesh is left unjudged, each will do what he likes, with there being no way possible to manage affairs of the church well. The self in each one of us must be dealt with. This teaching of the Scripture applies equally to assemblies as to individuals.

Questions

(1) Suppose a brother came to Shanghai with a letter of commendation from the assembly in Tsinan. He is later excommunicated by the assembly in Shanghai. Is it necessary for Shanghai to inquire of the brethren in Tsinan before excommunicating that brother?

When a brother comes with a letter of commendation from the assembly in Tsinan, he will be received accordingly by the assembly in Shanghai. If he is found out later to be unsaved, he can be excommunicated. He is received because the brethren in Tsinan have given him a letter of commendation. We must believe in the words of the brethren in Tsinan and receive him. But afterwards in dealing with him we have no need to notify the brethren in Tsinan. This is because after that brother is introduced and received, he is now a brother in the assembly in Shanghai. And hence, the assembly in Shanghai has the authority to deal with him.

(2) Can we go elsewhere to break bread? Is it contrary to Scriptural truth?

Suppose there are two groups in the same locality that have the breaking of bread. We need to discern which one stands on the ground of the church. If both stand on church ground, they ought to have fellowship and be one group. One group but separate meetings. Whoever is received at the Lord's table by one is automatically received by the other. There is no need to be received again because we are now one fellowship group.

(3) Is it all right if I break bread with a group of weak brethren and go to another place to hear a famous preacher?

It is not forbidden to go elsewhere to hear the word. But one thing must be clarified. Your fellowship with the people where you go to hear the word will be restricted. This is because unless the preachers as well as their works aim at the purpose of God, what they do may not be considered as God's work according to the Scriptures. I have already mentioned elsewhere that God's work is not an evangelistic band, an endeavor society, a Sunday school program, a Bible class, a revival meeting, and so forth. God's work from start to finish is one, which is to say, the Church. What God aims at doing in a locality is the establishing and building up of the local assembly there. Any attempt which falls short of this aim—failing to do that much—is not reckoned as God's work. I do not mean to say that evangelistic meetings, Bible classes, revival meetings, and so forth are not good. I am only saying that if these are all which are being done, without having the building of the local assembly as their objective, they come short of God's purpose. For such endeavors actually lower the purpose of God. All the works which God did as recorded in the book of Acts were never less than the contributing to the building up of the local assembly.

Today in the church there are people who teach the truth, who lead souls to Christ, who search the Scriptures, and proclaim the gospel. These things the believers must do. Nevertheless, we need to hold fast to God's purpose and to aim at the Church. What we are afraid of is that many works, though very good, fall short of God's work which is the Church. We believe there are indeed people with gifts outside of us; but we also believe that if we are more faithful, God will also raise up in our own midst such gifted persons. If we live in God's light, there will be no need to go elsewhere to hear the word of God.

(4) Some believers criticize the truths which we hold and keep themselves strictly to their own Bible class; yet they come to break bread with us and to speak at the breaking of bread meeting. How should we deal with such people?

If in a certain locality there exists such an exclusive type of Bible class, it does not meet according to the principle of the Church. Their work falls short of God's aim, and therefore it is not His work but a human imitation of it, since the work of God is always aimed at and centered in the Church. Though such a Bible class and so on are good and blessed by the Lord, these are not deemed to be His work. We may say that God's work is truly *in* them, because we cannot ignore the fact of what the Lord does in their works. Indeed, we would be offending God if we were to say there is not the work of God in their works. Nevertheless, the *purpose* of their works is not centered in building up the Church of God.

If these people come to break bread, we should be most happy to receive them. We are not receiving them according to the denomination which they represent, yet we cannot refuse them simply because they are still in their denomination.

If a person in the denomination is saved, we can receive him to break bread with us, but we must be careful in receiving him to preach. If he is not clear on church truth, we can have fellowship with him in life, but not necessarily in work. For we do not know what he will speak about. There are many people with whom we may have fellowship in life, but not in work. This is the principle which the apostle Paul held to.

Note also the following situation: "Now I beseech you, brethren, mark them that are causing the divisions and occasions of stumbling, contrary to the doctrine which ye learned; and turn away from them" (Rom. 16.17). Hence the brethren should avoid people who cause divisions. The elders can notify us of whom we should avoid and with whom we should fellowship. Let the brethren learn to obey.

(5) When we receive a person to the breaking of bread, should we not inquire about the following four things?—(1) Is he a saved person? (2) Has he committed the manifest sins mentioned in 1 Corinthians 5? (3) Is he willing to be committed to the group? and (4) Will he be open to fellowship with the brethren here? Suppose a person is saved and he does not have the sins which might otherwise keep him away from the table. Suppose, too, that he wants to break bread with us, yet he will not be responsible towards the group nor fellowship with the brethren. On the contrary, he tries to interfere with church affairs. How should we deal with such people?

Please note that (1) and (2) are the conditions for receiving a person to the Lord's table, but that (3) and (4) are those which relate to the discerning of the body. If a person does not discern the body, he eats and drinks judgment to himself (1 Cor. 11). This is something which all the elders or responsible brothers must clearly understand. As to the discerning of the body, this has two sides: (1) to discern this body as the body of the Lord Jesus. We break bread in order to remember the Lord Jesus himself. This is why we come to eat and to drink at His table. (2) to discern this body as being also the entire body of Christ. As we gather to break bread, we are not only conscious of all here who break bread together as the body of Christ but also of all those everywhere else who are redeemed by the precious blood. If a Japanese believer comes to our midst to break bread with us, we still must acknowledge him as a beloved brother in the Lord. Suppose England invades Tibet and the international atmosphere grows tense. When a brother from England comes to our midst to break bread with us, we must likewise consider him to be our beloved brother in Christ. We must not be influenced by human discrimination; instead, we must be governed by the relationship which exists within the body of Christ.

For this reason, therefore, when such a person who refuses to discern the body comes into our midst for the breaking of bread, you may discuss with him if he is willing to discern the body. Is he willing to be responsible to the church for all his actions? If he is unwilling, we still cannot keep him from breaking bread, because he is already saved. Yet he must be told that he will eat and drink judgment to himself if he does not discern the body, and thus it would be rather unprofitable for him spiritually.

(6) Will such eating and drinking judgment to oneself become so serious as to reach the point of death?

If the church group is holy and it knows how to exercise God's authority, such a thing may indeed happen. Why is the breaking of bread so serious? Because if you confess that this is the body of Christ and acknowledge that you are a part of it, and yet you fail to discern the body as mentioned earlier, then this means you are bearing false witness and such a witness will disgrace God. For the breaking of bread is a testimony to the angels, to the demons, and to all the principalities and authorities. The false testimony you may give will bring disgrace to God. He may be lenient towards an ignorant person, but He shall be severe with one who knowingly bears false witness.

(7) If a brother is sick, must he be anointed by the elders before he can be healed?

A believer may be sick due to various reasons: he may be ill through his carelessness towards natural environments or through Satanic attack or through his disjoining himself from the body of Christ. If a believer is disjoined from the body of Christ through his not holding fast the Head and not taking his proper position in the body, he needs to know first how he became disjoined before he asks the elders of the church to anoint him with oil.

Anointing means causing him to return to his rightful place in the body of Christ through the power of the Holy Spirit. We all know we are members of Christ's body. And just as a member is in the flow of the circulation of the life and blood of the physical body, so a member of the body of Christ is in the flow of the circulation of the life and blood of Christ. The running down of precious oil from Aaron's head to the entire body as spoken of in the Old Testament (Psalm 133) is a picture or type of this very matter. As long as a member stands in his or her place in the body, the precious oil will flow to that one. And thus will that member receive the protection of the precious oil and be kept from sickness. For all who stand in their rightful places in the body of Christ are under the anointing of the Head. The precious oil is on the head of Christ, from whence it flows to us. Having the oil, we have health. Having the oil, we have life. A believer is sick in this case because he has been disconnected from the body of Christ so that the life and anointing of the Head is unable to flow to him.

"Is any among you sick? let him call for the elders of the church; and let them pray over him, anointing him with oil in the name of the Lord" (James 5.14). It says here to call for the *elders* to anoint a person with oil, because the elders represent the church, and thus they represent the body of Christ. Anointing with oil is to bring this sick believer back under the anointing of the Head. If he is brought back under such anointing, his sickness shall be healed.

(8) Such being the case, can those who represent the church tell the brother who is sick that they will anoint him with oil so that he may be healed?

Indeed they can. Except that before the anointing there must first be the confession of sins and prayer: "Confess therefore your sins one to another" (James 5.16a). Such confession of sins is necessary because there has been an obstacle to the mutual relationship within the body. After sins are confessed and the cause for being disjoined is removed, the member is returned to his original place in the body. If there remains an obstacle, the anointing would be useless. Hence first let the obstacle be removed. Let all criticism and controversy with the brethren be cleared up. Even the elders need to confess sins one to another so that all possible obstacles are removed and the relationship in the body of Christ can be restored. Then the anointing with oil will cause the anointing on Christ's head to flow to that member.

(9) How should we deal with people who have not committed the sins in 1 Corinthians 5 but nonetheless continue to disturb the meetings of the assembly in spite of repeated warnings from the elders?

Notify all the brethren to keep away from them. For the elders especially bear spiritual responsibility in this area. If there happens to be such a person who disturbs the meetings, the elders should deal with him in prayer. We ought to know that it is a matter of great seriousness to deal with a brother through prayer. If the responsible brothers will indeed seriously deal with the situation in one accord, a most tragic and grave consequence will most likely come upon such a person, for God will use the authority which He has established to judge the case. When the Corinthian case appeared, Paul chided them for not being able to deal with it. Those who act as elders must know how to deal with such situations; otherwise, the flesh—if left unchecked—will become so corrupted as to more than likely incur very serious consequences later. Hence, let us all learn to be obedient people. With our flesh under control, we will not have much of a problem.

(10) What is meant by meeting on church ground? How do we know our group is standing on church ground?

Let me make an announcement: we are both most open and most exclusive in the areas of breaking bread and fellowship. Open, because we receive all the children of God without discrimination against anyone. Exclusive, because any church fellowship that on the one hand may actually practice many of the things which we practice—such as baptism, the breaking of bread, elders and deacons, and so forth—and yet on the other hand does not stand on church ground, is not good enough for us.

Just because a fellowship has the appearance of following the Scriptures does not mean that it is necessarily standing on the ground of the church. This question of church ground needs to be answered affirmatively before we can join ourselves with it.

What is meant by referring to a church group as standing on church ground?

Two things are essential: (a) It is *not a sect*. What is the difference between a sect and a church? A church includes all the believers, whereas a sect includes only part of the believers. A sect raises a wall in the church to separate itself off from others who also belong to the church. A sect is not able to stand on the ground of the church because (1) those in a sect take on a special name which the entire church body does not do; (2) those in a sect emphasize a special truth which the whole church body does not emphasize; and (3) those in a sect practice a special fellowship (that is to say, membership) other than the fellowship of the entire body of Christ. A group which stands on church ground has neither a special name other than the general name of the church, nor does it have any special truth nor special membership.

(b) It is *living out the body*. Although we may observe a group which does not have a special name or creed or membership and which—in its appearance—meets according to the Scriptures, we must inquire further if such a group lives out the life of the body. For not all who are not sects stand on the ground of the church. They may not be a sect negatively speaking, but positively speaking, they may not know what the body of Christ in the church truly is.

You should try to discern if a group takes up the responsibility of the local assembly in its locality. If there are other small gatherings in the locality of a similar nature, do those in the first group seek diligently to unite with them to become, together, the local assembly? Does the first group help the other gatherings to see the nature of a local assembly? Or do those in the first group let the scattering of the various gatherings continue without making any effort to unite them so that none can really represent the nature of the local assembly? Do those in the first group try their best to accommodate all the children of God, or do they build up a stronghold around themselves to take care of their small fellowship alone? If the latter is true, they are not standing on the ground of the church.

Now even if this group *has* taken up the responsibility of the local assembly, you will want to further inquire as to whether or not that group practices "localism"—that is to say, is it only concerned with its own locality by failing to recognize that the Church of God is universal and hence failing to maintain fellowship with other assemblies that stand on similar church ground? If it in fact *does* refuse to fellowship with other local assemblies elsewhere, thus depriving them of the opportunity to march forward together as one, it has not yet taken the church ground.

I suppose all of us have already come to know that there is only the local assembly in view in the Bible. Due to the outward ruinous appearance of the Church today, however, the division among God's people is so serious that no group of believers—including ourselves—can freely call itself the local assembly. We here, for example, can only say we are meeting on the ground of the local church. Though we are not "the local church," we nevertheless stand on local church ground.

(11) If there is spread a Lord's table anywhere which accepts all God's children, can we say that the brethren there stand on church ground?

The first thing to be settled is to understand what is meant by standing on church ground. We know that for any group of believers to be standing on church ground it must not be a sect; but this understanding is only a negative one. Positively understood, a group must manifest the life of the body of Christ, which is to say, that it is not independent but is willing to walk together with all non-sectarian brothers and sisters wherever found. Though the Church is now in ruin, there are still people who remain outside of man-made sects. We ought to walk together with all who do not belong to any sect. And by so doing we shall stand on the ground of the church.

Actually this expression of standing on church ground needs especially to be employed in our day when the ruin of the Church can be seen on every hand. When the Church was one, before there were sects and many man-made things, everybody stood on church ground and manifested the life of the body of Christ. But now the Church in its appearance is today quite desolate, and people have divided themselves into sects according to human opinions. There is therefore the need for some believers not to divide into sects and to stand on the ground of the church. If they do so, they will manifest on behalf of the whole Church the life of the body of Christ which it ought to exhibit.

Today in many places believers have seen the error of sectarianism, but they have not seen what the body of Christ is. It is good that they are non-sectarian; yet this is but negative in nature. Though the Church today does not have the appearance of unity, those who have been delivered from this disunity still have the obligation of walking according to the principle of the oneness of the Church. Hence even if somewhere a Lord's table is open to all God's children, we need to further inquire if that group's work and testimony and fellowship are joined with all who have been freed from sects. How can we, who do not belong to any sect, fail to be united together as in the time when there was no sect? All who do not belong to the sects must manifest the life of the body which the Church as a whole ought to have. For this reason, people who claim to be non-sectarian but still will not work and fellowship with all others who are themselves equally non-sectarian are really independent in nature. Though they are willing to receive all God's children at the Lord's table, they have neither stood on the ground of the church nor known what the body of Christ is. Such a table is in actual fact *not* the Lord's table because the loaf on that table does not represent all the saints.

3 How to Meet

There are different kinds of meetings, yet two things must be observed about all of them:

(a) *Arrive early*. It is most unkind towards others to be late to a meeting because you cause them to wait for you: "Wherefore, my brethren, when ye come together to eat, wait one for another" (1 Cor. 11.33). There are many who do indeed observe this Scripture verse; however, instead of their waiting for others, they let the others wait for them. Everyone must try to arrive early lest people have to wait for the latecomers.

The evils of late arrival are several in number: (i) It causes the meeting to have a late start and a late ending. This will inconvenience sisters who have responsibilities for cooking and taking care of children. (ii) In the breaking of bread meeting, hymns which have *already* been sung may be called for again by the late arrivals. This will create repetition. (iii) It has happened that a breaking of bread meeting may have already begun; nevertheless, latecomers may initiate new starts, thus resulting in having perhaps four or five different beginnings! We need to learn to be led by the Holy Spirit in how we remember the Lord. Each time at such a meeting for the remembering of the Lord, it may commence differently—sometimes it commences with the sufferings of the Lord, at other times it may commence with the forgiveness of our sins, and at still other times, with the glory of the Lord, and so on. Yet because the latecomers do not know how the meeting has started, their prayers and hymns may not at all fit in with the spirit of the meeting already in progress. For the above reasons, therefore, it is better to arrive early and then wait than it is to arrive late.

(b) *Stand to speak.* It is best in the meetings for the brethren to stand and speak. Speaking while seated does not produce sufficient sound to be easily heard; it may also conflict with the voices of other brothers, for when one who is seated mentions a hymn with his head bent down, he cannot observe whether some other brother has already simultaneously stood up to pray. Our ears are simply not as quick as our eyes. By our standing up, the incidence of having two persons speak at the same time can often be avoided. Hence let us remember that before anyone prays or speaks or mentions a hymn we should look around to see if anybody else has already stood up. Though this seems to be a small matter of etiquette, it is something which ought to be observed.

(1) Breaking of Bread Meeting

The first point to be noticed is that in a breaking of bread meeting, we come to remember the Lord; therefore, everything must be centered upon Him. We ought to know that prayer in the forms of asking and interceding are not suitable at such a time. Through our prayers we should praise and thank the Lord and not, at this time, remember our needs in prayer. Let it be pure praise and thanksgiving. According to the light given believers in the Scriptures, such a meeting is divided into two parts: before the breaking of the bread, the heavenly Father is put before us. Before the bread is broken, God will lead us into remembering the Lord himself. And hence, all praises and thanksgiving are centered upon the Lord. Before the bread is broken, what we see is the Lord Jesus as the only begotten Son because He alone is the Son. But after the bread is broken, we see the Lord Jesus as the firstborn Son, for we now have a part in the Son as the many sons. Before the bread is broken, the Lord Jesus is the grain of wheat; after the bread is broken, this grain of wheat has fallen into the ground and died and has thus borne many grains. In discerning the body of Christ, we see the Lord as the Firstborn who will lead many sons into glory as spoken of in Hebrews 2. He will lead many sons in praises in the midst of the congregation. This is not, however, a law which must be implemented in every meeting. Yet if we are willing to learn to be led of the Spirit, we will understand how in such a corporate spiritual exercise we will be led step by step to the Father.

On that "last night" the Lord Jesus first led His disciples in eating the Passover feast, then they sang a hymn and went out to the Mount of Olives. The so-called "songs of degrees" or "songs of ascents" is that collection of the 150 Old Testament Psalms which were sung after the children of Israel had kept the Passover and eaten the Passover feast. As they walked up the fifteen steps to the temple, they sang these psalms. Similarly, upon our having eaten the bread, we too should go up to praise God. Let the Lord himself lead us to approach the Father. Our hymns are all "songs of ascents"—that is to say, a rising of our spirits higher and higher after the bread is broken. This is true not only according to the teaching of the book of Hebrews, the example of our Lord, and the instruction of these psalms; it is also according to our personal spiritual experience. After we were saved, did we not thank and praise the Lord first, and then worship God?

The second point to be noticed in the breaking of bread meeting is to learn to follow the lead which has already been established. Though such a time is devoted to remembering the Lord, the meeting can begin on a variety of diverse notes. Sometimes the sufferings of the Lord are what is emphasized, at other times stress is laid on the glory of the Lord in what He has gone through during His earthly life. We need to recognize the start already made in the meeting and learn to follow the lead. Whether singing or praying, it is best to proceed along that line than to make a new start. Do not try to squeeze into the meeting the meaningful Scripture passage which you may have read that very morning in your private devotions or the favorite song which you usually love to sing. Sometimes the meeting is already ended—with the praises and thanks having been adequately offered; but then, suddenly, a brother will stand up to suggest a hymn or offer a prayer. All this is too personal. We must instead keep the unity of the meeting, for that is very precious. In the breaking of bread meeting, it really puts to the test just who is a good brother: whether one is concerned with only what is his or with the movement of the meeting!

In a meeting, we must close all our personal activities and follow the corporate movement. If it is but one person in a room, he may sing or pray as he pleases. In a meeting, though, there are more people than merely oneself. Therefore let us not inject too much of our own personal feeling into it. Of course, our thanks and praises are to be personal, for unless they are personal they are false. Nonetheless, though the personal element is always in a meeting, special attention must be paid to that which is corporate. We need to proceed together on one line of thought.

Concerning any word given at the breaking of bread meeting, let us keep in mind that the Lord must be the center. If the Scriptures are read, such must lead people to Him. If a word is given, it too must lead people to focus on the Lord. There is no meeting more important than that of the breaking of bread. In a ministry meeting, people listen concerning the Lord for their own benefit, but in the breaking of bread gathering, we go forth to meet the Lord and to remember Him. It is for the Lord himself.

(2) Bible Study Meeting

In a Bible study meeting, no one brother speaks; rather, all the brethren study together before God. One brother will read a portion of Scripture, and then the other brothers join in speaking and discussing, raising questions, and giving some explanations. Thus will the chapter be read verse by verse. I personally feel that it is a failure if there is not such a Bible study meeting in a local assembly.

In such a meeting, no one leads permanently. Some will get up and read the Scriptures, some will raise questions, and some will try to answer or explain. The principle which governs such a meeting is that nothing is done to enhance one's own self. Each one should set himself aside before he comes to the meeting. We must learn to express the life of the body. This is not only true regarding the Bible study meeting; it is likewise true regarding all other kinds of meetings. Everything is for the sake of the brethren. In the meeting, you are not trying to express yourself; nor are you waiting passively for others' help. You should learn instead to serve your brethren.

He who serves is greater than he who is served, so says the Lord. Every time each of us comes to a meeting, we should remember we come to be a servant of the brothers and sisters. We come to serve them, not merely to hear a message. We serve not because we are proud of ourselves as being greater and better than the rest, but because this is what we should do. Accordingly, let us not sit in a meeting and wait for other people to speak up first. We may start by asking a question to give people opportunity to answer or to follow the lead. Keep in mind that such a question is not asked only for one's own self or for one's own understanding. It is asked with the hope that others too may be profited. We can ask questions whose answers we already know as well as those which we do not know. Perhaps we know quite a lot, but some new brothers may not have the same knowledge. We should therefore ask questions for them.

In a ministry meeting, those who understand are greatly benefited, while those who do not understand gain little or nothing. We may say that such a time is mainly for people who have knowledge and wisdom (natural wisdom and knowledge are nothing in God's sight). People who are illiterate, dull and slow in understanding can only gain a little. But the Bible study meeting is designed to help the weakest of all believers. In such a meeting we can detect how much the brethren really know. Occasionally, some may ask questions totally unrelated —even nonsensical or laughable—in character. Even so, this represents their need. To us it is an insignificant thing, but to them it is a large matter.

Hence in such a meeting, never deem it too elementary to be profitable to us. Remember that we come to help the meeting. We come to be a servant. Perhaps your absence will cause a great loss to others, but our presence will demonstrate our approval and support of the meeting.

Do we not see that we have erred if we cannot help or serve the brethren? This is because we are mindful only of our spiritual growth and care and not for the welfare of the meeting as well as the well-being of the brethren. We are not willing to help and serve the brethren. In the meeting, all the brethren are expected to learn to be brothers and sisters to them so that all may grow together.

If there is any controversial matter, let it not be mentioned in the meeting. During the past year all our gatherings were blessed by God and showed real progress except on the one occasion when two brothers argued over a certain issue till their faces turned red. This was due to their not knowing how to be brothers. "Him that is weak in faith receive ye," said the apostle Paul, "yet not to doubtful disputations" (Rom. 14.1 mg.). This principle is most important. Any person who insists on arguing is being unkind to his brother. He is not helping his brother; he merely wishes to force through his own opinion. What shall a man be profited if his opinion prevails and yet his brother is not helped?

Consequently, in any meeting, our flesh needs to be bound

and self must be delivered to death. It is easy to say these words in ordinary days, but the flesh will be severely tested in the meeting. In ordinary times, we may be impressed by the gentleness or love or patience shown by a certain brother. In the meeting, however, we will discover whether he is really sweet or sour. Let us lay aside all doubtful matters and not argue over them. How unfortunate for any brother to consider his own view worthy of mandatory adoption.

Thus we can see that in a Bible study meeting, there is only one principle—which is that of laying down ourselves. Two bad symptoms are to be avoided in a meeting: pride and withdrawal. Pride due to looking at one's strength; withdrawal due to looking at one's weakness. Seeing his own strength, a person tends to speak much; seeing his own weakness, one tends to shut up. Actually, speaking or remaining silent is equally bad. Wherever self is, there is pride; wherever self is, there is withdrawal. All which is of the flesh must be laid down. If each one speaks to glorify the Lord, every problem is solved

(3) Gospel Meeting

There exists a great misconception among brothers and sisters regarding gospel meetings. Forgive me for mentioning this one matter: Frequently, brothers will call on the phone to inquire if there will be preaching of the gospel in the morning or in the afternoon. What they mean by this question is that if it is a gospel meeting they will not attend since they are already saved. This is a mistake. The issue lies not in whether it is to be a gospel meeting, but rather in whether I should attend in order to strengthen the hand of the brother who preaches so that he will not need to fight the battle alone. It should not be a matter of personal gain but one of a desire to help the brother as well as to help the meeting. Please realize that even if there is not any new word spoken, each time the same gospel is preached it is the glorious good news which none of the saved should ever tire of hearing. By sitting in the gospel meeting, you unknowingly have helped the one who preaches and have strengthened his hand. If you have never had the experience of preaching, you will not understand its significance. But if you do have any preaching experience, you will find great comfort in seeing a brother sitting there. By strengthening your brother you help the meeting, and so you work with God.

What will be the facial expressions of the brothers and sisters sitting in a gospel meeting? The case will often be that if something new is said, they will listen enraptured. If, however, there is nothing new, they will feel cheated in coming, though they may not openly express it. I am really surprised that such difficulty exists concerning a gospel meeting. I feel that God's gospel can be heard a hundred times without it ever losing its freshness, because each time the story of how God loves us is told, it sounds so precious to our ears. We ought to praise God forever for the gospel story.

Some brothers and sisters will simply sit there without showing the slightest trace of anything on their faces. They neither smile nor frown. They are so cool. Such an attitude cannot help the brother who preaches; quite the contrary, it causes that brother to feel bound. He wonders if he has said something wrong to make them react like this. How often some people come and sit there spreading death. There is a kind of facial expression which can freeze a meeting. Hence, when you attend a meeting, it would be good for you to sometimes say an amen to show your sympathy or to nod your head in agreement or to respond with a smile to indicate that you are being helped by what is preached. By so doing you will render spiritual help to the brother who does the preaching, in making him feel he is not there standing alone but is rather supported by all the brethren. All this is important to realize, for your attitude will affect the preacher.

When the word preached touches you, it is very appropriate for you to say an amen I would not object even if the sound were louder, for not only those in the meeting place say amen, even the angels are likewise responding with an amen.

This matter of our support of the one preaching I believe was the scene recorded in Acts 2 on the occasion when Peter rose up to speak. I love this passage of the Scriptures very much because what is noted there was not Peter alone, but the eleven also who stood with him. Though only Peter was speaking, the eleven stood with him to show their agreement. Do not therefore turn within yourself to see what you may attain or how your inner state may be affected. If the assembly life is good, your personal life will also be good.

(4) Prayer Meeting

In order to see things done or to have the greatest power, the prayer meeting is most helpful. It can best measure spiritual strength. I hope many brothers and sisters will come, and that there will be many prayer burdens.

In a prayer meeting, as with all church meetings, assembly life not only helps a Christian's spiritual life, it also manifests the life of the body of Christ. If we overlook the gathering of the saints, we overlook the life together. And such is a great failure.

At a prayer meeting, things to be prayed for should be mentioned and explained. There ought not be too much speaking. Before we mention anything, let us ask ourselves if we have previously prayed for it at home. If it has not been prayed for at home, do not bring it out to deceive the brethren. Any matter which has not been prayed for at home shows neither need nor worth for prayer. This is a principle, a law. Whatever has not been prayed for personally has no need to be prayed for corporately. Only after it has been prayed for privately and a sense of personal inadequacy still lingers can it then be mentioned publicly in a prayer meeting.

Prayers offered in prayer meetings are heard most as well as least by God. Personal prayers are often heard, but corporate prayers are heard even more. People frequently use words and express sentiments in a prayer meeting which they do not use in their inner chamber. Oftentimes they pray with many words and on many things in a prayer meeting which they never do in their inner chamber. This ought not be so. Actually, whatever has not been a burden to pray for in the inner chamber should not be brought to the prayer meeting to be prayed for there. Prayer without burden ought not be uttered because it will not be heard by God. What prayer you feel inwardly is also felt by God. The power of prayer offered in a prayer meeting with burden and with one accord far exceeds individual prayer. If this were not true, there would be little point in having public prayer. Prayers offered with one heart without anything discordant existing between believers are most effective. God will surely hear such prayers. Hence the truth of the statement when we say that prayer is work.

Do not pray too long and too much. It is indeed true that prayer is like casting a net, yet it is not one person who casts the net. In case you sense something is left unprayed for, you should secretly ask God to raise up somebody else to pray for it. When I was in England, a Christian friend told me a story about a prayer meeting. There was a brother who prayed for many things. He felt he had prayed too long and ought to stop. Yet he also felt there were still many things which should be prayed for. On the one hand, he was afraid that if he ceased praying, nobody else would continue his prayer; on the other hand, he was apprehensive lest if he continued in prayer, he would occupy too much time. Still, out of consideration for other people, he decided to let some other brother pray. So he silently prayed within himself thus: I as an individual have prayed long enough in the meeting, please secure another brother, Lord, to continue my prayer. As he finished his public praying, somebody else actually continued his prayer and prayed for all the things which waited to be prayed for. So I would say that even if your thoughts are strong and good and many, you too should ask God to raise up other people at the same meeting to pray. God will attend to this request, for He is a living God. In a prayer meeting, we should give other people the opportunity to pray. Thus shall we pray with one accord and in life.

Sometimes God will use one among the brothers and sisters to speak for them. All who are experienced in prayer know how very difficult it is to have suitable words to express a need. Often several persons have prayed for the same thing, and yet the burden is not discharged. So let us ask God to give us words to express our burden in prayer. Ask Him to raise up one among us who can express God's thought. At times there may be ten persons praying together for a certain matter, and all have prayed well. Nevertheless, the consensus among them still is that none has hit the mark. Suddenly one brother begins to pray; and as he prays, he hits the mark. Everybody senses that this is it, and all will say amen. This is praying in the Spirit. If there is no one who can express the inward need for all in a prayer meeting, that meeting is a failure. On the other hand, if people pray from 7:00 p.m. to 7:30 p.m. and have already arrived at the point of having had the burden discharged, all may go home for there is no need for further prayer. The words of the Holy Spirit are spoken by the Holy Spirit through man to express the mind of God. Such prayer is thorough and prevailing.

In 1926, I was severely ill in Foochow. My whole body turned purple. Three brothers and one sister came to my room to pray for me. The first one prayed with tears, yet I did not feel touched. The second one also prayed fervently, but I still did not sense anything. The third one was known as a prayer warrior, but his prayer too was of no avail. The fourth one to pray was that sister. As she opened her mouth, she prayed: "O God, people in hades cannot praise you, nor do you like them to praise you in hades" (cf. Ps. 115.17, 6.5; Is. 38.18). I instantly felt that this was it. Even before the prayer was ended, I knew I was well. The burden was lifted, and the sickness was healed. That very afternoon I got out of bed, and the next day I was on my way to travel for the Lord's work. Hence let us ask God to use us as a mouthpiece in the prayer meeting so that we may utter the words of the Holy Spirit to express the current burden and need of the brothers and sisters.

I will also mention what happened at the recently concluded conference. Our convocation began on the Lord's Day January 20. At the prayer meeting on the 17th, we prayed especially for this Victory Conference. Many brethren prayed fervently for many things, and I ardently responded with amens. However, there lingered a sense of need as if a burden had not been uttered. Later on, one brother opened his mouth and prayed: "O God, grant us good weather that it will not be too cold nor raining, nor snowing, and that we may also meet quietly." Everybody at the prayer meeting immediately felt touched, and the amens were louder than in the other prayers. Now before the conference commenced the weather had not been too good. Even in the evening of our prayer time (Thursday), it had been snowing. But on Friday before the conference, both rain and snow stopped. When did it rain again? The Thursday after our conference was concluded. During the whole time of the conference, it had not rained once. Furthermore, in the lane where we met, one family was holding a funeral. The day before the conference, on Saturday, they made a tremendous noise during their funeral observance. But on the second day they stopped. And only after our conference was over did they again begin to observe the funeral service with great noise. Had they done this during the conference, we would not have been able to meet quietly.

Hence in a prayer meeting, we need people to be the mouthpiece of the Holy Spirit. If we have such people, we will have no difficulty. For our difficulty is not knowing the need. Whenever the burden is lifted, the work is done.

(5) Meeting of Brothers or Sisters

Due to the vastness of Shanghai and the scatteredness of the brothers and sisters over the city, there is a special need to have meetings for brothers and for sisters for the sake of fellowship. At such meetings, particular attention is given to fellowship and care. There we may talk about how to be brothers as well as discuss affairs concerning the gathering. We can mention the problems which brothers and sisters from abroad may incur or the employment situation of the local brethren or any special need among the saints. These are important practical matters. Many things can be corrected in such meetings. We can never be individual, isolated believers; we must learn how to bear each other's burdens. Many are concerned only with their own personal salvation and spirituality; they care not at all how other brothers and sisters fare, for they have no interest in living together. Yet God has not created a special heaven for each one of us. He puts us in a body so that we may help each other and fellowship with one another.

Many poor brethren dare not visit the houses of the rich brethren, nor do the rich brethren like to visit the homes of the poor brethren. In society, there are such distinctions as rich and poor, master and servant; but in the church all these distinctions are abolished. All the differences in the flesh must go through the cross. This is what the cross does for us.

We must not bring to the church meeting that which the cross has already abolished and laid in the tomb. The cross has not only done away with the wall of partition between the Jews and the Gentiles and between the cultured and the uncultured, but it has also taken away the wall between freemen and bondmen (see Eph. 2.13-16; Col. 3.11; cf. Gal. 3.28). In other words, it has abolished all elements of social status. In the home there is the distinction between master and servant, but in the church there is *no* such distinction. If one brother is a servant in a home to another brother, he should obey his master and be a good servant in that brother's house. And the brother who is the master must also be a good master of the house. But in the brothers meeting or in the breaking of bread meeting, there is no such distinction as between master and servant.

Beware of going into extremes on both sides. The servant must not think that because his master is a brother he can therefore be disobedient; nor should the master fail to control the servant because he is a brother. For there is a difference in the family situation. A Christian must learn to live properly as a human being. To use another illustration, let us assume that a father and son are both Christians. In their home, they are father and son. In the church assembly, the son can consider his father as a brother. In the family, however, the son must not treat his father as only a brother.

Hence in a brothers meeting, that is to say, when the brothers in the church gather together, they should be brought to the place where they recognize that in the Lord there is neither the rich nor the poor, neither the noble nor the humble, neither master nor servant, neither parent nor children. All these social and class distinctions are abolished in the body of Christ.

In a brothers or sisters meeting, the purpose is for fellowship, for helping to solve practical problems, and for learning to live together. It is not for hearing messages. The danger of many revival meetings is that when the revivalists are gone, the people are scattered. So that God's way is to place all these individually saved people in the various meetings of the church so that they may be joined into one and may be able to help one another.

To emphasize the practical aspect of assembly life, I think that first and foremost the brethren should increase their communication. They must not only show concern but also actually look after each other. Even though there are many things which should be dealt with individually and personally, oftentimes you should also know the problem your brothers or your sisters have. For example: if a brother is unemployed, you should find out why he is unemployed. If he has honestly been laid off, you should mention it at the brothers meeting so that all may help him according to the teaching of James 2. What we need to note here is to do, and not only to believe. To believe alone is useless. Or on the other hand, if that brother lost his job due to dishonesty, then he should be exhorted and helped into repentance. Such matters are not convenient nor suitable to be mentioned in a prayer meeting, a breaking of bread meeting, or a gospel meeting; but they *can* be raised in a brothers meeting. If a matter touches upon a personal name, it should not be publicly announced—not even in the brothers meeting.

How can we take care of these needy people if we do not know their problems and weaknesses, if we do not know what things have happened in their homes, or whether they are sick or in want? We do not have a hired pastor to look after these people. On the contrary, every brother and sister must do this work. Let it not be that the poor brothers deliberately avoid fellowship with the rich brethren, nor that the rich brethren overlook the needs of the poor brethren. None can cease to be a brother or sister because he or she does not want to fellowship with some other believers. We must demonstrate our togetherness in assembly life by our being real brothers and sisters.

Questions

(1) What kind of meeting is the one described in 1 Corinthians 14?

It is a meeting for the exercising of spiritual gifts. Though we today may not have the riches of such spiritual gifts as was true in the early days, we nevertheless do meet in accordance with that principle.

(2) What type of meeting is pointed to in Hebrews 10.25: "not forsaking our own assembling together"?

There it includes all kinds of meetings.

(3) When is the proper time to actually break bread at a breaking of bread meeting?

The Lord's Supper is for the sake of remembering the Lord. Hence the earlier the bread is broken, the better. Do not wait till after Eutychus falls down before the bread is to be broken (Acts 20.9-12). In a breaking of bread meeting we should discover its high tide. It is almost unavoidable that people will bring their family and circumstantial problems, failures and weaknesses into the meeting. It therefore requires some singing or prayers at the start to deliver them from these things. As each spirit is set free and the praise reaches its high point, the time for the breaking of the bread is come. Why can we not break bread at once? This is due to our weakness. When the high tide is reached, the bread should immediately be broken; if not, the propitious moment for doing such will ebb from this point.

(4) Should we give our offering on the Lord's Day at the time of breaking bread?

This really is no problem. The Lord commands us to give on the first day of the week (see 1 Cor. 16.2). The breaking of bread and giving happen to be on the same day, but they are not necessarily to be at the same time.

(5) When should we meet for the Lord's Supper—morning, afternoon, or evening?

The teaching of the New Testament is that it is to be eaten in the evening. Usually breakfast is consumed in a hurry because people are anxious to go to work; for many, lunch is taken outside and not in their homes; only supper is the meal when the family gathers and eats at leisure.

I personally feel it is far better in China to have the Lord's Supper in the evening. This naturally will cause inconvenience to some sisters. Yet in view of the fact that in China the Sunday service in different denominations is usually conducted in the morning or in the afternoon, people might come to eat the bread and drink the cup simply out of habit if the Lord's Supper is held in the morning or in the afternoon, and hence it will be rather difficult to distinguish between the saved and the unsaved in that case. It will easily offend people if the bread and the cup are passed over them. But if the meeting is held in the evening, there will not be such a problem. People who would attend merely for the purpose of hearing sermons will not come.

(6) At the breaking of bread, do we need to lift up the cup and bless it as in 1 Corinthians 11?

The lifting up of the cup actually follows the tradition of the Roman Catholic Church. Their priests consider themselves as blessing the cup on behalf of the Lord Jesus. Hence, when they lift the cup, they intone the Lord, saying: "This is my body which is for you; . . . this is my blood which is poured out for you." Many of the Protestant denominations have also adopted this practice. But we cannot bless in His stead. We believe the Lord is in our midst, and it is still He who blesses. How we bless is but our using the voices of the brothers and sisters in saying to the Lord, "Lord, we thank you." I believe this is according to the Scriptures (1 Cor. 10.16). For a brother to stand in the place of the Lord Jesus is in reality to usurp His place. A brother who finally blesses the loaf and the cup is but a brother who serves as the mouthpiece of all the brethren in giving thanks to the Lord. So that really there is no need to lift up the bread and the cup. Any other brother who is in fellowship and is not hindered by evil may get up and give thanks for the bread and the cup for all the brethren.

(7) In the breaking of bread meetings should we stand, kneel, or sit when praying? Is it irreverent not to kneel?

The postures in prayer are raised by this question. The Bible pays little attention to whether we pray sitting, standing, or kneeling. It does not consider not kneeling as irreverent or that kneeling is the sole position for praying. The New Testament records that when the disciples in Tyre sent off Paul and his companions, they with their wives and children knelt down on the beach and prayed (Acts 21.5). But in the record of Matthew, as the Lord teaches us to pray He says: "Enter into thine inner chamber, and having shut thy door, pray" (6.6). He does not say kneel and pray. The Scriptures cite many occasions of praying with faces covered. The Bible also several times tells of praying to the Lord sitting. It as well speaks of praying with hands lifted up, such as in the case of Moses who on the top of the hill had his hands lifted up (Ex. 17.11). As a matter of fact, the Scriptures often speak of praying with hands lifted up, for the lifting up of hands indicates the asking of God. It serves the purpose of attracting God's attention. "Pray in every place," said Paul to Timothy, "lifting up holy hands" (1 Tim. 2.8). It is easy to pray in every place, but it is not so easy to kneel down and pray in every place. We have no problem in lifting up our hands to pray, but we find it impossible to kneel and pray, since there are places where we just cannot kneel. In my opinion, let this matter be left to personal conviction. If the conscience of some compels them to kneel and pray, let them pray kneeling. But to make kneeling a law is unnecessary.

(8) Who should prepare the bread used at the Lord's Supper?

According to the Scriptures, the bread should be prepared by the deacons—both male and female.

(9) Is it necessary to have a tablecloth as well as another cloth to cover the bread and the cup?

Having the bread and cup covered is a Roman Catholic tradition. They think the elements are not holy if they are not covered. But according to 1 Corinthians 11, the bread and the cup should not be covered, because the breaking of bread expresses the death of our Lord and is to exhibit the Lord's death. It is nothing less than a testimony. Why then should it be covered? As to having a tablecloth, this is a matter of absolute freedom. If the table is not too neat, it may be covered with a tablecloth.

(10) If we consider head covering to be a teaching of the Scriptures, why do we not also practice the "saluting of one another with a holy kiss"—which is likewise a Scriptural teaching?

The Bible says to "salute one another with a holy kiss" (Rom. 16.16). The command is not that of kissing one another, but rather that if any one *should* salute with a kiss, let it be holy. The apostle has not exhorted us to kiss one another, since kissing can easily become unholy. The emphasis is on the word holy, not on the word kiss. If there is kissing, let it be holy.

As regards head covering, let me say again that it is highly profitable. In the meeting, sisters should have their heads covered. They should have on themselves the sign of submission to authority—for the sake of the angels. And the authority here, in the original, points to positional authority. Why is it so? Because Satan is also an angel. His "self" demonstrated the first sin, and it was the cause of his fall. His self rose up to resist

God and to overthrow His authority. The most marvelous thing in the universe is authority. We ought to know the importance of God's authority. He uses His word to hold together all things. Even the *name* of Christ is full of authority. God put Satan under His authority, yet Satan tried to overturn God's authority. The great dragon mentioned in Revelation 12—also called the old serpent—drew within his tail the third part of the stars of heaven (v.4), which means that Satan carried one third of the angels in heaven into his rebellion against God's authority. This is a well-known fact in the universe. This is the story of how sin was first brought into the universe.

And how did sin enter the world for the second time? It was through Eve. As Eve was created by God, she was to have Adam as her head. Paul declares in 1 Timothy that "Adam was not beguiled, but the woman being beguiled hath fallen into transgression" (2.14). There is a similarity between the sin in the Garden of Eden and Satan's sin. This sin is that the woman rebelled against Adam her head. Before she received permission from Adam, she acted on her own. So that sin comes from rebelling against authority, for sin is lawlessness.

Due to the fact that Eve fell in the same principle as Satan had fallen, God so ordains that woman should "have a sign of authority on her head, because of the angels" (1 Cor. 11.10). This sign will serve as a testimony before the angels to let them see that we today no longer do what Eve did on that day. Naturally, many sisters find this hard to accept. It thus becomes a real test to the sisters. Yet if the flesh is willing to be judged, this should constitute no problem. In the Garden of Eden, the woman did not stand in her proper place; but now, in the church, the sisters ought to take their proper place.

(11) Should we exhort sisters who cut their hair to cover their heads?

These small things greatly test our conscience. The

first thing is to encourage them to have long hair. If they refuse to have long hair, there is no need to exhort them to cover their heads. For they have already indicated they do not care for the glory which God has given them. A sister has a double covering: one is the natural covering of the hair, the other is the sign of head covering. If the natural covering be overturned, what use will the sign of head covering be to her? Having a sign of covering on her head is something which she must do willingly.

(12) Can a brother wear a hat when he is praying or preaching?

In my own experience, I always take off my hat when I pray. I feel I will dishonor my head if I do not take off my hat. This does not mean that God will not hear if a brother prays with his head covered or a sister prays without her head covered. But our praying and prophesying have special relationship with the angels in the spiritual realm. Hence the brother ought not have his head covered. According to my personal view, talking to people on the road about the Lord is also related to the spiritual realm, and therefore it is better to take the hat off.

(13) What is the difference between prophesying and preaching?

Not all who can preach and edify people are prophets. For a prophet not only can edify people but also actually predict things. He is able to predict as well as to speak forth the mind of God.

(14) What must be done to the left-over bread and wine at a breaking of bread meeting?

These may be consumed either by some brethren or by fire.

(15) In the breaking of the bread, do we break a piece from the whole loaf or can we pick up some fragments in the plate?

There is no difference, since all come from the same loaf of bread.

4 The Boundary of a Local Assembly

We will now deal with the subject of the boundary of the local assembly—that is to say, how far-reaching is the sphere of a local assembly?

The authority of the elders, which we have mentioned before, is to be exercised within the local assembly, because elders are established for the local assembly. Their position and function are all related to the local assembly. Elders in Shanghai are not elders in Nanking or Peking. Whereas the gifts of God are for the whole Church, the offices are for the local assembly. There are no super elders who can control assemblies other than their local one. Elders can only govern a local assembly.

How extensive is the border of a local assembly? How large a place is required to form a local assembly? Please note that the Bible never divides the Church according to region, nor does it even place several churches under a regional church. Although there are seven churches in Asia being mentioned in Revelation, we do not find in God's word that Ephesus or Philadelphia had been chosen to control the other six churches. We only see seven churches represented by seven golden lampstands. In the Old Testament record there is mentioned the one lampstand with seven branches; but here in Revelation are seven lampstands—not one with seven branches but seven lampstands representing seven separate churches, each emitting light and each bearing responsibility directly to Christ.

Whichever church it may be, it accepts the rule of Christ and not the control of other churches. Each lampstand is independent in government, without it being managed by other lampstands. Each is responsible to its high priest, the Son of man who walks in the midst of the seven golden lampstands. None of them is subject to any of the other churches. Though they are seven churches, they do not join to form a united church and make themselves answerable to a regional or annual conference. We may say that each is a "congregation" which takes a locality as its limit.

The Bible usually takes a city, the smallest executive governmental area, as the boundary of a local assembly. A local assembly is the unit of the Church in God's word. It does not join with other assemblies and make the resulting larger church a central church. In other words, in the eyes of God, He has not made Rome as the central church. He never makes any local assembly the center of the churches to be in control of other assemblies. There is no center on earth in God's government. Even Jerusalem was not a center to the early churches.

This did not rule out the existence of regions in the biblical record. Some places were so similar in conditions and needs that they would receive the same treatment in the record. For instance, it is said of Paul that he "passed through the upper country" (Acts 19.1); again, "from Jerusalem, and round about even unto Illyricum" (Rom. 15.19). These are regions. Galatia, too, was not a single city, but a province. And hence the Bible mentions "the churches of Galatia" (1 Cor. 16.1). The book of Revelation records the seven churches *in Asia*, since Ephesus, Smyrna, Pergamum, Thyatira, Sardis, Philadelphia, and Laodicea were all located in the region of Asia. Asia is a region; Galatia is a province. Let us be clear that although the need, testimony and service of these local assemblies were closely akin to each other, no one church assumed a superior organization and authority over the other nearby churches. Some may think of Jerusalem as having been "the mother church." Actually there is no such thing as a mother church. To put it another way, each local assembly is locally governed, it being directly accountable to Christ and not answerable to any other organization or assembly. This is to say, in short, that a local assembly is to be the only—yea, is to be the highest and lowest—organization in a locality. There is nothing lower or higher than a local assembly. Since there is no higher court above it to which to appeal, it is the highest organization in a locality. And because it is the lowest unit of the church on earth, there is nothing lower.

The Bible does not endorse a centralized Rome that controls all the local assemblies. This is because Christ in heaven reserves for himself the position of being the Head. Each and every local church must maintain the testimony of the body of Christ, since each is a miniature manifestation of Christ's body. Each must be directly responsible to Christ and not to any other assembly. Each is under the rule of Christ and not under the control of any other organization.

God purposely set Jerusalem aside lest people would misconstrue that the Church on earth needed a center. He sent apostles out from Antioch (Acts 13) and not out from Jerusalem in order to avoid the misunderstanding that the church in Jerusalem was the mother church with all the other churches serving as her branches. Let us therefore never consider the assembly at Shanghai as the mother church. The assemblies in various localities are subject to Christ directly and not to any other assembly.

This truth concerning the independence of the local assembly is a balance to the truth of the inter-relatedness of the various assemblies in the body life. For God will not tell one assembly not to do something but then tell another assembly to do that very thing. He will guide one assembly in the same way as He guides other assemblies. We earlier saw how the Gentile churches were to imitate the churches in Judea. We also saw earlier how God ordains His churches not to move independently but to keep unity by paying attention to the movement of the body of Christ: for example, whoever has been excommunicated by one assembly should not be received by another assembly. One assembly is bound together with the other assemblies in that it should not act independently. It is not of God that any assembly should move freely on its own without considering the other assemblies. Yet, there is the other side of truth which declares that each assembly is directly responsible to the Head. How easy for us to go off-balance, but truth must be kept in balance.

Sometimes we may fall into the way of Rome. Whatever Rome decides, all the Roman Catholics must obey. But this is not the balance of truth. What we need is to accept the restraint of the other assemblies in that we agree to march forward together in matters of truth and on the other hand to see that we each are directly responsible to the Head. The churches mentioned in Revelation chapters 2 and 3 (Ephesus, Smyrna, Pergamum, Thyatira, Sardis, Philadelphia, and Laodicea) have their own golden lampstands respectively. Each is positioned in its own stand; none of them is somebody else's stand. Each maintains its own place and is accountable to God. And hence the Lord reprimands as well as commends Ephesus itself—He does not put the blame of Ephesus on Smyrna nor transfer the virtue of Ephesus to Smyrna. No church is responsible for any other church, and no church stands by the other church, because all are directly responsible to the Lord and all accept His rule. At the same time, however, God's word declares this: "He that hath an ear, let him hear what the Spirit saith *to the churches*" (Rev. 2.7). This illustrates the balance of truth.

On the one hand, the message is addressed to the angel of the church at Ephesus; but at the end of the message *to Ephesus*, it is said to be spoken as well *to the churches*. At the beginning of each of the seven letters, the letter is addressed to the particular angel of the individual churches respectively, but at the end of each letter it is made clear that each letter is for all the churches to hear. It commences with an individual church being directly responsible to God; it concludes with every other church needing to hear the word which God declares to each of the other churches. This indicates how all the churches must keep that which one church receives. As to the responsibility of each church, every one is individually responsible to God; as to the movement of all the churches, there needs to be a concerted action. This explains why the letter is sent to Ephesus but why it is also applicable to all the other churches. Such is the balance of truth.

In the Bible God has ordained that the lowest unit of the Church on earth is the local assembly, which at the same time is equally the highest. Every local assembly is a miniature manifestation of the Church universal. There is nothing larger or smaller than it. We need to be careful that whatever we do in Shanghai may be in step with all the churches in China. We need to seek not only to maintain the same step with all the churches in China but also to take the same step with all the local assemblies of the world. Nevertheless, whatever action the church in Shanghai takes, it is directly responsible to God. It is not to be controlled by any other organization. So far as the authority of the church in Shanghai is concerned, nothing is higher than the eldership. This is the boundary which God has ordained. In each city, there is the plurality of elders, but these elders may only govern the local assembly there and not extend their government to assemblies elsewhere. The boundary set by God is to appoint elders in every city; consequently, the authority of the elders cannot extend beyond the city limits. The Bible advocates the local assembly which is then governed only locally. May we maintain this balance of moving together with other assemblies as well as bearing responsibility directly towards God as a local assembly.

The Border of a Local Assembly

Concerning the border of a local assembly, in the New Testament God makes the city to be its boundary. So that the maximum sphere of a local assembly is a city and nothing larger than a city. In the biblical record, there is no church that controls a region, a province, or a county. The city always marks the limit of the church. A city was originally the aggregate of people who lived in the same locality. Let us realize that due to today's complicated life we have such divisions as county, township, village, and so forth. In the olden days, wherever the people congregated and lived and were protected—that was considered a city (Gen. 4.17). For various reasons, they lived in the city. In the first part of Genesis we find nothing smaller than the city. At the time when Joshua apportioned the land to the Hebrew people, we notice that the place where people lived was still called a city, only now sometimes villages were also mentioned (see Joshua 18.28). When the Lord Jesus sent out His disciples to preach the gospel, they were sent to cities (see Matt. 10). This is because in the biblical account a city was viewed as the lowest unit of the aggregate of people.

Thus the boundary of a local assembly in the Scriptures is according to the limit of such a city. Ephesus, Corinth, and Thessalonica, for example, were all such cities. The border of a local church never exceeds the limit of a city. The province of Asia was such a large area that it had seven churches. Galatia was a region, and hence the phrase "the churches in Galatia" was used. Corinth, on the other hand, was only a city, and so the whole church assembled together there (1 Cor. 14.23). The church in Corinth is but one church. Throughout the New Testament we see that all the local assemblies take the particular city limits as their border.

How wise is the way of God in keeping believers from confusion. For if He were to take the nation as the boundary of the church, the border of the church would then frequently be changed because a nation would fall and thus would the boundary of the church be altered. If God were to use the province as the boundary of the church, the border of the church would also be subject to change since provincial lines can often be altered too. Would not all these cause confusion? Instead, God in His word used neither province nor nation nor other political division as the unit of church boundary. He took instead the city or village as the church boundary because its border and name are not easily changed. We see national, regional, and provincial borders and names frequently altered, but the names and borders of cities and villages are the least influenced by political change. The names of many villages have remained the same for hundreds of years. Many cities may be ceded to other nations, yet they still remain as civic entities because they are the most durable of political units. For this reason, God has ordained the city limits to be the border of the local assembly. Although we have mentioned the village as a variant unit of church border, in actual fact the village is but a miniature city. Hence God's thought is still the city.

God makes cities the permanent unit of the local assembly. There is great profit in dividing church lines by this method without setting some higher control above it. For if there is sin or failure in one local assembly, it will not contaminate the other assemblies elsewhere. Had God put seven or eight churches under the authority of a few men, the failure of one or two among these men would undoubtedly have affected all these churches. If He had established a center in the province of Asia to control all seven of its churches, the failure of the center would have dragged all the other seven churches down with it. But these seven churches in Asia were respectively responsible to the Lord. Though five of them failed, there were yet Smyrna and Philadelphia which remained faithful. In this way God was able to preserve the weak and the good from the sinful and improper.

Dividing by City Line

What God first created was a garden—the Garden of Eden—and not a city. But what He finally is to obtain is to be the New Jerusalem, which is a city. So that the thought of the city was manifested only after the fall of man had occurred. Before man's fall, trees such as the tree of life and other fruit-bearing trees were planted in the Garden. And a living stream flowed out of the Garden. But since the fall of man, the work of God has ever been to transform the garden into a city. For a garden seems to have neither boundary nor protection. God purposely builds the city for the sake of protection as well as for boundary. It is to be separated, thus forbidding sin to enter its precincts. God has the city in mind not only for today, but also for the time of the millennium. The Scriptures make clear that some believers will rule five cities, some will rule over ten cities. And even at the time of the New Heaven and the New Earth, God still focuses on the city. For at that time there will be the city of New Jerusalem. He thus lifts up the city because it has a boundary, is separated, distinguishable, easily governed and not easily confused.

Wherever some believers are gathered together in a city, this gathering becomes the local assembly. Other assemblies in other cities cannot interfere with these saints' local affairs. The border of a local assembly is as extensive as the limits of the city. Its boundary, therefore, follows the line of the governmental extent of the city. For God has not left to the brethren or to the elders to decide on its border. The responsibility of the church is to adopt the city or village as determined by the government. The dimension of a city is the dimension of a local assembly. Cities vary in their sizes. Some like Nineveh require a three days' journey to traverse its city limits. Some are like Jerusalem whose radius is only about two miles (John 11.18, "fifteen furlongs"). Bethany is another place, but it does not belong to the city of Jerusalem. Although Jerusalem and Bethany are closely adjacent to each other, the first is a city which has its own border and the second is a village which likewise has its own border. And thus the Bible divides them according to their political divisions. In spite of the fact that some localities are larger while some are smaller, the church cannot make its own division but must follow the political or governmental division. For God uses the governmental division as the accepted dimension of today's local assembly.

How to Meet Separately in One City

We have seen how the assembly in the Scriptures takes a city or a village as its unit. In Shanghai, for example, we meet in two different places—Wen Teh Lane and Gordon Lane. What is the relationship between these two meetings? Before we deal with this question, let us first consider how the Bible solves this problem when there are too many people meeting in one city. On the Day of Pentecost, three thousand souls were added to the church in Jerusalem. Later on, five thousand were saved. There were consequently many believers in Jerusalem. Jerusalem was different from Corinth. In the latter city not too many people were saved, and hence the entire church could be assembled together in one place (1 Cor. 14.23). But in Jerusalem the entire church could not assemble together in one place because there were too many believers: first, three thousand, then an additional five thousand, and finally those who were being saved daily! They did not have such a huge facility. So that we see that even though they were all together as one, they broke bread in "homes" (see Acts 2.46). This was the difference between the church in Corinth and the church in Jerusalem. In Corinth they met in one place because they were comparatively few in number. In Jerusalem, however, they met in many "homes" because they were too many in number. Accordingly, when there are too many people in a local assembly, they may meet in many "homes." This is how it is shown to us in the book of Acts.

The people of a local assembly may meet in different homes, but they are still one church. For instance, if in Jerusalem people met in scores of places, can it be said that in Jerusalem there was one church or that there were scores of churches? The answer of the Bible is: there is but one church. For let us recall that God uses the entire city (no matter its size) as the border of the local assembly. The church in a city is always singular in number. In Jerusalem there was only one church. Though there may have been scores of meeting places, the government of the church in Jerusalem was nevertheless one. It had the same group of elders and deacons. The elders in the church in Jerusalem may have functioned as elders in these "homes," but they could not go to Samaria and function as elders there. This is because a local assembly takes the city as its boundary. Now this is our situation in Shanghai. According to the legal political division, Shanghai is but one city, and therefore there is but one church. Both the Wen Teh Lane meeting and the Gordon Lane meeting must together be reckoned as one church. When the number of a local assembly is increased, people can meet in different places. Some may ask what number should be reached before there are separate meetings? What is the limitation? Let us recall the incident of the distribution of the loaves by our Lord. Before He multiplied the loaves to feed the five thousand men, He caused the multitude to "sit down in companies, about fifty each" (Luke 9.14). "And they sat down in ranks, by hundreds, and by fifties" (Mark 6.40). In my opinion, since we are the Lord's sheep, it is easier to be fed by dividing into companies of fifties or hundreds. Such division has several advantages.

(1) The apostles in the early days of Acts did not have money to build a large meeting hall. So they followed the principle of "home meetings" though not necessarily dividing into

fifties and hundreds. Thus there was no difficulty in their finding places to meet. We today would rather not have a large central place but instead divide ourselves into fifties and hundreds.

(2) Having hundreds or thousands gathered together to break bread would have been time-consuming and also there would have been no cup and no loaf big enough for such a huge number of people. So it is evident that the many who were saved in the early days did not break bread all in one place. Even in our own day when we ourselves sometimes have two to three hundred people breaking bread together, it would take us one to two hours. Some people can wait but many may not have the strength to wait so long.

(3) For several hundreds assembling together, it is rather difficult to have good fellowship due to the limitation of time. On each occasion a person may know and fellowship with only one or two others. But by that method it would take months and months before a person could fellowship with all. How can the assembly grow in such a way? If, however, there are only fifty or a hundred gathered together, it is relatively easy to fellowship with one another, and it enhances the growth of the believers. It is also easier for the responsible brothers to take care of all the brethren. When the number becomes too large, it is difficult to give good care. This is therefore a principle we should practice.

It was for this reason, among others, that last year we started to meet in Gordon Lane as well as at Wen Teh Lane. Yet the meeting in Gordon Lane and the meeting in Wen Teh Lane are not two churches but are one church—one entire fellowship—meeting in two "homes." The responsible brothers in Wen Teh Lane are the same as those in Gordon Lane. When a brother travels from Shanghai to Nanking, he needs to have a letter of recommendation. But for him to go to Gordon Lane from Wen Teh Lane and vice versa, he does not need such a letter.

Concerning City Limits and Suburbs

"And the children of Israel gave unto the Levites out of their inheritance, according to the commandment of Jehovah, these cities with their suburbs" (Joshua 21.3). This passage speaks of cities with their suburbs. "Blessed shalt thou be in the city, and blessed shalt thou be in the field" (Deut. 28.3). This passage speaks of city and field. From the Old Testament record it is understood that every city had its suburbs as well as its fields. These suburbs and fields surrounded the city for the sake of providing the city with necessities. The food the city consumed came from the suburbs and fields. The city obviously could not exist by itself. In addition, the city had to be responsible for its suburbs and fields. Likewise today, the church in the city should bear responsibility not only for the city but also for the suburbs and fields. Whether it is preaching the gospel or building up the saints, the church in the city should take care of its suburbs and fields; for the latter support the former, and cause the number in the assembly to increase. In other words, the people in the church of the city should also take care of the people in its suburbs and fields. When people are saved in the suburbs, and they are not able to meet by themselves, bring them to the city to meet. This will support the meeting in the city and make it stronger. But after the brethren from the suburbs increase in number, and they have also learned to meet, let them become another "home" or even make the suburb as another "city" unit and begin a new assembly.

Questions

(1) Should we practice the laying on of hands today?

The Bible does mention the laying on of hands, but it is not the same as what people call laying on of hands today.

Nowadays, it is always viewed as a case of the "better" laying hands on the "lesser." But in the Scriptures there is equally the view that the "lesser" can lay hands on the "better" as well as the "better" can lay hands on the "lesser." As recorded in Acts 8, when the apostles Peter and John laid hands on the Samaritan believers, what they did was a case of the "better" laying hands on the "lesser." But Acts 13 tells us that in the church at Antioch, when several prophets and teachers ministered to the Lord and fasted, the Holy Spirit said to them: "Separate me Barnabas and Saul for the work whereunto I have called them" (v.2b). So they laid hands on Barnabas and Saul and sent them away. Now we know from this same passage that Paul and Barnabas were apostles, but they had hands of the prophets and teachers laid on them. Yet in Ephesians 4 the apostles are listed first, then the prophets and the teachers. And hence in Acts 13 we find the "lesser" laid hands on the "better."

The biblical conception of the laying on of hands is not what people today usually think of—the latter being an action of the "better" performed on the "lesser." In the Scriptures, laying on of hands is but an expression of fellowship, sympathy and union. The laying on of hands spoken of in Acts 8 shows that the Samaritans were also joined to the body of Christ even as their baptism testified to their being joined to the death of Christ. The laying on of hands told of in Acts 13 indicates that the church was united with Barnabas and Paul and was in full agreement and fellowship with them. Their going out was the going out of the whole church. Such kind of laying on of hands exhibits to us that it was not only Barnabas and Paul who went abroad to preach the gospel but that the whole church at Antioch went forth with them. So that what the two apostles did was related to the entire church at Antioch. Their laying on of hands spoke not only of their fellowship with the ones who received this token (Paul and Barnabas) but also of the fellowship of the ones who received the laying on of hands with the whole church at Antioch. If anyone would go out from one locality to work for the Lord, it is best if he is sent out by the laying on of hands.

Let us be careful in our wiping out all the traditions of men from Scriptural teaching just as people cleanse dust from the glass. Some do not wipe the dust off but instead break the glass because it is filled with dust. Many may suggest that since we talk about elders and deacons and the laying on of hands we are not different from any denomination. Let us see that there is actually nothing wrong with these things in themselves; but what is wrong is that which men have added on to them. Our purpose today is not to destroy the works of the denominations but to restore the things which God had originally ordained. We cannot forsake biblical realities because of human adulteration. We instead ought to ask if God has so commanded. When I go out to do spiritual work, how many times I expect the brethren to lay hands on me to show that I do not go out alone but that the entire church sends me out. They are one with me.

(2) When Paul laid hands on Timothy, he imparted a gift to Timothy. Is a gift received through the laying on of hands?

What is a gift? It is the ability of a member. In other words, if you are an eye in the body, your gift is seeing; if you are an ear in the body, your gift is hearing. When a person is joined to the body of Christ, he immediately receives a gift. Why, then, did the apostle lay hands on Timothy? In representing the body of Christ, the apostle recognized that Timothy was also a member of that body. It pleases God that such laying on of hands will activate a gift in the person. What Acts 13 expresses is also the union of the body of Christ, although it is not for the manifestation of gifts but for the demonstration of the principle of our working together. Never can prophets and teachers impart gifts to apostles. I believe the laying on of hands should be continued. Nevertheless, Paul warned Timothy to "lay hands hastily on no man, neither be partaker of other men's sins: keep thyself pure" (1 Tim. 5.22). Hebrews tells us to "not lay again a foundation" (6.1). Both baptism and laying on of hands are included in that foundation. And hence, if we neglect the laying on of hands there will be some flaw in the foundation.

(3) How about receiving people to the breaking of bread? "Him that is weak in faith receive ye" (Rom. 14.1). "Wherefore receive ye one another, even as Christ also received you" (Rom. 15.7). Receiving people is but a part of the procedure. The main question is whether or not there is faith itself, not merely how strong or weak their faith is. The other question is, Will God accept them? We need to know if God will accept them or not. We cannot accept those whom God does not accept.

Concerning this matter of receiving, I would like to mention a few things here:

(a) People who come with letters of recommendation. We should accept all who come with letters of recommendation, though we need to discern where these letters come from. Letters which come from places where their stand on the Christian faith is doubtful cannot be taken at their face value. We cannot accept people simply on the basis of these letters. But with respect to letters from places where their faith is known, we can believe and also accept the people recommended. We must believe that what these places do are what we too will do.

(b) People introduced by two or three witnesses. We can accept people who are introduced by two or three brethren. The problem lies in people who are passing by or in visitors who break bread with us only once. In my opinion, it is best if two or three brothers can talk with them to find out if they are saved before receiving them.

(c) There are a few things we ought to know before receiving anyone to break bread:

(1) if that person is saved;

(2) if he has committed any of the sins mentioned in 1 Corinthians 5 which are grounds for excommunication;

(3) if he knows that the breaking of bread is not only to remember the Lord but also to discern the body of Christ.

Numbers (1) and (2) are conditions, for a person must be saved and clean before he can partake of the bread. Number (3) is a teaching, the instruction of which he ought to have, that he may stand on the ground of the body of Christ. Otherwise, he will eat and drink judgment to himself.

If a person is saved and he has not committed the sins of 1 Corinthians 5, and even though he may not be able to discern the body, he still can be received, because we must receive those who are weak in faith. However, we should be faithful in instructing people to discern the body, yet without making it a condition for receiving people because this will make us a sect.

(4) After a person is saved, must he be baptized before he can take the bread?

In the case of a newly saved person, it is better for that one to first be baptized and then to break bread. In the Bible we do not find recorded any names of people who have believed for some time but were not baptized. For believing and baptism were simply joined together. Never was a person saved but kept from baptism for several months. Furthermore, we cannot make baptism a condition for breaking bread. Some are only sprinkled and do not know that baptism is a testimony. We ought to receive such people for they belong to God. We must not make baptism a condition for receiving people; we can only take it as a teaching. We cannot excommunicate people who are not baptized. When they truly see the cross, they will obey the truth and be baptized.

THE CHURCH AND THE WORK

II

The Church and the Work

II

Rethinking the Work

WATCHMAN NEE

Christian Fellowship Publishers, Inc.
New York

Publishing History for Volume Two, ***Rethinking the Work:***

First published in Chinese under this title by The Gospel Book Room (Shanghai, January 1938).

First published in English in Great Britain under the title *Concerning Our Missions* by The Witness and Testimony Publishers (London, April 1939). In the public domain.

First published in English in the United States under the title *Concerning Our Missions* by Zondervan Publishing House (Grand Rapids, later 1939).

Revised Edition published in English for the first time under the title *The Normal Christian Church Life* by International Students Press (Washington, D.C., 1962) and variously reprinted at different times since then under that same title.

Published in a paperback edition in English in the United States under the title *Concerning Our Missions* (n.p., [February 1980]).

First English-language edition published 1939 in Great Britain by The Witness and Testimony Publishers from whose Trustees Christian Fellowship Publishers, Inc. has received assurance of support for reprinting and adapting it to its original form under the title of the original Chinese edition.

Printed in the United States of America.

Available from the Publishers at:

11515 Allecingie Parkway
Richmond, Virginia 23235

Volume Two

Rethinking the Work

TRANSLATOR'S NOTE
to the
Revised and Enlarged English Edition (1982)

As indicated elsewhere, this second of three volumes on the church and the Work had originally been published in Chinese as *Rethinking the Work.* When the first English-language translation of the book was subsequently published in London under the title *Concerning Our Missions,* the original book's entire first chapter *as a chapter entity* (entitled "The Ministry and the Ministers") was deleted, although some of its text was incorporated into the English translation's first chapter ("The Apostles"), which chapter was actually the original Chinese edition's second chapter. Moreover, a subtopic (dealing with false apostles) to be found in the original Chinese version of the chapter entitled "The Apostles" was also deleted when *Concerning Our Missions* was published.

Now in order that there might be available to English-language readers the entire text of *Rethinking the Work,* all deleted materials cited above have in this present edition of the book been restored to the work and have been placed in their proper order in the text just as it had appeared in the earlier Chinese version. In addition, so as to avoid any repetition, that part of the original first chapter which had been incorporated into the first chapter of *Concerning Our Missions* has been deleted and reinserted at its proper place in the opening chapter* of this new edition now in the reader's hands.

With these various corrections made, therefore, this revised and enlarged edition of the London translation of the original Chinese work provides the reader for the first time with the *complete* text in English of Watchman Nee's *Rethinking the Work.*

Finally, the reader should be aware that as far as practicable, word spellings, abbreviations, capitalization, and the like that were characteristic of the earlier British edition of 1939 have been retained throughout this expanded version of the author's English-language translation, including all material previously deleted but now newly translated and restored. Moreover, unless otherwise indicated, the Revised Version of the Bible has been retained as the basic source for Biblical quotations throughout the text—except that in the new material restored or added, the American Standard Version (1901) has been used.

---

*Except for this reinsertion, the entire opening chapter entitled "The Ministry and the Ministers" has been translated and published into English *for the first time.* The same is true as well for the sub-topic entitled "The False Apostles," which has now been translated and restored to Chapter 2 of the present work.

CONTENTS

The Revised Version is used throughout unless otherwise stated.

Preface to First English Edition (1939)

After the publication of my book in Chinese, quite a number of missionaries asked for an English edition. I felt reluctant to comply, for personally I should prefer to have those books translated which better represent my ministry, rather than this one which is liable to be misunderstood and controverted. But that it was the Lord's mind seemed to be quite clear, and in that confidence I proceeded with the translation. The book as it now stands is a greatly abridged and slightly revised edition of the Chinese edition. Neither in expression nor in style is it as English as I should wish, but I trust that in this respect I may reckon on the leniency of its readers. If all we want is the Truth of God, then the difficulty of understanding the book should prove no serious barrier to the reading of it.

Because of the vastness of the subject and the importance of its issues, I have not found it easy either to write or translate the book. Since some of the same points have had to be dealt with in different parts of the book, it will be found necessary to read it right through if full understanding is to result. If, because of seemingly insurmountable difficulty, the book is laid aside before completed, a false position will result; whereas, by reading it right through, many, if not all, of the difficulties will be cleared up. Frequently the questions which arise at certain points are answered further on—sometimes much further on. So to do it justice, the reader is asked to finish reading it before passing judgment.

The book is not intended for anyone and everyone. It is for those who bear responsibility in the Lord's service. But, more than this, it is for such as honestly and truly mean business with God, for those whose hearts are open and have no padlocked mind or prejudices. The book may test one's sincerity and honesty to no small degree; but genuine hunger and desire to know the Lord's full thought will sustain the perusal to the end. I fully realize the many imperfections of this book (this is not a gesture, but a confession); but despite them all, I believe the Lord has shown something which is of importance to the whole Body of Christ.

The whole matter will grow upon the reader and become clearer with relaxed contemplation after the first reading. The door must not be closed with a snap of "Impossible!" or, "Ideal, but not practical!" By prayerful openness of heart, without argument or discussion, the Spirit of Truth should be given a chance, and then *what is of Him* will cause all our natural reactions to die away, and we shall know the Truth and the Truth shall make us free!

May I remind my readers that the book is not intended to be studied in a hypothetical way. I have quite a large number of fellow-workers who have been sent out and are working along the lines indicated, and there are a larger number of churches which have been formed and developed on the basis mentioned.* So what is set forth in these pages is no mere theory, or teaching, but something we have actually tested out.

One of the prayers I have offered in connection with this book is that the Lord should keep it from those who oppose and would use it as a chart for attack, and also from those who agree and would use it as a manual for service. I dread the latter far more than the former.

LONDON. W. NEE.
April, 1939.

*See Introduction.

Introduction

The content of the following pages is the substance of a number of talks to my younger fellow-workers during conferences held recently in Shanghai and Hankow. When the addresses were given, the present book was not in view, but only my immediate audience; and the fact that the messages were intended for the instruction of my young colleagues accounts for their intensely practical nature, and for the simplicity of the style adopted. At these two conferences we* sought in the first place to examine the teaching of God's Word concerning His churches and His Work, and in the second place to review our past missions in the light of our findings.

The talks proved of value to my younger brethren, and, as long-hand notes were taken, the messages were shared with others. This resulted in many requests that the addresses be put into book form. As the conferences were attended chiefly by my younger fellow-workers, I felt at liberty to instruct and counsel them, and to discuss quite freely a number of intimate and rather delicate matters. Had the addresses been intended for a wider audience, or for publication, I should have felt obliged to omit many matters that were mentioned, and to speak in an altogether different strain. I naturally hesitated when the suggestion was made to publish them, but the Lord made it clear that that was His mind, so I have no option but to

*The word "we" is used throughout this book as amongst fellow-workers, for it was so used by the Apostles in the Book of Acts.

acquiesce. I questioned the wisdom of preserving the original style of the addresses, with their bits of "elder-brotherly" counsel and their distinct personal strain; but as a number of friends testified to special help received through the more personal parts, I realized that the book would lose its greatest value if those were eliminated; therefore, though I send the addresses forth somewhat revised, they still remain, both in matter and style, very much as they were when originally delivered.

We trust the readers of this book will bear in mind that its messages, as originally given, were never meant for them. They were intended exclusively for the inner circle of my most intimate associates in the Work, but by request we share our findings with the wider circle of all our brethren. This book is something private made public; something originally intended for the few now extended to the many; so we trust our readers will pardon anything that seems unsuited to the wider public.

We should like to point out here the place of the teachings of this book in the great body of Divine Truth, for the former have spiritual value only as they are held in relation to the latter. During the past eighteen years, the Lord has led us through different experiences in order that we might learn a little of the principle as well as the fact of the Cross and Resurrection, and learn something of the Christ-life, the Lordship of Jesus, the corporate life of the Body, the ground of the Kingdom of God, and His Eternal Purpose. It is natural, therefore, that these things have been the burden of our ministry. But God's wine must have a wine-skin to contain it. In the Divine pattern, nothing is left for man to decide. God Himself has provided the best wine-skin for His wine, which will contain and preserve it without loss, hindrance, or misrepresentation. He has shown us His wine, but He has shown us his wine-skin also.

Our work, throughout the past years, has been according to certain definite principles; but never until now have we tried to define or teach them. We have sought rather, in the power of the Spirit, to stress those truths which are so dear to our hearts and which, we believe, have more direct bearing on the spiritual life of the believer and the Eternal Purpose of God. But the practical out-working of those truths in the Lord's service is by no means unimportant. Without that, everything is in the realm of theory, and spiritual development is impossible. So we would seek, by the grace of God, not only to pass on His good wine, but also the wine-skin He has provided for its preservation. The truths set forth in this book must therefore be regarded in relation to those taught throughout the eighteen years of our ministry, and as the *sequence*, not the introduction, to them.

Within the scope of these pages, it has been impossible to deal with all the questions relating to the subject of the book. Some I have already dealt with elsewhere, and others I hope to deal with at a later date. *The title of the book explains its nature.* It is not a treatise on missionary methods, but a *review* of our past work in the light of God's Will as we have discovered it in His Word. The Lord had most graciously led us by His Spirit in our past service for Him, but we wanted to be clear as to the foundations upon which all Divine work should rest. I realized that the primary need of my younger brethren was to be led of the Spirit and to receive revelation from Him, but I could not ignore their need of a solid *scriptural* basis fo. all their ministry; so together we talked freely of what we had been doing and how we had been doing it, and sought to compare our work and methods with what God had set before us in His Word. We examined the scriptural reasons for the means we employed, and the scriptural justification for the end we pursued; and we made a note of various lessons we had learned by observation as well as by experience. There was no thought of criticizing the labours of others, or even of making any suggestion to them how the Work of God ought to be conducted; we were merely seeking to learn from God's Word, from experience, and from observation, how to conduct the Work in the days to come, so that *we* might be workmen "approved unto God."

The book is written from the standpoint of a servant looking from the Work *towards the churches*. It does not deal with the specific ministry to which we believe the Lord has called us, but only with the general principles of the Work; nor does it deal with "the Church, which is His Body," but with the local churches and their relation to the Work. The book does not touch the principles of the Work, or the life of the churches; it is only a review of our past works, as the title suggests.

The truths referred to in this book have been gradually learned and practised during the past years. Numerous adjustments have been made as greater light has been received, and if we remain humble, and God still shows us mercy, we believe there will be further adjustments in the future. The Lord has graciously given us a goodly number of associates in the Work, all of whom have been sent forth on the basis mentioned in this book, and through their labours numerous churches have been established in different parts of China. Though vastly different conditions obtain in these many churches, and the believers connected with them differ greatly too—in background, education, social standing, and spiritual experience—yet we have found that if, under the absolute Lordship of Jesus, we come to see the heavenly pattern of church formation and government, then the scriptural methods are both practicable and fruitful.

Whilst the book itself may seem to deal with the technical side of Christianity, let us emphasize here that we are not aiming at mere technical correctness. It is spiritual reality we are after. But spirituality is not a matter of theory; it always issues in practice; and it is with spirituality in its practical outworking that this book deals.

It is wearisome to me, if not actually repulsive, to talk with folk who aim at perfect outward correctness, whilst they care little for that which is vital and spiritual. Missionary methods, as such, do not interest me at all. In fact, it is a deep grief to meet children of God who know practically nothing of the hatefulness of a life lived in the natural energy of man, and know little of vital experience of the Headship of Jesus Christ, yet all the while they are scrupulously careful to arrive at absolute correctness of method in God's service. Many a time we have been told, "We agree with you in everything." Far from it! In reality we do not agree at all! We hope this book will not fall into the hands of those who wish to improve their work by improving their methods, without adjusting their relationship to the Lord; but we do hope it will have a message for the humble ones who have learned to live in the power of the Spirit and have no confidence in the flesh.

It is death to have a wine-skin without wine, but it is loss to have wine without a wine-skin. We must have the wine-skin *after* we have the wine. Paul wrote the Ephesian Epistle, but he could also write the Corinthian Epistle; and Corinthians presents us with Ephesian truths in practical expression. Yes, the writer of Ephesians was also the writer of Corinthians! But why is it that the children of God have never had any serious contentions over Ephesian truths, but always over Corinthian truths? Because the sphere of Ephesians is the Heavenlies, and its truths are purely spiritual, so if there is any diversity of opinion concerning them, no one feels it much; but Corinthian teachings are practical and touch the earthly sphere, so if there is the slightest difference of opinion a reaction is felt at once. Yes, Corinthians is very practical! And it tests our obedience more than does Ephesians!

The danger, with those who know little about life and reality, is to emphasize mere outward correctness: but with those to whom life and reality are a matter of supreme importance, the temptation is to throw away the Divine pattern of things, thinking it legal and technical. They feel that they have the greater and can therefore well dispense with the lesser. As a result, the more spiritual a man is, the freer he feels to do as he thinks fit. He considers that he himself has authority to decide on outward matters, and rather fancies that to ignore God's commands regarding them is an indication that he has been delivered from legality and is walking in the liberty of the Spirit. But God has not only revealed the truths that concern our inner life. He has also revealed the truths relating to the outward expression of that life. God prizes the inner reality, but He does not ignore its outward expression. God has given us Ephesians, Romans and Colossians, but He has also given us Acts, the Epistles to Timothy and the Epistles to the Corinthians. We might deem it sufficient for God to instruct us through Romans, Ephesians and Colossians as to our life in Christ, but He has deemed it necessary to instruct us through Acts, Corinthians and Timothy, how to do His Work and how to organize His Church. God has left nothing to human imagination or human will. Man is afraid to use a thoughtless servant, but God does not care to use an over-thoughtful one; all He requires of man is simple obedience. "Who hath been his counsellor?" asked Paul (Rom. 11.34). Man would fain occupy the post, but God has no need of a counsellor. It is not our place to suggest how we think Divine Work should be done, but rather to ask in everything, "What is the Will of the Lord?"

The Pharisees cleansed the outside of the platter, but left the inside full of impurity. Our Lord rebuked them for setting so much store on outward things, and ignoring the inward; and many of God's people conclude from the Lord's rebuke that, providing we stress the inner side of spiritual truth, all is well; but God demands both inward and outward purity. To have the outer without the inner is spiritual death, but to have the inner without the outer is only spiritualized life. And spiritualization is not spirituality. Our Lord said, "*These* ye ought to have done, and not to have left the *other* undone." (Matt. 23.23). No matter how trifling any Divine command may seem, it is an expression of the Will of God; therefore we never dare treat it lightly. We cannot neglect the least of His commands with impunity. The importance of His requirements may vary, but everything that is of God has eternal purpose and eternal worth. Of course, the mere observance of outward forms of service has no spiritual value whatever. All spiritual truths, whether pertaining to the inner or the outer life, are liable to be legalized. Everything that is of God—whether outward or inward—if in the Spirit is life, if in the letter it is death. So the question is not, Is it outward or inward? but, Is it in the Spirit or in the letter? "The letter killeth, but the Spirit giveth life" (2 Cor. 3.6).

It is our desire to accept and proclaim the whole Word of God. We covet to be able to say with Paul, "I shrank not from declaring unto you the whole counsel of God" (Acts 20.27). We seek to follow the leading of God's Spirit, but at the same time we seek to pay attention to the examples shown us in His Word. The leading of the Spirit is precious, but if there is no example in the Word, then it is easy to substitute our fallible thoughts and unfounded feelings for the Spirit's leading, drifting into error without realizing it. If one is not prepared to obey God's Will in every direction, it is easy to do things contrary to His Word and still fancy one is being led of His Spirit. We emphasize the necessity of following both the leading of the Spirit and the examples of the Word, because by comparing our ways with the written Word we can discover the source of our leading. The Spirit's guidance will always harmonize with the Scriptures. God cannot lead a man one way in Acts and another way to-day. In externalities the leading may vary, but in principle it is always the same; for God's Will is eternal, therefore changeless. God is the Eternal God; He takes no cognizance of time, and His Will and Ways all bear the stamp of eternity. This being so, God could never act one way at one time and another way later on. Circumstances may differ and cases may differ, but in principle the Will and Ways of God are just the same to-day as they were in the days of the Acts.

God said to the Israelites: "Moses for your hardness of heart suffered you to put away your wives" (Matt. 19.8), but the Lord Jesus said, "What God hath joined together, let not man put asunder" (Matt. 19.6). Is there not a discrepancy here? No! "Moses for your hardness of heart suffered you to put away your wives; but from the beginning it hath not been so" (Matt. 19.8). It is not that in "the beginning" it was permissible, and later it became forbidden, and still later became permissible again, as though God were a changeable God. No, the Lord said, "*From the beginning* it hath not been so"—showing that God's Will had never altered. "From the beginning" right on until to-day it is just the same. Here is a most important principle. If we want to know the Mind of God, we must look at His commands in Genesis and not look at His permissions later on, because every later permission has this explanation, "for your hardness of heart." It is God's directive Will we want to discover, not His permissive Will. We want to see what God's purpose was "from the beginning." We want to see things as they were when they proceeded in all their purity from the Mind of God, not what they have become because of "hardness of heart" on the part of His people.

If we would understand the Will of God concerning His Church, then we must not look to see how He led His people last year, or ten years ago, or a hundred years ago, but we must return to the beginning, to the "genesis" of the Church, to see what He said and did then. It is there we find the highest expression of His Will. Acts is the "genesis" of the Church's history, and the Church in the time of Paul is the "genesis" of the Spirit's work. Conditions in the Church to-day are vastly different from what they were then, but these present conditions could never be our example, or our authoritative guide; we must return to "the beginning." Only what God has set forth as our example in the beginning is the eternal Will of God. It is the Divine standard and our pattern for all time.

A word of explanation may be needed regarding the examples God has given us in His Word. Christianity is not only built upon precepts, but also upon examples. God has revealed His Will, not only by giving orders, but by having certain things done in His Church, so that in the ages to come others might simply look at the pattern and know His Will. God has not only directed His people by means of abstract principles and objective regulations, but by concrete examples and subjective experience. God does use precepts to teach His people, but one of His chief methods of instruction is through history. God tells us how others knew and did His Will, so that we, by looking at their lives, may not only know His Will, but see how to do it too. He worked in their lives, producing in them what He Himself desired, and He bids us look at them, so that we may know what He is after.

Shall we, then, say that because God has not commanded a certain thing we need not do it? If we have seen His dealings with men in days past, if we have seen how He led His people and built up His Church, can we still plead ignorance of His Will? Is it necessary for a child to be told explicitly how to do everything? Must each item be separately mentioned of things permissible and not permissible? Are there not many things he can learn simply by watching his parents or his elder brothers and sisters? We learn more readily by what we see than by what we hear, and the impression upon us is deeper. That is why God has given us so much history in the Old Testament, and the Acts of the Apostles in the New. He knows we learn more easily by example than by precept, and examples have greater value than precepts, because precepts are abstract, whilst examples are precepts carried into effect. By looking at them, we not only know what God's precepts are, but we have a tangible demonstration of their outworking. If we try to eliminate examples from Christianity and leave only its precepts, then we have not much left. Precepts have their place, but examples have no less important a place, though obviously conformity to the Divine pattern in outward things is mere formality if there is no correspondence in inner life.

In closing, may I stress the fact that this is not a book on missionary methods. Methods are not to be despised, but in God's service what matters most is the man, not his methods. Unless the man is right, right methods will be of no use to him or to his work. Carnal methods are suited to carnal men, and spiritual methods to spiritual men. For carnal men to employ spiritual methods will only result in confusion and failure. This book is intended for those who, having learned something of the Cross, know the corruption of human nature, and seek to walk, not after the flesh, but after the Spirit. Its object is to help those who acknowledge the Lordship of Christ in all things, and are seeking to serve Him in the way of His own appointing, not of their choosing. To put it in other words, it is written for those who are already in the good of Ephesian truths, so that they may know how to express their service along Corinthian lines. May none of my readers use this book as a basis for external adjustments in their work, without letting the Cross deal drastically with their natural life.

In God's Work everything depends upon the kind of worker sent out and the kind of convert produced. On the part of the convert, a real Holy Ghost new birth is essential, and a vital relationship with God; and on the part of the worker, besides personal holiness and enduement for service, it is essential that he have an experimental knowledge of the meaning of committal to God and faith in His sovereign Providence; otherwise, no matter how scriptural the methods employed, the result will be emptiness and defeat.

To the Lord and to His people I commend this book, with the prayer that He may use it for His glory, as He sees fit.

SHANGHAI. W. NEE.

January, 1938.

1 The Ministry and the Ministers

The Work of God

God has one objective, and that is, to increase His Son. He purposes to have people come under the name of His Son and to share the life of His Son so that they become His own children. He designs to use these people for the increase of His Son in order that the personal Christ may also be the corporate Christ. For all the purposes of God are in His Son and all His works are intended to extend His Son!

The tragedy surrounding the events in the Garden of Eden lies in the fact that instead of receiving the life of God's Son man sinned, thereby turning himself against God and becoming a slave to Satan. And hence, thereafter the work of God first lay, negatively, in solving the question of man's sin by delivering him from the bondage of the devil, and, positively, in causing man to accept His Son's life. God would then be able to give increase to His Son so that His Son might fill all in all. Before the fall, God only required man to accept His life. But since his fall, man needs to have the double problem of sin and the power of Satan solved before he can receive the life of God. The redemptive work of God is therefore to deliver man from sin and Satan and to cause man to partake of His Son's life.

In order for us to understand God's redemptive work, we need to realize that man is today under the power of Satan.

Due to his following his own idea and thus committing sin, man made himself the enemy's prisoner of war. To deliver him from the power of the enemy, God sent His own Son, the Lord Jesus Christ, to the world to become a man. And as a man, Christ was led by the Holy Spirit to encounter Satan's temptations and won the victory. Being filled with the power of God, He drove away Satan and delivered men from the enemy's power everywhere. He died for us according to the righteousness of God. He shed His blood to cleanse us from all our sins. Originally God had His righteous judgment against sinners. But Christ received this judgment in our stead so that neither the righteous God nor the accusing Satan could have anything more to say. There is now absolute satisfaction, there is now total silence. The kingdom of Satan is now completely destroyed, since God's judgment has been fully executed. Satan no longer has any ground to attack men. Such redemption is perfect and eternal, never seen in the past nor to be seen in the future.

What is more is that our Lord includes in His death all those who believe in Him. His Cross is our cross. Our old man was crucified with Him on the Cross. Then, too, those who formerly had been in subjection to Satan have now passed out of his hand, with Satan unable to find his former subjects again.

Not only this, but our Lord also released His life through His death and has become food to us so that we might share in His life. As a result, the plan which God foreordained before the foundation of the world is now fulfilled in us. We who today have the Son have become the children of God. Through faith in Him we partake of Him, He thus becoming greatly increased and expanded.

Since the redemptive work of Christ is so complete, God has given Him all men as well as all authority of judgment. Today we have not yet seen Him executing His authority of judgment nor have we seen all men come to Him. Though He has all the authority of heaven and earth, we still nevertheless notice the power of the devil here. Why is this so?

The Church

This is because the question of the Church has not been resolved. In the Bible there is not only in view the personal Christ but also the corporate Christ. The first has the total victory, but the second has yet to experience this victory. The personal Christ is the Head of the corporate Christ. Christ is the Head, the Church is the Body. Christ plus the Church is the corporate Christ. Christ Himself has fully overcome, but the Church is yet to experience His victory. The triumph of the Head must be experienced by the Body.

Moreover, the Church has not fully known Christ, nor is she absolutely clear on the faith. Though the believers are people with Divine life, they are babes nonetheless and have yet to be fully grown up unto the measure of the stature of the fulness of Christ. The Church must arrive at a certain measure before she can satisfy God's heart. God does everything for the sake of Christ, because Christ is His objective. God wishes all the redeemed to receive life only from Christ, to know Him fully, and to be like Him completely. It is the Will of God that all the grace and life in the Head would flow into the Body. All the facts in Christ must become experiences in the Church.

Hence before Christ will bind Satan and bless the whole world by Himself, He must first establish His Church, thereby causing His people to partake of His victory, as well as arrive at the full measure ordained for them. Consequently, God has His own Work to do *today*. He is building the Body of Christ until all who compose it arrive at the unity of the faith and of the full knowledge of the Son of God, until they attain unto the measure of the stature of the fulness of Christ (see Eph. 4.12,13). Such an undertaking of building the Body of Christ is God's *current* Work. It occupies a large place in all the works of God. His today's Work is centered upon this one thing: He is especially concerned with the upbuilding of the Body of Christ.

The Work of the Ministry

For this important Work, God has chosen a number of men. This group of workers is responsible for His special Work. We do not mean to say that God has *no other* works today, nor do we mean to say that He has *no other* kinds of workers today. We simply maintain that God's current Work is preeminently concerned with building the Body of Christ. No doubt God has many, many other workers today, but this particular group of workers whose work is to build the body of Christ are His special workmen.

God has many works, and in His service there are many ministries. A ministry is that piece of work which God has particularly called someone to do. Some are called to perform this ministry, whilst others are called to perform other ministries. The number of ministries is very great since God uses people in many different areas. Nevertheless, the Scriptures show us that there is one special ministry which is distinct from all other ministries. Such a ministry is referred to in the Bible as "the Ministry" in distinctive contrast to the others. And the kind of gathering and building up of the Body of Christ associated with "the Ministry" is called "the work of the ministry" (Eph. 4.12 Darby). Many people there are who work the works of God, but only one group of people is entrusted with "the work of the Ministry." Many are the ministries which God apportions to men, but one class of men alone is involved in "the work of the Ministry."

Let us see how the Word of God addresses this matter. "But to each one of us has been given grace according to the measure of the gift of the Christ. Wherefore he says, Having ascended up on high, he has led captivity captive, and has given gifts to men. . . . And he has given some apostles, and some prophets, and some evangelists, and some shepherds and teachers, for the perfecting of the saints; with a view to the work of the ministry, with a view to the edifying of the body of Christ; until we all arrive at the unity of the faith and of the knowledge of the Son of God, at the fullgrown man, at the measure of the stature of the fulness of the Christ" (Eph. 4.7,8,11-13 Darby).

Here we see two things which Christ has done following His death, resurrection and ascension: (1) Due to His complete victory, Christ has so led His enemy captive that the latter can no longer accuse nor abuse his former slaves. Christ has already overcome and ascended on high. He has taken captive all forces which in the past have tyrannized men. Hence all who are in Christ also have total victory over Satan. Soon Christ will manifest His authority on earth; He will bind His enemy and cast him into the bottomless pit. (2) Before Christ does this binding and casting, He will first manifest this authority in the Church by giving gifts to all whom He has delivered from the enemy, thereby on the one hand proving man's elevation in Him and on the other hand enabling men to be an instrument of deliverance to other people.

The gifts mentioned here are not those of the Holy Spirit given to men personally, but as Head of the Church the Lord grants grace to certain individuals that they may become His *gifts to the Church* to serve the saints and to build up the Body. In other words, the Lord bestows a group of workers as His gift to the Church for her edification. They are especially called by Him to do the work of the Ministry. Formerly they were slaves to the enemy, but now they are completely delivered because of the death and resurrection of the Lord. They further are being appointed by the Ascended Lord to be His powerful vessels for the emancipation of other people, since they are given authority by the Lord to do the work of deliverance which He Himself had done. They are a delivered class of people who have now become instruments in the Hand of God to attack the enemy,

The intent of God is for all the redeemed to know Him and to be filled with His life and Holy Spirit without any mixture of the flesh. He accordingly needs some men whom He can use to do the Work of building up His people. While He waits for His enemies to be His footstool, He gives certain necessary gifts —that is, He gives His servants in the Ministry—to the Church for the gathering together of all whom He has called to share His Glory and for their being built up into His fulness.

One thing, however, must be noticed here: the gifts referred to here are not those which the Holy Spirit divides to each severally as He wills (see 1 Cor. 12.11); rather, these are persons whom the Lord sets up in the Church for her edification and profit. Concerning gifts, we must distinguish between those given by the Holy Spirit to individual believers and those given by the Lord to the Church, since the Bible does indeed speak of these different kinds of gifts. One kind is given to believers *individually*, the other is given to the Church *corporately*. The gifts we individually receive from the Holy Spirit enable us to serve God in performing particular works. Some may prophesy, some may teach, some speak in tongues, some may heal the sick, and so on. These are the gifts which the Holy Spirit grants to individuals. Those which the Lord gives to the Church, however, are different. For what He gives to the Church are persons who possess the gifts of the Holy Spirit.

Although today the Lord is in Glory, His heart yearns to gather the lost. Especially is He mindful of His saints (who are the Church), to whom He desires to give more of Himself so that they may be filled with Him. His thought is for His Church to receive all His various graces, to be led of the Holy Spirit, to know the Will of God, and to enter into the accomplished fact of His redemptive work. For the communication and supply of these blessings, He gives gifted persons to the Church. So that this work of the Ministry is different from all other ordinary ministries. Every believer is gifted, but only such gifted persons as herein described are called to perform this special Work.

Every believer receives a ministry from the Lord, but all such ministries are of the general kind; only the Ministry of these men of whom we have been speaking is special.* Such men are God's ministers, God's workers, who are appointed by the Lord to accomplish God's Work through this Ministry.

This group of special men includes the following: the apostles, the prophets, the evangelists, the shepherds (pastors) and teachers. Let us now discuss the differences amongst these four classes of men.**

These four classes of persons may be divided into two categories: the apostles and the prophets for one, the evangelists and the pastors and teachers form another. This is because the apostles and the prophets lay the foundation (see Eph. 2.20), whereas the evangelists and the pastors and teachers build on that foundation. The first set of two comes directly from the Lord and establishes the foundation of God's Heavenly Abode in an extra-ordinary fashion. The second set is comparatively more ordinary since the evangelists and the pastors and teachers save souls and edify the saints on the basis of the teachings of the apostles and the prophets.

There is another way to distinguish these four classes of persons. The apostles and the evangelists are more for the Gospel, whilst the prophets and the teachers are more for the Church. The prophets proclaim God's Word in a supernatural way, but

---

*Please note that the words "Ministry" and "Work" so identified in this book have reference to this special ministry and work.

**Strictly speaking, pastors and teachers are *one* gift, not two, because teaching and shepherding are closely related. In the enumeration of the gifts in Ephesians 4, apostles, prophets, and evangelists are all mentioned separately—whilst pastors and teachers are linked together Further, the first three are each prefixed by the word "some," whereas the word "some" is attached to pastors and teachers unitedly, thus—"some apostles," "some prophets," "some evangelists," and "some pastors and teachers," not "*some* pastors and *some* teachers." The fact that the word "some" is used only four times in this list indicates that there are only four classes of persons in question. Pastors and teachers are two in one.

the teachers expound God's truth less supernaturally. The ministry of the prophets and teachers is especially confined to one local assembly. Hence we find that as it pertained to the church at Antioch, these two classes of men were recorded as being there (Acts 13.1). On the other hand, the apostles are appointed especially to the ministry of preaching the Gospel. But whilst the evangelists preach the Gospel in one locality, the apostles are to preach the Gospel everywhere.

Though these four classes of persons are all God-given gifts to the Church, they do not necessarily represent by their class names the special spiritual gifts given to them severally by the Holy Spirit. We know that the prophesying of the prophets is a gift (see 1 Cor. 12.10 and Rom. 12.6) and that the teaching of the teachers is also a gift (see Rom. 12.7). But the Scriptures do not tell us what special gift makes the apostles. We do not even know what is the gift of the evangelists. There is the gift that is identified with the prophets and there is the gift that is identified with the teachers, but not the gift that is identified with either the apostles or the evangelists. So that whilst all four classes of men are in themselves gifts to the Church, only two amongst them are also personal gifts. Therefore, apart from the prophets and the teachers who respectively receive gifts of prophesying and of teaching, we are ignorant as to what special gifts the Holy Spirit bestows upon the apostles and the evangelists to equip them for their works. Nevertheless, all four are God's appointed workers in the Ministry. They receive their ministry from Him to do His special work of building up the Body of Christ. They bear special spiritual responsibility in the Church for the realization of God's purpose in this age.

Comparing Some Scripture Passages

In order to understand these ministers in "the work of the Ministry," it would be helpful to compare certain Scripture passages. In the Bible there are at least three passages which resemble the one in Eph. 4; namely 1 Cor. 12.8-10, 1 Cor. 12.28, and Rom. 12.6-8. In these three passages, various ministries, various persons, and various gifts are mentioned. Only in Ephesians, however, is the term "the Ministry" used. In order to know the distinction between Eph. 4 and the other passages, we must compare them.

"For to one is given through the Spirit the word of wisdom; and to another the word of knowledge, according to the same Spirit: to another faith, in the same Spirit; and to another gifts of healings, in the one Spirit; and to another workings of miracles; and to another prophecy; and to another discernings of spirits: to another divers kinds of tongues; and to another the interpretation of tongues" (1 Cor. 12.8-10).

"And God hath set some in the church, first apostles, secondly prophets, thirdly teachers, then miracles, then gifts of healings, helps, governments, divers kinds of tongues" (1 Cor. 12.28).

"And having gifts differing according to the grace that was given to us, whether prophecy, let us prophesy according to the proportion of our faith; or ministry, let us give ourselves to our ministry; or he that teacheth, to his teaching; or he that exhorteth, to his exhorting: he that giveth, let him do it with liberality; he that ruleth, with diligence; he that showeth mercy, with cheerfulness" (Rom. 12.6-8).

1 Cor. 12.8-10 enumerates the gifts given to *individual* believers. Eph. 4.11,12 speaks of the persons whom the Lord gives as gifts to the *Church*. The gifts in 1 Cor. 12 are *supernatural*, whilst the gifts in Rom. 12 are *ordinary* as a result of the Lord's grace and our faith. The nine gifts mentioned in 1 Cor. are those received when men are under the power of the Holy Spirit. Hence in verse 1 it says this: "Now concerning spirituals" (original Greek). The gifts in Rom. 12 are based upon the grace of God. God gives men grace so that they may manifest His grace by fulfilling their various functions as members of the Body. Consequently, the gifts enumerated are

neither miraculous nor Spirit-moved but are rather of life. Even "giveth" and "showeth mercy" are viewed as gifts, for all of them are gifts according to grace. In Eph. 4, however, those persons mentioned are the Lord's gifts given to the Church. The persons *themselves* are gifts, and the gifts they receive are such gifts as those enumerated in 1 Cor. 12 and Rom. 12. The emphasis of 1 Corinthians is power, whilst the emphasis in Romans is life. Ephesians speaks of the persons who possess these two different kinds of gifts, for the persons themselves are God's gifts to the Church.

"*The* Ministry" in Ephesians is unique and special. 1 Cor. 12 also speaks of ministry, but there it is the ministries (see verse 5, original Greek) which are of the common ordinary kind, of which the children of God receive severally before the Lord. The four gifts to the Church as cited in Eph. 4 are for "the work of the Ministry"; the nine gifts to individuals listed in 1 Cor. 12.8-10 are for the ministries as each person possesses a different gift for a different service.

1 Cor. 12.28 enumerates eight (or nine) classes of persons God has set in the Church. It is different from the gifts enumerated earlier in verses 8-10. For the earlier passage in 1 Cor. 12 refers to the *gifts* of the Holy Spirit, whilst verse 28 refers to the *workings* (or operations) of God. The first alludes to the gifts which the Holy Spirit gives to the church *local*, whereas the latter passage alludes to the workings of God in the Church *universal*. Verses 8-10 have reference to the gifts individuals receive from the Holy Spirit, but in verse 28 we see that God sets in the Church those men who have received gifts for His operation. So that there are eight (or nine) classes of persons cited in 1 Cor. 12.28 whom God has set in the Church, whereas in Ephesians there are only four classes of persons whom God gives to the Church for "the Ministry." In the Church of God there are many who function, yet the four classes of persons mentioned in Eph. 4 alone take part in the special work of building up the Body of Christ. All the others

have their usefulness and services, but only the four classes of persons enumerated in Ephesians are especially used for "the Ministry."

Of the four classes of persons in Ephesians, 1 Cor. 12 mentions three, the evangelists being left out. This is because the scope of Ephesians and Corinthians is not the same. The scope of the first is that of building up the Body of Christ, and therefore the evangelists are needed. They are listed prior to the pastors and teachers since they are the ones who initially bring people into the Body of Christ. Corinthians, however, deals with the workings of God *in* the Church, and hence it leaves the evangelists out of its list since the working of the evangelists is not *in* the Church but rather *for* the Church.

One more thing is worth noticing: Romans, Corinthians and Ephesians all touch upon the Body of Christ; and yet even here they have their differences. Romans and Corinthians consider all the believers as members of the Body; consequently, all have gifts and functions (though they are not the same). Ephesians tells us how this Body is built by gifts (in this case, gifts in the form of men); it does not regard the four classes of persons as members of the Body; it instead reckons them as people who build up the Body, and thus their position is different from that of the rest of God's children.

Analysis of These Four Classes of Persons

As noted earlier, teachers and pastors are regarded as one class of persons, because those who teach must also shepherd and those who shepherd must also teach. These two kinds of work are interrelated. Furthermore, the word "pastor" as applied to any person is found nowhere else in the New Testament, but the word "teacher" is used on four other occasions. In the New Testament we find reference elsewhere to an apostle (e.g. Paul), and a prophet (e.g. Agabus), and an evangelist (e.g. Philip), and a teacher (e.g. Manaen), but nowhere in

God's Word do we find anyone referred to as a pastor. This confirms the fact that these four classes are not spiritual gifts but are rather gifted persons, and it also confirms the fact that pastors and teachers are one class of men.

Teachers are men who have received the gift of teaching. This is not a miraculous gift, but a gift of grace, which accounts for the fact of its being omitted from the miraculous gifts in 1 Cor. 12.8-10 and included in the list of the gifts of grace in Rom. 12. It is a gift of grace which enables its possessors to understand the teachings of God's Word, and to discern His purposes, and thus equips them to instruct His people in doctrinal matters. In the church at Antioch there were several persons thus equipped, Paul being among the number. It is by the operation of God that such men are "set in the Church," and their position is next to that of the prophets. A teacher is an individual who has received the gift of teaching from God, and has been given by the Lord to His Church for its upbuilding.

The work of a teacher is to interpret to others the truths which have been revealed to him, and to lead God's people to an understanding of the Word, and encourage them to seek and receive for themselves Divine revelation through the Scriptures. The sphere of a teacher's work is mainly amongst the children of God, though at times they also teach the unsaved (1 Tim. 4.11, 6.2; 2 Tim. 2.2; Acts. 4.2-18; 5.21,25,28,42). The work of the teachers is more one of interpretation than of revelation, whereas the work of the prophets is more one of revelation than of interpretation. They seek to lead believers to an understanding of Divine truth, and they seek to lead unbelievers to an understanding of the Gospel.

Evangelists are also our Lord's gift to His Church, but exactly what their personal gifts are we do not know. Both the teachers and the prophets are set up by God. What enables a teacher to teach is the gift of teaching (Rom. 12.7), and what enables a prophet to prophesy is the gift of prophecy (1 Cor. 12.10). But the evangelists are different from the teachers and the prophets, for although they are also set up by God, we do not know what special gift God gives to enable them to be evangelists. For the Word of God does not speak of any evangelistic gift.

Even so, evangelists *are* one of the four classes of persons whom God has appointed to the Ministry. The Bible does refer once to Philip as being an evangelist (Acts 21.8), and Paul on one occasion encouraged Timothy to do the work of an evangelist and fill up the measure of his ministry (2 Tim. 4.5). Notice, however, that it is not the preaching of the Gospel but the doing the work of an evangelist; for the matter before us is not that of gift but of ministry. Evangelists are one of the ministries in the Ministry. Apart from the three occasions referred to, the noun "evangelist" is not found in Scripture, though we frequently meet the verb which is derived from the same root.

In the Word of God the place of prophets is more clearly defined than that of teachers and evangelists. Prophecy is mentioned amongst the gifts of grace (Rom. 12.6), and amongst the miraculous gifts we find it again (1 Cor. 12.10). God has set prophets in the Church universal (1 Cor. 12.28), but He has also given prophets for the Ministry (Eph. 4.11). There is both the gift of prophecy and the office of a prophet. The prophet is both a man set by God in His Church to occupy the prophetic office, and a man given by the Lord to His Church for the Ministry.

Let us notice especially that in the original Greek the word "prophecy" in both Rom. 12.6 and 1 Cor. 12.10 are verbal nouns. Thus, we are to understand the prophets along two different lines: one is to speak for God as men who are moved by the Holy Spirit and have received miraculous power; the other is to speak for God as men who have the power of the Holy Spirit in ordinary life. In the Old Testament period, a prophet was (1) to predict, (2) to preach, and (3) to pronounce God's Will towards individuals. According to the New Testament, however, a prophet still prophesies with miraculous power and preaches in spiritual power, but he no longer pronounces God's Will towards individuals. This is because all shall know of God in themselves (see Heb. 8.11). The words spoken by the prophets carry authority, for in prophesying or in preaching there is the power of the Holy Spirit. They receive from God revelations pertaining to future or present situations—these being either for warning or for edification.

Of the four classes of gifted men bestowed by the Lord upon His Church for its upbuilding, the apostles were quite different from the other three. The special position occupied by apostles is obvious to any reader of the New Testament. They were specially commissioned by God to found churches through the preaching of the Gospel, to bring revelation from God to His people, to give decisions in matters pertaining to doctrine and government, and to edify the saints and distribute the gifts. Both spiritually and geographically their sphere is vast. That their position is superior to that of prophets and teachers is clear from the Word: "God has set some in the church, *first* apostles" (1 Cor. 12.28). Also in the Ministry, the apostles head the list. For they are God's chosen workers and foremen. They are especially entrusted with the Work of God.

Ministry and Gift

Apostles belong to the Ministry, but they are quite different from the prophets, evangelists and teachers, because unlike these three, it is not their gifts that determine their office; i.e. they are not constituted apostles by receiving an apostolic gift.

It is important to note that apostleship is an office, not a gift. An office is what one receives as the result of a commission: a gift is what one receives on the basis of grace. "I was appointed . . . an apostle" (1 Tim. 2.7). "I was appointed . . . an apostle" (2 Tim. 1.11). We see here that apostles are commissioned. Being an apostle, therefore, is not something which is subject to receiving an apostolic gift but is that which is subject to receiving an apostolic commission.

What is the difference between office and gift? Whatever is commissioned is office and whatever speaks of enabling is gift. Natural gifts are what we naturally possess, whilst spiritual gifts are what we possess through the Holy Spirit. Office is the result of commission. Apostleship is an office. This is clearly told of in both First and Second Timothy.

God's Gift to the Church

There is not only difference between office and gift, even in gifts there is the distinction between personal gifts and gifts to the Church. Since we have just stated that apostleship is an office and not a gift, what does the Word of God mean when it says, "He gave some apostles" (Eph. 4.11)? Here we need to distinguish as to whether the term "apostle" signifies a personal gift or a gift to the Church; whether it signifies a spiritual ability obtained personally from God or a class of persons the Church receives from God. Let us remind ourselves of what we have said earlier, that apostles are a class of persons the Church has received from God; for no such thing as an apostolic gift is ever cited in the Scriptures. It is therefore not a question here of apostleship being a gift given to an apostle, but a gift given to the Church; it is not a spiritual gift given to a man, but a gifted *man* given to the Church. Eph. 4.11 does not say that the Lord gave an apostolic gift to any person, but that He gave men as apostles to His Church. Men have received gifts of the Spirit which have qualified them to become prophets and teachers, but no man has ever received a spiritual gift which has qualified him to be an apostle. Apostles are a class of people the Church has received as our Lord's gift for its upbuilding.

"For to one is given through the Spirit the word of wisdom; and to another the word of knowledge, according to the same

Spirit: to another faith, in the same Spirit; and to another gifts of healings, in the one Spirit; and to another workings of miracles; and to another prophecy; and to another discernings of spirits: to another divers kinds of tongues; and to another the interpretation of tongues" (1 Cor. 12.8-10). This passage enumerates the gifts of the Holy Spirit given to *individuals*. It lists the various gifts men receive in order to speak the word of wisdom or the word of knowledge, to be prophets or healers of sickness, and so on. But there is no mention of any apostolic gift, that is, the gift the Holy Spirit gives to men to make them apostles.

"And God hath set some in the church, first apostles, secondly prophets, thirdly teachers, then miracles, then gifts of healings, helps, governments, divers kinds of tongues" (1 Cor. 12.28). In the former passage which enumerates the gifts given to individuals (verses 8-10), the apostles are not included. In this passage which speaks of the *men* set up in the Church by God, we find that "apostles" heads the list of God's gifts to the Church. It is not that God has given His Church the gift of apostleship, but that He has given it *men* who are apostles; and He has not given the gifts of prophecy and teaching to His Church, but He has given it some *men* as prophets and some *men* as teachers. God has set different kinds of workers in His Church for its edification, one of which is apostles. They do not represent a certain kind of gift, they represent a certain class of persons.

The difference between the apostles, and the prophets and teachers, is that the latter two represent both gifts given by the Spirit to individuals and at the same time gifts given by the Lord to His Church, whereas apostles are men given by the Lord to His Church, but they do not represent any special personal gift of the Spirit.

By comparing these two passages in 1 Cor. 12, we can easily see that whatever gift is enumerated in the first passage is almost matched by whatever man is set forth in the second passage. The two seem to complement each other, except in the case of apostles—who are not listed in the gifts of the Holy Spirit but are listed first amongst the men whom God has set in the Church, since apostles are God's gift to the Church. Through them the spiritual blessings of God flow to the Church. Nothing is mentioned as to the supernatural enabling the apostles received from the Holy Spirit. They are especially related to God's workings in the Church.

The Church Universal and the Church Local

Something amazing is hinted at here. "And God hath set some in the church, first apostles, secondly prophets, thirdly teachers" (1 Cor. 12.28). What church is this? It is that which comprises all the children of God, both past and present, home and abroad; and therefore it is the Church universal. In this Church God has set "first apostles, secondly prophets, thirdly teachers." But in 1 Cor. 14.23 we read of "the whole church . . . assembled together." What church is this? Obviously, the local church, for the Church universal cannot gather together in one locality. It was in this local church that the brethren exercised their spiritual gifts. One of them would have "a psalm," another "a teaching," another "a revelation," another "a tongue," and another "an interpretation" (14.26), but more important than all these was the gift of prophecy (14.1).

In Chapter 12 apostles took precedence over the other ministers, but in Chapter 14 prophets took the precedence. In the Church universal apostles are first, but in the local church prophets are first. How does it come about that prophets take first place in the local church, since in the universal Church they only occupy the second place? Because in the Church universal the question is not of personal gifts of the Spirit, but of God's gift of *ministers* to the Church, and of these apostles rank first; but in the local church the question is one of *personal gifts* of the Spirit and of these prophecy is the chief, because *it is most important*.

Not only are the apostles left out of Chapter 14, they in addition are not even mentioned in the exercising of spiritual gifts. This is because, as we have seen, apostleship is not a personal gift. In the exercising of spiritual gifts, the prophets stand first; but in the listing of God's workers, the office of the apostle surpasses all. In 1 Cor. 14, there is no place for the apostles. For in the area of gifts, the gift of prophecy is the greatest; whereas in the area of office, there is none greater than the apostles. Hence in the assembling of the local church the greatest gift is that of prophecy because the prophets reveal the mind of God, both current and future. In the Church universal, however, the apostles have the highest office.

The Personal Gift of the Apostle

Who are the apostles, then? Apostles are those gifted persons whom God has chosen to be His fitted vessels by sending them out to preach the Word and to build up the Church. They are those gifted ones who have received a special office, they being appointed by God to travel around for the work of the Ministry. Although apostleship is an office, the apostles without doubt have their personal gifts.

An apostle may be a prophet or a teacher. Should he exercise his gift of prophecy or teaching in the local church, he does so in the capacity of a prophet or a teacher; but when he exercises his gifts in different places, he does so in the capacity of an apostle. The implication of apostleship is being sent by God to exercise gifts of ministry in different places. It is immaterial to his office what personal gift an apostle has, but it is essential to his office that he be sent of God. An apostle can exercise his spiritual gifts in any place, but he cannot exercise his apostolic gifts, because an apostle is such by office, not by gift.

Nevertheless, apostles do have personal gifts for their ministry. "Now there were at Antioch, in the church that was there, *prophets and teachers*, Barnabas, and Symeon that was called Niger, and Lucius of Cyrene, and Manaen the foster-brother of Herod the tetrarch, and Saul. And as they ministered to the Lord, and fasted, the Holy Ghost said, Separate me Barnabas and Saul for the work whereunto I have called them" (Acts 13.1-2). These five men all had the gifts of prophecy and teaching—a miraculous gift and a gift of grace. From that company of five *two* were sent by the Spirit to other parts, and *three* were left at Antioch. As we have already seen, the two sent out were thereafter *called apostles*. They received no apostolic gift, but they did receive an apostolic commission. It was their gifts that qualified them to be prophets and teachers, but it was their commission that qualified them to be apostles. The three who remained in Antioch *were still prophets and teachers*, not apostles, simply because they had not been sent out by the Spirit; the two became apostles, not because they had received any gift in addition to the gift of prophecy and teaching, but because they additionally received an office as a result of their commission. The gifts of all five were just the same, but the two received a Divine commission in addition to their gifts, and that qualified them for apostolic ministry.

In the beginning, the Lord Jesus called twelve disciples to Himself and gave them authority to cast out unclean spirits and to heal all manner of disease. Then the Scriptures follow this up by saying that this same group of men, now sent forth by the Lord, were called apostles (Matt. 10.1,2,5). The *gift* they received was a miraculous one, but the *office* they received was the apostleship. It was not because they became apostles that they were given a special apostolic gift. A mathematician, for example, is skilful in mathematics, though he may not necessarily be a professor of mathematics. He will not become a professor of mathematics until he is employed by a university. To have the knowledge of mathematics is an ability, to be a professor of mathematics is a position. Gift is spiritual ability, whilst apostleship is a position. If a person has gift but is not sent forth by God, he is not an apostle, just as a mathematician is not a professor until he is engaged to be such. Accordingly, apostles are not identified as such by their having any ability but by their having a special position. A professor must have ability, but his having ability does not guarantee him a position. Paul and Barnabas had the same gifts as Lucius, Symeon and Manaen; nevertheless, they became apostles and obtained a special position because they were commissioned by God.

The Sphere of Their Work

The sphere of an apostle's work is quite different from that of the other three special ministers. That prophets and teachers exercise their gifts in the local church is seen from the statement, "There were at Antioch, in the church that was there, prophets and teachers." You can find prophets and teachers in the local church, but not apostles, because they have been called to minister in different places, whilst the ministry of prophets and teachers is generally confined to one locality (1 Cor. 14.26,29).

As to evangelists, we do not know their special sphere, as very little is said of them in God's Word; but the story of Philip, the evangelist, throws some light on this class of ministers. Philip left his own locality and preached in Samaria, but whilst he did good work there, the Spirit did not fall upon any of his converts. It was not till the apostles came from Jerusalem and laid hands on them that the Spirit was poured out. This would *seem to indicate* that the local preaching of the Gospel is the work of an evangelist, but that the universal preaching of the Gospel is the work of an apostle. This does not imply that the labours of an evangelist are necessarily confined to one place, but it does mean that that is their usual sphere. In the same way the prophet Agabus prophesied in another place, but his special sphere of work was his own locality.

The Procedure of Divine Ordination

We know that certain men become prophets and teachers because they receive the gifts of prophecy and teaching. We do not know for sure what gift makes men evangelists. The apostles, however, are definitely an office and not a gift. They are specially called and commissioned by God to be such. It is quite adequate for persons to be prophets, teachers (and pastors), and evangelists so long as they have gifts. We do not read anywhere that aside from their gifts they must undergo any certain procedure of Divine ordination. Of the four classes of persons in the Ministry, three of them become such ministers directly through their gifts. Those who are so gifted become such persons.

The apostles, on the other hand, are different in this regard. Though they too belong to these four classes of persons in the Ministry, they are quite distinct from the other three in that they do not become apostles directly through any gift. The apostles may have gifts similar to those of the other three classes of persons, but they have a *special calling* and *special commission* which the latter classes do not have. So far as gift is concerned, an apostle may be a prophet; yet he is more than a prophet because he has received a special commission. The other three classes of persons join the Ministry through gift, but the apostles join the Ministry through *commission*.

Let us recognize that, in the local church, what is emphasized is gift and not office. And hence there is the biblical record of how the prophets exercised their gift, but there is no place in Scripture showing this concerning the apostles. Notwithstanding the fact that apostles are God's gift to the Church, they *themselves* do not gain anything. When a person gifted with prophecy exercises his gift of prophecy in different places to which he has been sent, he is an apostle. The individual gift of an apostle may not be prophecy; he may instead have the gift of healings. Even so, he is commissioned by

God to exercise his gift in various churches.

In Eph. 4 the church local and the Church universal are viewed together, and so the Body of Christ is employed as an all-inclusive term. There the apostles, the prophets, the teachers, and the evangelists are lumped together. Actually, though, the spheres of their work are different, since in at least the case of apostles, their sphere of work occurs not only in a local place but in other places as well.

The Ministry of the Ministers

God thus lays upon these two groups of men (the apostles and the rest) the responsibility of the work of the Ministry. According to His pleasure He gives gifts to some local brothers as prophets and teachers and evangelists that they may serve Him and His Church with these gifts. In addition, out of these gifted persons He chooses especially one class of men and sends them out to do the Work which He calls them to do. Besides their gifts they also receive an office. They become workers with a mandate. Just as the gifted brethren serve the local church with their gifts, so these specially commissioned brethren faithfully fulfill their ministry of building up the Body of Christ amongst various local churches.

Through these men God imparts His grace to His Church. And these men cause all the grace of the Head to flow into the Body by the gifts given them by the Holy Spirit. Ministry is nothing less than to supply Christ to the Church: ministry is to communicate the Christ they know to the Church: for the purpose of God lies in the Church gaining Christ through their gifts.

God has given these classes of persons to the Church for the perfecting of the saints with a view to the Work of the Ministry and the building up of the Body of Christ—until all believers attain unto a full-grown man, which is the measure of the stature of the fulness of Christ Who is the Head. As Christians we should grow into Christ by acknowledging Him as our Head and accepting His grace and command so that we may be filled increasingly with Him. For this very purpose, God through these men reveals Christ and His riches to all the members so that all may grow into Him Who is the Head of the Body, into the One Who is all and in all, into the one and only Glorious Man. The Church ought to know deeply the riches of Christ through the instrumentality of these men in order that she be no longer tossed to and fro with every wind of doctrine perpetrated by the wiles of the enemy (Eph. 4.14).

As the prophets serve the local church with their gift, even so, the apostles serve the churches in many places with their office. These two classes of persons are extremely important because both kinds of works—extra-local and local in nature—are in their hands. Hence the Bible tells us that God's holy temple is "built upon the foundation of the apostles and prophets" (Eph. 2.20).

The prophets, teachers and evangelists in the local church are but those who have such gifts. Because of their particular gifts they take part in the Ministry—in the building up of the Body of Christ; yet they do not occupy any office to govern the local church. The administrative responsibility of the church is vested in "the overseers and deacons" (Phil. 1.1 mg.). The elders occupy the highest office in a local church even as the prophets remain the most important gifted person in a local church. Yet in God's Work—in the work of the Ministry of building up the Body of Christ—there are these four classes of persons. But amongst them all, the apostles stand foremost since they have an office which the others do not have.

We see, then, that in local church government, the office of the elders is the highest; and that in the building up of the Body of Christ, the office of the apostles is the greatest. It is because of this that the New Testament, when speaking of solving a local problem which is also related to other churches, singles out "the apostles and the elders" (see Acts 15.2,4,6,23).

Even though the apostles are the greatest in God's Work, they have no position in the local church. Elders occupy the highest office in the church, but they have no part in the work of the Ministry. The prophets have the most important gift, nevertheless, they have neither office in the church nor overall responsibility in the Work.

In the local church two aspects must be equally emphasized: one is government, the other is edification. Government is a matter of office, and hence there are elders and deacons. Edification is a matter of gift, and hence there are prophets, evangelists, and pastors and teachers. The function of the elders is to take care of the daily government of the church, whilst the work of the prophets and teachers is to edify when the church assembles. In the event that some elders are also prophets and teachers, they may govern the church in its daily affairs as well as edify it in the meetings.

The apostles play no part in the daily administration of the church, neither do they take responsibility in the regular edification in the meetings. If any apostle is also a prophet or a teacher, and though he may not govern the church directly as do the elders, yet he can—during the time of meetings—edify the local church in his capacity of prophet or teacher.

To sum up, the office of the apostles requires them to go to many places to do the Work of the Lord. And by the various gifts they receive (such as their being prophets, teachers, etc.), they are able to build up the brethren in different local churches.

2 The Apostles

God is a God of works. Our Lord said, "My Father worketh even until now." And He has a definite purpose, toward the realization of which He directs all His works. He is the God "who worketh all things after the counsel of His own will." But God does not do everything directly by Himself. He works through His servants. Among the servants of God the Apostles are the most important ones. It will do us good if we look into the Word of God to know what it has to teach on the matter of the Apostles.

The First Apostle

In the fulness of time God sent forth His Son into the world to do His Work. He is known as the Christ of God, i.e. "the Anointed One." The term "Son" relates to His Person; the name "Christ" relates to His Office. He was the Son of God, but He was sent to be the Christ of God. "Christ" is the ministerial name of the Son of God. Our Lord did not come to the earth or to the Cross on His own initiative; He was anointed and set apart for the Work by God. He was not self-appointed, but sent. Frequently throughout the Gospel of John we find Him referring to God, not as "God," or "the Father," but as "the One Who sent me." He took the place of a sent one. If that is true in the case of the Son of God, how much more should it apply to His servants? If even the Son was not expected to take any initiative in God's Work, is it likely that we are expected to do so? The first principle to note in the Work of God is that all His workers are sent ones. If there is no Divine commission, there can be no Divine Work.

Scripture has a special name for a sent one, i.e. an apostle. The meaning of the Greek word is "the sent one." The Lord Himself is the first Apostle because He is the first one specially sent of God: hence the Word refers to Him as "*the* Apostle" (Heb. 3.1).

The Twelve

While our Lord fulfilled His Apostolic Ministry on earth, He was all the time aware that His life in the flesh was limited; so even as He pursued the Work committed to Him by the Father, He was preparing a group of men to continue it after His departure. These men were also termed apostles. They were not volunteers; they were sent ones. We cannot overemphasize this fact that all Divine Work is by commission, not by choice.

From amongst whom did our Lord choose these apostles? They were chosen from amongst His disciples. All those sent out by the Lord were already disciples. Not all disciples are necessarily apostles, but all apostles are necessarily disciples; not all disciples are chosen for the Work, but those who are chosen are always selected from amongst the disciples of the Lord. An apostle then must have two callings; in the first place he must be called to be a disciple and in the second place he must be called to be an apostle. His first calling is from amongst the children of the world to be a follower of the Lord: his second calling is from amongst the followers of the Lord to be a sent one of the Lord.

Those apostles chosen by our Lord during His earthly ministry occupy a special place in Scripture, and they also occupy a special place in the purpose of God, because they were with the Son of God while He lived in the flesh. They were not just called apostles, they were called "the Twelve Apostles." They occupied a special place in the Word of God, and they occupy a special place in the plan of God. Our Lord told Peter that one day they should "sit on thrones judging the twelve tribes of Israel" (Luke 22.30). "*The* Apostle" has His throne, and "the Twelve Apostles" are going to have their thrones too. This is a privilege not granted to other apostles. When Judas lost his office and God led the remaining eleven to choose one to make up the number, we read that they cast lots and the lot fell upon Matthias, "and he was numbered with the *eleven* Apostles" (Acts 1.26). In the next chapter we find the Holy Spirit inspiring the writer of the Acts to say, "Peter, standing up with the *eleven*" (Acts 2.14), which shows that the Holy Spirit recognized Matthias to be one of the Twelve. Here we see that the number of these apostles was fixed; God did not want more than twelve, nor would He have less. In the Book of Revelation we find that the ultimate position which they occupy is again a special one—"And the wall of the city had twelve foundations and in them the names of the Twelve Apostles of the Lamb" (Rev. 21.14). Even in the new heaven and the new earth the Twelve enjoy a place of peculiar privilege, which is relegated to no other workers for God.

The Apostles in Scripture Days

The Lord as an apostle was unique, the Twelve, as apostles, were also unique; but neither "*the* Apostle" nor "the Twelve Apostles" could abide on the earth forever. When our Lord departed, He left the Twelve to continue His Work; now that the Twelve have departed, who are here to carry it on?

The Lord has gone, but the Spirit has come. The Holy Spirit is come to bear all responsibility for the Work of God on earth. The Son was working for the Father; the Spirit is working for the Son. The Son came to accomplish the Will of the

Father: the Spirit has come to accomplish the Will of the Son. The Son came to glorify the Father: the Spirit has come to glorify the Son. The Father appointed Christ to be "*the* Apostle": the Son while on earth appointed "the Twelve" to be Apostles. Now the Son has returned to the Father, and the Spirit is on earth appointing men to be apostles. The apostles appointed by the Holy Spirit cannot join the ranks of those appointed by the Son, but they are apostles for all that. The apostles we read of in the fourth chapter of Ephesians are clearly not the original Twelve, for *those* were appointed when the Lord was still on earth, whilst *these* date their appointment to apostleship *after* the ascension of the Lord; they were the gifts of the Lord Jesus to His Church *after* His glorification. The Apostles *then* were the personal followers of the Lord Jesus, but the apostles *now* are ministers for the building up of the Body of Christ. We must differentiate clearly between the Apostles who were witnesses to the Resurrection of Christ (Acts 1.22,26), and the apostles who are ministers for the edifying of the Body of Christ, for the Body of Christ was not in existence before the Cross. There is no doubt that later on the Twelve received the Ephesian commission, but the Twelve, as the Twelve, were quite distinct from the apostles mentioned in Ephesians. It is evident then that God has *other* apostles besides the original Twelve.

Immediately after the outpouring of the Spirit we see the Twelve Apostles carrying on the work. Until the twelfth chapter of Acts they are seen as the chief workers; but with the opening of the thirteenth chapter we see the Holy Spirit beginning to manifest Himself as the Agent of Christ and the Lord of the Church. In that chapter we are told that in Antioch, when certain prophets and teachers were ministering to the Lord and fasting, the Holy Spirit said, "Separate me *now* Barnabas and Saul for the Work to which I have called them" (Acts 13.2, Darby). *Now* is the time that the Spirit begins to send men forth. At this point two new workers were commissioned by the Holy Ghost.

After these two were sent out by the Spirit how were they designated? When Barnabas and Paul were working in Iconium, "the multitude of the city was divided; and part held with the Jews, and part with the *apostles*" (Acts 14.4). The two sent forth in the previous chapter are in this chapter referred to as "apostles," and in the same chapter (verse 14), the designation "the *apostles*" is used in apposition to "Paul and Barnabas," which proves conclusively that the two men commissioned by the Holy Spirit were also apostles. They were not among the Twelve, but they were apostles nevertheless.

Who then are apostles? Apostles are God's workmen, sent out by the Holy Spirit to do the Work to which He has called them. The responsibility of the Work is in their hands. Broadly speaking, all believers are responsible for the Work of God, but apostles are a group of people specially set apart for the Work. In a peculiar sense the responsibility of the Work is upon them.

Now we see the teaching of the Scriptures as touching apostles. God appointed His Son to be "*the* Apostle": Christ appointed His disciples to be "the Twelve Apostles": and the Holy Spirit appointed a group of men (apart from the Twelve) to be the Body-building apostles. The first Apostle is unique: there is only one; the Twelve Apostles are also in a class by themselves: there are only twelve; but there is another order of apostles, chosen by the Holy Spirit, and as long as the building up of the Church goes on and the Holy Ghost's presence on earth continues, the choosing and sending forth of this order of apostles will continue too.

In the Word of God we find numerous other apostles besides Barnabas and Paul. There are many belonging to the new order chosen and sent forth by the Spirit of God. In 1 Cor. 4.9, we read: "God hath set forth us the apostles last." To whom do the words "us the apostles" refer? The pronoun "us" implies that there was at least one other apostle besides the writer. If we study the context, we note that Apollos was with Paul when he wrote (verse 6), and Sosthenes was a joint writer with Paul of the Epistle. So it seems clear that the "us" here refers either to Apollos or to Sosthenes, or to both. It follows then that either or both of these two must have been apostles.

Rom. 16.7: "Salute Andronicus and Junia, my kinsmen and my fellow-prisoners, who are of note among the apostles." The clause "who are of note among the apostles" does not mean that they were regarded as notable by the apostles, but rather that among the apostles they were notable ones. Here you have not only another two apostles, but another two notable apostles.

1 Thess. 2.6: "We might have been burdensome, as the apostles of Christ." The "we" here refers clearly to the writers of the Thessalonian letter, i.e. Paul, Silvanus and Timothy (1.1), which indicates that Paul's two young fellow-workers were also apostles.

1 Cor. 15.5-7: "He was seen of Cephas, *then of the Twelve*; after that, he was seen of about five hundred brethren at once; . . . after that, he was seen of James; *then of all the apostles*." Besides the Twelve Apostles there was a group known as "all the apostles." It is obvious, then, that apart from the Twelve, there were other apostles.

Paul never claimed that he was the last apostle and that after him there were no others. Let us read carefully what he said: "Last of all he was seen of me also . . . for I am the least of the apostles, that am not meet to be called an apostle" (1 Cor. 15.8,9). Notice how Paul used the words "last" and "least." He did not say that he was the last apostle, he only said he was the least apostle. If he were the last, there could be no more after him, but he was only the least.

In the Book of Revelation it is said of the Ephesian church: "Thou hast tried them which say they are apostles, and are not, and hast found them liars" (2.2). It seems clear from this verse that the early churches expected to have other apostles apart from the original Twelve, because, when the Book of Revelation was written, John was the only survivor of the Twelve, and by that time even Paul had already been martyred. If there were to be only twelve apostles, and John was the only one left, then no one would have been foolish enough to pose as an apostle, and no one foolish enough to be deceived; and where would have been the need to "try" them? If John were the only apostle, then testing would be simple indeed! If any one was not John, he was not an apostle!

The Meaning of Apostleship

Since the meaning of the word "apostle" is "the sent one," the meaning of apostleship is quite plain, i.e. the office of the sent one. Apostles are not primarily men of special gifts, they are men of special commission. Everyone who is sent of God is an apostle. Many called of God are not as gifted as Paul, but if they have received a commission from God, they are just as truly apostles as he was. The apostles were gifted men, but their apostleship was not based upon their gifts; it was based upon their commission. Of course, God will not send anyone who is unequipped, but equipment does not constitute apostleship. If God cared to send out a man totally unequipped, that man would be as much an apostle as a fully equipped one, since apostleship is not based on human qualification but on Divine commission. It is futile for anyone to assume the office of an apostle simply because he thinks he has the needed gifts or ability. It takes more than mere gift and ability to constitute men apostles; it takes nothing less than God Himself, God's Will and God's call. No man can attain to apostleship through natural or other qualifications; God must make him an apostle if he is ever to be one. Whether or not a man is going to be of any spiritual worth, and his work serve any spiritual end, depends upon the sending of God. "A man sent of God" should be the main characteristic of our entering upon His service, and of all our subsequent movements.

Let us turn to the Scriptures. In Luke 11.49 we read: "I will send them prophets and apostles, and some of them they shall slay and persecute." From the Book of Genesis to the Book of Malachi we do not come across anyone who was explicitly called an apostle, yet the men here referred to as apostles lived between the time of Abel and Zecharias (verse 51), so it is clear that even in Old Testament times God had His apostles.

Our Lord said, "The servant is not greater than his Lord: neither the apostle (Greek) than he that sent him" (John 13.16). Here we have a definition of the term "apostle." It implies being sent out—that is all; and that is everything. However good human intention may be, it can never take the place of Divine commission. To-day those who have been sent out by the Lord to preach the Gospel and to establish churches call themselves missionaries, not apostles; but the word "missionary" means the very same thing as "apostle," i.e. "the sent one." It is the Latin form of the Greek equivalent, "apostolos." Since the meaning of the two words is exactly the same, I fail to see the reason why the *true* sent ones of to-day prefer to call themselves "missionaries" rather than "apostles."

The Evidence of Apostleship

Is there any evidence that one is really commissioned of God to be an apostle? In 1 Cor. 9.1-2, Paul is dealing with our question in writing to the Corinthian saints, and it is obvious from his argument that apostleship has its credentials. "The seal of my apostleship are ye in the Lord," he writes, as if to say, "If God had not sent me to Corinth, then you would not be saved to-day, and there would be no church in your city." If God has called a man to be an apostle, it will be manifest in the fruit of his labours. Wherever you have the commission of God, there you have the authority of God: wherever you have the authority of God, there you have the power of God: and wherever you have the power of God, there you have spiritual fruits. The fruit of our labours proves the validity of our commission. And yet it must be noted that Paul's thought is not that apostleship implies numerous converts, but that it represents spiritual values to the Lord, for He could never send anyone forth for a lesser purpose. The Lord is out for spiritual values, and the object of apostleship is to secure them. In this case the Corinthians represent these values. But did not Paul say here, "Have I not seen Jesus our Lord?" Then is it only those who have seen the Lord Jesus in His resurrection manifestations who are qualified to become apostles? Let us follow carefully the trend of Paul's argument: In verse 1 he asks four questions: (1) "Am I not free?" (2) "Am I not an apostle?" (3) "Have I not seen Jesus our Lord?" (4) "Are not ye my work in the Lord?" An affirmative answer to all four questions was taken for granted, for Paul's case demanded such an answer. Notice that in pursuing his argument in the second verse Paul drops two of his questions and follows out the other two. He drops the first and third, and takes up the second and fourth, linking them together. For the purpose of his reasoning he sets aside, "Am I not free?" and, "Have I not seen Jesus our Lord?" and replies to the question, "Am I not an apostle?" and, "Are not ye my work in the Lord?" Paul was clearly seeking to demonstrate the genuineness of his commission from the blessing that attended his labours, not from his being free or from his having seen the Lord.

Of the four questions asked by Paul, three relate to his person and one to his work. These three are on the same plane, and are quite independent of one another. Paul was not arguing that because he was free and because he was an apostle, therefore he had seen the Lord: nor was he reasoning that because he was an apostle and because he had seen the Lord, therefore he was free: no more was he seeking to demonstrate that because he was free and had seen the Lord, therefore he was an apostle. The facts are he *was* free, he *was* an apostle, and he *had* seen the Lord. These facts had *no* essential connection one with the other, and it is absurd to connect them. It would be as reasonable to argue that Paul's apostleship was based upon his being free, as that it was based upon his seeing the Lord. If he was not seeking to prove his apostleship from the fact of his freedom, no more was he seeking to prove it from his having seen the Lord. Apostleship is not based on having seen the Lord in His resurrection manifestations.

Then what is the meaning of 1 Cor. 15.5-9? "He was seen of Cephas, then of the Twelve: After that, he was seen of above five hundred brethren at once; . . . after that he was seen of James; then of all the apostles. And last of all he was seen of me also." The object of this passage is not to produce evidence of apostleship, but evidence of the resurrection of the Lord. Paul is recording the different persons to whom the Lord appeared; he is not teaching what *effect* was produced upon these persons by His appearing. Cephas and James saw the Lord, but they were Cephas and James after they saw the Lord, just as they were Cephas and James before; they did not become Cephas and James by seeing Him. The same applies to the Twelve Apostles and the five hundred brethren. Seeing the Lord did not constitute them Apostles. They were twelve Apostles before they saw the Lord, and they were twelve Apostles after they saw the Lord. The same argument applies in Paul's case. The facts were, he had seen the Lord, and he was the least of the apostles; but it was not seeing the Lord that constituted him the least of the apostles. The five hundred brethren were not apostles before they saw the Lord, nor were they after. Seeing the Lord in His resurrection manifestations did not constitute them apostles. They were simply "brethren" before, and they were simply "brethren" after. The Word of God nowhere teaches that seeing the Lord is the qualification for apostleship.

But apostleship has its credentials. In 2 Cor. 12.11-12, Paul writes, "In nothing am I behind the very chiefest apostles . . . truly the signs of an apostle were wrought among you in all patience, in signs, and wonders, and mighty deeds." There was abundant evidence of the genuineness of Paul's apostolic commission: and the signs of an apostle will never be lacking where there is truly an apostolic call. From the above passage we infer that the evidence of apostleship lies in a two-fold power—spiritual and miraculous. Endurance is the greatest proof of spiritual power, and it is one of the signs of an apostle. It is the ability to endure steadfastly under continuous pressure that tests the reality of an apostolic call. A true apostle needs to be "strengthened with all power, according to the might of his glory, unto all patience and longsuffering with joy" (Col. 1.11). Yes, it takes nothing short of "*all* power according to the *might* of his glory" to produce "all patience and longsuffering with joy." But the reality of Paul's apostleship was not only attested by his patient endurance under intense and prolonged pressure, it was evidenced also by the miraculous power he possessed. Miraculous power to change situations in the physical world is a necessary manifestation of our knowledge of God in the spiritual realm, and this applies not to heathen lands only, but to every land. To profess to be sent ones of the omnipotent God, and yet stand helpless before situations that challenge His power, is a sad contradiction. Not all who can work wonders are apostles, for the gifts of healing and of miracle-working are given to members of the Body (1 Cor. 12.28) who have no special commission, but miraculous as well as spiritual power is part of the equipment of all who have a true apostolic commission.

The False Apostles

False apostles are present now as well as having been present in the days of the early Church. "Such men are false apostles, deceitful workers, fashioning themselves into apostles of Christ" (2 Cor. 11.13). The Bible thus mentions explicitly false apostles. It does not say these were false *disciples*, since they could very well have been truly born-again disciples. They probably took on godliness as a way of gain, expecting to enrich themselves at the expense of the Corinthian believers. And hence Paul warned the believers at Corinth to be on guard. At times some real apostles may think of reaping some profit from the result of their work. Such persons as these become false apostles. And accordingly, the Bible calls for the testing of these apostles. Thus we find the Lord saying to the church in Ephesus that the believers there did "try them that call themselves apostles, and they are not, and didst find them false" (Rev. 2.2). The Lord commended the Ephesian believers for doing so.

The greatest test for a false apostle is money. Whoever is not clear of money and harbors the ulterior motive of gain in his heart is doubtless a false apostle. A false apostle will be one who either seeks for fame or for wealth. In sending relief to the saints in Jerusalem, Paul especially appointed two other brothers to accompany him and his apostolic party: "avoiding this, that any man should blame us in the matter of this bounty which is ministered by us: for we take thought for things honorable, not only in the sight of the Lord, but also in the sight of men" (2 Cor. 8.20,21). All who are greedy of money are false apostles. Whenever money has its hold on us, our work shall cease to be wholly for the Lord. And thus there is the possibility of our turning from being real apostles to becoming false ones! We need to learn how to test those who call themselves apostles and are not, just as the Ephesian believers did.

Thank God that the Holy Spirit is still here. Thank God that it is not because I do not possess a special gift that I cannot be an apostle. Thank God, too, that it is not because I have seen the Lord with my fleshly eyes that I can therefore be an apostle. And thank God that if I have the Lord's call and commission, I can be this or that apostle, irrespective of my being a prophet or teacher or an evangelist—or my being none of these. Today, it is not a question of gift nor a matter of seeing the Lord in the flesh but the fact of having the Lord's commission. If there is a commission from the Lord, one can be an apostle after the order of Paul and Barnabas. Though we cannot be among the Twelve, nevertheless we are still apostles. We may not be ranked among the great apostles, but we can still be among the least of them; for this number of apostleship is unfilled. Whoever is commissioned and sent forth by the Lord has a place in it.

Women Apostles

Have women any place amongst the ranks of the apostles? Scripture indicates that they have. There were no women amongst the Twelve sent forth by the Lord, but a woman is mentioned amongst the number of the apostles who were sent forth by the Spirit after the Lord's ascension. Rom. 16.7 speaks of two notable apostles, Andronicus and Junia, and good authorities agree that "Junia" is a woman's name.* So here we have a sister as an apostle and a notable apostle at that.

---

*It should be noted that whether "Junia" is in the masculine or feminine gender in the original Greek is still a subject of controversy to this day among Greek and Bible scholars.—*Translator, 1982 edition*

3 The Separation and Movements of the Apostles

The church in Antioch is the model church shown us in God's Word, because it was the first to come into being after the founding of the churches connected with the Jews and the Gentiles. In the second chapter of Acts we see the church in connection with the Jews established in Jerusalem, and in the tenth chapter we see the church in connection with the Gentiles established in the house of Cornelius. It was just after the establishment of these churches that the church in Antioch was founded. In its transition stage the church in Jerusalem was not altogether free from Judaism, but the church in Antioch from the very outset stood on absolutely clear Church ground. It is of no little significance that "the disciples were called Christians *first* in Antioch" (Acts 11.26). It was there that the peculiar characteristics of the Christian and the Christian Church were first clearly manifested, for which reason it may be regarded as the pattern church for this dispensation. Its prophets and teachers were model prophets and teachers, and the apostles it sent forth were model apostles. Not only are the men sent forth an example to us, but the mode of their sending forth is our example too. Since the first recorded sending out of apostles by the Holy Spirit was from Antioch, we shall do well to look carefully into its details.

Since the completion of the New Testament the Holy Spirit has called many of God's children to serve Him throughout the world, but, strictly speaking, none of these can be regarded as our examples. We must always look at the first act of the Holy Spirit in any given direction to discover His pattern for us in that particular direction; therefore in order to see what example the Church must follow to-day in the sending forth of apostles, let us examine carefully the first recorded sending forth of workers from the first church established on absolutely clear Church ground.

The Holy Spirit's Call

In the first two verses of Acts 13 we read: "Now there were in the church that was at Antioch certain prophets and teachers; as Barnabas and Simeon that was called Niger, and Lucius of Cyrene, and Manaen, which had been brought up with Herod the tetrarch, and Saul. As they ministered to the Lord, and fasted, the Holy Ghost said, Separate me Barnabas and Saul for the work whereunto I have called them." Let us note a few facts here. There was a local church in Antioch, there were certain prophets and teachers who were ministers in that church, and it was from amongst those that the Holy Spirit separated two for another sphere of service. Barnabas and Saul were two ministers of the Lord already engaged in the Ministry when the call of the Spirit came. The Holy Spirit only sends to other parts such as are already equipped for the Work and are bearing responsibility where they are, not those who are burying their talents and neglecting local needs whilst they dream of some future day when the call will come to special service. Barnabas and Saul were bearing the burden of the local situation when the Spirit put the burden of other parts upon them; their hands were full of local work when He thrust them out to work further afield. Let us note first that the Holy Spirit chooses apostles from amongst the prophets and teachers.

"And as they ministered to the Lord, and fasted, the Holy

Ghost said, Separate me Barnabas and Saul for the work whereunto I have called them." These prophets and teachers ministered so whole-heartedly to the Lord, that when occasion demanded they even ignored the legitimate claims of their physical being and fasted. What filled the thoughts of those prophets and teachers at Antioch was ministry to the Lord, not work for Him. Their devotion was to the Lord Himself, not to His service. No one can truly work for the Lord who has not first learned to minister to Him. It was while Barnabas and Saul ministered to the Lord that the voice of the Spirit was heard calling them to special service.

It was to the Divine call they responded, not to the call of human need. They had heard no reports of man-eaters or head-hunting savages; their compassions had not been stirred by doleful tales of child-marriage, or foot-binding, or opium-smoking. They had heard no voice but the voice of the Spirit; they had seen no claims but the claims of Christ. No appeal had been made to their natural heroism or love of adventure; they knew only one appeal—the appeal of their Lord. It was the Lordship of Christ that claimed their service, and it was on His authority alone that they went forth. Their call was a spiritual call, no natural factor entered into it. It was the Holy Spirit who said, "Separate me Barnabas and Saul for the work whereunto I have called them." All spiritual work must begin with the Spirit's call; all Divine work must be divinely initiated. The plan conceived for the work may be splendid, the reason adequate, the need urgent, and the man chosen to carry it out may be eminently suitable; but if the Holy Spirit has not said, "Separate me that man for the work to which I have called him," he can never be an apostle. He may be a prophet or a teacher, but he is no apostle. Of old all true apostles were separated by the Holy Ghost for the work to which He called them, and to-day all true apostles must just as surely be set apart for the work by Him. God desires the service of His children, but

He makes conscripts, He wants no volunteers. The Work is His, and He is its only legitimate Originator. Human intention, however good, can never take the place of Divine initiation. Earnest desires for the salvation of sinners, or the edification of saints, will never qualify a man for God's Work. One qualification, and only one, is necessary—God must send him.

It was the Holy Spirit who said, "Separate me Barnabas and Saul for the work whereunto *I have called them*." Only the Divine call can qualify for the apostolic office. In earthly governments there can be no service without commission, and the same holds true in the government of God. The tragedy in Christian work to-day is that so many of the workers have simply *gone* out, they have not been sent. It is Divine commission that constitutes the call to Divine work. Personal desire, friendly persuasions, the advice of one's elders and the urge of opportunity—all these are factors on the natural plane, and they can never take the place of a spiritual call. That is something which must be registered in the human spirit by the Spirit of God.

When Barnabas and Saul were sent forth, the Spirit first called them, then the brethren confirmed the call. The brethren may say you have a call, and circumstances may seem to indicate it, but the question is, have *you* yourself heard the call? If *you* are to go forth, then *you* are the one who must first hear the voice of the Spirit. We dare not disregard the opinion of the brethren, but their opinion is no substitute for a personal call from God. Even if they are confident that we have a call, and in that same confidence a company of God's people gladly send us forth to the work, unless we ourselves know a direct speaking of God into our hearts, on the basis of the new covenant, then we go forth as the messengers of men, not as the apostles of God.

If God desires the service of any child of His, He Himself will call him to it, and He Himself will send him forth. The first requirement in Divine work is a Divine call. Everything hinges on this. A Divine call gives God His rightful place, for it recognises Him as the Originator of the work. Where there is no call from God, the work undertaken is not of Divine origin, and it has no spiritual value. Divine work must be Divinely initiated. A worker may be called directly by the Spirit, or indirectly through the reading of the Word, through preaching, or through circumstances; but whatever means God may use to make His will known to man, *His* voice must be the one heard through every other voice; *He* must be the one who speaks, no matter through what instrument the call may come. We must never be independent of the other members of the Body, but we must never forget that we receive all our directions from the Head; so we must be careful to preserve our spiritual independence, even whilst we cultivate a spirit of mutual dependence amongst the members. It is wrong to reject the opinion of fellow-workers under the pretext of doing the Will of God, but it is also wrong to accept their opinions as a substitute for the direct instructions of the Spirit of God.

Separation of Workers

Yes, it was the Holy Spirit who called Barnabas and Saul, but He said to the other prophets and teachers as well as to them, "Separate me Barnabas and Saul for the Work whereunto I have called them." The Holy Spirit spoke directly to the apostles, but He also spoke indirectly through the prophets and teachers. What was said privately to the two was confirmed publicly through the other three. All apostles must have a personal revelation of God's Will, but to make that alone the basis of their going forth is not sufficient. On the one hand the opinion of others, however spiritual and however experienced, can never be a substitute for a direct call from God: on the other hand, a personal call, however definite, requires the confirmation of the representative members of the Body of Christ in the locality from which the workers go out.

Let us observe that the Holy Spirit did not say to the *church* in Antioch, "Separate me Barnabas and Saul"; it was to the prophets and teachers He spoke. For God to make His Will known to the entire assembly would scarcely have been practicable. Some of its members were spiritually mature, but others were only babes in Christ. Some were whole-heartedly devoted to the Lord, but it is highly improbable that all the members sought the Lord with such singleness of purpose that they could clearly differentiate between His Will and their own ideas, therefore God spoke to a representative company in the church, to men of spiritual experience who were utterly devoted to His interests.

And here was the result—"When they had fasted and prayed and laid their hands on them, they sent them away" (Acts 13.3). The setting apart of the apostles by the prophets and teachers followed the call which came to them from the Spirit. The call was personal, the separation was corporate; and the one was not complete without the other. A direct call from God, and a confirmation of that call in the setting apart of the called ones by the prophets and teachers, is God's provision against free-lances in His service.

The calling of an apostle is the Holy Spirit speaking directly to the one called; the separating of an apostle is the Holy Spirit speaking indirectly through the fellow-workers of the called one. It is the Holy Spirit Who takes the initiative both in the calling and separation of workers; therefore, if the representative brethren of any assembly set men apart for the service of the Lord, they must ask themselves, Are we doing this on our own initiative, or as representing the Spirit of God? If they move without absolute assurance that they are acting on behalf of the Holy Ghost, then the separation of the worker has no spiritual value. They must be able to say of every worker they send forth, He was sent out by the Holy Ghost, not by man. No separation of workers should be done hastily or lightly. It was for this reason that fasting and prayer preceded the sending forth of Barnabas and Saul.

When Barnabas and Saul were separated for the Work there was prayer and fasting and the laying on of hands. The prayer and fasting was not merely in view of the immediate need of clear discernment regarding the Will of God, but in view also of the coming need when the apostles would actually go forth. And the laying on of hands was not by way of ordination, for Barnabas and Saul were already ordained by the Holy Ghost; here, as in the Old Testament, it was an expression of the perfect oneness of the two parties represented. It was as though the three sending forth the two said to them: When you two members of the Body of Christ go forth, all the other members go with you. Your going is our going, and your work is our work. The laying on of hands was a testimony to the oneness of the Body of Christ. It meant that those who remained behind were one with those who went forth, and in full sympathy with them; and that, as they went, those at the base pledged themselves to follow them continually with prayerful interest and loving sympathy.

As regards all sent ones, they must pay attention to these two aspects in their separation for the service of God. On the one hand there must be a direct call from God and a personal recognition of that call; on the other hand there must be a confirmation of that call by the representative members of the Body of Christ. And as regards all who are responsible for the sending forth of others, they must on the one hand be in a position to receive the revelation of the Spirit and to discern the mind of the Lord; on the other hand they must be able to enter sympathetically into the experience of those whom they, as the representative members of the Body of Christ, send forth in the Name of the Lord. The principle that governed the sending forth of the first apostles still governs the sending forth of all apostles who are truly appointed by the Spirit to the Work of God.

The Expression of the Body

On what ground did these prophets and teachers set certain men apart as apostles, and whom did these prophets and teachers represent? Why did they, and not the entire church, separate those workers? What is the significance of such separation, and what is the qualification required on the part of those who assume responsibility in the matter?

The first thing we must realize is that God has incorporated all His children into one Body. He recognizes no division of His people in various "churches" and missions. He has designed that all who are His shall live a corporate life, the life of a body amongst whose many members there is mutual consideration, mutual love and mutual understanding. And He has purposed that not only the life, but also the ministry of His children, should be on the principle of the body, that it should be a matter of mutual helpfulness, mutual edification, and mutual service—the activity of the many members of one body. There are two aspects of the Body of Christ—life and ministry. The first half of Eph. 4 speaks of the Body in relation to its ministry; the second half speaks of the Body in relation to its life. "From whom all the body fitly framed and knit together through that which every joint supplieth, according to the working in due measure of each several part, maketh the increase of the body unto the building up of itself in love" (verse 16). Here it is work that is under consideration; but in verse 25 the question is clearly one of life: "Wherefore putting away falsehood, speak ye truth each one with his neighbour: for we are members of one another." In Rom. 12 we see how the members should care one for another, so that the thought there again is the manifestation of the one life; but in 1 Cor. 12 we see how the members should serve one another, so the thought in that passage is the manifestation of the one ministry.

When we speak of the one Body we emphasize the oneness of the life of all God's children: when we speak of its many members we emphasize the diversity of functions in that unity. The characteristic of the former is life: the charactertistic of the latter is work. In a physical body the members differ one from another, yet they function as one, because they share one life and have the upbuilding of the whole body as their one aim.

Because the Body of Christ has these two different aspects—life and ministry—it consequently has two different outward manifestations. The church in a locality is used to express the life of the Body, and the gifts in the Church are used to express the ministry of its members. In other words, each local church should stand on the ground of the Body, regarding itself as an expression of the oneness of the life of the Body, and it should on no account admit of division, since it exists as the manifestation of an indivisible life. The various ministers of the Church should likewise stand on the ground of the Body, regarding themselves as an expression of the oneness of its varied ministries; and perfect fellowship and co-operation should characterize all their activity, for though their functions are diverse, their ministry is really one. No local church should divide into different sects, or affiliate with other churches under a denomination, thus departing from the ground of the Body; and no group of ministers should unite to form a separate unit, standing on other than Body ground. All their work should be performed as members of the Body, and not as members of an organization existing in distinction from it. A worker may employ his gifts in the capacity of an officer of an organization, but in so doing he departs from the ground of the Body.

A cursory reading of Eph. 4.11-12 might lead us to conclude that apostles, prophets, evangelists, pastors and teachers functioned outside the Body, because they were given by the Lord to His Church for her upbuilding (verse 12); but the sixteenth verse makes it clear that they do not stand outside the Body to build it up: they seek to build it up from within. They themselves are part of the Body, and it is only as they take their rightful place in it, as ministering members, that the whole Body is edified.

That churches are the local expression of the Body of Christ is an established fact, so we need not go into that here; but some explanation is called for regarding the gifted ministers whom God has set in the Church as the expression of the Ministry of the Body. In 1 Cor. 12 Paul is clearly dealing with the question of Christian service. He likens the workers to different members of a body, and shows that each member has its specific use, and all serve the body as belonging to it, not as distinct from it. In verse 27 he writes, "Now ye are the Body of Christ, and severally members thereof"; and in the following verse he says, "And God hath set in the church, first apostles, secondly prophets, thirdly teachers, then miracles, then gifts of healing, helps, governments, divers kinds of tongues." A study of these two verses makes it clear that the gifted *ministers* of verse 28 are the *members* of verse 27, and that the *Church* of verse 28 is the *Body* of verse 27; therefore, what ministers are to the Church, members are to the Body. They hold their position in the Body on account of their functions (the "hearing" and "smelling" of verse 17). The gifted ministers are the functioning members of the Body, and all their operations are as members. They are to the Church what hands, feet, mouth and head are to the physical body. God's servants do not minister to the Church as apart from it, but as its members. They are *in* the Body, serving it by the use of those faculties which they, as members, possess. A church in any locality is an expression of the one life of the Body, while its ministers are the expression of the difference and yet oneness of its ministry.

1 Cor. 12 deals with the subject of the Body of Christ, not in its life-aspect but in its work-aspect. The whole chapter is taken up with the question of ministry, and that ministry is spoken of as the functioning of the different members, from which it is evident that in the thought of God all ministry is on Body ground. Ministry is the practical expression of the Body, an expression of the diversity in unity of its various members. Therefore we see that when the life-aspect of the Body of Christ is expressed, there you have a local church, and when the work aspect is expressed, there you have a manifestation of the gifts God has given to His Church.

In reading 1 Cor. 12.28 one cannot but be arrested by the striking difference between the description of the first three gifts and the remaining five. Paul, under the inspiration of the Spirit, takes special care in enumerating them—"first apostles; secondly prophets; thirdly teachers." The first three are specifically numbered, but not the rest; and they are quite distinct in their nature as well as their numbering. They are men, the rest are things. The three first-named gifts of the Lord to His Church—apostles, prophets and teachers—stand apart from all the others; they are ministers of God's Word, and their function, to edify the Body of Christ, is the most important function in the Church. *They are the representatives of the Ministry of the Body.*

The only scriptural record of the sending forth of *apostles* is found in Acts 13, and there we see that it is the *prophets* and *teachers* who set them apart for their ministry. Scripture provides no precedent for the separation and sending forth of men by one or more individuals, or by any mission or organization; even the sending out of workers by a local church is a thing unknown in the Word of God. The only example provided us there is the separating and sending forth of apostles by the prophets and teachers.

What is the significance of this? In Antioch the prophets

and teachers were chosen of God to separate Barnabas and Saul for His service, because they were the ministering members of the church, and this separation of the apostles was *a question of ministry rather than life*. Had it related to life, and not specifically to service, then it would have been the concern of the whole local church, not merely of its ministering members. But let it be noted that, though Barnabas and Saul were not separated for the Work by the entire church, they were not sent out as representatives of a few select members, but as representatives of the whole Body. Their being separated by the prophets and teachers implied that they did not go out on individualistic lines, or on the basis of any organization, but on the ground of the Ministry of the Body. The emphasis, as we have seen, was on ministry, not on life, but it was a ministry representing the whole Church, not representing any particular section of it. This is clearly expressed by the laying on of hands.

As we have seen, the laying on of hands speaks of oneness (Lev. 1.4), and the only oneness known amongst the children of God is the oneness of the Body of Christ; therefore, in laying hands upon the apostles, the prophets and teachers definitely stood on the ground of the Body, acting as its representative members. Their action identified the whole Church with the apostles, and identified the apostles with the whole Church. These prophets and teachers did not stand on individual ground to send the apostles forth as their personal representatives, nor did they stand on the ground of any select company to send them out as representatives of that particular company; but they stood on the ground of the Body, as its ministering members, and set these two apart for the work of the Gospel. In their turn the two, being thus separated, went forth, not to represent any particular individuals or any special organization, but to represent the Body of Christ, and the Body of Christ alone. All work that is truly scriptural and truly spiritual must be out from the Body and must minister to the Body. The

Body must be the ground on which the worker stands, and it alone must be the sphere in which he works.

On two different occasions Paul had the laying on of hands; first when he believed on the Lord (Acts 9.17), then on the occasion under consideration, when he was sent out from Antioch. The former expressed his identification with the life of the Body: the latter his identification with the Ministry of the Body. The first proclaimed him a member of the Body by receiving life from the Head; the second proclaimed him a ministering member, working not as an isolated individual, but in relation to the other members, as a part of one great whole.

In sending Barnabas and Saul from Antioch, the prophets and teachers stood for no "church" or mission; they represented the Ministry of the Body. They were not the whole Church, they were only a group of God's servants; they bore no special name, they were bound by no particular organization, and they were subject to no fixed rules. They simply submitted themselves to the control of the Spirit and separated those whom *He* had separated for the Work to which *He* had called them. They themselves were not the Body, but they stood on the ground of the Body, under the authority of the Head. Under that authority, and on that ground, they separated men to be apostles; and under the same authority, and on the same ground, others can do the same. The separation of apostles on this principle will mean that the men sent out may differ, those who send them may differ, and the time and place of their sending may differ too; but since all is under the direction of the one Head, and on the ground of the one Body, there will still be no division. If Antioch sends men out on the basis of the Body, and Jerusalem sends men out on the basis of the Body, there will still be inward oneness despite all outward diversity. How grand it would be if there were no representatives of different earthly bodies, but only representatives of *the* Body, the Body of Christ. If thousands of local churches, with thousands of prophets and teachers, each sent out thousands of different workers, there would be a vast outward diversity, but there could still be perfect inward unity if all were sent out under the direction of the one Head and on the ground of the one Body.

That Christ is the Head of the Church is a recognized fact, but that fact needs emphasis in relation to the ministry as well as the life of the Church. Christian ministry is the ministry of the whole Church, not merely of one section of it. We must see to it that our work is on no lesser basis than the Body of Christ, otherwise we lose the Headship of Christ, for Christ is not the Head of any system, or mission, or organization: He is the Head of the Church. If we belong to any human organization, then the Divine Headship ceases to be expressed in our work.

In Scripture we find no trace of man-made organizations sending out men to preach the Gospel; we only find representatives of the Ministry of the Church, under the guidance of the Spirit and on the ground of the Body, sending out those whom the Spirit has already separated for the Work. If those responsible for the sending out of workers sent them out, not as their own representatives or the representatives of any organization, but only as representatives of the Body of Christ: and if those sent out stood on the ground of no particular "church" or mission, but on the ground of *the* Church alone, then no matter from what places the workers came or to what places they went, co-operation and unity would always be possible and much confusion in the Work would be avoided.

Their Movements

After the apostles were called by the Spirit and were separated for the Work by the representative members of the Body, what did they do? We need to recall that those who separated them only expressed identification and sympathy by the laying on of hands; they had no authority to control the apostles. Those prophets and teachers at the base assumed no official responsibility in regard to their movements, their methods of work, or the supply of their financial needs. In Scripture we nowhere find that apostles are under the control of any individual or any organized company. They had no regulations to adhere to and no superiors to obey. The Holy Spirit called them, and they followed His leading and guidance; He alone was their Director.

In Chapters 13 and 14 of the Book of Acts we find the first scriptural record of missionary movements. Though to-day the places we visit and the conditions we meet may be vastly different from those of the Scripture record, yet in principle the experience of the first apostles may well serve as our example. Let us glance for a moment at these two chapters.

"So they, being sent forth by the Holy Ghost, went down to Seleucia; and from thence they sailed to Cyprus. And when they were at Salamis, they proclaimed the word of God in the synagogues of the Jews: and they had also John as their attendant. And when they had gone through the whole island unto Paphos, they found a certain sorcerer" (13.4-6). From the very outset constant movement characterized those sent ones. A true apostle is a traveller, not a settler.

"Now Paul and his company set sail from Paphos and came to Perga in Pamphylia: and John departed from them and returned to Jerusalem. But they, passing through from Perga, came to Antioch of Pisidia; and they went into the synagague on the sabbath day and sat down" (13.13-14). (The Antioch mentioned here is not the same as the Antioch from which Barnabas and Saul set forth on their first missionary tour.) The apostles were constantly on the move, proclaiming the Word of God wherever they went, but until they reached Antioch in Pisidia we are not told anything of the result of their labours. From this point there is a definite development in the Work.

"Now when the synagogue broke up, many of the Jews and of the devout proselytes followed Paul and Barnabas: who, speaking to them, urged them to continue in the grace of God" (13.43). Here is the outcome of a short period of witness in Antioch of Pisidia—many of the Jews and religious proselytes believed. A week later almost the whole city gathered together to hear the Word (verse 44); but this enthusiastic response on the part of the people provoked the Jews to jealousy, and they opposed the apostles (verse 45). At this point the apostles turned to the Gentiles (verse 46), and "as many as were ordained to eternal life believed" (verse 48). On the previous Sabbath a number of Jews had received the Word of life: this Sabbath a number of Gentiles believed on the Lord; so not long after the arrival of the apostles in Antioch of Pisidia we find a church there.

But the apostles did not argue, "Now we have a group of believers here, we must stay awhile and shepherd them." They founded a local church at Antioch of Pisidia, but they did not stay to build it up. On they went again, publishing the Word of the Lord "throughout all the region" (verse 49). Their objective was not one city, but "all the region." The modern custom of settling down in one place to shepherd a particular flock has no precedent in Scripture.

Persecution followed (verse 50). The opponents of the Gospel message expelled the apostles from their coasts, and they answered by shaking the dust from their feet (verse 51). Many a present-day missionary has no dust to shake from his feet! But those who gather no dust lack the characteristic of an apostle. The early apostles never settled down in comfortable homes, nor did they stop for long to pastor the churches they founded; they were constantly itinerating. To be an apostle means to be a sent one, i.e. to be always going out. A stationary apostle is a contradiction in terms. A true apostle is one who in times of persecution will always have dust to shake off his feet.

What effect had this early departure of the apostles upon the infant church? Here was a group of new believers, mere babes in Christ, and their fathers in the faith forsook them in their infancy. Did they argue, Why should the apostles take fright at persecution and leave us to face the opposition alone?

Did they plead with the apostles to remain awhile and care for their spiritual welfare? Did they reason, If you leave us now we shall be as sheep without a shepherd? If both of you cannot stay, surely one at least can remain behind and look after us. The persecution is so intense, we shall never get through without your help. How amazing the Scripture record is: "And the disciples were filled with joy and the Holy Ghost" (verse 52).

There was no mourning amongst the disciples when the apostles went, but great gladness. The disciples were glad, for they knew the Lord; and they might well rejoice, because the apostles' departure meant an opportunity for others to hear the Gospel. What was loss to them was gain to Iconium. Those believers were not like the believers of to-day, hoping for a settled pastor to instruct them, solve their problems and shelter them from trouble; and those apostles were not like the apostles of to-day; they were pioneers, not settlers. They did not wait till believers were mature before they left them. They dared to leave them in mere infancy, for they believed in *the power of the life of God* within them.

But those disciples were not only filled with joy, they were filled with the Holy Ghost. The apostles might go, but the Spirit remained. Had the apostles remained to pastor them, it would have mattered little whether they were filled with the Spirit or not. If they had had a pastor to throw light on all their problems they would have felt little need of the Spirit's instruction, and they would have felt little need of His power if they had had one in their midst who was bearing all responsibility for the spiritual side of the work whilst they attended to the secular. In Scripture there is not the slightest hint that apostles should settle down to pastor those they have led to the Lord. There are pastors in Scripture, but they are simply brethren raised up of God from *amongst* the local saints to care for their fellow-believers. One of the reasons why so many present-day converts are not filled with the Spirit is because the apostles settle down to shepherd them and take upon themselves the responsibility that belongs to the Holy Ghost.

Praise God that the apostles "moved on to Iconium," for "a great multitude of both Jews and Greeks believed" (14.1). Before long "the multitude of the city was divided; and part held with the Jews, and part with the apostles" (verse 4). The saved were obviously "a great multitude," since their coming out from the unsaved so vitally affected the place as to cause a division in the city. Only a short time after the apostles left Antioch in Pisidia, there was a church established in Iconium; and here, as in the previous place, opposition was intense. The apostles might well have argued that to leave "a great multitude" of mere babes in Christ exposed to fierce persecution, was heartless, and bad policy besides. But the apostles were true to their apostolic calling, and off they went "to cities of Lycaonia, Lystra and Derbe" (verse 6). And what did they do when they came to Lystra? As elsewhere, so here, "they preached the Gospel" (verse 7); and as elsewhere, so here, there was opposition and persecution (verse 19). It is difficult to estimate the number of believers at Lystra, but judging by the remark that the disciples "encircled" Paul (verse 20, Darby), there must have been at least half a dozen, and there may have been scores or even hundreds. So now there is a church in Lystra!

Does Paul stay to shepherd them awhile, or at least to tend them till the fierceness of the opposition had subsided? No! "On the morrow he went forth with Barnabas to Derbe" (verse 20). And there again the Glad Tidings are proclaimed and there again they "made many disciples" (verse 21). So another church is formed! And with the founding of a church in Derbe the first missionary tour of the apostles closes.

Looking back over these two chapters, we note that a fundamental principle governs the movements of the apostles. They travel from place to place, according to the leading of the

Spirit, preaching the Gospel and founding churches. Nowhere do we find them settling down to shepherd and instruct the converts, or to bear any local responsibility in the churches they have founded. In days of peace the apostles were on the move, and in days of persecution likewise. "Go!" was the word of the Lord, and "Go!" was the watchword of the apostles. The outstanding trait of a sent one is that he is always on the move.

On Their Return

But the question arises, How were these new converts shepherded and instructed? How were the newly-founded churches established? In studying the Word we find that the missionary tour of the apostles consisted of an outward and a return journey. On their outward journey their first concern was to found churches: on their return journey their chief business was to build them up.

Having "made many disciples, they returned to Lystra, and to Iconium, and to Antioch, confirming the souls of the disciples, exhorting them to continue in the faith, and that through many tribulations we must enter into the kingdom of God" (14.21-22). Here we see Paul and Barnabas returning to do some construction work in the churches already founded; but as before on their outward journey, so now on their return, they never settle down in any one place.

It is clear then that the apostles did not just move from place to place founding churches, they also did definite construction work. Merely to found churches without establishing them would be like leaving new-born babes to their own resources. The point to note here is, that whilst the instruction of the new converts and the building up of the churches was a very vital part of the apostles' work, they did it, not by settling down in one place, but rather by *visiting the places* where they had been before. Neither in their initial work of preaching the

Gospel, nor in their subsequent work of establishing the churches, did the apostles take up their permanent abode in any one place.

Before they left a place where a church had been founded and some construction work done, they appointed elders to bear responsibility there (14.23). This is one of the most important parts of an apostle's work. (This subject will be dealt with more fully in a subsequent chapter.)

Thus the early apostles worked, and the blessing of the Lord rested on their labours. We shall do well if we follow in their steps, but we must realize clearly that even though we adopt apostolic methods, unless we have apostolic consecration, apostolic faith and apostolic power, we shall still fail to see apostolic results. We dare not under-estimate the value of apostolic methods—they are absolutely essential if we are to have apostolic fruits—but we must not overlook the need of apostolic spirituality, and we must not fear apostolic persecution.

Back to Antioch

"And thence they sailed to Antioch, from whence they had been committed to the grace of God for the work which they had fulfilled. And when they were come, and had gathered the church together, they rehearsed all things that God had done with them, and how that he had opened a door of faith unto the Gentiles" (14.26-7). On their return to Antioch the apostles "rehearsed all things that God had done with them." It was from Antioch that Paul and Barnabas had gone out, so it was only fitting that on their return they should give an account of the Lord's dealings with them to those from whom they had gone forth. To give reports of the Work to those who are truly bearing the burden with us, is sanctioned by God's Word. It is not only permissible, but necessary, that the children of God at the base should be informed of His doings on the field; but we do well to make sure that our reports are not in the nature of advertisements.

In the matter of reporting, we should on the one hand avoid all unnatural reticence and soulish seclusiveness; on the other hand we must carefully guard against the intrusion of any personal interest. In all reports of the Work our aim should be to glorify God and bring spiritual enrichment to those who share them. To utilize reports as a means of propaganda, with material returns in view, is base in the extreme, and unworthy of any Christian. When the motive is to glorify God and benefit His children, but at the same time to make known the needs of the Work with a view to receiving material help, it is still far from acceptable to the Lord, and is unworthy of His servants. Our aim should be this alone—that God shall be glorified and His children blessed. If there were this perfect purity of motive in our reports, how differently many of them would be worded!

Each time we write or speak of our work let us ask ourselves these questions: (1) Am I reporting with a view to gain publicity for myself and my work? (2) Am I reporting with the double object of glorifying the Lord *and* advertising the work? (3) Am I reporting with this aim *alone*, that God shall be glorified and His children blessed? May the Lord give us grace to report with unmixed motives and perfect purity of heart!

4 The Elders Appointed by the Apostles

"Elders" is a designation of Old Testament origin. We find reference made in the Old Testament to the elders of Israel and also to the elders of different cities; and in the Gospels we meet the term again, but still in relation to the Israelites. Even the elders referred to in the first part of Acts are of the Old Testament order (4.5,8,23; 6.12).

When were elders first instituted in the Church? Acts 11.30 refers to them in connection with the church in Jerusalem, and this is the first mention of elders in connection with any church; but though their existence is mentioned, nothing is said of their origin. Not till Acts 14.23, when we read of Paul and Barnabas returning from their first missionary journey, do we discover who they were, how they were appointed, and by whom. "When they had appointed for them elders in every church, and had prayed with fasting, they commended them to the Lord. . . ."

The Appointment

We have seen that the apostles themselves could not remain with the new believers to shepherd them and to bear the responsibility of the work locally; how then were the new converts cared for, and how was the work carried on? The apostles did not request that men be sent from Antioch to shepherd the flocks, nor did one of themselves remain behind to bear the burden of the local churches; what they did was simply this: "When they had appointed for them elders in every church, and had prayed with fasting, they commended them to the Lord on whom they had believed" (verse 23). Wherever a church had been founded on their outward journey, they appointed elders on their return journey. They did not wait until any arbitrary standard was reached before appointing elders in a church, but "in *every* church" they chose a few of the more mature members to care for their fellow-believers.

The apostolic procedure was quite simple. The apostles visited a place, founded a church, left that church for awhile, then returned to establish it. In the interval certain developments would naturally take place. When the apostles left, some of the professing believers would leave too: others would continue to attend the meetings, and would prove themselves to be truly the Lord's, but would make no appreciable progress: others again would eagerly press on in the knowledge of the Lord and show real concern for His interests. Those who had more spiritual life than others would spontaneously come to the fore, and take responsibility for their weaker brethren. It was because they had proved themselves to be elders that the apostles appointed them to hold office as elders, and it was their business to shepherd and instruct the other believers, and to superintend and control the church affairs.

Nowhere did the apostles settle down and assume responsibility for the local church, but in every church they founded they chose from amongst the *local* believers faithful ones upon whom such responsibility could be placed. When they had chosen elders in each church, with prayer and fasting they committed them to the Lord, just as, with prayer and fasting, they themselves had been committed to the Lord by the prophets and teachers when they were sent out on their apostolic ministry. If this committal of elders to the Lord is to be of spiritual value, and no mere official ceremony, a vital knowledge of the Lord will be required on the part of the apostles. It is easy to become so occupied with the problems and needs of the situation, that one instinctively takes the burden upon oneself, even whilst admitting the truth that the Lord is responsible for His own Church. We need to know Christ as Head of His Church in no mere intellectual way if we are to let all its management pass out of *our* hands at the very outset. Only an utter distrust of themselves, and a living trust in God, could enable the early apostles to commit the affairs of every local church into the hands of local men who had but recently come to know the Lord. All who are engaged in apostolic work, and are seeking to follow the example of the first apostles in leaving the churches to the management of the local elders, must be spiritually equipped for the task; for if things pass out of human hands and are not committed in faith to Divine hands, the result will be disaster. Oh, how we need a living faith and a living knowledge of the living God!

The Word of God makes it clear that the oversight of a church is not the work of apostles, but of elders. Although Paul stayed in Corinth for over a year, in Rome for two years, and in Ephesus for three years, yet in none of these places did he assume responsibility for the work of the local church. In Scripture we read of the elders of Ephesus, but never of the apostles *of* Ephesus; and we find no mention made of the apostles *of* Philippi, but we do find reference to the bishops of Philippi. Apostles are responsible for their own particular ministry, but not for the churches which are the fruit of their ministry. All the fruit of the apostles' work had to be handed over to the care of local elders.

In God's plan provision has been made for the building up of local churches, and in that plan pastors have a place; but it was never His thought that apostles should assume the role of pastors. He purposed that apostles should be responsible for the work in *different* places, whilst elders were to bear responsibility in *one* place. The characteristic of an apostle is *going*: the characteristic of an elder is *staying*. It is not necessary that elders resign their ordinary professions and devote themselves exclusively to their duties in connection with the church. They are simply *local* men, following their usual pursuits and at the same time bearing special responsibilities in the church. Should local affairs increase, they may devote themselves entirely to spiritual work, but the characteristic of an elder is not that he is a "full-time Christian worker"; it is merely that, as a local brother, he bears responsibility in the local church. Locality determines the boundary of a church, and it is for that reason that the elders are always chosen from amongst the maturer believers in any place, and not transferred from other places. Thus the local character of the churches of God is preserved, and consequently also their independent government and spiritual unity.

According to the usual conception of things, one would think it necessary for a considerable time to elapse between the founding of a church and the appointment of elders, but that is not according to God's pattern. The first missionary tour of the apostles covered less than two years, and during that period the apostles preached the Gospel, led sinners to the Lord, formed churches, and appointed elders wherever a church had been formed. The elders were chosen on the apostles' return journey, not on their first visit to any place; but the interval between their two visits was never long, at most a matter of months. On their return journey the apostles would naturally find some places progressing more favourably than others, but they did not reason that, because of the low state of any church, they would make an exception and appoint no elders. They appointed elders "in *every* church." Some may ask, If all the members of a church are in a low spiritual condition, how is it possible to appoint elders amongst them? It may solve the problem of many if they only consider the implication of the term "elder." The existence of an "elder" implies the existence of a junior. The word "elder" is relative, not absolute. Amongst the group of men in their seventy-ninth year it takes a man in his eightieth year to be their "elder"; but it only takes a child of eight to be "elder" to a company of children of seven. Even amongst the spiritually immature there are bound to be those who, in comparison with them, are more mature, and have spiritual possibilities, which is all the qualification they require to be their "elders."

A church may come far short of the ideal, but we cannot on that account deprive it of the status of a church. Our responsibility is to minister to it and so seek to bring it nearer the ideal. In the same way, even the comparatively advanced ones in a locality may not reach the ideal of elders, but we cannot for that reason deprive them of the status of elders. In comparison with the elders of other places they may seem very immature, but if they are more advanced than the other believers in the same locality, then in their own church they *are* elders. We must remember that the office of an elder according to Scripture is limited to a locality. Being an elder in Nanking does not qualify a man to be an elder in Shanghai; but even if his spiritual state be far from what it should, provided he is in advance of his fellow-believers in the same church, then he is qualified to be an elder there. You can only have pattern elders where you have a pattern church. Where a church is immature, the elders will naturally be immature; where a church is mature, the elders will also be mature. The model elders of 1 Tim. 3, and of Titus 1, are to be found in model churches.

The appointing of comparatively spiritual brothers to be elders is a principle set forth in the Word of God, though it runs counter to the modern conception of things; but even whilst we recognize this principle, we must not seek to apply it in any legal way. That would spell death. We must force nothing, but must be continually open to the leading of the Spirit. He will indicate the right time for the appointment of elders in any church. Should there be no leading of the Holy Spirit, and circumstances not permit of an immediate appointment of elders on the second visit of the apostles, then a Titus could be left behind to see to their appointment later. This is the first subject dealt with in the book of Titus, and it is a most important one. Paul gives Titus injunctions to "establish" elders in every city in Crete (Titus 1.5).

In the appointment of elders the apostles did not follow their personal preferences; they only appointed those whom God had already chosen. That is why Paul could say to the elders in Ephesus, "The Holy Ghost hath made you bishops" (Acts 20.28). The apostles did not take the initiative in the matter. They merely established as elders those whom the Holy Spirit *had already* made overseers in the church. In a man-made organization the appointment of an individual to office entitles him to occupy that office; but not so in the Church of God. Everything there is on a spiritual basis, and it is only Divine appointment that qualifies a man for office. If the Holy Ghost does not make men bishops, then no apostolic appointment will ever avail to do so. In the Church of God everything is under the sovereignty of the Spirit; man is ruled out. Elders are not men who think themselves capable to control church affairs, or men whom the apostles consider suitable, but men whom the *Holy Ghost* has set to be overseers in the Church. Those whom the Spirit chooses to be shepherds of the flock, to them He also gives grace and gifts to qualify them for spiritual leadership. It is their spiritual call and their spiritual equipment, not their official appointment, that constitutes them elders. In a spiritual sense they are already elders before they hold the position officially, and it is because they actually *are* elders that they are publicly appointed to be elders. In the early Church it was the Holy Spirit Who first signified His choice of elders, then the apostles confirmed the choice by appointing them to office.

Apostles and Elders

Elders were local men appointed to oversee affairs in the

local church. Their sphere of office was limited by the locality. An elder in Ephesus was not an elder in Smyrna, and an elder in Smyrna was not an elder in Ephesus. In Scripture there are no local apostles, nor are there any extra-local elders; all elders are local, and all apostles are extra-local. The Word of God nowhere speaks of apostles managing the affairs of a local church, and it nowhere speaks of elders managing the affairs of several local churches. The apostles were the ministers of all the churches, but they had control of none; the elders were confined to one church and they controlled affairs in that one. The duty of apostles was to found churches. Once a church was established, all responsibility was handed over to the local elders, and from that day the apostles exercised no control whatever in its affairs. All management was in the hands of the elders, and if they thought right they could even refuse an apostle entry into their church. Should such a thing occur, the apostle would have no authority to insist on being received, since all local authority had already passed from his hands into the hands of the elders.

How did Paul deal with the adulterous believer in Corinth? He did not just notify the church that *he* had excommunicated the man. The utmost he could do was to instruct its members regarding the seriousness of the situation and seek to admonish them to remove the wicked person from their midst (1 Cor. 5.13). If the church was right spiritually they would pay attention to Paul, but if they disregarded his exhortations, whilst they would be wrong spiritually, they would not be wrong legally. In the event of their despising his counsel, Paul could only bring his spiritual authority to bear on the situation. In the Name of the Lord Jesus he could "deliver such a one unto Satan for the destruction of the flesh" (verse 5). He had no official authority to discipline him, but he had spiritual authority to deal with the case. He had his spiritual "rod."

The affairs of the local church are entirely independent of the apostles. Once elders have been appointed, all control passes into their hands, and whilst thereafter an apostle may still instruct and persuade, he can never interfere. But this did not hinder Paul from speaking authoritatively to the Corinthians. Even a casual reader will notice how authoritative his statements were in both epistles. It was quite within his province to pass judgment where doctrinal and moral questions were concerned, and when Paul did so he was most emphatic; but the actual enforcing of such judgments was outside his province and entirely a matter for the local church.

An apostle can deal with the disorders of a church whenever his advice and counsel are sought, as was the case with Paul and the church in Corinth. It was because of their enquiries that he could say to them, "And the rest will I set in order whensoever I come" (1 Cor. 11.34). But the point to note here is that "the rest" of the matters which Paul intended to "set in order" on his arrival in Corinth were to be attended to in the same way as those he had dealt with in his Epistle, and they were dealt with *doctrinally*. In like manner as he had instructed them concerning certain affairs there, so he would instruct them concerning the remaining matters on his arrival; but the Corinthians themselves, not Paul, were the ones who would have *to deal* with the situation.

Since Peter and John were apostles, how did it come about that they were elders of the church in Jerusalem? (1 Pet. 5.1; 2 John 1; 3 John 1). They were elders as well as apostles because they were not only responsible for the Work in different places, but also for the church in *their own* place. When they went out they ministered in the capacity of apostles, bearing the responsibility of the Work in other parts; when they returned home they performed the duties of elders, bearing the responsibility of the local church. (Only such apostles as are not itinerating *much* could be elders of the church in their own locality.) When Peter and John were away from their own church they were apostles, when they returned they were elders. It was not on the ground of their being apostles that they were elders in

Jerusalem; they were elders there solely on the ground of their being local men of greater spiritual maturity than their brethren.

There is no precedent in Scripture for a *visiting* apostle to settle down as elder in any church he visits; but, provided circumstances permit of his being frequently at home, he could be an elder in his own locality, on the ground of his being a local brother. If the local character of the churches of God is to be preserved, then the extra-local character of the apostles must also be preserved.

Paul was sent out from Antioch and he founded a church in Ephesus. We know he did not hold the office of elder in any church, but it would have been possible for him to be an elder in Antioch, not in Ephesus. He spent three years in Ephesus, but he worked there in the capacity of an apostle, not an elder, i.e. he assumed no responsibility and exercised no authority in local affairs, but simply devoted himself to his apostolic ministry. Let us note carefully that *there are no elders in the universal Church and no apostles in the local church.*

Their Responsibilities

It is the responsibility of every saved man to serve the Lord according to his capacity and in his own sphere. God did not appoint elders to do the work on behalf of their brethren; after the appointment of elders, as before, it is still the brethren's duty and privilege to serve the Lord. Elders are also called "bishops" (Acts 20.28; Titus 1.5,7). The term "elder" relates to their person; the term "bishop" to their work. "Bishop" means "overseer," and an overseer is not one who works instead of others, but one who supervises others as they work. God intended that every Christian should be a "Christian worker," and He appointed some to take the oversight of the work so that it might be carried on efficiently. It was never His thought that the majority of the believers should devote themselves exclusively to secular affairs and leave the church matters to a group of spiritual specialists. This point cannot be overemphasized. Elders are not a group of men who contract to do the church work on behalf of its members; they are only the head-men who superintend affairs. It is their business to encourage the backward and restrain the forward ones, never doing the work instead of them, but simply directing them in the doing of it.

The responsibility of an elder relates to matters temporal and spiritual. They are appointed to "rule," and also to "instruct" and "shepherd." "Let the elders that rule well be counted worthy of double honour, especially those who labour in the word and in teaching" (1 Tim. 5.17). "Tend the flock of God which is among you, exercising the oversight, not of constraint, but willingly, according unto God; nor yet for filthy lucre, but of a ready mind; neither as lording it over the charge allotted to you, but making yourselves ensamples to the flock" (1 Pet. 5.2,3).

The Word of God uses the term "rule" in connection with the responsibilities of an elder. The ordering of church government, the management of business affairs and the care of material things, are all under their control. But we must remember that a scriptural church does not consist of an active and a passive group of brethren, the former controlling the latter, and the latter simply submitting to their control, or the former bearing all the burden whilst the latter settle down in ease to enjoy the benefit of their labours. "That the members should . . . care one for another" is God's purpose for His Church (1 Cor. 12.24). Every church after God's own heart bears the stamp of "one another" on all its life and activity; mutuality is its outstanding characteristic. If the elders lose sight of that, then their ruling the church will soon be changed to *lording* it over the church. Even while the elders exercise control in church affairs, they must remember that they are only fellow-members with the other believers; Christ alone is the Head. They were not appointed to be "lords" of their brethren, but to be their "*examples.*" What is an example? It is a pattern for others to follow. Since they were to be a pattern to the brethren, then obviously it was neither God's thought for them to do all the work and the brethren none, nor for the brethren to do the work whilst they simply stood by and commanded. For the elders to be a pattern to the brethren implied that the brethren worked and the elders worked as well; and it implied that the elders worked with special diligence and care, so that the brethren should have a good example to follow. They were overseers, but they were not "lords" of their brethren, standing aloof and commanding; *and* they did direct the work, but they did it more by example than by command. Such is the scriptural conception of the rule of the elders.

But their responsibility does not merely relate to the material side of church affairs. If God has equipped them with spiritual gifts, then they should also bear spiritual responsibility. Paul wrote to Timothy, "Let the elders that rule well be counted worthy of double honour, especially those who labour in the word and in teaching" (1 Tim. 5.17). It is the responsibility of all elders to control the affairs of the church, but such as have special gifts (as of prophecy or teaching) are free to exercise these for the spiritual edification of the church. Paul wrote to Titus that an elder should "be able both to exhort in the sound doctrine, and to convict the gainsayers" (Titus 1.9). The preaching and teaching in the local church is not the business of apostles but of local brethren who are in the Ministry, especially if they are elders. As we have already seen, the management of a church is a matter of local responsibility, so also is teaching and preaching.

On the spiritual side of the work the elders not only help to build up the church by teaching and preaching, but by pastoral work. To shepherd the flock is peculiarly the work of elders. Paul said to the Ephesian elders: "Take heed unto yourselves, and to all the flock, in the which the Holy Ghost hath made you bishops, to feed the church of God" (Acts 20.28). And Peter wrote in the same strain to the elders among the saints of the Dispersion, "Tend the flock of God which is among you" (1 Pet. 5.2). The present-day conception of pastors is far removed from the thought of God. God's thought was that men chosen *from among the local brethren* should pastor the flock, not that men coming from other parts should preach the Gospel, found churches, and then settle down to care for those churches. A clear understanding of the respective responsibilities of apostles and elders would clear away many of the difficulties that exist in the Church to-day.

The Plurality of Elders

This work of ruling, teaching and shepherding the flock, which we have seen to be the special duty of the elders, does not devolve upon one man only in any place. To have pastors in a church is scriptural, but the present-day pastoral system is quite unscriptural; it is an invention of man.

In Scripture we see that there was always more than one elder or bishop in a local church. It is not God's will that one believer should be singled out from all the others to occupy a place of special prominence, whilst the others passively submit to his will. If the management of the entire church rests upon one man, how easy it is for him to become self-conceited, esteeming himself above measure and suppressing the other brethren (3 John). God has ordained that several elders together share the work of the church, so that no one individual should be able to run things according to his own pleasure, treating the church as his own peculiar property and leaving the impress of his personality upon all its life and work. To place the responsibility in the hands of several brethren, rather than in the hands of one individual, is God's way of safeguarding His Church against the evils that result from the domination of a strong personality. God has purposed that several brothers should unitedly bear responsibility in the church, so that even in controlling its affairs they have to depend one upon the other and submit one to the other. Thus, in an experimental way, they will discover the meaning of bearing the Cross, and they will have opportunity to give practical expression to the truth of the Body of Christ. As they honour one another and trust one another to the leading of the Spirit, none taking the place of the Head, but each regarding the others as fellow-members, the element of "mutuality," which is the peculiar feature of the Church, will be preserved.

5 | The Churches Founded by the Apostles

The Church and the Churches

The Word of God teaches us that the Church is one. Why then did the apostles found separate churches in each of the places they visited? If the *Church* is the Body of Christ, it cannot but be one. Then how does it come about that we speak of *churches*?

The word "church" means "the called out ones." The term is used twice in the Gospels, once in the sixteenth chapter of Matthew and once in the eighteenth, and we meet it quite frequently in the Acts and in the Epistles. In the Gospels the word is used on both occasions by our Lord, but it is employed in a somewhat different sense each time.

"Thou art Peter, and upon this rock I will build my church; and the gates of Hades shall not prevail against it" (Matt. 16.18). What church is this? Peter confessed that Jesus was the Christ, the Son of the living God, and our Lord declared that He would build His Church upon this confession—the confession that, as to His Person He is the Son of God, and as to His work He is the Christ of God. This Church comprises all the saved, without reference to time or space, i.e. all who in the Purpose of God are redeemed by virtue of the shed Blood of the Lord Jesus, and are born again by the operation of His Spirit. This is the Church universal, the Church of God, the Body of Christ.

"And if he refuse to hear them, tell it unto the church" (Matt. 18.17). The word "church" is used here in quite a different sense from the eighteenth verse of Matt. 16. The sphere of the church referred to here is clearly not as wide as the sphere of the Church mentioned in the previous passage. The Church there is a Church that knows nothing of time or place, but the church here is obviously limited both to time and place, for it is one that can hear you speak. The Church mentioned in Chapter 16 includes all the children of God in every locality, whilst the church mentioned in Chapter 18 includes only the children of God living in one locality; and it is because it is limited to one place that it is possible for you to tell your difficulties to the believers of whom it is composed. Obviously the church here is local, not universal, for no one could speak at one time to all the children of God throughout the universe. It is only possible to speak at one time to the believers living in one place.

We have clearly two different aspects of the Church before us—the Church and the churches, the universal Church and the local churches. The Church is invisible: the churches are visible; the Church has no organization: the churches are organized; the Church is spiritual: the churches are spiritual and yet physical; the Church is purely an organism: the churches are an organism, yet at the same time they are organized, which is seen by the fact that elders and deacons hold office there.*

All Church difficulties arise in connection with the local churches, not with the universal Church. The latter is invisible and spiritual, therefore beyond the reach of man, whilst the former is visible and organized, therefore still liable to be touched by human hands. The heavenly Church is so far removed from the world that it is possible to remain unaffected

*Throughout this book it would be well for the reader to distinguish clearly between the Church and the church

by it, but the earthly churches are so close to us, that if problems arise there we feel them acutely. The invisible Church does not test our obedience to God, but the visible churches test us severely by facing us with issues on the intensely practical plane of our earthly life.

The Basis of the Churches

In the Word of God we find "the Church of God" spoken of in the singular (1 Cor. 10.32), but we find the same Word referring to the "churches of God" in the plural (1 Thess. 2.14). How has this unity become a plurality? How has the Church which is essentially one become many? The Church of God has been divided* into the churches of God on the one ground of difference of locality. Locality is the only scriptural basis for the division of the Church into churches.

The seven churches in Asia, referred to in the Book of Revelation, comprised the church in Ephesus, the church in Smyrna, the church in Pergamos, the church in Thyatira, the church in Sardis, the church in Philadelphia and the church in Laodicea. They were seven churches, not one. Each was distinct from the others on the ground of the difference of locality. It was only because the believers did not reside in one place that they did not belong to one church. There were seven different churches simply for this reason, that the believers lived in seven different places. Ephesus, Smyrna, Pergamos, Thyatira, Sardis, Philadelphia and Laodicea are clearly all the names of places. Not only were the seven churches in Asia founded on the basis of locality, but all the churches mentioned in Scripture were founded on that same basis. Throughout the Word of God we can find no name attached to a church save the name of a place, e.g. the church in Jerusalem, the church in Lystra, the church in Derbe, the church in Co-

*The word "divided" is used here in its purest sense

losse, the church in Troas, the church in Thessalonica, the church in Antioch. This fact cannot be over-emphasized that *in Scripture no other name but the name of a locality is ever connected with a church, and division of the Church into churches is solely on the ground of difference of locality.*

Spiritually the Church of God is one, therefore it cannot be divided; but physically its members* are scattered throughout the earth, therefore they cannot possibly live in one place. Yet it is essential that there be a physical gathering together of believers. It is not enough that they be present "in the spirit," they must also be present "in the flesh." Now a church is composed of all "the called-out ones assembled" in one place for worship, prayer, fellowship and ministry. This assembling together is absolutely essential to the life of a church. Without it there may be believers scattered throughout the area, but there is really no church. *The Church* exists because of the existence of its members, and it does not require that they meet in a physical way; but it is essential to the very existence of *a church* that its members gather together in a physical way. It is in this latter sense that the word "church" is used in 1 Cor. 14. The phrase "in the church" (verses 19, 23, 28) means "in the church meetings." A church is a church assembled. These believers are not separated from other believers in any respect but that of their dwelling-places. As long as they continue in the flesh they will be limited by space, and this physical limitation, which, in the very nature of things makes it impossible for God's people to meet in one place, is the only basis sanctioned by God for the forming of separate churches. Christians belong to different churches for the sole reason that they live in different places. That division is merely external. In reality the Church as the Body of Christ cannot be divided, therefore even

*The grudge which certain writers bear against the use of the word "member" in connection with the word "church" is merely a matter of terms, not of facts

when the Word of God refers to the different assemblies of His people, the places named vary, but it is still "the church" in every one of these places, e.g. "*the church* in Ephesus," "*the church* in Smyrna," "*the church* in Pergamos," etc.

In the New Testament there is one method and one alone of dividing the Church into churches, and that God-ordained method is division on the basis of locality. All other methods are man-made, not God-given. May the Spirit of God engrave this truth deeply on our hearts, that the only reason for the division of God's children into different churches is because of the different places in which they live.

What is a New Testament church? It is not a building, a Gospel-hall, a preaching centre, a mission, a work, an organization, a system, a denomination, or a sect. It is the meeting together for worship, prayer, fellowship and mutual edification, of all the people of God in a given locality, on the ground that they are Christians in the same locality. People may apply the term "church" to any of the above, but they are no church for all that. The Church is the Body of Christ; a church is a miniature Body of Christ. All the believers in a locality form the church in that locality, and in a small way they ought to show forth what the Church should show forth. They are the Body of Christ in that locality, so they have to learn how to come under the Headship of the Lord, and how to manifest oneness amongst all the members, guarding carefully against schism and division.

The Boundary of a Locality

We have seen that all the churches in Scripture are local churches, but the question naturally arises, What is a scriptural locality? If we note what places are mentioned in God's Word in connection with the founding of churches, then we shall be able to determine what the extent of a place must be to justify its being regarded as a unit for the forming of a church.

In Scripture the localities which determine the boundary of a church are *neither countries, nor provinces, nor districts.* Nowhere do we read of a national church, or a provincial church, or of a district church. We read of the church in Ephesus, the church in Rome, the church in Jerusalem, the church in Corinth, the church in Philippi, the church in Iconium, etc. Now what kind of places are Ephesus, Rome, Jerusalem, Corinth, Philippi and Iconium? They are neither countries, nor provinces, nor districts, but simply places of convenient size for people to live together in a certain measure of safety and sociability. In modern language we should call them cities. That cities were the boundaries of churches in the apostolic days is evident from the fact that on the one hand Paul and Barnabas "appointed . . . for them elders *in every church*" (Acts 14.23), and on the other hand Paul instructed Titus to "appoint elders *in every city*" (Titus 1.5).

In the Word of God we see no church that extends beyond the area of a city, nor do we find any church which does not cover the entire area. A city is the scriptural unit of locality. From the Books of Genesis and Joshua we learn that "cities" in olden days were the places where people grouped together to live; they were also the smallest unit of civil administration, and each possessed an independent name. Any place is qualified to be a unit for the founding of a church which is a place where people group together to live, a place with an independent name, and a place which is the smallest political unit. Such a place is a scriptural "city" and is the boundary of a local church. Large cities such as Rome and Jerusalem are only units, whilst small cities such as Iconium and Troas are likewise units. Apart from such places where people live a community life, there is no scriptural unit of the churches of God.

Questions will naturally arise concerning large cities such as London. Do they reckon one "unit-locality," or more than one? London is clearly not a "city" in the scriptural sense of the term, and it cannot therefore be regarded as a unit. Even people living in London talk about going "into the city," or "into town," which reveals the fact that, in their thinking, "London" and "the city" are not synonymous. The political and postal authorities, as well as the man on the street, regard London as more than one unit. They divide it respectively into boroughs and postal districts. What they regard as an administrative unit, we may well regard as a church unit.

As to country-places which could not technically be termed "cities," they may also be regarded as "unit-localities." It is said of our Lord, when on earth, that He went out into the "cities and villages" (Luke 13.22), from which we see that country-places, as well as towns, are considered to be separate units.

This division of churches according to locality is a demonstration of the marvellous wisdom of God. Had God ordained that the Church be divided into churches with country as their boundary, then in the event of one country being vanquished and absorbed by another, the church would have to change its sphere. Were a province to mark the limit of a church, the sphere of the churches would be frequently altered because of the frequent change of provincial boundary. The same holds good in respect of a district. The most stable of all political units is a village, a town, or a city. Governments, dynasties and countries may change, but cities are seldom affected by any political change. There are cities that have passed from one country to another and still have their original name, and there are cities in existence to-day that have retained the same name for centuries. So we see the Divine wisdom in decreeing that a locality should fix the boundary of a church.

Since the limits of a locality mark the limits of a church, then no church can be narrower than a locality, and none wider. The Word of God recognizes only two churches, the universal Church and the local church; there is no third church whose sphere is narrower than the local, or else wider than the local and yet narrower than the universal Church. A local church admits of no possible division, and it admits of no possible extension. You cannot narrow its sphere by dividing it into several smaller churches, nor can you widen its sphere by linking several local churches together. Any church smaller than a local church is not a scriptural church, and any church larger than a local church, and yet smaller than the universal Church, is not a scriptural church either.

Not Narrower than a Locality

We read in 1 Cor. 1.2 of "the church of God which is at Corinth." Corinth was a "unit-locality" and the church in Corinth a "unit-church." When discord crept in, and its members were on the point of splitting the church into four different factions, Paul wrote rebuking them: "Each one of you saith, I am of Paul; and I of Apollos; and I of Cephas; and I of Christ." "Are ye not carnal?" (1 Cor. 1.12; 3.4). Had these people formed four different groups they would have been sects, not churches, for Corinth was a city, and that is the smallest unit which warrants the forming of a church. The Church of God in Corinth could not cover a lesser area than the whole city, nor could it comprise a lesser number of Christians than all the Christians who lived there. This is Paul's definition of the church in Corinth—"even them that are sanctified in Christ Jesus, called to be saints" (1.2). To form a church in an area smaller than a "unit-locality" is to form it on a smaller basis than a scriptural unit, and it follows that it cannot be a scriptural church. Any group of believers less than all the believers in a place is not qualified to be a separate church. The unit of the church must correspond with the unit of the locality. *A church must cover the same area as the locality in which it is found.* If a church is smaller than a locality, then it is not a scriptural church, it is a sect.

To say, "I am of Paul," or "I am of Cephas," is obviously sectarian; but to say "I am of Christ" is sectarian too, though less obviously so. The confession, "I am of Christ," is good as a confession, but it is not an adequate basis for forming a separate church, since it excludes some of the children of God in a given locality by including only a certain section who say, "I am of Christ." That every believer belongs to Christ is a fact, whether that fact be declared or not; and to differentiate between those who proclaim it and those who do not, is condemned by God as "carnal." It is the fact that matters, not the declaration of it. The sphere of a church in any place does not merely include those in that place who say, "I am of Christ," but all in that place who *are* of Christ. It extends over the entire area of the locality, and includes the entire number of the Christians in the locality.

To take one's stand as belonging to Christ alone is perfectly right, but to divide between Christians who take that stand and Christians who do not, is altogether wrong. To brand as sectarian those who say, "I am of Paul," or "I am of Cephas," and feel spiritually superior as we separate ourselves from them and have fellowship only with those who say, "I am of Christ," makes us guilty of the very sin we condemn in others. If we make non-sectarianism the basis of our fellowship, then we are dividing the church on a ground other than the one ordained of God, and thereby we form another sect. The scriptural ground for a church *is a locality and not non-sectarianism.* Any fellowship that is not as wide as the locality is sectarian. All Christians who live in the same place as I, are in the same church as I, and I dare exclude none. I acknowledge as my brother, and as a fellow-member of my church, every child of God who lives in my locality.

There were a great number of believers in Jerusalem. We read of a multitude who turned to the Lord, yet they are all referred to as "*the church* in Jerusalem," not "*the churches* in Jerusalem." Jerusalem was a *single place*, therefore it could only reckon as a *single unit* for the founding of a single church. You cannot divide the church unless you can divide the place. If there is only one locality there can only be one church. In

Corinth there was only *the* church in Corinth: in Hankow there is only *the* church in Hankow. We do not read of "the churches in Jerusalem," or, "the churches in Ephesus," or, "the churches in Corinth." Each of these was only reckoned one place, therefore it was only permissible to have one church in each. As long as Jerusalem, Ephesus and Corinth remain "unit-localities," just so long do they remain "unit-churches." *If a locality is indivisible, then the church formed in that locality is indivisible.*

Not Wider than a Locality

We have just seen that the boundary of a church cannot be narrower than the locality to which it belongs. On the other hand, its boundary cannot be wider than the locality. In the Word of God we never read of "the church in Macedonia," or "the church in Galatia," or "the church in Judea," or "the church in Galilee." Why? Because Macedonia and Galilee are provinces, and Judea and Galatia are districts. A province is not a scriptural unit of locality, neither is a district; both include a number of units, therefore they include a number of separate churches and do not constitute one church. A provincial church or a district church is not according to Scripture, since it does not divide on the ground of locality, but combines a number of localities. It is because all scriptural churches are local churches that there is no mention of state churches, provincial churches, or district churches in the Word of God.

"Then had the churches rest throughout all Judea and Galilee and Samaria" (Acts 9.31, A.V.). The Holy Spirit did not speak here of "the church," but of "the church*es*." Because there were a number of localities there were also a number of churches. It was not God's plan to unite the churches of different places into one church, but to have a separate church in each place. There were as many churches as there were places.

"He went through Syria and Cilicia, confirming the churches" (Acts 15.41). Again the reference is not to one single church, because Syria and Cilicia were vast districts, each comprising a number of different places. It is permissible in political circles to unite many different places into a district and call it Syria or Cilicia, but God does not unite the believers in a number of different places and call them "the church in Syria," or "the church in Cilicia." There may be unions or combines in the commercial or political world, but God sanctions no combine amongst the churches. *Each separate place must have a separate church.*

"All the churches of the Gentiles" (Rom. 16.4). The churches of God were not formed on national but on local lines; therefore there is no mention of "the church of the Gentiles," but of "the churches of the Gentiles."

"The churches of Asia salute you" (1 Cor. 16.19). "The churches of Macedonia" (2 Cor. 8). "The churches of Galatia" (Gal. 1.2). "I . . . was still unknown by face unto the churches of Judea which were in Christ" (Gal. 1.21-2). Asia, Macedonia, Galatia and Judea were all areas comprising more than one "locality-unit," therefore the Word of God refers to "the churches" in these areas. A church according to the Divine thought is always a church in one locality; any other kind of church is a product of the human mind.

God sanctions no division of the church within any one locality, and He sanctions no denominational combine of the churches in a number of localities. In Scripture there is always one church in one place, never several churches in one place, nor one church in several places. God does not recognize any fellowship of His children on a basis narrower, or wider, than that of a locality.

Nanking is a city, so is Soochow. Because each is a separate unit, therefore, each has a separate church. The two places are both in the same country, and even in the same province, but because they are two separate cities they must form two separate churches. Politically Glasgow and Nanking do not belong to the same province, or even the same country, yet the relationship between Nanking and Soochow is exactly the same as between Nanking and Glasgow. Nanking and Soochow are *as* truly separate units *as* Nanking and Glasgow are. In the division of churches the question of country or province does not arise, it is all a question of cities. Two cities of the same country, or the same province, have no closer relationship than two cities of different countries or different provinces. God's intention is that a church in any one locality should be a unit, and in their relationship one to the other the different churches must preserve their local character.

When God's people throughout the earth really see the local character of the churches, then they will appreciate their oneness in Christ as never before. The churches of God are local, *intensely local.* If any factor enters in to destroy their local character, then they cease to be scriptural churches.

The Independence of the Churches

It was never God's purpose that a number of churches in different places should be combined under any denomination or organization, but rather that each one should be independent of the other. Their responsibilities were to be independent and their government likewise. When our Lord sent messages to His children in Asia, He did not address them as "the church in Asia," but "the seven churches which are in Asia." His rebuke of Ephesus could not be applied to Smyrna, because Smyrna was independent of Ephesus; the confusion in Pergamos could not be laid to the charge of Philadelphia, because Philadelphia was independent of Pergamos; and the pride of Laodicea could not be attributed to Sardis, because Sardis was independent of Laodicea. Each church stood on its own merits and bore its own responsibility. Since God's children lived in seven different cities, they consequently belonged to seven different churches; and since each was independent of the other, each had its own special commendation, or exhortation, or rebuke.

And not only were there these seven churches on earth, there were seven candlesticks representing them in heaven. In the Old Testament there was only one candlestick with seven different branches, but in the New Testament there were seven distinct candlesticks. Had the New Testament representation been the same as the Old, then believers in the seven Asiatic churches might have united to form one church; but there are now seven separate candlesticks, each upon its own base, so that the Lord is able to walk "*in the midst* of the candlesticks" (Rev. 2.1). Therefore, though all churches stand under the authority of the one Head and express the life of the one Body (for they are all made of gold), still they are not united by any outward organization, but each stands on its own base, bearing its own responsibility, maintaining its local independence.

Among the Churches

This does not imply that the different local churches have nothing to do with one another, and that each can simply do as it pleases without considering the rest, for the ground of a church is the ground of the Body. Although they are unit-churches in outward management, still their inner life is one, and the Lord has made their members the members of one Body. There is no outward organization forming them into one big combine, but there is a strong inward bond uniting them in the Lord. They have a oneness of life which knows nothing of the bounds of locality, and which leads the separate churches to uniform action, despite the absence of all outward organization. In organization the churches are totally independent one of the other, but in life they are one, and consequently interdependent. If one church receives revelation, the others should seek to profit by it: if one is in difficulty, the others should come to its succour; but whilst the churches minister one to the other, they should always preserve their independence of government and responsibility.

On the one hand, each church is directly under the authority of the Lord and responsible to Him alone; on the other hand, each must not only listen to His direct speaking, but to His speaking through the others. "He that hath an ear, let him hear what the Spirit saith to the churches," is our Lord's injunction to all (Rev. 2 and 3). In the introduction of His letters to the seven churches we find our Lord addressing the angel of each church, but at their close we find that His message to one particular church was also a message to all the churches. From this it is clear that what one church ought to do, all the churches ought to do. The responsibility of the churches is individual, but their actions should be uniform. This balance of truth ought to be carefully preserved.

We find the same teaching in the Epistles. "For this cause have I sent unto you Timothy . . . who shall put you in remembrance of my ways which be in Christ, even as I teach everywhere in every church" (1 Cor. 4.17). What Paul has taught "everywhere in every church," the Corinthians are called upon to lay to heart. There is not one kind of instruction for Corinth, and another kind of instruction for another place. What the Apostles have been teaching to some of the churches, the believers in other churches must also note. And that applies to commandments as well as to matters of doctrine. "As the Lord hath distributed to each man . . . so let him walk. And so ordain I in all the churches" (1 Cor. 7.17). The Lord could never give a command to one church, which in any way contradicted His command to another church. His requirements of one group of His children were His requirements of all His children. "But if any man seemeth to be contentious, we have no such custom, neither the churches of God" (1 Cor. 11.16). The church in Corinth was apt to strike out on individual lines. All the other churches were going on together with the Lord, it was only Corinth that was out of step; so Paul sought to bring it into line with the others. To-day, alas! it is not just one church that has departed from God's way, but the majority of the churches. It is a tragedy that to-day an injunction to follow "all the churches" would lead, not into, but away from, the Will of God!

"Now concerning the collection for the saints, as I gave order to the churches of Galatia, so also do ye" (1 Cor. 16.1). Paul is saying in effect, "Although you are independent of other churches, yet you must not disregard their example." A willingness to help one another, and to learn from one another, should mark the relationship between the various churches. What the more mature churches have learned from the Lord, the less experienced should be ready to learn from them. "For ye, brethren, became imitators of the churches of God which are in Judea in Christ Jesus," wrote Paul to the Thessalonians (1 Thess. 2.14). The church in Thessalonica was younger than the churches in Judea, therefore it was only fitting that they should learn from them.

There is a beautiful balance in the teaching of God's Word regarding the relationship between the various churches. On the one hand, they are totally independent one of another in matters relating to responsibility, government, and organization; on the other hand, they are to learn one from another and to keep pace one with another. But in everything it is essential to have both the guidance of the Holy Spirit and the pattern in God's Holy Word.

The Highest Court

Since there is a spiritual relatedness between the various local churches, no one church must strike out on an individualistic line, and taking advantage of its independence, decide things after its own good pleasure; it must rather cultivate relationship with the other churches, seeking their sympathy and working with their spiritual good in view. On the other hand, since each is totally independent of the other, the decision of a church in any locality is absolutely final. There is no higher court of appeal; the local church is the supreme court. There is no organization to whose control it must submit, nor is there any organization over which it exercises control. It has neither superiors nor subordinates. If any one is received or refused by a local church, its judgment in the matter must be regarded as absolutely decisive. Even should the decision be wrong, all that can be done is to appeal for a reconsideration of the case. The local church is the highest church authority. If other churches object to its decisions, all they can do is to resort to persuasion and exhortation. There is no alternative course, because the relationship which exists between the churches is purely spiritual, not official.

If a brother who has been disciplined in Nanking removes to Soochow, and there proves himself to be innocent of the charge brought against him, then Soochow has full authority to receive him, despite the judgment of Nanking. Soochow is responsible for its actions to God, not to Nanking. Soochow is an independent church, and has therefore full authority to act as it deems best. But because there is a spiritual relationship with Nanking, it is well for the brother in question not to be received before its wrong judgment is pointed out to Nanking. If Nanking's relationship with the Lord is right, then it will pay attention to what Soochow has to say, but if it refuses to do so, Soochow cannot press anything against Nanking, because Nanking as a local church is directly responsible to the Lord alone, and has full authority to decide and act independently of Soochow. If the churches are spiritual there will be no difficulty in their relationship one with the other, but if they are not, and difficulties should arise, we must not seek to solve them by interfering in any way with their independence, for it is ordained by an all-wise God.

The organization of no one church is superior to another,

nor is its authority greater. Many Christians regard Jerusalem as the mother-church, possessing supreme authority, but such a conception has its source in the human mind, not in the Divine Word. Every church is locally governed and is directly responsible to God, not to any other church or organization. A local church is the highest Christian institution on earth. There is none above it to whom appeal can be made. A local church is the lowest scriptural unit, but it is also the highest scriptural organization. Scripture warrants no centralization in Rome which could give Rome authority over other local churches. This is God's safeguard against any infringement of the rights of His Son. Christ is Head of the Church, and there is no other head in heaven or on earth.

There must be a spiritual relatedness amongst the churches if the testimony of the Body is to be preserved, but there must at the same time be an absolute independence of government if the testimony of the Head is to be maintained. Each church is under the immediate control of Christ, and is directly responsible to Him alone.

Then why, when a question arose concerning circumcision, did Paul and Barnabas go to Jerusalem to see the apostles and elders there? Because those who were responsible for the erroneous teaching in Antioch had come from Jerusalem. *Jerusalem was the place where this problem originated, therefore it was to Jerusalem the apostles went to have it settled.* If a boy were caught in mischief, we would report his misdeeds to his father. In going to Jerusalem Paul and Barnabas were bringing the case to those who had control of the brethren who had created trouble, and once they brought the matter to the responsible source, a speedy settlement was effected. The elders in question were not the elders *in* Jerusalem, but the elders *of* Jerusalem; and the apostles were not the apostles *of* Jerusalem but the apostles *in* Jerusalem. The former were the representatives of the church, the latter the representatives of the Work. Paul and Barnabas referred the matter to the apostles and elders, because the apostles had been responsible for teaching in the churches, and the elders for any decisions come to regarding local matters. When the apostles and elders both repudiated responsibility concerning the teaching propagated by these troublesome brethren from Jerusalem, Paul and Barnabas on their later visits to different places were able to show to the churches there "the decrees of the apostles and elders at Jerusalem" (Acts 16.4). We must not infer from this that the elders of Jerusalem had any authority over other churches, but merely that they, as well as the apostles, repudiated the teaching of those who had gone out *from them*. Besides, in Jerusalem some of the apostles occupied the double office of elder and apostle.

How to Preserve the Local Character of the Churches

Since the churches of God are local, we must be careful to preserve their local character, their local sphere and their local boundary. Once a church loses these, it ceases to be a scriptural church. Two things call for special attention if the local nature of a church is to be safe-guarded.

In the first place, no apostle must exercise control in any official capacity over a church. That is contrary to God's order, and destroys its local nature by putting the impress of an extra-local minister upon it. No apostle has the authority to establish a private church in any place. The church belongs to the locality, not to the worker. When people are saved by the instrumentality of any man, they belong to the church in the place where they live, not to the man through whom they were saved, nor to the organization he represents. If one or more churches are founded by a certain apostle, and that apostle exercises authority over them as belonging in a special sense to him or his society, then those churches become sects, for they do not separate themselves from other Christians (saved through the instrumentality of other apostles) on the ground of difference of locality, but on the ground of the difference of instrumentality of salvation. Thus apostles become the heads of different denominations, and their sphere the sphere of their respective denominations, whilst the churches over which they exercise control become sects, each bearing the particular characteristic of its leader instead of the characteristic of a church local.

The epistle to the Corinthians throws light on this subject. There was division amongst the believers in Corinth simply because they failed to realize the local character of the church and sought to make different apostles—Paul, Apollos, and Cephas—the ground of their fellowship. Had they understood the Divinely ordained basis for the division of the Church, they could never have said, "I belong to Paul," or "I belong to Apollos," or "I belong to Cephas," for, despite their especial love for certain leaders, they would have realized that they belonged not to any one of them, but to the church in the locality in which they lived.

No worker may exercise control over a church or attach his name to it, or the name of the society he represents. The Divine disapproval will always rest on the "church of Paul," or "the church of Apollos," or "the church of Cephas." In the history of the Church it has frequently happened that when God has given special light or experience to any individual that individual has stressed the particular truth revealed or experienced, and gathered people round him who appreciated his teaching, with the result that the leader, or the truth he emphasized, has become the ground of fellowship. Thus sects have multiplied. If God's people could only see that the object of all ministry is the founding of local churches and not the grouping of Christians around any particular individual, or truth, or experience, or under any particular organization, then the forming of sects would be avoided. We who serve the Lord must be willing to let go our hold upon all those to whom we have ministered, and let all the fruits of our ministry pass into local churches governed entirely by local men. We must be scrupulously careful not to let the colouring of our personality destroy the local character of the church, and we must always serve the church, never control it. An apostle is servant of all and master of none. No church belongs to the worker, it belongs to the locality. Had it been clearly seen by the men who have been used of God throughout the history of the Church, that all the churches of God belong to their respective localities, and not to any worker or organization used in their founding, then we should not have so many different denominations to-day.

Another thing is essential for the preservation of the local character of the church—its sphere must not become wider than the sphere of a locality. The current method of linking up companies of believers in different places who hold the same doctrinal views, and forming them into a church, has no scriptural foundation. The same applies to the custom of regarding any mission as a centre, linking together all those saved or helped by them to constitute a "church" of that mission. Such so-called churches are really sects, because they are confined by the bounds of a particular creed, or a particular mission, not by and within the bounds of locality.

The reason why God does not sanction the establishing of churches which combine companies of believers in different places is because the Divinely-ordained basis for the forming of churches is thereby destroyed. Any "church" formed with a mission as its centre is bound to be other than local. Because wherever there is a centre there is also a sphere, and if the centre of the church is a mission then obviously its sphere is not the scriptural sphere of locality but the sphere of the mission. It clearly lacks the characteristic of a church, and can only be regarded as a sect. In the Purpose of God, Jesus Christ is the *centre* of all the churches, and the locality is their sphere.

Whenever a special leader, or a specific doctrine, or some experience, or creed, or organization, becomes a centre for drawing together the believers of different places, then because the centre of such a church federation is other thwn Christ, it follows that its sphere will be other than local; and whenever the Divinely-appointed sphere of locality is displaced by a sphere of human invention, there the Divine approval cannot rest. The believers within such a sphere may truly love the Lord, but they have another centre apart from Him, and it is only natural that the second centre becomes the controlling one. It is contrary to human nature to stress what we have in common with others; we always emphasize what is ours in particular. Christ is the common centre of all the churches, but any company of believers that have a leader, a doctrine, an experience, a creed, or an organization as their centre of fellowship, will find that *that* centre becomes *the* centre, and it is that centre by which they determine who belong to them and who do not. The centre always determines the sphere, and the second centre creates a sphere which divides those who attach themselves to it from those who do not.

Any thing that becomes a centre to unite believers of different places, will create a sphere which includes all believers who attach themselves to that centre and excludes all who do not. This dividing line will destroy the God-appointed boundary of locality, and consequently destroy the very nature of the churches of God. Therefore the children of God must see to it that they have no centre of union apart from Christ, because any extra-local union of believers around a centre other than the Lord enlarges the sphere of fellowship beyond the sphere of locality, and thus the specific characteristic of the churches of God is lost. *There are no other churches in Scripture but local churches!*

The Benefits of Independence

The Divine method of making locality the boundary line between the different churches has various obvious advantages:

(1) If each church is locally governed, and all authority is in

the hands of the local elders, there is no scope for an able and ambitious false prophet to display his organizing genius by forming the different companies of believers into one vast federation, and then satisfy his ambition by constituting himself its head. Rome could never sway the power it does today had the churches of God maintained their local ground. Where churches are not affiliated, and where local authority is in the hands of local elders, a pope is an impossibility. Where there are only local churches there can be no Roman Church. It is the federation of different companies of believers that has brought such evils as dabbling in politics into the Church of God. There is power in a federated "church," but it is carnal power, not spiritual. God's thought for His Church is that she should be like a mustard-seed on earth, full of vitality, yet scarcely noticed. It is federation that has brought the Church of today to the state of Thyatira. The failure of Protestantism is that it has substituted organized churches—State and Dissenting—for the Church of Rome, instead of returning to the Divinely-ordained local churches.

(2) Further, if the churches retain their local character, the spread of heresy and error will be avoided, for if a church is local, heresy and error will be local too. Rome is a splendid illustration of the reverse side of this truth. The prevalence of Romish error is because of Romish federation. The sphere of the federated churches is vast, consequently the error is widespread. It is a comparatively simple matter to "quarantine" a local church, but to isolate error in a vast federation of churches is quite another proposition.

(3) The greatest advantage of having locality as the boundary of the churches is that it precludes all possibility of sects. You may have your special doctrines and I mine, but as long as we are out to maintain the scriptural character of the churches by making locality the only dividing line between them, then it is impossible for us to establish any church for the propagation of our particular beliefs. As long as a church preserves its local

character, it is protected against denominationalism, but as soon as it loses that, it is veering in the direction of sectarianism. A believer is sectarian when he belongs to anyone, or anything, apart from the Lord and the locality. Sects and denominations can only be established when the local character of the church is destroyed.

In the wisdom of God He has decreed that all His churches be local. This is the Divine method of safeguarding them against sects. Obviously it can only protect the Church against sectarianism in expression. It is still possible for a sectarian spirit to exist in a non-sectarian church, and only the Spirit of God can deal with that. May we all learn to walk after the Spirit and not after the flesh, so that both in outward expression and inward condition the churches of God may be well-pleasing to Him.

6 The Basis of Union and Division

The Forming of Local Churches

In the previous chapter we observed that the word "church" was only mentioned twice in the Gospels. It is used frequently in the Book of Acts, but we are never explicitly told there how a church was formed. The second chapter speaks of the salvation of about three thousand men, and the fourth chapter of a further five thousand, but nothing whatever is said about these believers forming a church. Without a single word of explanation they are referred to in the following chapter as "the church"—"And great fear came upon the whole church" (5.11). Here the Scriptures call the children of God "the church," without even mentioning how the church came into being. In Acts 8.1, immediately after the death of Stephen, the word is again used, and the connection in this case is clearer than before. "There arose on that day a great persecution against the church which was in Jerusalem." From this passage it is obvious that the believers in Jerusalem are the church in Jerusalem. So we know now what the church is. It consists of all the saved ones in a given locality.

Later on, in the course of the apostles' first missionary tour, many people were saved in different places through the preaching of the Gospel. Nothing is mentioned about their being formed into churches, but in Acts 14.23, it is said of Paul and Barnabas that "they . . . appointed for them elders in every church." The groups of believers in these different places are called churches, without any explanation whatever as to how they came to be churches. They *were* groups of believers, so they simply *were* churches. Whenever a number of people in any place were saved, they spontaneously became the church in that place. Without introduction or explanation of any kind, the Word of God presents such a group of believers to us as a church. The scriptural method of founding a church is simply by preaching the Gospel; nothing further is necessary, or even permissible. If people hear the Gospel and receive the Lord as their Saviour, then they *are* a church; there is no need of any further procedure in order to *become* a church.

If in a given place anyone believes on the Lord, as a matter of course he is a constituent of the church in that place; there is no further step necessary in order to make him a constituent. No subsequent "joining" is required of him. Provided he belongs to the Lord, he already belongs to the church in that locality; and since he *already* belongs to the church, his belonging cannot be made subject to any condition. If, before recognizing a believer as a member of the church, we insist that he "join" us, or that he resign his connection elsewhere, then "our church" is decidedly not one of the churches of God. If we impose any conditions of membership upon a believer in the locality, we are immediately in an unscriptural position, because his being a member of the local church is conditioned only by his being a believer in the locality. All the saved ones who belong to the place in which we live belong to the same church as we do. I mean by the church a scriptural church, and not a man-made organization. *A local church is a church which comprises all the children of God in a given locality.*

Let us note well that the ground of our receiving anyone into the church is that the Lord has already received that one. "Him that is weak in faith receive ye . . . for God hath received him" (Rom. 14.1,3). "Wherefore receive ye one another, even as Christ also received you" (15.7). Our receiving anyone is merely our recognition that the Lord has already received him. Our receiving him does not make him a member of the church; rather it is that we receive him because he is already a member. If he is the Lord's, he is in the church: if he is not the Lord's, he is not in the church. If we demand anything beyond his reception by the Lord before admitting him to fellowship, then we are not a church at all, but only a sect.

Within and Without the Circle

In any place where the Gospel has been proclaimed and people have believed on the Lord, they are the church in that place, and they are our brethren. In the days of the apostles the question of belonging or not belonging to a church was simple in the extreme; but things are not so simple in our days, for the question has been complicated by many so-called churches that exclude those who should be in the church, and include those who should be outside. What sort of a person can be rightly considered a constituent of the church? What is the minimum requirement we can insist upon for admission to church fellowship? Unless the qualifications for church membership are clearly defined, there will always be the danger of excluding from the church those who truly belong to it and including those who do not.

Before we proceed to discover who really belong to a local church and who do not, let us first enquire who belong to the universal Church and who do not, since the condition of membership in *a* church is essentially the same as in *the* Church. When we know what kind of persons belong to *the* Church, then we know also what kind of persons belong to *a* church.

How can we know who is a Christian and who not? "If any man hath not the Spirit of Christ he is none of his" (Rom. 8.9). According to the Word of God every person in whose heart Christ dwells by His Spirit is a true Christian. Christians may differ from one another in a thousand respects, but in this fundamental matter there is no difference between them; one and all have the Spirit of Christ dwelling within them. If we wish to know who belongs to the Lord, then we only need to discover whether he has the Spirit of Christ or not. Whoever has the Spirit of Christ is inside the Church circle, and whoever has not the Spirit of Christ is outside the circle. A participant of the Spirit of God is an essential part of the Church of God: a non-participant of the Spirit of God has no part in the Church. In the Church universal it is thus: in the church local it is also thus. "Try your own selves, whether ye be in the faith; prove your own selves. Or know ye not as to your own selves, that Jesus Christ is in you? unless indeed ye be reprobate" (2 Cor. 13.5). There is a subjective line of demarcation between the Church and the world; all within that line are saved, and all without that line are lost. This line of demarcation is the indwelling Spirit of Christ.

The Unity of the Spirit

The Church of God includes a vast number of believers, living at different times, and scattered in different places throughout the earth. How has it come about that all have been united into *one* universal Church? With such disparity in age, social position, education, background, outlook and temperament, how could all these people become one Church? What is the secret of the unity of the saints? By what means has Christianity caused these people, with their thousand differences, to become truly one? It is not that, having a grand convention and agreeing to be one, Christians become united. Christian unity is no human product, its origin is purely Divine. This mighty mysterious unity is planted in the hearts of all believers the moment they receive the Lord. It is "the unity of the Spirit" (Eph. 4.3).

The Spirit who dwells in the heart of every believer is one

Spirit, therefore He makes all those in whom He dwells to be one, even as He Himself is one. Christians may differ from one another in innumerable ways, but all Christians of all ages, with their countless differences, have this one fundamental likeness—the Spirit of God dwells in every one of them. *This is the secret of the oneness of believers, and this is the secret of their separation from the world.* The reason for Christian unity and for Christian separation is one.

It is this inherent unity that makes all believers one, and it is this inherent unity that accounts for the impossibility of division between believers, except for geographical reasons. Those who have not got this are outsiders; those who have got it are our brethren. If you have the Spirit of Christ and I have the Spirit of Christ, then we both belong to the same Church. There is no need to *be* united, we *are* united by the one Spirit who dwells in us both. Paul besought all believers to endeavour "to keep the unity of the Spirit" (Eph. 4.3); he did not exhort us to "have" the unity, but merely to keep it. We have it already, for obviously we cannot "keep" what we do not have. God has never told us to become one with other believers; we already *are* one, therefore we do not need to create unity, we only need to maintain it.

We cannot *make* this unity, since by the Spirit we *are* one in Christ, and we cannot *break* it, because it is an eternal fact in Christ; but we can destroy *the effects* of it, so that its expression in the Church is lost. Alas! that we have not only failed to preserve this precious unity, but have actually so destroyed the fruits of it, that there is little outward trace of unity amongst the children of God.

How are we going to determine who are our brothers and our fellow-members in the Church of God? Not by enquiring if they hold the same doctrinal views as we, or have had the same spiritual experiences; nor by seeing if their customs, mode of living, interests and preferences tally with ours. We merely enquire, Are they indwelt by the Spirit of God or not? We cannot insist on unity of opinions, or unity of experience, or any other unity amongst believers except the unity of the Spirit. That unity there can, and always must be, amongst the children of God. All who have this unity are in the Church.

In your travels has it not sometimes happened that on boat or train you have met a stranger, and after only a few moments conversation you have found a pure love for him welling up in your heart? That spontaneous outgoing of love was because of the one Spirit dwelling in both hearts. Such inner spiritual oneness transcends all social, racial and national differences.

How can we know whether or not a person has this unity of the Spirit? In the verse immediately following Paul's exhortation to "keep the unity of the Spirit," he explains what those have in common who possess this unity. We cannot expect believers to be alike in everything, but there are seven things which all true believers share, and by the existence or absence of these we can know whether or not a person has the unity of the Spirit. Many other things are of great importance, but these seven are vital. They are indispensable to spiritual fellowship, and they are at once the minimum and the maximum requirements that can be made of any person who professes to be a fellow-believer.

Seven Factors in Spiritual Unity

"There is one body, and one spirit, even as also ye were called in one hope of your calling; one Lord, one faith, one baptism, one God and Father of all, who is over all, and through all, and in all" (Eph. 4.4-6). A person is constituted a member of the Church on the ground that he possesses the unity of the Spirit, and that will result in his being one with all believers on the above seven points. They are the seven elements in the unity of the Spirit, which is the common heritage of all the children of God. In drawing a line of demarcation between those who belong to the Church and those who do not, we must require nothing beyond these seven lest we exclude any who belong to the family of God; and we dare not require anything less, lest we include any who do not belong to the Divine family. All in whom these seven are found belong to the Church; all who lack any of them do not belong to the Church.

(1) *One Body.* The question of unity begins with the question of membership of the Body of Christ. The sphere of our fellowship is the sphere of the Body. Those who are outside that sphere have no spiritual relationship with us, but those who are inside that sphere are all in fellowship with us. We cannot make any choice of fellowship in the Body, accepting some members and rejecting others. We are all part of the one Body, and nothing can possibly separate us from it, or from one another. Anyone who has received Christ belongs to the Body, and he and we are one. If we do not wish to extend fellowship to anyone, we must first make sure that he does not belong to the Body; if he does, we have no reason to reject him (unless for such disciplinary reasons as are clearly laid down in the Word of God).

(2) *One Spirit.* If anyone seeks fellowship with us, however he may differ from us in experience or outlook, provided he has the same Spirit as we have, he is entitled to be received as a brother. If he has received the Spirit of Christ, and we have received the Spirit of Christ, then we are one in the Lord, and nothing must divide us.

(3) *One Hope.* This hope, which is common to all the children of God, is not a general hope, but the hope of our calling, i.e. the hope of our calling as Christians. What is our hope as Christians? We hope to be with the Lord for ever in glory. There is not a single soul who is truly the Lord's in whose heart there is not this hope, for to have Christ in us is to have "the hope of glory" in us (Col. 1.27). If anyone claims to be the Lord's, but has no hope of heaven or glory, his is a mere empty profession. All who share this one hope are one, and since we

have the hope of being together in glory for all eternity, how can we be divided in time? If we are going to share the same future, shall we not gladly share the same present?

(4) *One Lord.* There is only one Lord, the Lord Jesus, and all who recognize that God has made Jesus of Nazareth to be both Lord and Christ are one in Him. If anyone confesses Jesus to be Lord, then his Lord is our Lord, and since we serve the same Lord, nothing whatever can separate us.

(5) *One Faith.* The faith here spoken of is *the* faith—not our beliefs in regard to the interpretation of Scripture, but the faith through which we have been saved, which is the common possession of all believers, i.e. the faith that Jesus is the Son of God (who died for the salvation of sinners and lives again to give life to the dead). Anyone who lacks this vital faith does not belong to the Lord, but all who possess it are the Lord's. The children of God may follow many different lines of scriptural interpretation, but in regard to this fundamental faith they are one. Those who lack this faith have no part in the family of God, but all who possess it we recognize as our brothers in the Lord.

(6) *One Baptism.* Is it by immersion or by sprinkling? Is it single or triune? There are various modes of baptism accepted by the children of God, so if we make the form of baptism the dividing line between those who belong to the church and those who do not, we shall exclude many true believers from our fellowship. There are children of God who even believe that a material baptism is not necessary, but since they *are* the children of God, we dare not on that account exclude them from our fellowship. What then is the significance of the "one baptism" mentioned in this passage? Paul throws light on the subject in his first letter to the Corinthians. "Is Christ divided? Was Paul crucified for you? or were ye baptized into the name of Paul?" (1.13). The emphasis is not on the mode of baptism, but on the *name* into which we are baptized. The first question is not whether you are sprinkled or immersed, dipped once or

thrice, baptized literally or spiritually, the important point is, into *whose name* have you been baptized? If you are baptized into the Name of the Lord, that is your qualification for church membership. If anyone is baptized into the Name of the Lord, I welcome him as my brother, whatever be the mode of his baptism. *By this we do not imply that it is of no consequence whether we are sprinkled or immersed, or whether our baptism is spiritual or literal. The Word of God teaches that baptism is literal, and is by immersion,* but the point here is that the mode of baptism is not the ground of our fellowship, but the Name into which we are baptized. All who are baptized into the Name of the Lord are one in Him.

(7) *One God.* Do we believe in the same personal, supernatural God as our Father? If so, then we belong to one family, and there is no adequate reason for our being divided.

The above seven points are the seven factors in that Divine unity which is the possession of all the members of the Divine family, and they constitute the only test of Christian profession. They are the possession of every true Christian, no matter to what place or period he belongs. Like a seven-fold cord the unity of the Spirit binds all the believers throughout the world; and however diverse their character or circumstances, provided they have these seven expressions of an inner oneness, then nothing can possibly separate them.

If we impose any conditions of fellowship beyond these seven—which are but the outcome of the one spiritual life, then we are guilty of sectarianism, for we are making a division between those who are manifestly children of God. If we apply any test but these seven, e.g. baptism by immersion, or certain interpretations of prophecy, or a special line of holiness teaching, or a "pentecostal" experience, or the resigning from any denominational church—then we are imposing conditions other than those stipulated in the Word of God. All who have these seven points in common with us are our brothers, whatever their spiritual experience, or doctrinal views, or "church" relationships. Our unity is not based on our appreciation of the truth of our oneness, nor on our coming out from all that would contradict our oneness, but upon the *actual fact* of our oneness, which is made real in our experience by the indwelling Spirit of Christ.

Local Churches

Now what is true of the universal Church is also true of a local church. The universal Church comprises all those who have the unity of the Spirit; the local church comprises all those who, *in a given locality*, have the unity of the Spirit. The Church of God and the churches of God do not differ in nature, but only in extent. The former consists of all throughout the universe who are indwelt by the Spirit of God: the latter consists of all in one locality who are indwelt by the Spirit.

Anyone wishing to belong to a church in a given locality must answer two requirements—he must be a child of God, and he must live in that particular locality. Membership in *the Church of God* is conditioned only by being a child of God, but membership in a *church of God* is conditioned, firstly, by being a child of God and, secondly, by living in a given locality.

In nature the Church is indivisible as God Himself is indivisible, therefore the division of the Church into churches is not a division in nature, life, or essence, but only in government, organization and management. Because the earthly church is composed of a vast number of individuals, a measure of organization is indispensable. It is a physical impossibility for all the people of God, scattered throughout the world, to live and meet in one place; and it is for that reason alone that the Church of God has been divided into churches.

We must realize clearly that the nature of all the local churches is the same throughout the whole earth. It is not that the constituents of one local church are of one kind, and the constituents of another local church are of another kind. In nature there is no difference whatever; the only difference is in the localities that determine their respective boundaries. The Church is indivisible, therefore in nature the churches are indivisible too; it is only in outward sphere that there is any possibility of dividing them. Physical limitations make geographical divisions inevitable, but the spiritual oneness of believers overcomes all barriers of space.

Locality is the Divinely-appointed ground for the division of the Church, because it is the only inevitable division. Every barrier between all believers in the world is avoidable, except this one. As long as believers remain in the flesh they cannot exist apart from their dwelling-places, therefore the churches which consist of such believers cannot but be restricted by their dwellings. Geographical distinctions are natural, not arbitrary, and it is simply because the physical limitations of the children of God make geographical divisions inevitable, that God has ordained that His Church be divided into churches on the ground of locality. Such division is scriptural, and all other divisions are carnal. *Any division of the children of God other than geographical implies not merely a division of sphere, but a division of nature. Local division is the only division which does not touch the life of the Church.*

Most believers of to-day are so utterly blind to the scriptural basis of a church that if one asks another, "To what church do you belong?" the first thought of the one questioned is of the specific line of teaching he approves of, or the group of people with whom he has special fellowship, or how his group of Christians is different from others, or perhaps the name that particular group bears, or the form of organization they have adopted—in short, *anything but the place* in which he lives. Few would answer that question with: "I belong to the church in Ephesus," or, "I belong to the church in Shanghai," or "I belong to the church in Los Angeles." It is our being in Christ that separates us from the world, and it is our being in a given locality that separates us from other believers. It is only because we reside in a different place from them that we belong to a different church. The only reason why I do not belong to the same church as other believers is because I do not live in the same place as they do. If I wish to be in the same church, then I must change my residence to the same place. If, on the other hand, I wish to be in a different church from others in my locality, then the only solution to my problem is to move to a different locality. Difference of locality is the only justification for division amongst believers.

Seven Forbidden Grounds of Division

On the positive side we have just seen the ground on which God has ordained that His Church be divided. Now, on the negative side, we shall see on what ground the Church ought not to be divided.

(1) *Spiritual Leaders.* "Now this I mean, that each one of you saith, I am of Paul; and I of Apollos; and I of Cephas; and I of Christ" (1 Cor. 1.12). Here Paul points out the carnality of the Corinthian believers in attempting to divide the church of God in Corinth, which, by the Divine ordering, was indivisible, being already the smallest scriptural unit upon which any church could be established. They sought to divide the church on the ground of a few leaders who had been specially used of God in their midst. Cephas was a zealous minister of the Gospel, Paul was a man who had suffered much for his Lord's sake, and Apollos was one whom God certainly used in His service; but though all three had been indisputably owned of God in Corinth, God could never permit the church there to make them a ground of division. He ordained that His Church be divided on the basis of localities, not of persons. It was all right to have a church in Corinth and a church in Ephesus, and quite all right to have several churches in Galatia and a number in Macedonia, for difference of locality justified divi-

sion into these various churches; and it was also all right for the believers to esteem those leaders whom God had used amongst them; but it would have been quite wrong to divide the churches according to the respective leaders by whom they had been helped.

Paul, Cephas and Apollos were true-hearted servants of God who allowed no party-spirit to separate them; it was their devotees who were responsible for the separation. Hero-worship is a tendency of human nature, which delights to show preference for those who appeal to its tastes. Because so many of God's children know little or nothing of the power of the Cross to deal with the flesh, this tendency of man-worship has expressed itself frequently in the Church of God, and much havoc has been wrought in consequence. It is in keeping with God's Will that we should learn from spiritual men and profit by their leadership, but it is altogether contrary to His Will that we should divide the Church according to the men we admire. *The only scriptural basis for the forming of a church is difference of locality, not difference of leaders.*

(2) *Instruments of Salvation.* Spiritual leaders are no adequate reason for dividing the Church, neither are the instruments used of God in our salvation. Some of the Corinthian believers proclaimed themselves to be "of Cephas," others "of Paul," others "of Apollos." They traced the beginning of their spiritual history to these men, and so thought they belonged to them. It is both natural and common for persons saved through the instrumentality of a worker, or a society, to reckon themselves as belonging to such a worker or society: and it is likewise both natural and common for an individual, or a mission, through whose means people have been saved, to reckon the saved ones as belonging to them. It is natural, but not spiritual: it is common, but, nevertheless, contrary to God's Will. Alas! that so many of God's servants have not yet realized that they are servants of the local church, not masters of a private "church." *Churches are divided on the ground of geog-*

raphy, not on the ground of the instruments of our salvation.

(3) *Non-sectarianism.* Some Christians think they know better than to say, "I am of Cephas," or, "I am of Paul," or, "I am of Apollos"; they say, "I am of Christ." Such Christians despise the others as sectarian, and on that ground start another community. Their attitude is—*You* are sectarian: *I* am non-sectarian; *You* are hero-worshippers: *We* worship the Lord alone.

But God's Word does not only condemn those who say, "I am of Cephas," "I am of Paul," or, "I am of Apollos": it just as definitely and just as clearly denounces those who say, "I am of Christ." It is not wrong to reckon oneself as belonging only to Christ: it is right and even essential; nor is it wrong to repudiate all schism amongst the children of God: it is highly commendable. God does not condemn this class of Christians for either of these two things, he condemns them for the very sin they condemn in others—their sectarianism. As a protest against division amongst the children of God, many believers seek to divide those who do not divide as from those who do, and never dream that they themselves are divisive! Their ground of division may be more plausible than that of others who divide on the ground of doctrinal differences, or personal preference for certain leaders, but the fact remains that they *are* dividing the children of God. Even whilst they repudiate schism elsewhere, they are schismatic themselves.

You say, "I am of Christ"; do you mean to say others are not? It is perfectly legitimate for you to say, "I am of Christ" if your remark merely implies to whom you belong; but if it implies, "I am not sectarian; I stand quite differently from you sectarians," then it is making a difference between them and other Christians. The very thought of *distinguishing* between the children of God has its springs in the carnal nature of man, and is sectarian. If we look on other believers as sectarian and consider ourselves to be non-sectarian, we are immediately differentiating between God's people and thereby manifesting a divisive spirit even in the very act of condemning division. No matter by what means we distinguish between the members of God's family—even if it be on the pretext of Christ Himself—we are guilty of schism in the Body.

What then is right? All exclusiveness is wrong: all inclusiveness (of true children of God) is right. Denominations are not scriptural, and we ought to have no part in them, but if we adopt an attitude of criticism, and think, *They* are denominational, *I* am undenominational; *they* belong to sects, *I* belong to Christ alone—such differentiating is definitely sectarian.

Yes, praise God I *am* of Christ, but my fellowship is not merely with those who *say*, "I am of Christ," but with all who *are* of Christ. What is of vital importance is not the confession, but the fact. Although these other believers *say* they are of Paul, of Cephas and of Apollos, yet *in fact* they are of Christ. I do not so much mind what they *say*, but I very much mind what they *are*. I do not enquire whether they are denominational or undenominational, sectarian or unsectarian, I only enquire, Are they of Christ? If they are of Christ, then they are my brethren.

Our personal standing should be undenominational, but the basis of our fellowship is not undenominationalism. *We ourselves should be non-sectarian, but we dare not insist on non-sectarianism as a condition of fellowship. Our only ground of fellowship is Christ.* Our fellowship must be with *all the believers* in a locality, not merely with *all the unsectarian believers* in that locality. *They* may make denominational differences, but *we* must not make undenominational requirements. We dare not differentiate between ourselves and them because they differentiate between themselves and others. They are the children of God, and because they make distinctions between themselves and other children of God, they do not on that account cease to be the children of God. Their denominationalism or sectarianism will mean that severe limitations are imposed upon the Lord as to His purpose and mind for them, and this will mean that they will never go beyond a certain measure of spiritual growth and fullness. Blessing there may be, but fullness of Divine purpose never.

All believers living in the same locality belong to the same church. This is an unchanging principle. We dare not alter "all the believers in a locality" to "all the undenominational believers in a locality." If we make undenominationalism or unsectarianism the boundary of our church, instead of locality, then we lose our local standing as a church and become a sect. It is not a denominational church, nor an interdenominational church, nor even an undenominational church we are after, but a *local* church. The difference between a local church and an undenominational church is as vast as the difference between heaven and earth. A local church is undenominational, but an undenominational church is denominational. The "church in Corinth" is scriptural, but "the church of all those who say, 'I am of Christ' in Corinth" is unscriptural. Our work is positive and constructive, not negative and destructive. We are out to establish churches, not to destroy denominations. Human nature is prone to go to extremes; it is so easy for us either to be undenominational ourselves and demand undenominationalism of others, or else to tolerate denominationalism in others and gradually become denominational ourselves. We ourselves *must* be undenominational, but we must not demand undenominationalism of other Christians as the basis of our fellowship.

Therefore, if we come to a place where Christ is not named, we must preach the Gospel, win men to the Lord, and found a local church. If we come to a place where there are already Christians, but on various grounds these believers separate themselves into denominational "churches," our task is just the same as in the other place—we must preach the Gospel, lead men to the Lord, and form them into a church on the scriptural ground of locality. All the while we must maintain an attitude of inclusiveness, not exclusiveness, towards those believers who are in different sects, for they, as we, are children of God, and they live in the same locality, therefore they belong to the same church as we do. For ourselves, we cannot join any sect or remain in one, for our church connection can only be on local ground, but in regard to others we must not make leaving a sect the condition of fellowship with those believers who are in a sect. That will make undenominationalism our church ground, instead of locality. Let us be clear on this point, that an undenominational church is not a local church; there is a vast difference between the two. A local church is undenominational, and it is positive and inclusive, but an undenominational church is not a local church, and it is negative and exclusive.

Let us be clear as to our position. We are not out to establish undenominational churches, but local churches. We are seeking to do a positive work. If believers can be led to see what a local church is—the expression of the Body of Christ in a locality—they will certainly not remain in any sect. On the other hand it is possible for them to see all the evils of sectarianism, and leave them, without knowing what a local church is. We must help those, to whom God has been pleased to use us, to understand clearly the truth regarding local churches, and not to lay emphasis on the question of denominations. They must realize that whenever they use the term "we" in relation to the children of God, they must include all the children of God, not merely those who are meeting with them. If when we say "our brethren" we do not include all the children of God, but only those who continually meet with us, then we are schismatic.

I do not condone sectarianism, and I do not believe we should belong to any sect, but it is not our business to get people to leave them. If we make it our chief concern to lead people to a real knowledge of the Lord and the power of His Cross, then they will gladly abandon themselves to Him, and will learn to walk in the Spirit, repudiating the things of the flesh; and we shall find there will be no need to stress the question of denominations, for the Spirit Himself will enlighten them. If a believer has not learned the way of the Cross and the walk in the Spirit, what is gained by his coming out of a sect?

(4) *Doctrinal Differences.* In the Greek the word rendered "heresies" in Gal. 5.20 does not necessarily convey the thought of error, but rather of division on the ground of doctrine. The Interlinear New Testament translates it as "sects," whilst Darby in his new translation renders it "schools of opinion." The whole thought here is not of the difference between truth and error, but of division based upon doctrine. My teaching may be right or it may be wrong, but if I make it a cause of division, then I am guilty of the "heresy" spoken of here.

God forbids any division on doctrinal grounds. Some believe that rapture is pre-tribulation, others that it is post-tribulation; some believe that all the saints will enter the Kingdom, others believe that only a section will enter; some believe that baptism is by immersion, others that it is by sprinkling; some believe that supernatural manifestations are a necessary accompaniment to the baptism in the Holy Ghost, whilst others do not; but none of these doctrinal views constitute a scriptural basis for separating the children of God. Though some may be right and others wrong, God does not sanction any division on account of difference as to such beliefs.* If a group of believers splits off from a local church in their zeal for certain teaching according to the Word of God, the new "church" they establish may have more scriptural teaching, but it could never be a scriptural church. To bring error into a church is carnal, but to divide a church on account of error may also be carnal. It is carnality that so often destroys the oneness of the church in any place.

---

*We are not, of course, dealing here with the foundations of the Faith, the essential doctrines of the Divine Persons, faith in Christ, Atonement, etc., but subsequent matters.

If we wish to maintain a scriptural position, then we must see to it that the churches we found in various places *only represent localities, not doctrines.* If our "church" is not separated from other children of God on the ground of locality alone, but stands for the propagation of some particular doctrine, then we are decidedly a sect, however true to the Word of God our teaching may be. The purpose of God is that a church should represent the children of God in a locality, not represent some specific truth there. *A church of God in any place comprises all the children of God in that place, not merely those who hold the same doctrinal views.*

Should we arrive at a place where a church has already been established on clear local ground, and discover that its members hold views which we consider unscriptural, or that they consider the views we hold as unscriptural, if we then refuse to recognise them as the church of God in that locality and withdraw from fellowship, we are divisive. The question is not whether they agree with our presentation of truth, but whether they are standing on clear church ground.

If our hearts are set to preach the local character of the churches of God, we cannot fail to come up against problems in our work. Unless the Cross operates mightily, what endless possibilities of friction there will be if we include in one church all the believers in the locality with all their varying views. How the flesh would like just to include those holding the same views, and to exclude all whose views differ from ours. To have constant and close association with people whose interpretation of Scripture does not tally with ours, is hard for the flesh, but good for the spirit. God does not use division to solve the problem, He uses the Cross. He would have us submit to the Cross, so that through the very difficulties of the situation, the meekness and patience and love of Christ may be deeply wrought into our lives. Under the circumstances, if we do not know the Cross, we shall probably argue, lose our temper, and finally go our own way. We may have right views, but God is giving us an opportunity to display a right attitude; we may believe aright, but God is testing us to see if we love aright. It is easy to have a mind well stored with scriptural teaching, and a heart devoid of true love. Those who differ from us will be a means in God's hand to test whether we have spiritual experience, or only scriptural knowledge, to test whether the truths we proclaim are a matter of life to us, or mere theory.

Rom. 14 shows us how to deal with those whose views differ from ours. What would we do if in our church there were vegetarians and Sabbatarians? Why, we should consider it almost intolerable if in the same church some of the believers kept the Lord's Day and others the Sabbath, and some ate meat freely, whilst others were strict vegetarians. That was exactly the situation Paul was facing. Let us note his conclusions. "But him that is weak in faith receive ye, yet not to doubtful disputations" (verse 1). "Who art thou that judgest the servant of another? To his own lord he standeth or falleth. Yea, he shall be made to stand; for the Lord hath power to make him stand" (verse 4). "Let us not therefore judge one another any more: but judge ye this rather, that no man put a stumbling-block in his brother's way, or an occasion of falling" (verse 13). Oh, for Christian tolerance! Oh, for largeness of heart! Alas! that many of God's children are so zealous for their pet doctrines that they immediately label as heretics, and treat accordingly, all whose interpretation of Scripture differs from theirs. God would have us walk in love toward all who hold views contrary to those that are dear to us (verse 15).

This does not mean that all the members of a church can hold whatever views they please, but it does mean that the solution to the problem of doctrinal differences does not lie in forming separate parties according to the different views held, but in walking in love toward those whose outlook differs from ours. By patient teaching we may yet be able to help all to "the unity of the faith" (Eph. 4.13). As we wait patiently on the Lord, He may grant grace to the others to change their views, or He may grant us grace to see that we are not such good teachers as we thought we were. Nothing so tests the spirituality of a teacher as opposition to his teaching.

The teachers must learn humility, but so must all the other believers. When they recognize their position in the Body, they will know that it is not given to everyone to determine matters of doctrine. They must learn to submit to those who have been equipped of God for the specific ministry of teaching His people. Spiritual gifts and spiritual experience are necessary for spiritual teaching, consequently not everyone can teach.

"Fulfil ye my joy, that ye be of the same mind, having the same love, being of one accord, of one mind; doing nothing through faction or vain-glory, but in lowliness of mind each counting other better than himself; not looking each of you to his own things, but each of you also to the things of others" (Phil. 2.2-4). When the churches have laid to heart what Paul wrote to the church in Philippi, then it will be perfectly possible to have only one church in one locality with no friction whatever amongst its many members.

(5) *Racial Differences.* "For in one spirit were we all baptized into one body, whether Jews or Greeks, whether bond or free; and were all made to drink of one Spirit" (1 Cor. 12.13). Jews have always had the strongest racial prejudice of all peoples. They regarded other nations as unclean, and were forbidden even to eat with them; but Paul made it very clear, in writing to the Corinthians, that in the Church both Jew and Gentile are one. All distinctions "in Adam" have been done away with "in Christ." *A racial "church" has no recognition in the Word of God. Church membership is determined by domicile, not by race.*

To-day in the large cosmopolitan cities of the world there are churches for the whites and churches for the blacks, churches for the Europeans and churches for the Asiatics. These have originated through failure to understand that the boundary of a church is a city. God does not permit any division of His children on the ground of difference of colour, custom, or mode of living. No matter to what race they belong, if they belong to the same locality they belong to the same church. God has placed believers of different races in one locality, so that, by transcending all external differences, they might in one church show forth the one life and the one Spirit of His Son. All that comes to us by nature is overcome by grace; all that was ours "in Adam" has been ruled out "in Christ." The whole matter hinges here—are all carnal differences done away with in Christ, or is there still a place for the flesh in the Church? Are our resources in Christ sufficient to overcome all natural barriers? Let us remember that the church in any locality includes all the believers living there and excludes all who live elsewhere.

(6) *National Differences.* Jews and Gentiles represent national as well as racial distinctions, but in the Church of God there is neither Jew nor Greek. There is no racial distinction there, and there is no national distinction either. All believers living in one place, no matter what their nationality, belong to the one church. In the natural realm there is a difference between Chinese, French, British and Americans, but in the spiritual realm there is none. If a Chinese believer lives in Nanking, he belongs to the church in Nanking. If a French believer lives in Nanking, he also belongs to the church in Nanking. The same holds good for Britishers, Americans, and all other nationals, provided they are born again. The Word of God recognizes "the church in Rome," "the church in Ephesus" and "the church in Thessalonica," but it does not recognize the Jewish church, or the Chinese church, or the Anglican church. The reason why the names of cities appear in Scripture in connection with the churches of God is because the difference of dwelling-place is the only difference recognized by God amongst His children. Their life is essentially one, and is therefore indivisible, but the place in which that life is lived cannot but vary as long as they remain in the flesh.

Since the churches are all local, if a believer—whatever his nationality—removes from one place to another, he immediately becomes a member of the church in the latter place, and has no church connection in the place of his former residence. You cannot live in one place and be the member of a church in another. There is no extraterritoriality in connection with the churches of God. As soon as you exceed the city limit, you exceed the church limit. If a Chinese brother moves from Nanking to Hankow, he becomes a member of the church in Hankow; in like manner, a British brother coming from London to Hankow immediately becomes a member of the church in Hankow. A change of residence necessarily involves a change of church, whereas naturalization has no effect on church membership.

Our fellow-workers who have gone from China to the South Sea Islands must be careful not to form an "Overseas Chinese church" there. It is possible to have an "Overseas Chinese Chamber of Commerce," or, an "Overseas Chinese College," or, an "Overseas Chinese Club." Anything you like can be "Overseas Chinese," but not a church. A church is always local! If you go to any city in a foreign land then it follows as a matter of course that you belong to the church in that city. There is nothing Chinese about the churches of God.

How glorious it would be if the saved in every city could overlook all natural differences and only consider their spiritual oneness. "We are the believers in Christ in such-and-such a place" is the finest confession a company of Christians can make. Whether Christ is in you or not, determines whether or not you belong to the Church; where you live determines the particular church to which you belong. The question put by God to the world is, Do they belong to Christ? The question put by God to believers is, Where do they live? Not nationality but locality is the question raised. *The churches of God are built on city ground, not on national ground.*

The usual conception of an indigenous church, whilst quite

right in some respects, is fundamentally wrong at the most vital point. Since the Divine method of dividing the Church is according to locality, not nationality, then all differentiation between Christian and heathen countries is contrary to God's thought. The Church of God knows neither Jew nor Greek, therefore it knows neither native nor foreigner, neither heathen country nor Christian country. The Scriptures differentiate between cities, not between countries, heathen and Christian; so if we would be in full accord with the mind of God, we must make no difference whatever between the Chinese and foreign church, between Chinese and foreign workers, or between Chinese and foreign funds.

The thought of the indigenous church is that the natives of a country should be self-governing, self-supporting, and self-propagating, whilst the thought of God is that the believers *in a city—whether native or foreign—should be self-governing, self-supporting, and self-propagating.* Take, for instance, Peking. The theory of the indigenous church distinguishes between Chinese and foreigners in Peking, whereas the Word of God distinguishes between the believers in Peking—whether Chinese or foreign—and the believers in other cities. That is why in Scripture we read of the *churches* of the Gentiles, but never of the *church* of the Gentiles. The attempt to form all Chinese believers into one church shows a lack of understanding in regard to the Divine basis of forming churches.

On the one hand there is no church of the Gentiles in Scripture; on the other hand we read of "the church of the Thessalon*ians*." It is suggestive that this is the only expression of its kind used in the New Testament. The Word does not speak of the church of the Greeks (a race, or nation), but of the church of the Thessalonians (a city). There is no such thing in the thought of God as the church of the Chinese, but there is such a thing as the church of the Pekinese; Scripture knows nothing of the church of the French, but it does recognize the church of the Parisians. A clear apprehension of the Divine basis of church formation—according to the difference of cities and not of countries—will save us from the misconception of the indigenous church. There should be no distinction whatever between Chinese and foreign Christians, between Chinese and foreign workers, or between Chinese and foreign money in any given locality.

(7) *Social Distinctions.* In Paul's day, from a social point of view, there was a great gulf fixed between a free-man and a slave, yet they worshipped side by side in the same church. In our day, if a rickshaw coolie and the President of our Republic both belong to Christ and live in the same place, then they belong to the same church. There may be a mission for rickshaw coolies, but there can never be a church for rickshaw coolies. *Social distinctions are no adequate basis for forming a separate church. In the Church of God there is "neither bond nor free."*

In Scripture we have at least seven definite things referred to which are forbidden by God as reasons for dividing His Church. As a matter of fact these seven points are only typical of all other reasons the human mind may devise for dividing the Church of God. The two millenniums of Church history are a sad record of human inventions to destroy the Church's unity.

Overcomers

The sphere of the church is local, and the local church should on no account be divided. The question naturally arises, if the spiritual life of a local (*not denominational*) church is very low, can a few of the more spiritual members not gather together and form another assembly? The answer from the Word of God is emphatically, No! God's Word only warrants the establishment of churches on local ground. Even lack of spirituality is no adequate reason for dividing the church. Should local methods, government and organization be far from ideal, that still constitutes no reason for division. Even wrong teaching (2 John 9 excepted) is no ground for those who know better to form a separate church. We must lay it to heart that the difference of locality is *the only ground* for dividing the Church of God; no other ground is scriptural.

We who live in the same locality cannot but belong to the same church. This is something from which there is no escape. If I am dissatisfied with the local church, the only thing I can do is to change my locality, then automatically I change my church. *We can leave a denomination, but we can never leave a church.* To leave a sect is justifiable, but to leave a church—whether on account of unspirituality, wrong doctrine, or bad organization—is utterly unjustifiable. If you leave the local church and form a separate assembly, you may have greater spirituality, purer teaching and better government; but *you have no church*, you have only a sect.

In the second and third chapters of Revelation we see seven different churches in seven different localities. Only two were not rebuked but actually praised by the Lord; the other five were all definitely censured. Spiritually those five were in a sad state. They were weak, defeated churches; but they were churches for all that, not sects. Spiritually they were wrong, but positionally they were right; therefore God only commanded those in them to be *overcomers*. The Lord said not a word about leaving the church. A local church is a church which you cannot leave, you must remain in it. If you are more spiritual than the other members, then you should use your spiritual influence and your authority in prayer to revive that church. If the church does not respond, you have only two alternatives; you must either remain there, keeping yourself undefiled, or else you must change your abode. *But this does not apply to a sect.* It is futile to seek by a wrong application of these two chapters to keep Spirit-taught believers within a sect, for the seven churches referred to are *local churches*, not sectarian "churches." However weak they may have been, they were still on the scriptural ground of the Body in the locality. The Word of God has never authorized anyone to leave a church. All groups of believers who base their fellowship on other ground than that of locality are sects, even though they may term themselves churches. It is all right to leave a sect, but it is never right to leave a local church. If you leave a local church, you do so without the authority of the Lord, and you become guilty of the sin of schism in the Body.

What a tragedy it is when a few spiritual members leave a local church, and form another assembly, simply because the other members are weak and immature. Those stronger members should remain in that church as overcomers, seeking to help their weaker brothers and sisters, and claiming the situation there for the Lord. Oh! how prone we are to despise the believers we consider inferior to us, and how we delight to associate with those whose fellowship we find specially congenial. Pride of heart, and a selfish enjoyment in spiritual things, cause us to overlook the fact that a church in any given place should consist of all the children of God in that place; so we narrow down Christian fellowship and make selection amongst the children of God. This is sectarianism, and it is a grief of heart to the Lord.

7 The Work and the Churches

The Apostles and the Churches

In regard to the universal Church, God first brought it into being, and thereafter set apostles to minister to it (1 Cor. 12.28); but in regard to the local churches the order was quite otherwise. The appointment of apostles preceded the founding of local churches. Our Lord *first* commissioned the Twelve Apostles, and *thereafter* the church in Jerusalem came into existence; the Holy Ghost *first* called two apostles—Paul and Barnabas—to the Work, and *thereafter* a number of churches sprang into being in different places. So it is clear that the apostolic ministry *precedes* the existence of the local churches, and consequently it is obvious that the Work of apostles does not belong to the local churches.

As we have already observed, the Holy Spirit said, "Separate me Barnabas and Saul for *the Work* whereunto I have called them." The service that followed the apostles' separation, which we generally refer to as their missionary campaigns, the Holy Spirit referred to as "the Work." "The Work" was the object of the Spirit's call, and all that was accomplished by Paul and his associates in after days, all that for which they were responsible, was included in this one term, "the Work." (The term, "the Work," is used in a specific sense in this book, and relates to all that is included in the missionary efforts of the apostles.)

Since churches are the result of the Work, they cannot possibly include it. If we are to understand the mind of God concerning His Work, then we must differentiate clearly between the Work and the churches. These two are quite distinct in Scripture, and we must avoid confusing them, otherwise we shall make serious mistakes, and the outworking of God's purposes will be hindered. The word "churches" appears frequently in Scripture, so it has been easy for us to arrive at a clear understanding of its meaning and content, but the word "Work" is not often used in the specific sense in which it is employed here, with the result that we have paid little heed to it. But the Spirit has used the expression in an inclusive way to cover all that related to the purpose of the apostolic call. Let us then abide by the term which the Spirit has chosen to employ.

It has been iterated and reiterated, but let us point it out once again, that the churches are local, and nothing outside the locality must interfere with them, nor must they interfere with anything beyond that sphere. Church affairs are to be managed by local men who, on account of their comparative spiritual maturity, have been appointed to be elders. As the Work of the apostles is to preach the Gospel and found churches, not to take responsibility in the churches already established, their office is not a church office. If they go to work in a place where no church exists, then they should seek to found one by the proclamation of the Gospel, but if one exists already, then their Work must be distinct from it. In the Will of God "the church" and "the Work" follow two distinct lines.

The Work belongs to the apostles, whilst the churches belong to the local believers. The apostles are responsible for the Work in any place, and the church is responsible for all the children of God there. In the matter of church-fellowship the apostles regard themselves as the *brethren* of all the believers in the city, but in the matter of Work, they regard themselves as its personnel, and maintain a distinction between themselves and the church. As members of the Body, they meet for mutual edification with all their fellow-members in the locality; but as ministering members of the Body, their specific ministry constitutes them a group of workers apart from the church. It is wrong for the apostles to interfere with the affairs of the church, but it is equally wrong for the church to interfere with the affairs of the Work. The apostles manage the Work; the elders manage the church. It follows then that we must be clear about our call. Has God called us to be elders, or to be apostles? If elders, then our responsibility is confined to local affairs: if apostles, then our responsibility is extra-local: if elders, then our sphere is the church: if apostles, then our sphere lies beyond the church, in the Work.

The reason why God called apostles, and entrusted the Work to them, is because He wished to preserve the local character of the church. If any church exercises control over Work in another locality, it at once becomes extra-local, and thereby loses its specific characteristic as a church. The responsibility of the Work in different places is committed to apostles, whose sphere extends beyond the locality; and the responsibility of the church is committed to elders, whose sphere is confined to the locality. An Ephesian elder is an elder in Ephesus, but he ceases to be one when he comes to Philippi, and *vice versa*. Eldership is limited to locality. When Paul was at Miletus he wished to see the representative members of the church in Ephesus, so he sent for the Ephesian elders, but no request was sent to the Ephesian apostle, for the simple reason that there was none. The apostles belong to different places, not to one place alone, whereas the sphere of the elders is strictly local, for which reason they take no official responsibility beyond the place in which they live. Whenever the church tries to control the Work, it loses its local character; whenever an apostle tries to control a church he loses his extra-local character. Much confusion has arisen because the Divine line of demarcation between the churches and the Work has been lost sight of.

Responsibility—Spiritual and Official

Just as the apostles have *spiritual* but no *official* responsibility regarding the church, so the elders, and the whole church, have *spiritual* but no *official* responsibility regarding the Work. It is commendable if a local church seeks to help in the Work; but it is under no official obligation to do so. If the members of the church are spiritual, they cannot but regard the Work of God as their work, in which case they will count it a joy to help in any way. They will recognize that, whilst the official responsibility for the Work rests on the apostles, the spiritual responsibility is shared by all the children of God, and consequently by them. *There is a vast difference between spiritual and official responsibility.* In the matter of official responsibility there are certain prescribed duties, and one is in the wrong if one fails to perform them; but in the matter of spiritual responsibility there are no legal obligations, therefore any neglect of responsibility does not register as an official shortcoming, but it does register a low spiritual state. From an official point of view, the responsibility of the Work rests upon the apostles. If they lack the needed help they cannot demand it, but if the church is spiritual, its members will see the meaning of the Body and will gladly assist in the Work and give towards it. If the church fails in spiritual responsibility the apostles may have difficulties which they should not have, and the church will suffer spiritually. On the other hand, the responsibility of the church rests officially upon the elders, therefore the apostles should not take upon themselves to do anything directly there. They may and should assist the church by their counsel and exhortations, and if the local believers are spiritual they will willingly receive such help; but should they be unspiritual, and in consequence reject the proffered help of the apostles, their failure is spiritual and not official, and the apostles have no option but to leave them to their own resources. The church does not come within the sphere of the

Work and is consequently outside the sphere of their authority. Again let us repeat, the churches are local, intensely local: the Work is extra-local, and always extra-local.

Representatives of the Ministry of the Body—Individuals, not Churches

There is a definite Divine reason for the fact that the Work is entrusted to individual apostles and not to local churches; but before we enter into that, let us examine the fundamental difference between the activities of a church as a body and the activities of a brother as an individual. It may be all right for a brother (or for several brothers) to go into business, but it would be all wrong for a church to do so. It might be quite in order for one or more brothers to open a restaurant or an hotel, but that would not be in order for a church. What may be perfectly permissible in the case of brothers, as individuals, is not necessarily permissible in the case of a church, as a company. The business of the churches consists in the *mutual* care of their various members, such as the conduct of meetings for breaking of bread, for the exercise of spiritual gifts, for the study of the Word, for prayer, for fellowship and for Gospel preaching. The Work is beyond the sphere of any church as *a* corporate body; it is the responsibility of individuals, though *not of individuals as such*.

There is no scriptural precedent for such work being undertaken by a church, as, for instance, hospitals, or schools, or even something on a more definitely spiritual plane such as foreign missions. It is perfectly in order for one or more members of a church to run a hospital, or a school, or to be responsible for mission-work, but not for any church as a whole. A church exists for the purpose of mutual help in one place, not for the purpose of bearing the responsibility of work in different places. According to God's Word, all the Work is the personal concern of individual brothers called and commissioned by God, *as members of the Body*, and not the concern of any church as a body. The responsibility of the Work is always borne by one or more individuals.

The important point to note is that the Body of Christ in its ministry-aspect is not represented by local churches, but by *individuals* who are the gifts given by God to His Church. A local church has not been chosen by God to represent the Body *where ministry is in view*. When God wants any representatives of the Body to express its ministry, He chooses certain individuals, who are the functioning members, to represent that Body. The whole thing is clear in the last part of 1 Cor. 12.

It was never the thought of God that His Work should be done on any other basis than that of the Body, because it is actually the natural functioning of the Body of Christ. It is the activity, under the direction of the Head, of those members who possess special faculties. We have already pointed out that the local church represents the Body in its life-aspect, and the functioning members represent the Body in its ministry-aspect. The local church is called to manifest not so much the service, as the life of the Body, whilst the apostles, prophets and teachers, as such, are called to manifest not so much the life, as the service of the Body. That is the reason why God did not entrust the Work to any local church as a body, but to individuals. But it is the latter, not the former, who represent the Body, if the latter are functioning members of the Body.

Therefore we find that the two apostles who went out from Antioch were not sent forth to the Work by the *whole church* but by *several ministers in the church*, because in the matter of service and Work it is the latter, not the former, who represent the Body. So the Work is the responsibility of individuals who are called and commissioned by God, and not the responsibility of the whole church.

But, let it be clearly understood, by individuals we do not mean individuals as individuals, but as functioning members *representing the Body*. God has never sanctioned that anyone take up an individualistic line in His work. Free-lancing, without due co-ordination with other members of the Body, has never been a Divine mode of work. This cannot be too strongly emphasized; nor can it be too strongly emphasized that in His Work God uses individuals to represent the Body, not local churches. Therefore, whilst the Work is the responsibility of individuals, it is not the business of just any individual who cares to take it up, but only of such as are called and sent forth by God, and are equipped with spiritual gifts for the task. Only those who represent the ministry of the Body can bear the official responsibility of the Work. The Work *is* undertaken by individuals, but only by such as represent the Body in its ministry-aspect, for they, not the entire church, are responsible for it. It is not individuals, as individuals, that undertake the Work, but individuals as representing the Body of Christ.

If our work is that of an apostle, it must be clearly distinguished from the local church. It may seem quite unimportant to some that any distinction be made between the Work and the church. They may think it of no consequence that the responsibility of the Work be in the hands of individual members, not the whole church, and that the apostles be responsible only for the Work, not for the church; but the principle is a scriptural principle, and its outworking is of great importance and has tremendous effects, as we shall presently see.

"His Own Hired Dwelling"

The church in Rome is a good illustration of the foregoing. Before Paul visited Rome he had written to the church there expressing an intense desire to see them (Rom. 1.10,11). From his letter it is obvious that a church had been established in that city prior to his arrival. When he actually reached Rome the church there did not hand over local responsibility to him, nor did they say (as a church to-day probably would), "Now that an apostle has come into our midst, he must take over the responsibility and be our pastor." Instead, we find this amazing record in the Word, "And he remained two whole years in his own hired lodging, and received all who came to him, preaching the kingdom of God, and teaching the things concerning the Lord Jesus Christ, with all freedom unhinderedly" (Acts 28.30,31, Darby). Why did Paul live in "his own hired lodging" and preach and teach from there and not from the already existing church. Some may suggest that because he was a prisoner he would not have been allowed to take meetings in the church; but there would have been little difference between taking meetings in the church and in the house. If he was granted permission to rent a house and preach and teach there, why should he have been refused permission to preach and teach in connection with the church? Moreover we need to remember that the Word does *not* state the *reason* why Paul hired a house and preached and taught there, it *only* mentions the *fact*. The fact is that he did rent a house and did preach and teach there, and that fact is enough for us. It is enough for our guidance. Further, God has made it clear that he was under no necessity to do so. No pressure whatever was brought to bear upon him, for he acted "*with all freedom unhinderedly*."

Then what is the meaning of the hired house? We must remember the Divine economy of words in Scripture, and we must realize that neither the occurrence, nor the record of it, was accidental. There is no room for chance happenings or unimportant records in God's Word. All that is written there is written for our learning, and even a seemingly casual remark may enfold a precious lesson. Moreover, this book is the Book of the Acts of the Apostles, who moved under the direct guidance of the Holy Spirit, so the record in question is also one of the acts of the Apostles, and is therefore not a chance happening, but an act under the guidance of the Holy Spirit. Here in two short sentences we have an important principle, viz. that the apostolic Work and the local church are quite distinct. A church had already been established in Rome, therefore the members must have had at least one meeting-place, *but they did not request Paul to take control of the local church, nor did they make their place of meeting to be Paul's centre of Work.* Paul had his own Work in his own hired house quite apart from the church, and apart from their meeting-place, and he did not take over the responsibility of the local church affairs.

Every apostle must learn to live in "his own hired dwelling" and work with that as his centre, leaving the responsibility of the local church to the local brethren.* The Work of God belongs to the workers, but the church of God belongs to the locality. Any Work in a given place is only temporary, but any church in a given place is always permanent. The Work is movable: the church is stationary. When God indicates that an apostle should move, his Work moves with him, but the church remains. When Paul thought of leaving Corinth, the Lord showed him he had further ministry for him in the city, so Paul remained for eighteen months—not permanently. When Paul left Corinth, his Work left; but the church in Corinth continued, although the fruits of his Work were left in the church. A church should not be influenced by the movements of the workers. Whether they are present or absent, the church should move steadily forward. Every one of God's workmen must have a clean-cut line of demarcation between his Work and the church in the place of his labours.

The Work of the apostles and the work of the local church run parallel; they do not converge. When the apostles are working in any place their Work goes on side by side with the

---

*Note: This does not mean that an apostle will not go into a local church and minister. See later, pp. 226-28.

work of the church; the two never coincide, nor can the one ever be a substitute for the other. On leaving a place an apostle should hand over all the fruit of his Work to the local church. It is not God's Will that the Work of an apostle should take the place of the work of the church, or be in any wise identified with it.

The principle of Paul living in his own hired house shows clearly that the work of the church is unaffected by the presence or absence of an apostle. After Paul's arrival in Rome the work of the church went on as before, independently of him. Since it was neither dependent on him for its origin or its continuance, it would be unaffected by his departure. Work is work, and church is church, and these two lines never converge, but keep running parallel one to the other.

Suppose we go to Kweiyang to work, what should be our procedure? On arrival in Kweiyang we either live in an inn, or rent a room, and we begin to preach the Gospel. When men are saved what shall we do? We must encourage them to read the Word, to pray, to give, to witness and to assemble for fellowship and ministry. One of the tragic mistakes of the past hundred years of foreign missions in China (God be merciful to me if I say anything amiss!) is that after a worker led men to Christ, he prepared a place and invited them to come there for meetings, instead of encouraging them to assemble by themselves. Efforts have been made to encourage the young believers to read the Word *themselves*, pray by *themselves*, witness *themselves*, but never to *meet by themselves*. Workers never think of reading, praying and witnessing for them, but they do not see any harm in arranging meetings for them. We need to show the new converts that such duties as reading, praying, witnessing, giving, *and assembling together*, are the minimum requirement of Christians. We should teach them to have *their own* meetings in *their own* meeting-place. Let us say to them, "Just as we cannot read the Word, or pray, or witness for you, so we cannot take the responsibility of preparing a meeting-place for you and leading your meetings." You must look out for suitable premises and conduct your own meetings. *Your* meetings are *your* responsibility, and a regular assembling of yourselves is one of your chief duties and privileges.

Many workers regard their meetings and the meetings of the church as one and the same thing, but they are not. (*See* Chapter 10). Therefore, as soon as a few believers are saved, we must instruct them to take full responsibility for their private reading, prayer and witness, and also for the public meetings of the church.

As for ourselves, whilst we go on working and keep our Work distinct from the work of the church, we must go and have fellowship with the believers in *their* various local gatherings. We must go and break bread with them, join with them in the exercise of spiritual gifts, and take part in their prayer meetings. When there is no church in the place to which God has sent us, we are only workers there, but as soon as there is a local church, we are brothers as well as workers. In our capacity as workers we can take no responsibility in the local church, but in our capacity as local brothers we go and meet with all the members of the church as their *fellow*-members.

As soon as there is a local church in the place of our labours, we automatically become members. Here is the chief point to observe in the relationship between the church and the Work—the worker must leave the believers to initiate and conduct their own meetings in their own meeting-place, and then he must go to *them* and take part in *their* meetings, not ask them to come to *him* and take part in *his* meetings. Otherwise we shall become settlers in one place and shall change our office from apostle to pastor; and when eventually we leave, we shall require to find a successor to carry on the church-work. If we keep "church" and "Work" parallel and do not let the two lines converge, we shall find that no adjustment will be needed in the church when we depart, for it will not have lost a "pastor," but only a brother. Unless we differentiate clearly in our own minds between church and Work, we shall mix the Work with the church and the church with the Work; there will be confusion in both directions, and the growth both of the church and the Work will be arrested.

"Self-government, self-support and self-propagation" has been the slogan of many workers for a number of years now. The need to deal with these matters has arisen because of the confusion between the church and the Work. In a mission, when people are saved, then the missionaries prepare a hall for them, arrange for prayer meetings and Bible classes, and some of them go as far as to manage the business and spiritual affairs of the church as well. The mission does the work of the local church! Therefore it is not surprising that in process of time problems arise in connection with self-government, self-support and self-propagation. In the very nature of things, such problems would never have come up for consideration if the principles shown us in God's Word had been adhered to from the very beginning.

Anyone who cares enough to be a Christian ought to be taught from the outset what the implications are. Believers must pray *themselves*, study the Word *themselves* and assemble *themselves*, not merely go to a meeting-place prepared *by others* and sit down and listen to *others* preach. Going to a mission-compound or mission-hall to hear the Word is not scriptural assembling, because it is in the hands of a missionary, or of his mission, not in the hands of the local church. It is a mixture of Work and church. If from the outset Christians learned to gather together according to the Scriptures, many problems would be avoided.

The Results of the Work

When a servant of God reaches a new place his first business must be to found a local church, unless there is one already in existence, in which case his one concern must be to help the church. The one aim of the Work in any place is the building up of the church in that place. All the fruit of a worker's labours must go to the increase of the church. The Work in any place exists for the church alone, not for itself. The apostle's goal is to build up the church, not to build up his work or any group of people that may have sent him out.

Wherein lies the failure of missions to-day? They keep the results of their work in their own hands. In other words, they have reckoned *their* converts as members of *their* mission, or of *their* mission-church, instead of building them into, or handing them over, to the local churches. The result is, the mission extends all the while and becomes quite an imposing organization, but local churches are scarcely to be found. And because there are no local churches, the mission has to send workers to different places as "pastors" of the various companies of Christians. So church is not church, and Work is not Work, but both are a medley of the two. There seems to be no scriptural warrant for forming companies of workers into missions; nevertheless, to regard a mission as an apostolic company is not definitely unscriptural, but for missions to enlarge their own organization instead of establishing local churches is distinctly so.

Two Lines of Work

An apostle should go and work in a certain place if the local church invites him, or if he himself has received a revelation from the Lord to work there. In the latter case, if there is a church in the place, he can write notifying them of his coming, just as Paul notified the churches in Corinth and in Rome. These are the two lines which regulate the Work of an apostle—he must either have a direct revelation of God's Will, or an indirect revelation through the invitation of a church.

Wherever an apostle goes he must learn to bear his own

responsibility, having his own hired dwelling. It may be all right to work in a place, living as the guest of the local church, but it would not be right to impose upon them by taking advantage of their hospitality over an extended period. If a worker expects to stay for any length of time in one place, then he must have his own centre of Work, and he must not only bear his own personal responsibilities, but also all responsibilities in connection with the Work. A local church must bear entire responsibility for *its* own work, and so must the worker for *his*. The church as such must not be involved in any financial outlay in connection with the Work; the worker alone is liable for all expenses incurred, and he must learn from the very outset of his ministry to look to the Lord for the supply of his needs. Of course, if the church is spiritual its members will recognize their spiritual responsibility, and will be willing to assist in material ways so that the Work of God may go forward, but the worker should take nothing for granted and should bear the entire financial burden, so that it may be manifest that the church and the Work are absolutely distinct.

When an apostle comes to a place where a local church already exists, he must never forget that no church authority rests with him. Should he desire to work in a place where the local church does not wish to have him, then all he can do is to pass on to some other part. The church has full authority either to receive or reject a worker. Even should the worker in question have been used of God to found the very church that rejects him, he can claim no authority in the church on that account.

Should he know unmistakably that God has led him to work in that place, yet the local church refuse to welcome him, if they persist in their attitude, then he must obey the command of God and go and work there despite them. But he must not gather believers around him, nor must he on any account form a separate church. There can only be one church in one place.

If he forms a separate company of believers where a local church already exists, he will be forming a sect and not a church. Churches are founded on the ground of locality, not on the ground of receiving a certain apostle. Even if the local church refused to receive him, and his Work had to be done without its sympathy and co-operation, or even despite its opposition, still all the results of his labours must be for their benefit. Despite its attitude to the apostle personally, all the fruit of his labours must be contributed to that church. The sole aim of all Work for God is the increase and up-building of the local churches. If they welcome the worker, the result of his labours go to them; if they reject him, it goes to them just the same.

We require deeper spiritual experience, and clearer spiritual light, if we are to be workers acceptable to God and to His Church. If we wish to overcome difficulties we must learn to overcome by spirituality, not by official authority. If we are spiritual we shall submit to the authority of the local churches. It is lack of submission on the part of God's servants that is responsible for the forming of numerous sects. Many so-called churches have been established because workers have been rejected by the churches and have gathered groups of people around them, who have supported them and the doctrines they taught. Such procedure is sectarian.

If we are truly led of God, surely we can trust God to open doors for us. If a church receives us, let us praise Him; if not, let us look confidently to Him to unlock closed doors. Many servants of God trust Him to open up spiritual truths to them, but they cannot trust Him to open doors for the reception of those truths. They have faith to believe God will give them light, but they have no faith to believe that He will also supply the keys to open human hearts to the light He has given. So they resort to carnal methods, and the consequence is much division amongst the children of God. If God Himself does not remove the obstacles in our circumstances, then we must quietly remain where we are, and not have recourse to natural means, which will assuredly work havoc in the Church of God.

The Specific Ministries of the Word

All God's servants are engaged in the ministry of building up the Body of Christ, but it does not follow that because all are in the ministry of the Word that all ministries are the same. Everyone has a different line of ministry. Time and again God has raised up some new witness, or group of witnesses, giving them fresh light from His Word, so that they could bear a special testimony for Him in the particular time and circumstances in which they live. All such ministry is new and specific and is of great value to the Church; but we must bear it well in mind that if God commits a specific ministry to any man relating to certain truths, he must not make his particular ministry, or his particular line of truth, the basis of a new "church." No servant of God should cherish the ambition that his truth be accepted as *the* truth. If doors are closed to it, let him wait patiently upon God who gave it till He opens doors for its reception. No separate "church" must be formed to bear a separate testimony. The Work of God does not sanction the establishment of a church for the propagation of any particular line of teaching. It knows only one kind of church—the local church; not a sectarian church, but a New Testament church.

Let us lay it to heart, that *our Work is for our ministry and our ministry is for the churches*. No church should be under a specific ministry, but all ministries should be under the church. What havoc has been wrought in the Church because so many of her ministers have sought to bring the churches under their ministry, rather than by their ministry serve the churches. As soon as the churches are brought under any ministry, they cease to be local and become sectarian.

When a specific ministry has been raised up of God to meet

a specific need in His Church, what should be the attitude of the minister? Whenever a new truth is proclaimed it will have new followers. The worker to whom God has given fresh light upon His truth should encourage all who receive that truth to swell the ranks of the local church, not to range themselves around him; otherwise the churches will be made to serve the ministry, not the ministry the churches, and the "churches" established will be ministerial "churches," not local ones. The sphere of a church is not the sphere of any ministry, but the sphere of the locality. Wherever ministry is made the occasion for the forming of a church, there you have the beginning of a new denomination. From the study of Church history we can see that almost all new ministries have led to new followings, and new followings have resulted in new organizations. Thus ministerial "churches" have been established and denominations multiplied.

If the Lord delays His coming and His servants remain true to Him, He will certainly raise up new ministries in the Word. He will open up special truths to meet the specific needs of His children. Some of the hearers will question the truths, others reject them and others condemn, whilst there will be those who gladly respond. What should the attitude of God's servants be? They must be fully persuaded in their own minds that *there can only be one church in one place*, and that all truth is for the enrichment of that church. If it receives the truths God's ministers proclaim, let them praise Him; if not, let them praise Him still. No thought must be entertained of forming a separate "church" comprising those believers who support the special doctrines emphasized. If in the local church a number of people receive their teaching, *then they must still remain there*. No divisive work must be done in the local church. Those who receive the truth may use their spiritual teaching and spiritual power to help their fellow-members, but they must not use any divisive methods to support the truth they have embraced. If we always bear in mind that the churches of

God are only formed on the basis of locality, much division amongst the children of God will be avoided.

Should God entrust us with a special ministry and lead us to a place where no church exists, our first duty is to establish one in the locality, and then contribute our ministry to it. We can establish local churches and contribute our ministry to such churches, but we dare not establish ministerial churches.

Let me illustrate the relation between various ministries and various local churches. One man is a florist, another a grocer. The most obvious way for them to extend their business is to establish branches in various districts. The florist opens branch-shops to sell flowers, and the grocer opens branch-shops to sell groceries. This is just like the various ministers trying to establish "churches" according to their ministry. God's plan for His Church is on quite a different line. It is not that the grocer and the florist each seek to open as many branches as they possibly can in order to sell their respective commodities, but that the grocer or the florist, arriving in any place, opens a department-store, and having duly established it, he contributes his goods to it, and other tradesmen coming along contribute their wares to the same store. A department-store does not just deal in one line of goods, it has a varied stock. The thought of God is not that we should open branch florist-shops or branch grocery-stores, or stores that specialize in other lines, but department-stores. His plan is that His servants should just establish a local church, and then contribute their different ministries to that church. The church is not controlled by *one* ministry but served by *all* the ministries. If any company of God's people are open to receive one truth only, then they are a sect.

As apostles our first concern on arrival in a place which has no church is to found one there. As soon as it has been formed we should seek to serve it with whatever ministry the Lord has entrusted to us, and then leave it. We dare to exercise our ministry faithfully, but, having done so, we dare to leave the church open to other ministry. This should be the attitude of all God's workmen. We should never cherish the hope that only "our" teaching will be accepted by any church. There must be no thought of dominating a church by our personality or by our ministry; the field must be left clear for all God's servants. There is no need to build a wall of protection around "our" particular "flock" to secure them *against* the teachings of others. If we do so, we are working along popish lines. We can safely trust God to protect our ministry, and we must remember that for "the perfecting of the saints" the varied ministries of all God's faithful servants are necessary. Local responsibility is with the elders; *they* must watch the interests of the flock in the matter of ministries.

Institutions of Faith

It must not be inferred from the foregoing that God has no other workmen but apostles and the various ministers of the Word. Those who work in the ministry of the Word are only a section of God's servants. The Work is not the only work. God has many servants who are bearing the burden of various works of faith, such as schools, orphanages and hospitals. Looked at superficially, their work does not seem as spiritual as the Work of the apostles or ministers we have just referred to, but in reality it is. Although such faith workers do not go forth as apostles, or teach the Word like the special ministers, yet they are used just as definitely as the others to strengthen the Church of God.

George Muller's orphanage is just such a faith work. It has resulted in the salvation of many souls. The question arises, where should the fruits of such a work go? Not into an orphanage-"church," but into the local church. A work such as that is not a unit sufficiently large to form a church. It is the city which is a church unit, not an institution. No matter how prosperous a work of faith may be, and no matter how many souls may be saved through it, no church can be formed on such a basis; for should there be various workers in one city engaged in various kinds of work, then there would be as many churches as there were such institutions. The boundary of a church is a city, not any institution in a city.

Several years ago I was in Tsinan. Some brothers in Cheloo University asked me if I thought it time for them to commence a meeting for the breaking of bread. I asked, "Do you represent Cheloo University or Tsinan city?" They answered, "Cheloo." "Then I do not think it is right," I said. Of course they wanted to know why, so I explained: "The Word of God sanctions the forming of a church in Tsinan, but not in Cheloo. The sphere of Cheloo is too narrow to justify the existence of a separate church. The standard scriptural unit for the forming of a church is a city, not a university."

The fruits resulting from various institutions of faith must not be retained by such institutions. All must be handed over to the local church. Workers must not argue that because they have been the means of salvation to certain souls, therefore they have a special claim upon them and special responsibility for them, and consequently withhold them from uniting with their fellow-believers in the locality. Even though there may be regular prayers, and preaching, and a variety of meetings in connection with a Christian institution, those can never serve as a substitute for church fellowship, and no such institution, however spiritual, can be regarded as a church, since it is not founded on the Divinely appointed basis of locality. All Christians engaged in efforts of this kind must differentiate clearly between church and Work, and they must realize that any sphere narrower than a locality does not justify the forming of a separate church. They dare not pride themselves on their successful work and think it will serve well as a church, but they must humbly join in fellowship with all the other members of the Body of Christ in the place where they live.

All the various God-given ministries have one aim, the

establishing of local churches. In the thought of God only one company of people exists, and all His designs of grace centre in that one company—His Church. The Work is not a goal in itself, it is only a means to an end. If we regard our work as an end, then our purpose is at variance with God's, for His end is the Church. What we regard as an end in itself is only the means to His end.

There are three things which we must bear clearly in mind. (1) The Work and other works are the special concern of the workers, not of the churches, and the sphere of any work is not wide enough to justify its being regarded as a church. (2) All workers must be humble enough to take the place of brothers in the local church. In the sphere of their Work they hold the position of God's servants, but in the sphere of the church they are only brethren. In the church there are only children of God, therefore none of its members are "workers," all are brethren. (3) The goal of all Work is the establishment of local churches. If we make our Work the basis of a separate unit of God's people, then we are building up a sect, not a church.

8 Among the Workers

The churches in Scripture are intensely local. We never find any federation of churches there; they are all independent units. The position is quite otherwise as regards the workers. Amongst them we find a certain amount of association; we see here a little group, and there another, linked together for the Work. Paul and those with him—as for instance Luke, Silas, Timothy, Titus and Apollos—formed one group; Peter, James and John, and those with them, formed another. One group came out from Antioch, another from Jerusalem. Paul refers to "those who were with me" (Acts 20.34), which indicates that whilst there was no organization of the workers into different missions, still they had their own special associates in the Work. Even in the beginning, when our Lord chose the Twelve, He sent them out two by two. *All* were fellow-workers, but *each* had his special fellow-worker. Such grouping of workers was ordained and ordered by the Lord.

These apostolic companies were not formed along partisan or doctrinal lines; they were formed under the Sovereignty of the Spirit, Who so ordered the circumstances of the different workers as to link them together in the Work. It was not that they were really divided from other workers, but merely that in the Spirit's ordering of their ways, they had not been led into special association with them. It was the Holy Spirit, not men, who said, "Separate me Barnabas *and* Saul." Everything hinged on the Sovereignty of the Spirit. The apostolic companies were subject to the Will and ordering of the Lord. As we have seen, the Twelve were divided into pairs, but it was not left to their personal discretion to choose their associates, it was the Lord Who coupled them together and sent them forth. Each had a special fellow-worker, but that fellow-worker was of the Lord's appointing, not of their choosing. It was not because of natural affinity that they associated specially with some, nor was it because of difference in doctrine or practice that they did not associate specially with others. The deciding factor was *always* the ordering of the Lord.

We recognize that the Lord is the Head of the Church, and that the apostles were the first order "set" by the Lord in the Church (1 Cor. 12.18). Although they were formed into associations, having their special fellow-workers appointed by the Lord, still they had no special name, system, or organization. They did not make a company smaller than the Body to be the basis of their Work; all was on the ground of the Body; therefore, although on account of difference of locality and the providential ordering of their ways, they formed different groups, still they had no organization outside the Body; their Work was always an expression of the ministry of the Body. They were constituted into separate companies, but each company stood on the ground of the Body, expressing the ministry of the Body.

The Lord is the Head of the Body and *not the Head of any organization*; therefore whether we work for a society, a mission, or an institution, and not for the Body alone, we lose the Headship of the Lord. We must see clearly that the Work is the Work of the Body of Christ and that, whilst the Lord did divide His workers into different companies (not different organizations), their Work was always on the ground of the Body. And we must recognize that every individual worker and every company represents the ministry of the Body of Christ, each office held being held in the Body, and for the furtherance of the Work of God. Then, and only then, can we have one ministry—the up-building of the Body of Christ. If we recognized clearly the oneness of the Body, what blessed results we should see! Wherever the principle of the oneness of the Body operates, all possibility of rivalry is ruled out. It does not matter if I decrease and you increase; there will neither be jealousy on my part, nor pride on yours. Once we see that all the Work and all its fruits are for the increase of the Body of Christ, then no man will be counted yours and no man mine; it will not matter then whether you are used or I. All carnal strife amongst the workers of God will be at an end once the Body is clearly seen as the principle of the Work. But life and work in the Body necessitates drastic dealings with the flesh, and that in turn necessitates a deep knowledge of the Cross of Christ.

The early apostles were never free-lances, they worked together. In the story of Pentecost we read of "Peter standing up with the Eleven" (Acts 2.14). At the Beautiful Gate we see Peter and John working together, and again they were the two who visited Samaria. When Peter went to the house of Cornelius, six other brethren accompanied him. When the apostles went out it was always in companies, or at least in couples, never alone. Their Work was not individual, but corporate. As to those with Paul at Antioch and elsewhere, it is unfortunate that so much emphasis has been placed upon Paul as an individual, with the result that his fellow-workers are almost lost sight of. We see that at Troas Luke joined their company and was of one mind with Paul in considering that the Macedonian cry should be responded to, and later on when they returned from Macedonia they brought with them as fellow-workers Sopater, Aristarchus, Secundus, Gaius, Timothy, Tychicus, and Trophimus. Later on we find Apollos, Priscilla, and Aquila joining them: still later we find Paul sending Timothy to Corinth and encouraging Apollos and Titus to go there; and some time afterwards we see Epaphroditus joining them as a fellow-worker. And it is good to read at the head of Paul's epistles words like these: "Paul and his brother Sosthenes," "Paul and his brother Timothy," "Paul, Silas and Timothy."

So, on the one hand we see no trace of organized missions in Scripture, nor do we on the other hand see any workers going out on individual lines, each being a law to himself. They are formed into companies, but such companies are on a spiritual basis, not on the basis of organization. Scripture gives no warrant on the one hand for an organized mission, nor does it on the other hand sanction free-lance work; the one is as far from the thought of God as the other. Therefore, whilst we must guard against the snare of man-made organizations, we must also guard against the danger of being too individualistic. We must not be organized into a mission and thus become schismatic; at the same time we must have associates in the Work with whom we co-operate on a spiritual basis, and thus maintain the testimony of the Body.

We need to emphasize this fact, that the apostles worked in association with others, but their companies were not organized. Their relationship one to another was only spiritual. They loved and served the same Lord, they had one call and one commission, and they were of one mind. The Lord united them, therefore they became fellow-workers. Some were together from the outset, others joined at a later date. They were one company, yet they had no organization, and there was no distribution of offices or positions. Those who joined them did not come in response to some "Wanted" advertisement, nor did they come because they were equipped by a special course of training. On their journeys the Lord so ordered circumstances that they met; He drew them one to another, and being of one mind and one spirit, linked together by the Lord, they spontaneously became fellow-workers. In order to join such a company there was no need of first passing an examination, or of fulfilling some special conditions, or of going through certain forms or ceremonies. The Lord was the One Who determined everything. He ordered; man only concurred. In such groups none held special positions or offices; there was no director, or chairman, or superintendent. Whatever ministry the Lord had given them, that constituted their position. *They received no appointments from the association.* The relationship which existed between its members was purely spiritual, not official. They were constituted fellow-workers, not by a human organization, but by a spiritual bond.

Spiritual Authority

Before considering the question of spiritual authority, let us read a few passages of Scripture bearing on the relationship between the workers, as they throw considerable light on our subject. "Timothy . . . would Paul have to go forth with him" (Acts 16.1-4). "When he (Paul) had seen the vision, straightway *we* sought to go forth into Macedonia, *concluding* that God had called us for to preach the Gospel unto them" (Acts 16.9,10). "But they that conducted Paul brought him as far as Athens; and receiving a *commandment* unto Silas and Timothy that they should come to him with all speed, they departed" (Acts 17.15). "Paul . . . *determined* to return through Macedonia. And there accompanied Him . . ." (Acts 20.3-5). "We, going before to the ship, set sail for Assos, there intending to take in Paul: for so had he *appointed* . . ." (Acts 20.13-14). "If Timothy come, see that he be with you without fear. . . . Set him forward on his journey in peace that he may come to me. . . . But as touching Apollos the brother, I *besought* him much to come unto you" (1 Cor. 16.10-12). "We *exhorted* Titus" (2 Cor. 8.6). "Titus . . . accepted our *exhortation*. . . . And we have *sent* together with him the brother" (2 Cor. 8.16-18). "We have *sent* with them our brother" (2 Cor. 8.22). "Tychicus, the beloved brother . . . I have *sent* unto you" (Eph. 6.21,22). "But I counted it necessary to *send* Epaphroditus" (Phil 2.25). "All my affairs shall Tychicus make known unto you" (Col. 4.7). "Luke, the beloved physician, and Demas salute you" (Col. 4.14). "And *say to* Archippus, Take heed to the ministry" (Col. 4.17). "We . . . *sent* Timothy" (1 Thess. 3.1-2). "*Do thy diligence* to come shortly unto me. . . . Take Mark, and *bring* him with thee. . . . But Tychicus I *sent* to Ephesus" (2 Tim. 4.9-13). "Trophimus *I left* at Miletus sick. *Do thy diligence* to come before winter" (2 Tim. 4.20-21). "For this cause *left I* thee in Crete, that thou shouldest set in order the things that were wanting, and appoint elders in every city, as I *gave thee charge*" (Titus 1.5). "When I *send* Artemas unto thee, or Tychicus, *give diligence* to come unto me to Nicopolis: for there have I determined to winter. *Set forward* Zenas the lawyer and Apollos on their journey *diligently*, that nothing be wanting unto them" (Titus 3.12-13).

The above Scriptures show us that among the workers of God dependence upon Him does not render us independent of one another. We saw that Paul *left* Titus in Crete to complete the work he himself had left unfinished, and that he afterwards *sent* Artemas and Tychicus to replace him when he instructed him to proceed to Nicopolis. On various occasions he appointed Timothy and Tychicus to do certain work, and we read that he *persuaded* Titus and Apollos to remain in Corinth. We observe that these workers not only learned to work in teams, but the less experienced learned to submit to the direction of the more spiritual. God's workers must learn to be "left," to be "sent" and to be "persuaded."

It is important to recognize the difference between official and spiritual authority. In an organization all authority is official, not spiritual. In a good organization the one who holds office has both official and spiritual authority; in a bad organization the authority wielded is only official. But in any organization, no matter whether the office-bearer *himself* has spiritual authority or not, the authority he holds in the organization is actually only official. What is the meaning of official authority? It means that because a man holds office, therefore he exercises authority. The authority is exercised solely on account of the office he holds. As long as the office-bearer retains his position, just so long can he exert his authority; as soon as he resigns office his authority ceases. Such authority is altogether objective, it is not inherent in the man himself. It is connected not with the person, but merely with his position. If he holds the office of superintendent, it follows as a matter of course that he superintends affairs, no matter whether he is spiritually qualified to do so or not; if he holds the office of director, then automatically he directs, even if lack of spirituality should really disqualify him from exercising control over other lives. The life of an organization is position; it is position that determines authority.

But in Divinely constituted companies of workers there is no organization. Authority *is* exercised amongst them, but such authority is spiritual, not official. It is an authority based upon spirituality, an authority which is the outcome of a deep knowledge of the Lord, and intimate fellowship with Him. Spiritual life is the source of such authority. The reason why Paul could direct others was not because of his superior position, but because of his greater spirituality. If he had lost his spirituality, he would have lost his authority. In an organization those who are spiritual do not necessarily hold any office, and those who hold office are not necessarily spiritual; but in Scripture it is otherwise. There it is those who know the Lord who superintend affairs. It is those who are spiritual that direct others, and if those others are spiritual, they will recognize spiritual authority and will submit to it. In an organization its workers are obliged to obey, but in a spiritual association they are not, and from an official point of view no fault can be found with them if they do not obey. In a spiritual association there is no compulsion; direction and submission alike are on the ground of spirituality.

Apart from the question of spiritual authority there is also the question of different ministries. All servants of the Lord are in the Ministry, and each has his own special ministry. In an organization, positions are allotted by man, but in spiritual work ministries are appointed by the Lord. Because of difference of ministry, we must on the one hand obey the Lord, and on the other we must obey the brethren. Such obedience is not on the ground of their superior position, but because their ministry differs from ours, and yet both are intimately related. If the head is moving the tips of my fingers, the muscles of my arms cannot take an independent attitude and refuse to move with them. The principle of being in one Body necessitates the closely related members to move with one another. In moving with the other members, we are not really obeying them; we are obeying the Head. In many things we can claim a direct guidance from the Head, but in just as many things the Head moves others and we simply *move with them*. Their movement is reason enough for us to fall in. It is most important to recognize this relatedness of various ministries in the Body of Christ. We have to know our ministry and to recognize the ministry of others, so that we can move as one obeying those who have a greater ministry. Since our ministry is interrelated in such a way, we dare not take an individual or independent attitude.

All positions held by God's ministers are spiritual, not official. Alas! men have only seen half the truth, so they try to organize the Work, appoint a director to superintend the service of others, but their directing is based upon their position in the organization, not upon their position in the Ministry. The reason why Paul could direct others was because the ministry committed to him by the Lord put him in a position of authority over them; and the reason why Titus, Timothy and Tychicus could submit to being directed was because the ministry committed to them by the Lord put them in a position under his authority. Unfortunately the directing of to-day is neither based upon depth of spirituality nor greatness of ministry.

Timothy was a man of God. He lived close to the Lord, obeying and serving Him faithfully, yet many a time he was sent here or there by Paul. He did not say, Do you think I am incapable of working by myself? Do you think I do not know how to preach the Gospel and how to found churches? Do you think I do not know how to go about things? Yes! Timothy knew much, yet he was willing to obey Paul. In spiritual work there is such a thing as being directed by others; there is the position of a Paul, and there is also the position of a Timothy, but these are spiritual, not official, positions.

To-day we must learn on the one hand to maintain a right relationship with our fellow-workers, and on the other hand to be guided by the Holy Spirit. We must maintain both relationships, and also maintain the balance between the two. In the first and second epistles to Timothy there are many passages which illustrate how fellow-workers should co-operate, and how a younger worker should submit to an older. A young Timothy ought to obey the commands of the Holy Spirit, but he ought also to receive the instructions of an elderly Paul. Timothy was sent out by Paul, Timothy was left by Paul at Ephesus, and Timothy obeyed Paul in the Lord. Here is an example for young servants of God. It is most important in His Work to learn how to be led by the Spirit and how, at the same time, to co-operate with our fellow-workers. The responsibility must not be wholly upon Timothy, neither must it rest wholly upon Paul. In the Work Timothy must learn to fit in with Paul, and Paul must also learn to fit in with Timothy. Not only must the younger learn to submit to the instructions of the elder, but the elder must learn how to instruct the younger. The one who is in a position to "leave," or "send," or "persuade" others, must learn not to follow the dictates of his own nature, acting according to personal inclination or desire, for in that case he will make it difficult for those under his authority. Paul must direct Timothy in such a way that he will not find it hard to obey both the Holy Spirit and the Apostle.

God's servants must work together in companies, but there is a kind of co-working which is to be avoided, i.e. co-working in a man-made organization which restricts its members so that they cannot really respond to the leading of the Spirit. When workers are entirely subject to the direction of men, then their work is not the outcome of a spiritual burden placed on them by God, but merely the doing of a piece of work in response to the dictates of those holding higher positions than they. The trouble to-day is that men are taking the place of the Holy Spirit, and the will of men in official position is taking the place of the Will of God. Workers have no direct knowledge of the Divine Will, but simply do the will of those in authority over them, without bearing any personal burden from the Lord for His Work.

There are others again who know the mind of God, have a call from Him, and depend entirely upon Him for the meeting of all their needs; but whilst they know what it is to be led of Him individually, they fancy they can just go their own way and do their own work in independence of others.

The teaching of God's Word is that, on the one hand, human organizations must not control the servants of God; on the other hand, His servants must learn to submit to a *spiritual* authority which is based on the difference of ministry. There is no organized co-operation, yet there is a spiritual fellowship and a spiritual oneness. Individualism and human organization alike are out of line with the Will of God. We should seek to know His Will, not independently, but in conjunction with the other ministering members of the Body. The call of Paul and Barnabas was on this principle. It was not a case of two prophets and teachers only, but of five, waiting upon God to know His Will. Acts 13 gives us a good example of a working company, all the workers being mutually related, and the guidance of one confirmed by the others.

The Sphere of the Work

The sphere of the Work, unlike the sphere of the local church, is very wide. Some of the workers are sent to Ephesus, some go to Paul at Nicopolis, some stay on in Corinth, some are left in Miletus, some remain in Crete, some return to Thessalonica and others go on to Galatia. Such is the Work! We see here not the movements of the local church but of the Work, for the movements of the local church are always confined to one locality. Ephesus only manages the affairs of Ephesus, and Rome the affairs of Rome. The church confines herself to matters in her own locality. There is no need for the church in Ephesus to send a man to Corinth, or for the church in Corinth to leave a man in Rome. The church here is local, the Work extra-local. Ephesus, Corinth and Rome are all the concern of the workers. The church only manages the affairs in any given locality, but the workers of God regard as their "parish" the sphere which *the Lord has measured out* to them.

No Central Control but Fellowship

In Scripture the workers were formed into companies, but that does not imply that *all* the apostles formed themselves into *one* company and placed everything under one *central control*. Although Paul had "those with him," and Peter his associates, they comprised only a number of apostles, not all the apostles. That all the apostles should combine into one company is not shown in the Word of God. It is quite in order for scores of men, or even hundreds, who have received the same trust from God, to join together in the same work; but in the Scriptures we find no centralization of authority for the control of *all* the apostles. There is a company of apostles, but it is not great enough to include *all* the apostles. That is Romish, not scriptural.

The parties referred to in Phil. 1.15-17; 2 Cor.

11.12,13,22,23; Gal. 4.17 all indicate that the Work in the early days was not centralized. Had it been centralized, those groups could not have remained in existence, for they could have been dealt with effectively. The Scriptures show that in Divine Work there is no universal organization or central control, which accounts for the fact that the Apostle had no authority to deal with those groups of people who were creating such difficulty in the churches.

The explanation is this, God does not wish the power of organization to take the place of the power of the Holy Ghost. Even though there be no central control, provided all the workers follow the leading of the Spirit, everything will run smoothly and satisfactorily and there will be the co-ordination of a body. Whenever people cease to obey the Spirit and labour in the power of the flesh, then it is best if the Work is simply allowed to fall to pieces. A good organization often serves as a bad substitute for the power of the Holy Ghost, by holding a work together even after all its vitality is gone. When life has departed from the work and the scaffolding of organization still supports it, its collapse is prevented; but that is doubtful gain, for a splendid outward organization may be blinding God's servants to a deep inward need. God would rather His Work be discontinued than that it go on with such a counterfeit for spiritual power. When the glory of God had departed from the temple He Himself left it to utter ruin. God desires that the outward and inward conditions should correspond, so that if death invades a work His workers may awaken at once to their need and in humility of heart seek His face.

Central control has many evils. It makes it easy for God's servants to disregard the leading of the Spirit, and readily develops into a Popish system, becoming a great worldly power. It is a scriptural fact that they are formed into companies, but they are not formed into one single company.

However, that does not mean that every company could just go on independently, knowing no relatedness or fellowship with other companies. The principle of the oneness of the Body holds good here as in all other relationships between the children of God. In Scripture we not only see the principle of "the laying on of hands," but also that of giving "the right hands" (Gal. 2.9). The former speaks of *identification*: the latter of *fellowship*. In Antioch hands were laid on Paul and Barnabas; in Jerusalem there was no laying on of hands, but the right hands of fellowship given them by James, Cephas and John. In Antioch the sphere in view was *one* apostolic company, and the point *emphasized* was identification; consequently hands were laid on them. But in Jerusalem the sphere in view was the relationship between *different* apostolic companies, and the point *emphasized* was fellowship; consequently the right hands were extended to them.

Many are called to work for the Lord, but their sphere of service is not the same, so it follows that their associates cannot be the same. But the various companies must all be identified with the Body, coming under the Headship of the Lord, and having fellowship amongst themselves. There is no laying on of hands between Antioch and Jerusalem, but there is the giving of the right hands of fellowship. So the Word of God does not warrant the forming of one central company, neither does it warrant the forming of various scattered, unrelated and isolated companies. There is no one central place for the laying on of hands, nor is there *merely* the laying on of hands and nothing else in any one of the various groups; but amongst them there is also the giving of the right hands of fellowship one to the other. Each company should recognize what God is doing with the other companies and should extend fellowship to them, acknowledging that they are also ministers in the Body. Under the ordering of God they may work in different companies, but all must work as one Body. The extending of the right hands of fellowship implies a recognition that other people are in the Body and we are in fellowship with them, working together in a related way, as becomes functioning members of the same Body. "When they saw that I had been intrusted with the gospel of the uncircumcision . . . and when they perceived the grace that was given unto me, James and Cephas and John, they who were reputed to be pillars, gave to me and Barnabas the right hands of fellowship, that we should go unto the Gentiles, and they unto the circumcision" (Gal. 2.7-9). The unrelated, scattered, disrupted and conflicting organizations in Christendom, which do not recognize the principle of the Body, and do not come under the Sovereignty and Headship of Christ, are never according to the Mind of the Lord.

Co-operation Among the Workers

The question naturally arises, how should workers and working associations co-operate? To one company God gives one kind of ministry, and to another an altogether different form of ministry. How should the various groups co-work? Peter and his associates, and Paul and those with him, were appointed to different spheres, but in the event of their Work overlapping, how should they act? Since there is no centralization of work, yet at the same time there are various groups of workers, how should these different groups co-operate? We must note two fundamental points in regard to the Work:

(1) The first responsibility of every worker—no matter what his ministry or what his special line of work—whenever he comes to a place where there is no *local* church, is to establish one in the locality. (What applies to the individual worker applies also to any group of workers.)

(2) Should he come to a place where a local church already exists, then all his teaching and all his experience must be contributed to that church, that it may be strengthened and edified, and no attempt should be made to attach that church to himself or to the society he represents.

If a worker goes to a place where there is no church and

founds one there for the propagation of his particular doctrine, then we cannot co-operate with him because he is building up a sect, and not a church. On the other hand, should a worker go to a place where there is already a local church, and instead of contributing his teaching and experience to its up-building, seek to make it a branch-church of the society to which he belongs, then again it is impossible for us to co-operate, because he is building up a denomination. The basis of fellowship in the church is the common possession of life in Christ, and living in the same locality. *The basis of co-operation in the Work is the common aim of the founding and building up of local churches.* Denominational affiliations do not hinder us from reckoning anyone as belonging to the Body, but the aim of denominational extension will certainly keep us from any co-operation in the service of God. The greatest harm a worker can do is, instead of establishing and edifying the local churches, to attach to his society the believers he finds in a place, or to form those brought to the Lord through his labours into a branch of his particular denomination. Both these modes of procedure are condemned by the Word of God.

Paul came from Antioch to Corinth and there he preached the Gospel. People believed and were saved, and soon there was a group of saints in Corinth. Into what kind of church did Paul form them? Into the church in Corinth. Paul did not establish an Antiochian church in Corinth. He did not form a branch-church of Antioch in Corinth, but simply established a church in Corinth. Thereafter Peter came to Corinth and preached the Gospel, with the result that another group of people believed. Did Peter say, Paul came from Antioch, but I am come from Jerusalem, so I must set up another church: I will establish a Jerusalemic church in Corinth, or, I will form a branch-church of Jerusalem here in Corinth? No, he contributed all those he led to the Lord to the already existing local church in Corinth. After a while Apollos came along. Again people were saved, and again all the saved ones were added to the local church. So in Corinth there was only one church of God; there were no schismatic denominations. Had Paul established the precedent of founding a church in Corinth to enlarge the sphere of the church from which he went out, calling it the Antiochian church in Corinth, then when Peter came to Corinth he might well have argued, It is all right for Paul to found an Antiochian church in Corinth since *he* came from Antioch, but I have nothing to do with Antioch; *my* church is in Jerusalem, so I must establish a Jerusalemic church here. Apollos coming to Corinth would in turn follow their example and establish another church as a branch of the one from which *he* came out. If every worker tried to form a branch of the church he represented, then sects and denominations would be utterly inevitable. If the aim of a worker in any place is not to establish a local church there, but to enlarge the church from which he has gone out, then he is not establishing a church of God in that locality, but only building up his own society. Under such circumstances there is *no possibility of co-operation*.

Conditions have greatly changed since the days of the early apostles. Christianity has lost its original purity, and everything connected with it is in a false and confused state. Despite that fact, our work to-day is still the same as in the days of the early apostles—to found and build up local churches, the local expressions of the Body of Christ. So if we are in a place where there is no church, we should seek the Lord's face that He may enable us to win souls for Himself and form them into a local church. If we are in a place where there are missions, or churches, standing on sectarian or denominational ground, but no church standing on the ground of the Body and the locality, then our duty is just the same, i.e. to found and build a local church. Many will still persist in their old ways, hence the persons standing on clear church ground may be far fewer than the total number of Christians in the locality; but the area of the ground on which they stand is just as wide as that on which the church ought to stand, so it is still our duty to maintain that ground. We can only co-operate with those who are building up the Body of Christ as expressed in local churches, and not with those who are building up something else. Denominational connection does not hinder us from fellowship in the Lord, but denominational extension does hinder us from co-operation in the Work of God.

Here is the most important principle in the Work of God—a worker must not seek to establish a branch of the church from which he goes out, but to establish a church in the locality to which he comes. He does not make the church in the place to which he goes to be an extension of the church in the place from which he comes, but he founds a church in that locality. Wherever he goes, he establishes a church in *that* place. He does not extend the church of his place of origin, but establishes the church in the place of his adoption. Since in Scripture all churches are local, Jerusalem and Antioch can have no branch-churches. We cannot extend one local church to another locality, we can only form a *new* church in that locality. The church which the apostles established in Ephesus is the church in Ephesus: the church which they established in Philippi is the church in Philippi: the churches which they established in other places are the churches of those different places. There is no precedent in Scripture for establishing any other than local churches. It is all right to extend *the* Church of God, but it is all wrong to extend *a* local church of God. What is the place in which I intend to work? It is the church in *that* place I must seek to establish.

Now there are two kinds of workers, viz., those who stand on scriptural ground, and those who stand on denominational or mission ground. But even with those who stand on denominational or mission ground, the principle of co-operation is just the same—the one aim of founding and building up the local church.

The work of evangelization is primarily for the salvation of sinners, but its spontaneous result is a church in the place where such work is done. The immediate object is the salvation of men, but the ultimate result is the formation of churches. The danger which confronts the missionary is to form those he has led to the Lord into a branch of the society he represents. Since workers represent different societies, they naturally form different branches of their respective societies, and the consequence is great confusion in the Work and churches of God. The immediate aim of the various workers is no doubt the same (what preacher does not hope that many souls will be won to the Lord?)· but there is a lack of clarity and definiteness regarding the ultimate issue. Some workers, praise God, are out to establish local churches, others, alas! are out to extend their own denomination, or to form mission churches.

This is a point on which my fellow-workers and I cannot see eye to eye with many of God's children. From the depths of our hearts we thank God that in the past century He has sent so many of His faithful servants to China, so that those who were sitting in darkness should hear the Gospel and believe in the Lord. Their self-sacrifice, their diligence and their godliness has truly been an example to us. Many a time, as we looked at the faces of missionaries suffering for the Gospel's sake, we have been moved to pray, "Lord, make us to live like them." May God bless and reward them! We acknowledge that we are utterly unworthy to have any part in the Work of God, but by the grace of God we are what we are, and since God in His grace has called us to His service, we cannot but seek to be faithful. We have nothing to criticize, and much to admire, as far as the Gospel-work of our missionary brethren is concerned, yet we cannot but question their methods in dealing with the fruits of such work. For in the past hundred years it has not resulted in the building up of local churches but in the forming of missionary churches, or of branch-churches of the various denominations which the missionaries represented. In our opinion this is contrary to the Word of God. There is no such thing in Scripture as the building up of denominations; we only find local churches there. May God forgive me if I am wrong!

Local Churches and Mission Churches

Permit me to mention a personal incident. Some time ago I met a certain missionary in Shanghai who asked me if it would not be possible for me to co-operate with his Mission. Not knowing quite what to say, I did not commit myself. Later on I came across him in another part of the country, and again he repeated his question and asked if I had anything against the Mission. I answered: "I dare not criticize your Mission, though I do not believe it is according to the full thought of God. I believe it was God's Will to establish it so that the servants of God in Western lands could come to China to preach the Gospel. I have nothing to say regarding the Mission as a body, for the Scriptures speak of companies of workers, and if you feel it should be organized, should have officers, and should bear a specific name, you must answer to God and not to man for that. Who am I that I should criticize the servants of the Lord? But whilst I do not criticize, I cannot copy, because God has not revealed that as His Will and way for me. Regarding the Mission as a mission, I have nothing to say, but I have serious questions regarding the churches formed by the Mission. To illustrate, you represent the 'X' Mission. Now, do those saved by your instrumentality become the 'X' Church, or do they become the church of the particular locality in which they live? It may be all right for missionaries to belong to the 'X' Mission, but it is all wrong for them to form the fruits of the Mission into the 'X' Church. The Word of God has not definitely forbidden the forming of an 'X' Mission, but it clearly does not sanction the founding of other than local churches."

Then I mentioned the apostolic examples, pointing out that they always sought to found or build up churches in the locality of their labours with the fruit of such labours. They never used such fruit to form branches of the companies in which they worked, otherwise the Church of God would have been rent by numerous factions from its very inception.

I then took as an illustration the work at T——. "There at T——," I said, "God has used you to win many souls. If the people saved by your instrumentality are the church in T—— I shall certainly join them, no matter what their spiritual state, or what their form of organization; otherwise I should be guilty of sectarianism. But if you build up an 'X' Church in T—— with the people saved there, then you are not building the Church of God in T——, and such a 'church' I regret to say I cannot join. I shall be obliged to work separately in T—— unless there is a church there standing on the scriptural ground of locality.

"If we are all out to establish local churches, then there is every possibility of co-operation. It is permissible to establish an 'X' Mission, but it is not scriptural to establish an 'X' Church. Suppose your 'X' Mission coming to T—— establishes an 'X' Church, thereafter various other missions come to T—— each establishing a separate mission 'church.' That would be the same as Paul establishing an Antiochian church in Corinth, and Peter coming along shortly after and establishing a Jerusalemic church there. On such a basis co-operation is impossible, for we should be disregarding the pattern which God has clearly shown us in His Word—the establishment of local churches.

"If we come to a place to found a church, then it must be local, intensely local, without anything extraneous to rob it in the slightest of its local character. If you come to T—— with the establishing of the church in T—— as your one aim, and I come to T—— with the establishing of the church in T—— as my one aim, then co-operation will be no problem. Even if a hundred and one missionaries, representing a hundred and one Missions, all come to T—— with this as their one aim, to establish the church in T——, then there will be no possibility of sectarianism, and co-operation will be a matter of course. If the aim of the 'X' Mission is only to preach the Gospel, then it is possible for us to co-work; but if there is a two-fold aim—the preaching of the Gospel and the extension of the Mission—then co-operation is not possible. If a worker seeks on the one hand to preach the Gospel, and on the other hand to extend his own society, it is impossible for us to co-work." Whether or not a man is out to establish local churches determines whether or not we can co-operate with him. No matter to what mission a man may belong, if he comes to a place not seeking to establish his own "church," but a church in the locality, then we are perfectly willing to work with him. Although we are not a mission, we are quite prepared to co-operate with any mission if they have no private end in view, but only the one end which God has shown as His Will regarding His Work.

May God grant us grace to see that His churches are all local churches.

9 The Question of Finance

It is a remarkable fact that, whilst the Book of Acts supplies many minute details regarding the work of an apostle, the one subject which from a human standpoint is of paramount importance in the carrying on of any work is not dealt with at all. No information whatever is given as to how the needs of the work, or the personal needs of the workers, were supplied. This is certainly amazing! What men consider of supreme importance, the apostles regarded of least consequence. In the early days of the Church God's sent ones went out under the constraint of Divine love. Their work was not just their profession, and their faith in God was not intellectual, but spiritual: not just theoretical, but intensely practical. The love and the faithfulness of God were realities to them, and that being so, no question arose in their minds concerning the supply of their temporal needs. To-day as then, the matter of finance will present no problems to those who have a vital faith in God and a real love for Him.

This question of finance has most important issues, so let us devote a little time to it. In grace God is the greatest power, but in the world mammon is the greatest. If God's servants do not clearly settle the question of finance, then they leave a vast number of other questions unsettled too. Once the financial problem is solved, it is amazing how many other problems are automatically solved with it. The attitude of Christian workers to financial matters will be a fairly good indication as to whether or not they have been commissioned of God. If the work is of God it will be spiritual, and if the work is spiritual the way of supply will be spiritual. If supplies are not on a spiritual plane then the work itself will speedily drift on to the plane of secular business. If spirituality does not characterize the financial side of the work, then the spirituality of its other departments is merely theoretical. There is no feature of the work that touches practical issues as truly as its finance. You can be theoretical in any other department, but not in that one.

The Importance of the Life of Faith

Every worker, no matter what his ministry, must exercise faith for the meeting of all his personal needs and all the needs of his work. In God's Word we read of no worker asking for, or receiving, a salary for his services. Paul made no contract with the church in Ephesus, or with any other church, that he should receive a certain remuneration for a certain period of service. That God's servants should look to human sources for the supply of their needs has no precedent in Scripture. We do read there of a Balaam who sought to make merchandise of his gift of prophecy, but he is denounced in no uncertain terms; and we read also of a Gehazi who sought to make gain of the grace of God, but he was stricken with leprosy for his sin. No servant of God should look to any human agency, whether an individual or a society, for the meeting of his temporal needs. If they can be met by the labour of his own hands, or from a private income, *well and good*; otherwise he should be directly dependent on God alone for their supply, as were the early apostles. The Twelve Apostles sent out by the Lord had no fixed salary, nor had any of the apostles sent out by the Spirit; they simply looked to the Lord to meet all their requirements. The apostles of to-day, like those of the early days, should regard no man as their employer, but should trust Him Who has sent them forth to bear the responsibility of all that the doing of His Will involves, in temporal as well as spiritual matters.

If a man can trust God, let him go out and work for Him; if not, let him stay at home, for he lacks the first qualification for the Work. There is an idea prevalent that if a worker has a settled income he can be more at leisure for the work, and consequently will do it better; but as a matter of fact, in spiritual work there is need for an unsettled income, because that necessitates intimate fellowship with God, constant clear revelation of His Will, and direct Divine support. In worldly business, all a worker needs by way of equipment is will and talent; but human zeal and natural gift are no equipment for spiritual service. Utter dependence on God is necessary if the work is to be according to His Will, therefore God wishes His workers to be *cast on* Him alone for financial supplies, so that they cannot but walk in close communion with Him and learn to trust Him continually. A settled income does not foster trust in God and fellowship with Him; but utter dependence on Him for the meeting of one's needs certainly does. The more unsettled a worker's living is, the more he will be cast on God; and the more an attitude of trustful dependence on God is cultivated, the more spiritual the work will be. So it is clear that the nature of the work and the source of its supply are closely related. If a worker receives a definite salary from man, the work produced can never be purely Divine.

Faith is a most important factor in God's service, for without it there can be no truly spiritual work; but our faith requires training and strengthening, and material needs are a means used in God's hand toward that end. We may profess to have faith in God for a vast variety of intangible things, and we may deceive ourselves into believing we really trust Him when we have no trust at all, simply because there is nothing concrete to demonstrate our distrust; but when it comes to financial needs, the matter is so practical that the reality of our faith is put to the test at once. If we cannot trust God to supply our temporal needs, then we cannot trust Him to supply our spiritual needs; but if we truly prove His trustworthiness in the very practical realm of material wants, we shall be able also to trust Him when spiritual difficulties arise either in connection with the Work or with our personal lives. What a contradiction it is if we proclaim to others that God is the living God, yet we ourselves dare not trust Him for the meeting of our material needs.

Further, he who holds the purse holds authority. If we are supported by men our work will be controlled by men. It is only to be expected that if we receive an income from a certain source we should have to account for our doings to such a source. Whenever our trust is in men, our work cannot but be influenced by men. It is a serious misconception to fancy that we can take money from men to do the Work of God. If we are supported by men, then we must seek to please men, and it is often impossible at the same time both to please men and God.

In His own Work God must have the sole direction. That is why He wishes us to depend on no human source for financial supplies. Many of us have experienced that again and again God has controlled us through money matters. When we have been in the centre of His Will, supplies have been sure, but as soon as we have been out of vital touch with Him, they have been uncertain. At times we have fancied God would have us do a certain thing, but He has showed us it was not His Will by withholding financial supplies. So we have been under the constant direction of the Lord, and such direction is most precious. If we cease to be dependent on Him, how can our trust be developed?

The first question anyone should face who believes himself truly called of God is the financial question. If he cannot look to the Lord alone for the meeting of his daily wants, then he is not qualified to be engaged in His Work, for if he is not financially independent of men, the work cannot be independent of men either. If he cannot trust God for the supply of needed funds, can he trust Him in all the problems and difficulties of the Work? If we are utterly dependent on God for our supplies, then we are responsible to Him alone for our work, and in that case it need not come under human direction. May I advise all who are not prepared for the walk of faith, to continue with their secular duties and not engage in spiritual service? Every worker for God must be able to trust Him.

If we have real faith in God, then we have to bear all the responsibility of our own needs and the needs of the Work. We must not secretly hope for help from some human source. We must have faith in God alone, not in God plus man. If the brethren show their love, let us thank God, but if they do not, let us thank Him still. It is a shameful thing for a servant of God to have one eye on Him and one eye on man or circumstance. It is unworthy of any Christian worker to profess to trust in God and yet hope for help from other sources. This is sheer disbelief. I have constantly said, and say it again, that as soon as our eyes turn to the brethren, we bring disgrace on our fellow-workers and on the Name of the Lord. Our living by faith must be absolutely real, and not deteriorate into a "living by charity." We dare to be utterly independent of men in financial matters, because we dare to believe utterly in God; we dare to cast away all hope in them, because we have full confidence in Him.

If our hope is in men, then when their resources dry up ours will dry up too. We have no "Board" behind us, but we have a "Rock" beneath us; and no one standing on this Rock will ever be put to shame. Men and circumstances may change, but we shall carry on in a steady course if our reliance is on God. All the silver and the gold are His, and none who walk in His Will can ever come to want. We are apt to trust in the children of the Lord who in bygone days have sent us gifts, but they will pass away. We must keep our eyes fixed on the unchanging God Whose grace and faithfulness continue for ever.

The two initial steps in the Work of God are—first, the prayer of faith for needed funds, then the actual commencement of the Work. To-day, alas! many of God's servants have no faith, yet they seek to serve Him. They commence the work without having the essential qualification for it, therefore what they do has no spiritual value. Faith is the first essential in any work for God, and it should be exercised in relation to material as well as other needs. If there is no faith for funds, then no matter how good the work is, sooner or later it will fail. When money stops the work will stop too.

Living of the Gospel

Our Lord said, "The labourer is worthy of his hire" (Luke 10.7); and Paul wrote to the Corinthians, "Even so did the Lord ordain that they which proclaim the Gospel should live of the Gospel" (1 Cor. 9.14). What is the meaning of living of the Gospel? It does not mean that God's servant should receive a definite allowance from the church, for the modern system of paid service in the work of God was unknown in Paul's day. What it does mean is that the preachers of the Gospel *may receive gifts* from the brethren; but no stipulations are made in connection with such gifts. No definite period of time is named, no definite sum of money, and no definite responsibility; all is a matter of free-will. As the hearts of believers are touched by God, they give gifts to His servants, so that whilst these servants receive gifts *through* men, their trust is still entirely in God. It is upon *Him* their eyes are fixed, it is to *Him* their needs are told, and it is *He* Who touches the hearts of *His* children to give. That is what Paul meant when he spoke of living of the Gospel. Paul himself received the gift from the church in Philippi (Phil. 4.16), and when he was in Corinth he was helped by the brothers in Macedonia (2 Cor. 11.9). These are examples of living of the Gospel. Paul received occasional gifts from individuals and from churches, but he received no definite remuneration for his preaching.

Yes, "the labourer is worthy of his hire," and he should certainly live of the Gospel. But we do well to ask ourselves, Whose labourers are we? If we are the labourers of men, then let us look to men for our support; but if we are the labourers of God, then we must look to no other but Him, though He may meet our needs through our fellow-men. The whole question hinges here, Has God called us and sent us out? If the call and the commission have come from Him, then He must and surely will be responsible for all that our obedience to Him involves. When we make our needs known to Him He will certainly hear, and He will move the hearts of men to supply us with all we need. If we are only volunteers in God's service, then God will not be responsible for the liabilities we incur, so we shall be unable to live of the Gospel.

When Miss M. E. Barber thought of coming to China to serve the Lord, she foresaw the difficulties of a woman setting out on her own for a foreign country, so she asked advice of Mr. Wilkinson of the Mildmay Mission to the Jews, who said, "A foreign country, no promise of support, no backing of any society – all these present no problem. The question is here: Are you going on your own initiative, or are you being sent by God?" "God is sending me," she replied. "Then no more questions are necessary," he said, "for if *God* sends you *He* must be responsible." Yes, if we go on our own initiative, then distress and shame await us, but if we go as sent ones of God, all responsibility will be His, and we need never enquire how He is going to discharge it.

But in Corinth Paul did not live of the Gospel, he made tents with his own hands. So there are evidently two ways by which the needs of God's servants may be met—either they look to God to touch the hearts of His children to give what is needful, or they earn it by doing part-time "secular" work. To work with our hands may be very good, but we require to note that Paul does not regard that as the usual thing. It is something exceptional, a course to be resorted to in special circumstances.

"If we sowed unto you spiritual things, is it a great matter if we shall reap your carnal things? If others partake of this right over you, do not we yet more? Nevertheless we did not use this right; but we bear all things, that we may cause no hindrance to the Gospel of Christ. Know ye not that they which minister about sacred things eat of the things of the temple, and they which wait upon the altar have their portion with the altar? Even so did the Lord ordain that they which proclaim the Gospel should live of the Gospel. But I have used none of these things: and I write not these things that it may be done so in my case: for it were good for me rather to die, than that any man should make my glorying void. . . . What, then, is my reward? That, when I preach the Gospel, I may make the Gospel without charge, so as not to use to the full my right in the Gospel" (1 Cor. 9.11-15,18). There are certain rights which are the privilege of all preachers of the Gospel. Paul did not receive anything from Corinth, because he was in special circumstances at the time; but though he did not avail himself of his privileges as a Gospel preacher on that occasion, that he did so at other times is quite clear. "Or did I commit a sin in abasing myself that ye might be exalted, because I preached to you the Gospel of God for naught? I robbed other churches, taking wages of them that I might minister unto you; and when I was present with you and was in want I was not a burden on any man: for the brethren, when they came from Macedonia, supplied the measure of my wants: and in everything I kept myself from being burdensome unto you, and so will I keep myself. As the truth of Christ is in me, no man shall stop me of this glorying *in the regions of Achaia*" (2 Cor. 11.7-10).

The Principle of Receiving Gifts

It is not permissible to receive a definite salary from a church, and at times it is not even permissible to receive an indefinite gift. Paul was demonstrating this principle in not receiving anything from the Corinthian church. If anyone gives us a gift out of pity for us, then for the Lord's sake we dare not accept it; or if gifts are offered, the reception of which would either bring us under obligation to the givers, or bring us under their control, we must refuse them too. All the servants of God must not only trust Him entirely for the supply of their needs, but when gifts are freely offered them, they must be able to discern clearly whether or not such gifts could be received by God.

In the Old Testament the tithes of the Israelites were handed over to the Levites. The Israelites made their offerings to God, not to the Levites, but the latter stood in the place of God to receive the offerings. To-day we are standing in the position of the Levites, and the gifts that are proffered to us are really offered to God. We do not receive gifts from any man, therefore we are under obligation to none. If anyone wants thanks, he must seek it from God, for God is the One Who receives the offerings. Therefore whenever a gift is given to us it is essential for us to be clear whether or not God could receive that gift. If God could not receive it, neither dare we. We dare not accept gifts indiscriminately lest we put God into a false position. (I say this reverently.) There are many people whose lives are not well-pleasing to God, how then could God receive their offerings? If He cannot, then we dare not do so in His stead. We should only receive money when our doing so involves no obligation on our part, and on God's part no misrepresentation of His nature.

It may happen at times that the gift is right, and also the attitude of the giver; but on the strength of his gift the giver may consider himself entitled to a say in the work. It is quite in order for the offerer to specify in what direction his offering be used, but it is not in order for him to decide how the work should be done. No servant of God must sacrifice his liberty to follow the Divine leading by accepting any money which puts him under human control. A giver is at perfect liberty to stipulate to what use his gift should be put, but as soon as it is given, he should take hands off, and not seek to utilize it as a means of exercising indirect control over the work. If he can trust a servant of God let him trust him; if not, then he need not give his money to him.

In secular work the man who supplies the means exercises authority in the realm to which his means is devoted, but not so in spiritual work. All authority in the Work rests with the *one who has been called of God to do it*. In the spiritual realm it is the worker who controls the money, not the money the worker. The one to whom the call has come, and to whom the Work has been entrusted by God, is the one to whom God will reveal the way the Work must be carried out, and he dare not receive money from anyone who would use his gift to interfere with the Lord's Will as it is revealed to him concerning the Work. If a giver is *spiritual*, we shall gladly seek his counsel, but his advice can be sought *solely on the ground of his spirituality, not on the ground of his gift*. If he can trust us, and if he is clear the Lord is leading him to give it to us, then we may receive his offering; otherwise let him keep his money, and let us go on with God's Work in the way He has directed, looking to Him alone to supply its needs and ours.

In all our service for God we must maintain an attitude of utter dependence on Him. Whether funds be abundant or low, let us steadfastly pursue our work, recognizing it as a trust committed to us by God, and a matter for which we must answer to Him alone. "Am I seeking to please men? If I were still pleasing men, I should not be a servant of Christ" (Gal. 1.10). We must remain absolutely independent of men as regards the financial side of the Work, but even in our independence we must preserve an attitude of true humility and willingness to accept advice from every member of the Body who is in close contact with the Head; and we should expect through them confirmation of the leading we have received direct from God. But all the counsel we seek and receive from others is on account of their spirituality, not on account of their financial position. We are willing to seek advice of the richest member of the Body, neither because of nor despite his money, and we are just as ready to seek the counsel of the poorest member, neither because of nor despite his poverty. In matters of finance we must maintain this ground, that it is God alone we have to do with. Let Paul's boasting be ours too!

Attitude towards the Gentiles

The principle is, "taking nothing of the Gentiles" (3 John 7). We dare not receive any support for the Work of God from those who do not know Him. If God has not accepted a man, He can never accept his money, and only what God can accept dare His servants accept. If anyone engaged in God's service accepts money for the furtherance of the Work from an unsaved man, then he virtually places God under obligation to sinners. Let us never receive money on God's behalf which would enable a sinner before the Great White Throne to charge God with having taken advantage of him. However, this does not mean that we need reject even the hospitality of the Gentiles. If in the providence of God we visit some Miletus, then we should do well to accept the hospitality of a friendly Publius. But this must be definitely under the ordering of God, not as a matter of regular occurrence. Our principle should always be to take nothing from the Gentiles. When we begin to use their money our work will have fallen into a sorry state.

The Churches and the Workers

Should the churches provide for the needs of the workers? God's Word supplies a clear answer to our question. We see there that the money collected by the churches is used in three different ways:

(1) For the poor saints. The Scriptures pay much attention to the needy children of God, and a large proportion of the local offerings goes to relieve their distress.

(2) For the elders of the local church. Circumstances may make it necessary for elders to give up their ordinary business in order to devote themselves wholly to the interests of the church, in which case the local brothers should realize their financial responsibility towards them, and seek at least in some measure to make up to them what they have sacrificed for the church's sake (1 Tim. 5.17,18).

(3) For the working brothers and the Work. This must be regarded as an offering to God, not as a salary paid to them.

"I robbed other churches, taking wages of them, that I might minister unto you; and when I was present with you and was in want, I was not a burden on any man; for the brethren, when they came from Macedonia, supplied the measure of my want; and in everything I kept myself from being burdensome unto you, and so will I keep myself" (2 Cor. 11.8-9). "And ye yourselves also know, ye Philippians, that in the beginning of the Gospel, when I departed from Macedonia, no church had fellowship with me in the matter of giving and receiving, but ye only. . . . But I have all things, and abound: I am filled, having received from Epaphroditus the things that came from you, an odour of a sweet smell, a sacrifice acceptable, well-pleasing to God" (Phil. 4.15,18). Where the members of a church are spiritual, they cannot but care for the interests of the Lord in places beyond their own locality, and the love of the Lord will constrain them to give both to the workers and to the Work. If the members are unspiritual they will probably reason that, since the church and the Work are separate, they have no obligations towards the Work, and it is enough that they bear responsibility for the church. But those members who are spiritual will always be alive to their responsibility in regard to the Work and the workers, and will never seek to evade it on the ground that they have no official responsibility. They will count it both a duty and a delight to further the Lord's interests by their gifts.

Whilst in the Epistles the churches are encouraged to give to the poor saints and also to the local elders and teachers, there is no mention made of encouraging the giving to the apostles, or to the Work in which they were engaged. The reason is obvious. The writers of the epistles were themselves apostles, therefore it would not have been fitting for them to invite gifts for themselves or their work, nor had they any liberty from the Lord to do so. It was quite in order for them to encourage the believers to give to others, but for the meeting of their own needs and the needs of the Work they could only look to God. As they cared for the needs of others, He did not overlook their needs, and He Himself moved the hearts of His saints to supply all that was required. So the workers of to-day should do as the apostles did of old, concern themselves only with the needs of others, and God will make all their concerns His.

That was a great and noble statement that our brother Paul made to the Philippians. He dared to say to those who were almost his sole supporters: "I have all things and abound.' Paul gave no hint of need, but took the position of a wealthy child of a wealthy Father, and he had no fears that by doing so further supplies would not be forthcoming. It was all very well for apostles to say to an unbeliever who himself was in distress: "Silver and gold have I none," but it would never have done for a needy apostle to say that to believers who would be ready to respond to an appeal for help. It is a dishonour to the Lord if any representative of His discloses needs that would provoke pity on the part of others. If we have a living faith in

God, we shall always make our boast in Him, and we shall dare to proclaim under every circumstance, "I have all things and abound." There is nothing petty or mean about God's true servants; they are all great souls. The following lines were penned by Miss M. E. Barber on Psalm 23.5 when she had used her last dollar:

There is always something over,
When we trust our gracious Lord;
Every cup He fills o'erfloweth,
His great rivers all are broad.
Nothing narrow, nothing stinted,
Ever issued from His store;
To His own He gives full measure,
Running over, evermore.

There is always something over,
When we, from the Father's Hand,
Take our portion with thanksgiving,
Praising for the path He planned.
Satisfaction, full and deepening,
Fills the soul, and lights the eye,
When the heart has trusted Jesus
All its need to satisfy.

There is always something over,
When we tell of all His love;
Unplumbed depths still lie beneath us,
Unscaled heights rise far above.
Human lips can never utter
All His wondrous tenderness.
We can only praise and wonder
And His Name for ever bless.

We are the representatives of God in this world, and we are

here to prove His faithfulness; therefore above all in financial matters we must be totally independent of men, and wholly dependent upon God. Our attitude, our words and our actions must all declare that He alone is our Source of supply. If there is any weakness here, He will be robbed of the glory that is His due. As God's servants, we must show forth the abundant resources of our God. We must not be afraid to *appear* wealthy before people. We must never be untrue, but such an attitude is perfectly consistent with honesty. Let us keep our financial needs secret, even if our secrecy should lead men to conclude that we are well off when we have nothing at all. He Who sees in secret will take note of all our needs, and He will meet them, not in stinted measure, but "according to His riches in glory by Christ Jesus" (Phil. 4.19). We dare to make things difficult for God, because He requires no assistance from us in order to perform His miracles.

From the study of God's Word we note two things concerning the attitude of His children to financial matters. On the one hand, workers should be careful to disclose their needs to none but God; on the other hand, the churches should be faithful in remembering the needs both of the workers and their work, and they should not only send gifts to those who are working in their vicinity, or to those who have been called out from their midst, but, like the Philippians and the Macedonians, they should frequently minister to a far-off Paul. The horizon of the churches should be much wider than it is. The present method of a church supporting its own "minister" or its own missionary, was a thing unknown in apostolic days. If, with the present-day facilities for transmitting money to distant parts, the children of God only minister to the material needs of those in their own locality, they certainly lack spiritual insight and largeness of heart. On the part of the workers there must be no expectation from man, and on the part of the churches there should be a faithful remembrance of the Work and the workers both at home and abroad. It is essential to the spiritual life of the churches that they take a practical interest in the Work. *God has no use for an unbelieving worker, nor has He any use for a loveless church.*

The distinction between the church and the Work must be clearly defined in the mind of the worker, especially as regards financial matters. Should a worker pay a short visit to any place on the invitation of the church, then it is quite right for him to receive their hospitality; but should he stay for an indefinite period, then he must bear the burden alone before God, otherwise his faith in God will wane. Even should a brother willingly offer free hospitality, it ought to be declined, for the life of faith must be carefully maintained. It is right for the brethren to give occasional gifts to the workers, as the Philippians did to Paul, but they must not bear the responsibility of any. The churches have no official obligations regarding the workers, and the latter must see to it that the former do not take such obligations upon themselves. God permits us to accept gifts, but it is not His Will that others become responsible for us. Gifts of love may be sent to the workers from their brethren in the Lord, but no believers must regard themselves as under any legal obligations towards them. Not only have the churches no official responsibility towards the workers, they are not even responsible for their board, lodgings, or travelling expenses. The entire financial responsibility of the work rests upon those to whom it has been committed by God.

"We wronged no man, we corrupted no man, we took advantage of no man" (2 Cor. 7.2). "I will not be a burden to you" (2 Cor. 12.14). "For neither at any time were we found using words of flattery, as ye know, nor a cloke of covetousness, God is witness" (1 Thess. 2.5). "Neither did we eat bread for nought at any man's hand, but in labour and travail, working night and day, that we might not burden any of you" (2 Thess. 3.8). From these passages we see clearly the attitude of the apostle. He was not willing to impose any burden upon others or in any way to take advantage of them. And this must be our attitude too. Not only should we receive no salary, we should be careful not to take the slightest advantage of any of our brethren. Apostles should be willing to be taken advantage of, but on no account should they ever take advantage of others. *It is a shameful thing to profess trust in God and yet play the role of a pauper, disclosing one's needs and provoking others to pity.* A servant of God who really sees the glory of God, and his own glorious position as one of His workmen, can well afford to be independent of others, and even liberal. It is only right for us to enjoy the hospitality of our brethren for awhile, but we should most rigidly guard against taking advantage of them in trifles such as a night's lodging, an odd meal, or the use of light and coal, or of household utensils, or even of a daily paper. Nothing reveals smallness of character so readily as taking petty advantages. If we are not careful in such matters we may as well relinquish our task.

All the movements of workers vitally affect the Work, and unless we have a living trust in God our movements are liable to be determined by prospective incomes. Money has great power to influence men, and unless we have true faith in God and a true heart to do His Will, we are likely to be influenced by the rise and fall of funds. If our movements are governed by financial supplies, then we are hirelings working for pay, or beggars seeking alms, and we are a disgrace to the Name of the Lord. We should never go to a place because of the bright financial prospects of working there, nor should we refrain from going because the financial outlook is dark. In all our movements we must ask ourselves, Am I in the Will of God; or am I influenced at all by financial considerations? We are out to serve the Lord, not to make a living.

The Workers and their Work

Let us be clear that we must not only bear the burden of our own personal needs, but of the needs of the Work as well.

If God has called us to a certain work, then all financial outlay connected with it is our affair. Wherever we go, we are responsible for all expenses relating to it, from its inception to its close. If we are called of God to do pioneering work, though the expenses of rent, furniture, travelling, etc. may amount to a goodly sum, we alone are responsible for them. He is not worthy to be called God's servant who cannot be responsible for his own needs and the needs of the work to which God has called him. Not the local church, but the one to which the work has been committed, must bear all financial burdens connected with it.

Another point to which we must give attention is a clear discrimination between gifts intended for personal use and gifts given for the work. It may seem superfluous to mention it, and yet it needs emphasis, that no money given for the Work should be used by the worker to meet his personal needs. It must either be used to defray expenses in connection with his own work, or be sent on to another worker. We must learn righteousness in relation to all money matters. If there is any lack in connection with the Work, the worker must bear the burden, and if there is any overplus, he cannot divert it to the meeting of his own requirements.

When I had just commenced to serve the Lord I read an incident in Hudson Taylor's life which was a great help to me. If I remember it aright, this is the gist of it: Mr. Taylor was in St. Louis, U.S.A., and was due in Springfield for meetings. The carriage taking him to the station was delayed, with the result that when he arrived there the train had already left, and there seemed no possible way for him to keep his appointment. But, turning to Dr. J. H. Brookes, he said, "My Father runs the trains, I'll be there in time." Upon inquiry of the agent, they found a train leaving St. Louis in another direction, which crossed the line going to Springfield; but the train on the other line always left ten minutes before this train arrived, as they were opposing roads. Without a moment's hesitation, Mr.

Taylor said he would go that way, in spite of the fact that the agent told him they never made connections there. While they waited, a gentleman came to the station and handed Mr. Taylor some money. He turned to Dr. Brookes with the remark, "Do you not see that my Father has just sent me my train fare!" meaning that, even if he should arrive in time for the other train, he could not take it. Dr. Brookes was amazed. He knew Mr. Taylor had quite a good sum of money in hand, which had been given him for his work in China, so he asked, "What do you mean by saying you have no money for your fare?" Mr. Taylor replied, "I never use anything for personal expenses that is specified for the Work. The money earmarked for my own use has just come in!" For almost the first time in the history of that road the St. Louis train arrived ahead of the other, and Mr. Taylor was able to keep his appointment at Springfield!

Making our Needs Known

As we have already said, an apostle may encourage God's people to remember the needs of the saints and of the elders, but he can mention nothing of his own needs or the needs of the Work. Let him only draw the attention of the churches to the wants of others, and God will draw their attention to his wants. Let him be concerned about the needs of the saints and elders, and God will use the saints and elders to draw the attention of the churches to his needs.

We must avoid all propaganda in connection with the Work. With utter honesty of heart we must trust in God and make our requirements known to Him alone. Should the Lord so lead, we may tell to His glory what He has wrought through us. (*See* Acts 14.27; 15.3, 4). But nothing must be done by way of advertisement, in the hope of receiving material help. This is displeasing to God and hurtful to ourselves. If in any financial matter our faith grows weak, we shall find it fail when difficulties arising in connection with the Work put it to the test. Besides, if we know anything of the power of the Cross to deal with the self-life, how can we resort to propaganda for our work and so take things out of the hands of God and carry them on by our own efforts?

I know of works which, at their inception, were on a pure faith basis, and the blessing of the Lord rested on them. Soon the workers felt the need of extending the Work, and actually extended it beyond their usual income. Consequently they had to resort to indirect advertisement in order to meet their liabilities. Let us beware of extending the Work ourselves, for if the extension is of man, we shall have to use man-made methods to meet the new demands. If *God* sees the Work needs extension, *He* Himself will extend it, and if *He* extends it, *He* will be responsible to meet the increased needs. It is because human methods are employed to extend a work, that human means must be devised to meet its fresh requirements; so advertisement and propaganda are resorted to in order to solve the problem. Circular letters, reports, magazines, deputation-work, special agents and special business centres, have been means much used of Christian workers to increase funds for the Work. Men are not willing to let God extend it in His own time, and because they cannot wait patiently for its spontaneous development, but force an artificial growth, they have to resort to natural activity to meet the demands of that growth. *They* have hastened developments, so *they* have to devise ways and means of procuring increased supplies. The spontaneous growth of the Work of God does not necessitate any activities of human nature, for *God* meets all demands which *He* creates.

Advertisement has been developed to a fine art in this age, but if we have to take our cue from business men and use up-to-date advertising methods to make our work a success, then let us give up our ministry and change our calling. The wisdom of the world declares that "the end justifies the means," but it is never so in the spiritual realm. Our end must be spiritual, but our means must be spiritual too. The Cross is no mere symbol; it is a fact and a principle which must govern all God's Work.

We must let the Holy Spirit hinder us where He will, and not seek to urge things forward by touching Divine Work with human hands. There is no need for us to devise means to draw attention to our work. God in His Sovereignty and Providence can well bear all responsibility. If *He* moves men to help us, then all is well, but if *we* seek to move men ourselves, both we and the Work will suffer loss. If we truly believe God we shall leave the matter wholly in His hands.

We are all trusting God for our living, but what need is there to make it known? I feel repelled when I hear God's servants emphasize the fact that they are living by faith. Do we really believe in God's Sovereignty and in His Providence? If we do, surely we can trust *Him to make our needs known* to His saints, and so to order things that our needs can be met without our trying to make them known. Even should people conclude from our mode of living that we have a private income, and in consequence withhold their gifts, we do not mind. I would counsel my younger brethren in the ministry not to talk of their personal needs, or of their faith in God, so that they may the better be able to prove Him. The more faith there is, the less talk there will be about it.

Among the Fellow-Workers

In the Old Testament we read that though the Levites stood in the place of God to receive tithes from all His people, they themselves offered tithes to Him. The servant of the Lord should learn to give as well as to receive. We praise God for the generous way the workers in days past have given to their fellow-labourers, but we still need to be more thoughtful for the material needs of all our brethren in the Work. We must remember the words of Paul: "These hands have ministered to my wants and to those who were with me" (Acts 20.34). We must not merely hope to have sufficient to spend on ourselves and our work, but must look to God to provide us with sufficient to give to others too. If we are only occupied with the thought of our personal needs and the needs of our work, and forget the needs of our fellow-workers, the plane of our spiritual life is too low. Like Paul, we must constantly think of those with us, and help to minister to their wants. If anyone amongst us is only a receiver and not a giver, he is unworthy of Him Who sent him and those who labour with him.

The scope of our thinking along the line of material needs should always be on the basis of "my wants and the wants of those with me." The money God sends to me is not only for me, but also for "those with me." A brother once suggested that God would surely supply the needs of all our fellow-workers, so we need not feel too concerned about them, especially as we are not a mission and have no financial obligations towards them. But our brother forgot that we are not only responsible for our own needs and the needs of our work, but in a spiritual way we, like Paul, are responsible also for "those with us." Whether we are good fellow-workers or not will be evidenced by the measure of our thoughtfulness for our brethren in the Work.

Since we are not a mission, and have no man-made organization, no head-quarters, no centralization of funds and consequently no distributing-centre, how can the needs of all our fellow-workers be supplied? This question has been repeatedly put to me by interested brethren. The answer is this, all needs will be met if each one realizes his three-fold financial responsibility; firstly, in regard to his personal and family needs: secondly, in regard to the needs of his work: and thirdly, in regard to the needs of his fellow-labourers. We must not only look to God to supply our own wants and all those related to our work, but we must look to Him just as definitely to send us extra funds to enable us to have something to send to our associates in the Work. Of course we have no official obligation towards them, but we cannot ignore our spiritual responsibility.

The requirements of workers vary, and the requirements of the Work vary too, besides which, the power of prayer differs in different individuals, and the measure of faith differs also. It follows therefore that our income will not be the same; but every one of us should definitely exercise faith for the supply of sufficient funds to be able to distribute to the necessities of others. The amounts we receive and give may differ, but the same principle applies to us all. Working on such a basis no head-quarters is necessary; for each of us acts as a sort of head-quarters and distributing-centre. Of course that does not mean we must send an equal share to all who are associated with us; that is a matter of individual guidance. We trust in the Sovereignty and Providence of God, and we leave it to Him to regulate the passing on of gifts so that none will have an overplus and none be left in want. Should God lead us to send money regularly to any particular worker, it would be well to send it through one brother this time and another next time, so that the giver will receive less attention from the receiver.

The principle of God's government in relation to financial things is, "he that gathered much had nothing over; and he that gathered little had no lack" (2 Cor. 8.15). Anyone who has gathered much must be willing to have nothing over, for only then can he who has gathered little have no lack. Some of us have proved in experience that when we bear the burden for those who gather little, God sees to it that we gather much; but if we only think of our own needs, the utmost we can hope for is to gather little and have no lack. It is a privilege to be able to help your brethren in the Work, and to be able to give away even the greater proportion of your income. Those who have only learned to take seldom receive; but those who have learned to give are always receiving and have always more to give. The more money you spend on others, the more your income will increase; the more you try to save, the more you will be troubled by "rust" and "thieves" (Matt. 6.19,20).

We must not confine our giving to those immediately associated with us, but must remember workers in other parts and seek to minister to their needs. We must constantly keep the thought of other workers and their needs before the brethren among whom we labour, and encourage them to help them, never fearing that God will bless other workers more than us. We must leave no room for fear or jealousy. Do we really believe in the Sovereignty of God? If so, we shall never fear that anything God has intended for us shall fail to reach us. The needs of Paul and his fellow-workers were great, and though he only brought the needs of the saints and the elders before the churches, God looked after his needs and the needs of those with him.

If your work is to be conducted along lines well-pleasing to God, then it is absolutely essential that the Sovereignty of God be a working factor in your experience, and no mere theory. When you know His Sovereignty, then even if men seem to move around you at random and circumstances appear to whirl at the mercy of chance, you will still be confident in the assurance that God is ordering every detail of your way for His glory and for your good. The needs of others may be known to men, whilst none may know or even care about your wants, but you will have no anxiety if the Sovereignty of God is a reality to you; for then you will see all those haphazard circumstances, and all those indifferent folk, and even the opposing hosts of evil, being silently harnessed to His Will; and all those unrelated forces will become related as one to serve His Purpose, and to serve the purposes of those whose will is one with His. Yes, "We know that to them that love God all things work together for good, even to them that are called according to His Purpose" (Rom. 8.28).

So the question is not, Are our needs small or great? or, Are they known or unknown? but simply this, Are we in the Will of

God? Our faith may be tested, and our patience too, but if we are willing to leave things in God's hands and quietly wait for Him, then we shall not fail to see a careful timing of events and an exquisite dove-tailing of circumstances, and, emerging from a meaningless maze, we shall behold a perfect correspondence between our need and the supply.

Why not a Faith Mission?

Some have asked, "Since you believe all God's servants should trust Him for their daily needs, and since you have quite a company of fellow-workers, why do you not become an organized faith mission?"

For two reasons: firstly, in God's Word all association of workers is on a spiritual, not on an official basis. As soon as you have an official organization, then you change the spiritual relationship which exists amongst the fellow-workers into an official relationship. Secondly, dependence upon God alone for the meeting of all material needs does not demand as active a faith on the part of an official organization as it does on the part of individuals who are only related in a spiritual fellowship. It is much easier to trust God as a mission than to trust Him as an individual. In Scripture we see individual faith, but we see no such thing as organization-faith. In an organization there is bound to be some income, and every member is sure to receive a share, whether he exercises faith or not. This opens the way for people to join the mission who have no active faith in God; and in the case of those who have faith when they join, there is the likelihood of personal trust in the Lord gradually growing weak through lack of exercise, since supplies come with a certain measure of regularity whether the individual members of the mission exercise faith or not. It is very easy to lose faith in God and simply trust an organization. Those who know the frailty of the flesh realize how prone we are to depend on anything and anyone but God. It is much easier to put our expectation in remittances from the mission than in ravens from heaven. Beloved, is not this the truth? If I have said anything amiss, may God and men both forgive me.

Because of our proneness to look at the bucket and forget the fountain, God has frequently to change His means of supply to keep our eyes fixed on the source. So the heavens that before sent us welcome showers become as brass, the streams that refreshed us are allowed to dry up, and the ravens that brought our daily food visit us no longer; but then God surprises us by meeting our needs through a poor widow woman, and so we prove the marvellous resources of God. Organization-faith does not stimulate personal trust in God, and that is what He is out to develop.

I know that in an organized body many difficulties vanish automatically. Humanly speaking, it ensures a much greater income, for many of God's children prefer to give to organizations rather than to individuals; besides, organized work comes much more to the notice of the children of God than unorganized. But questions such as these challenge us continually: Do you really believe in God? Must scriptural principles be sacrificed to convenience? Do you really want God's best with all its accompanying difficulties? We do, and so we have no alternative but to work on the ground of the Body of Christ in spiritual association with all others who stand on that same ground.

But we wish to point out that, though we ourselves are not a mission, we are not opposed to missions. Our testimony is positive, not negative. We believe that in God's Word the different groups of sent-out ones who were associated in the Work all stood on the ground of the Body, and that no such group was organized into a mission; still, if our brethren feel led of God to form such an organization, we have nothing to say against it; we only say, God bless them! For us to form a mission because others of God's children do so would be wrong, since we see no scriptural ground for it, and have no leading of the

Spirit in that direction. But whether we work in a fellowship whose relationships are only spiritual, or in an organization whose relationships are official, may God make us absolutely one in this, that we do not seek the increase or extension of the companies in which we work, but make it our one aim to work exclusively for the founding and up-building of the local churches

10 The Organization of Local Churches

Having already observed the difference between the Work and the churches, between the apostles and the elders, between the basis of a scriptural church and sects, we can now proceed to see how a local church is organized.

According to the present-day conception, three things are regarded as essential to the existence of a church, apart from the group of Christians who constitute its members. These three are—a "minister," a church building and "church services." The Christian world would query the existence of a church if even one of these three were lacking.

What would one think nowadays of a church without a "minister"? Call him "pastor," or anything else you like, but such a man you certainly must have. As a rule he is specially trained for church work, but he may either be a local man, or a worker transferred from some other place. Whatever his background and qualifications, he gives himself exclusively to the affairs of the church. Thus the churches are divided into two classes—the "clergy" who make it their business to attend to spiritual matters, and the "laity," who devote themselves to secular things. Then of course there must be church services, for which the minister is responsible, and the most essential of these is the Sunday-morning gathering. You may call it a "service," or a "meeting," or whatever you choose, but such a gathering there must be at least every Sunday, when the church-members sit in their pews and listen to the sermon their minister has prepared. And naturally there must be a church building. You may term it "hall," "meeting-place," "chapel," or "church"; but whatever you care to call it, such a place there must be; otherwise, how could you ever "go to church" on Sundays? But what is considered as essential to a church nowadays, was considered totally unnecessary in the early days of the Church's history. Let us see what the Word of God has to say on the matter.

The "Minister," or Worker, in Church Government

"Paul and Timothy, servants of Jesus Christ, to all the saints in Christ Jesus which are at Philippi, with the bishops and deacons" (Phil. 1.1). In not a single scriptural church do we find any mention of a "minister" controlling its affairs; such a position is always occupied by a group of local elders. And nowhere do we get a clearer or more comprehensive presentation of the personnel of a church than in the verse just quoted from the Philippian letter. The church consists of "all the saints," "the bishops" and "the deacons." The "deacons" are the men appointed to "serve tables" (Acts 6.2-6), i.e. those who care exclusively for the business side of things. The "bishops" are the elders, who take the oversight of all church matters. (Acts 20.17,28 and Titus 1.5,7 make this quite clear.) And besides "the bishops" and "the deacons," there are "all the saints." These three classes comprise the entire church, and no other class of person can be introduced into any church without making it an unscriptural organization.

Before we go on to consider the elders, let us glance for a moment at the deacons. They do not occupy such an important position as the elders, who rule the church; they are chosen by the church to *serve* it. They are the executors who carry out the decisions of the Holy Spirit through the elders and the church. Because the deacons have actually more to do with assembly life than with the Work, we deem it sufficient just to make this brief mention of them.

There are two points in connection with the elders that call for special attention. Firstly, they are chosen from amongst the common *brethren*. They are not workers who have a special call from God to devote themselves exclusively to spiritual work. As a rule they have their families, and their business duties, and are just ordinary believers of good reputation. Secondly, elders are chosen from amongst the *local brethren*. They are *not* transferred from other places, but are set apart just in the place where they live, and they are not called to leave their ordinary occupations, but simply to devote their spare time to the responsibilities of the church. The members of the church are local men, and as elders are chosen from amongst the ordinary members, it follows that they are also local men (Acts 14.23; Titus 1.5).

And since all scriptural elders are local brothers, if we transfer a man from some other place to control a church, we are departing from scriptural ground. Here again we see the difference between the churches and the Work. A brother may be transferred to another place to take care of the Work there, but no brother can be sent out of his own locality to bear the burdens of the church in another place. The churches of God are all governed by elders, and elders are *all* chosen from amongst the local brethren.

If a group of men are saved in a certain place, and a worker is left in charge of them, then it is inaccurate to refer to that company as a church. If affairs are still in the hands of the worker and have not passed into the hands of the local brothers, then it is still his *work*, it is not a *church*. Let us make this distinction clear, the Work is always in the hands of the workers, and the church is always in the hands of the local brethren. Whenever a worker is in control of affairs, then it is a question of Work, not of a church.

It has been pointed out before that in God's Word there are local elders, but no local apostles. When Paul left Titus in Crete, his object was not that Titus should manage church affairs there, but that he should appoint elders in every place so that *they* could take charge of affairs. The business of the worker is to found churches and appoint elders, never to take direct responsibility in the churches. If in any place an apostle takes responsibility for the affairs of the local church, he either changes the nature of his office or the nature of the church. No apostle coming from another place is qualified for the office of local elder; the post can only be occupied by local men.

Let us who have been called of God to the Work be absolutely clear on this point, that we were never called to settle down as pastors in any place. We may revisit the churches we have founded, and help the believers we formerly led to the Lord, but we can never become their "minister" and bear the responsibility of spiritual affairs on their behalf. They must be satisfied with the elders appointed by the apostles and learn to honour and obey them. Obviously it needs more grace on the part of the believers to submit themselves to others of their own number and of their own rank, than to yield to the control of a man who comes from another place and has special qualifications for spiritual work. But God has so ordained it, and we bow to His wisdom.

The relationship between the Work and the church is really very simple. A worker preaches the Gospel, souls are saved, and after a short lapse of time a few of the comparatively advanced ones are chosen from amongst them to be responsible for local affairs. Thus a church is established! The apostle then follows the leading of the Spirit to another place, and history is repeated there. So the spiritual life and activity of the local church develops, because the believers bear their own responsibility; and the Work extends steadily because the apostles are free to move from place to place preaching the Gospel and founding new churches.

The first question usually asked in connection with a church is, "Who is the minister?" The thought in the questioner's mind is, "Who is the man responsible for ministering and administering spiritual things in this church?" The clerical system of church management is exceedingly popular, but the whole thought is foreign to Scripture, where we find the responsibility of the church committed to elders, not to "ministers," as such; and the elders only take oversight of the church work, they do not perform it on behalf of the brethren. If, in a company of believers, the minister is active and the church-members are all passive, then that company is a mission, not a church. In a church all the members are active. The difference between the elders and the other members is that the latter work, whilst the former both work themselves *and also* oversee the others as they work. Since the question of elders has been dealt with elsewhere, we shall make no further reference to it here.

The Meeting-Place

Another thing which is considered of vital importance to the existence of a church is a church building. The thought of a church is so frequently associated with a church building, that the building itself is often referred to as "the church." But in God's Word it is the living believers who are called "the church," not the bricks and mortar (*see* Acts 5.11; Matt. 18.17). According to Scripture it is not even necessary for a church to have a place definitely set apart for fellowship. The Jews always had their special meeting-places, and wherever they went they made a point of building a synagogue in which to worship God. The first apostles were Jews, and the Jewish tendency to build special places of worship was natural to them. Had Christianity required that places be set apart for the specific purpose of worshipping the Lord, the early apostles, with their Jewish background and natural tendencies, would have been ready enough to build them. The amazing thing is that, not only did they not put up special buildings, but they seem to have ignored the whole subject intentionally. It is Judaism, not Christianity, which teaches that there must be sanctified places for Divine worship. The temple of the New Testament is not a material edifice; it consists of living persons, all believers in the Lord. Because the New Testament temple is spiritual, therefore the question of meeting-places for believers, or places of worship, is one of minor importance. Let us turn to the New Testament and see how the question of meeting-places is dealt with there.

When our Lord was on earth He met with His disciples at times on the hill-side and at times by the sea; He gathered them around Him now in a house, again in a boat, and there were times when He drew apart with them in an upper room; but there was no "consecrated" place, where He habitually met with His own. At Pentecost the disciples were gathered in an upper room, and after Pentecost they either met all together in the Temple (Acts 2.46), or separately in different houses (Acts 2.46), or at times in Solomon's Porch (Acts 5.12). They met for prayer in various homes, Mary's being one of them (Acts 12.12), and we read that on a certain occasion they were assembled in a room on the third floor of a building (Acts 20.8). Judging from these passages, the believers assembled in a great variety of places and had no official meeting-place; they simply made use of any building that suited their needs, whether a private home, or just a room in a house, or else a wide space like Solomon's Porch. They had no buildings specially set apart for church use; they had nothing which would correspond to the "church" of to-day.

"And upon the first day of the week, when we were gathered together to break bread, Paul discoursed with them. . . . And there were many lights in the upper chamber, where we were gathered together. And there sat in the window a certain young man named Eutychus" (Acts 20.7-9). In Troas we find the believers meeting in the third story of a building. There is a delightfully unofficial air about this gathering, such a contrast to the present-day conventional services, with the church members all sitting stiffly in their pews. But this Troas meeting was a truly scriptural one. There was no official stamp upon it; it bore the marks of real life, in its perfect naturalness and pure simplicity. It was quite all right for some of the saints to sit on the window-ledge, or for others to sit on the floor, as Mary did of old. In our assemblies we must return to the principle of the "upper room." The ground floor is a place for business, a place for men to come and go; but there is more of a home atmosphere about the upper room, and the gatherings of God's children are family affairs. The Last Supper was in an upper room, so was Pentecost, and so again was the meeting here. God wants the intimacy of the "upper room" to mark the gatherings of His children, not the stiff formality of an imposing public edifice.

That is why in the Word of God we find His children meeting in the family atmosphere of a private home. We read of the church in the house of Priscilla and Aquila (Rom. 16.5; 1 Cor. 16.19), the church in the house of Nymphas (Col. 4.15), and the church in the house of Philemon (Philem. 2). The New Testament mentions at least these three different churches that were in the homes of believers. How did churches come to be in such homes? If in a certain place there were a few believers, and one of them had a house large enough to accommodate them all, they quite naturally assembled there, and the Christians in that locality were called "the church in the house of So-and-so."

Everything must begin at the beginning. When a church is founded, the believers from the very outset must learn to meet by themselves, either in their own homes or in some other building which they are able to secure. Of course, not every church is a church in a "house," but a church in a "house" should be encouraged rather than considered as a drawback. If the number of believers is great and the sphere of the locality wide, they might need to meet, as the saints in Jerusalem did, in different "houses" (which may mean homes, halls, or any other building) instead of in one house. There was only one church in Jerusalem, but its members assembled in different "houses." The principle of "houses" still applies to-day. This does not mean that the whole church will always meet separately; in fact, *it is important, and of great profit*, for all the believers to gather together quite regularly in one place (1 Cor. 14.23). To make such meetings possible, they could either borrow or rent a public place for the occasion, or, if they have sufficient means, they could acquire a hall permanently for the purpose. But the meeting-place for the believers could generally be in a private home. If this is not available, and not suitable, of course other buildings could be acquired. But we should try to encourage meetings in the homes of the Christians.

The grand edifices of to-day, with their lofty spires, speak of the world and the flesh rather than of the Spirit, and in many ways they are not nearly as well suited to the purpose of Christian assembly as the private homes of God's people. In the first place, people feel much freer to speak of spiritual things in the unconventional atmosphere of a home than in a spacious church building where everything is conducted in a formal manner; besides, there is not the same possibility for mutual intercourse there. Somehow, as soon as people enter those special buildings, they involuntarily settle down to passivity, and wait to be preached to. A family atmosphere should pervade all gatherings of the children of God, so that the brothers even feel free to ask questions (1 Cor. 14.35). Everything should be under the control of the Spirit, but there should be the liberty of the Spirit too. Further, if the churches are in the private homes of the brethren, they naturally feel that all the interests of the church are their interests. There is a sense of closeness of relationship between themselves and the church. Many Christians feel that church affairs are something quite beyond them. They have no intimate concern in them, because in the first place they have their "minister" who is specially responsible for all such affairs, and then they have a great church building which seems so remote from their homes, and where matters are conducted so systematically and with such precision that one feels overpowered and bound in spirit.

Still further, the meetings in believers' homes can be a fruitful testimony to the neighbours around, and they provide an opportunity for witness and Gospel preaching. Many who are not willing to go to a "church" will be glad to go to a private house. And the influence is most helpful for the families of the Christians. From early days the children will be surrounded by a spiritual atmosphere, and will have constant opportunity to see the reality of eternal things. Again, if meetings are in the homes of the Christians, the Church is saved much material loss. One of the reasons why, during the first three centuries of Church history, the Christians survived the Roman persecutions, was because they had no special buildings for worship, but met in cellars and caves and other inconspicuous places. Such meeting-places are not readily discovered by their persecutors; but the large and costly edifices of to-day would be easily located and destroyed, and the churches would be speedily wiped out. The imposing structures of our modern times convey an impression of the world rather than of the Christ whose Name they bear. *(The halls and other buildings required for the Work are quite another matter; we are speaking here only of the churches.)*

So the scriptural method of church organization is simple in the extreme. As soon as there are a few believers in a place, they begin to meet in one of their homes. If numbers increase so that it becomes impracticable to meet in one house, then they can meet in several different houses, but the entire company of believers can meet together once in a while in some public place. A hall for such purposes could either be borrowed, rented, or built, according to the financial condition of the church; but we must remember that the ideal meeting-places of the saints are their own private homes.

Meetings connected with the Work are arranged along totally different lines, and are entirely under the auspices of the workers. They are on the principle of Paul's own hired house in Rome. As we have seen, when Paul reached Rome a church was already in existence there, and the believers already had their regular gatherings. Paul did not use the meeting-place of the church for his work, but rented a separate place, as he stayed for a prolonged period in Rome. In Troas he only stayed for a week, so he rented no place there, but simply accepted the hospitality of the church. When he went away the special meetings he had been conducting there ceased, but the brethren in Troas still continued their own meetings. If a worker intends to remain for a considerable period in any place, then he must procure a separate centre for his work and not make use of the church's meeting-place; and *frequently such a centre will demand more extensive accommodation than the meeting-place of the church*. If the Lord calls some of His servants to maintain a permanent testimony in a given place, then the call for a special building in connection with the Work may be much greater than the need of premises is in connection with the church. It is almost essential to have a hall if the Work is to be carried on in any place, whereas the homes of the brethren will nearly always meet the needs of the church meetings.

The Meeting

Before we consider the question of meeting, let us first say a few words concerning the nature of the Church. Christ is the Head of the Church and "we, who are many, are one body in Christ, and severally members one of another" (Rom. 12.5). Apart from Christ, the Church has no head; all believers are only members, and they are "members one of another." "Mutuality" expresses the nature of the Church, for all the relationships amongst believers are of one member to another, never of a head to the members. All those who compose a church take their place as members of the Body, not one occupying the position of head. The whole life of the church, and all its activities, must be stamped by this characteristic of "mutuality."

But the nature of the Work is quite different from that of the church. In the Work there are active and passive groups. The apostles are active, and those amongst whom they labour are passive, whereas in the church all are active. In the Work activity is one-sided; in the church it is all-around.

When we recognize the fundamental difference between the nature of the Work and the church, then we shall easily understand the scriptural teaching concerning the meetings which we are about to consider. There are two different kinds of meetings in Scripture—the church meeting and the apostolic meeting. If we are to differentiate clearly between the two, we must first understand the different nature of church and Work. Once we see that clearly, a glance at the nature of any meeting will make it obvious to what sphere it belongs; but if we fail to realize the distinction, we shall constantly confuse the church with the Work. In the early Church there were meetings which were definitely connected with the churches, and others that were just as definitely connected with the Work. In the latter only one man spoke, and all the others constituted his audience. One stood before the others, and by his preaching directed the thoughts and hearts of those who sat quietly listening. This type of meeting can be recognized at once as a meeting connected with the apostolic Work, because it bears the character of the Work, i.e. activity on the one side and passivity on the other. There is no stamp of "mutuality" about it. In the church meetings, "*each one* hath a psalm, hath a teaching, hath a revelation, hath a tongue, hath an interpretation" (1 Cor. 14.26). Here it is not a case of one leading and all the others following, but of each one contributing his share of spiritual helpfulness. True, only a few of those present take part, but all may; only a few are actual contributors to the meeting, but all are potential contributors. The Scriptures show these two distinct kinds of meetings—apostolic meetings, which are led by one man, and church meetings, in which all the local brethren are free to take part.

The apostolic meetings may be divided into two classes—for believers and for unbelievers. The meeting which was held immediately after the Church came into existence was an apostolic meeting for unbelievers (Acts 2.14). The gatherings in Solomon's Porch (Acts 3.11) and in the house of Cornelius (Acts 10) were of the same nature, and there are still other records of similar meetings in the Book of Acts. They were clearly apostolic meetings, not church meetings, because one man spoke and all the others listened. Paul's preaching at Troas was to the brethren (Acts 20). Whether it was in the church or not, it was still apostolic in nature, for it was one-sided, the apostle alone speaking to the whole assembly, and not the various members taking part for their mutual edification. Paul preached to the brethren at Troas because he was passing through that place, and any apostle passing through a place as he did would be free to respond to an invitation from the brethren to help them spiritually. Then when Paul was in Rome the believers came to his hired room to hear him witness (Acts 28.23,30,31). This work again is specifically apostolic in nature, because one man is active, whilst the others are passive.

The second kind of meeting is mentioned in the First Epistle to the Corinthians:

> If therefore the whole church be assembled together, and all speak with tongues, and there come in men unlearned or unbelieving, will they not say that ye are mad? . . . What is it then, brethren? When ye come together, each one hath a psalm, hath a teaching, hath a

> revelation, hath a tongue, hath an interpretation. Let all things be done unto edifying. If any man speaketh in a tongue, let it be by two, or at the most three, and that in turn; and let one interpret: but if there be no interpreter, let him keep silence in the church; and let him speak to himself, and to God. And let the prophets speak by two or three, and let the others discern. But if a revelation be made to another sitting by, let the first keep silence. For ye all can prophesy one by one, that all may learn, and all may be comforted; and the spirits of the prophets are subject to the prophets; for God is not a God of confusion, but of peace; as in all the churches of the saints (1 Cor. 14.23,26-33).

This is obviously a church meeting, because it is not one man leading whilst all the others follow, but each gifted one contributing to the meeting as the Spirit directs. In the apostolic meetings there is a definite distinction between the preacher and his audience, but in this kind of meeting any *gifted* member of the church may be preacher and any may be audience. Nothing is determined by man, and each takes part as the Spirit leads. It is not an "all-man" ministry, but a Holy Ghost ministry. The prophets and teachers minister the Word as the Lord gives it, whilst others minister to the assembly in other ways. Not all can prophesy and teach, but all can seek to prophesy and teach (verse 1). An opportunity is given to each member of the church to help others, and an opportunity is given to each one to be helped. One brother may speak at one stage of the gathering and another later on; you may be chosen of the Spirit to help the brethren this time, and I next time. Everything in the meeting is governed throughout by the principle of "two or three" (verses 27, 29). Even the same "two or three" prophets are not permanently appointed to minister to the meetings, but at each meeting the Spirit chooses any two or three from amongst all the prophets present. That such assemblies are assemblies of the church is seen at a glance, because the stamp of mutuality is clearly upon all the proceedings

There is only one verse in the New Testament which speaks of the importance of Christians meeting together; it is Heb. 10.25: "Not forsaking the assembling of ourselves together, as the custom of some is, but exhorting one another; and so much the more, as ye see the day drawing nigh." This verse shows that the object of such assembling is to exhort "one another." This is obviously not an apostolic meeting, for it is not a case of one man exhorting the entire assembly, but all the members bearing equal responsibility to exhort one another. A church meeting has the stamp of "one another" upon it.

There are several purposes for which the church meets, as recorded in Scripture. First, for prayer (Acts 2.42; 4.24, 31; 12.5); second, for reading (Col. 4.16; 1 Thess. 5.27; Acts 2.42; 15.21,30,31); third, for the breaking of bread—which are not meetings presided over by a single individual who bears all responsibility, since reference is made to "the cup of blessing which *we* bless . . . the bread which *we* break" (1 Cor. 10.16,17)—(Acts 2.42; 20.7); and fourth, for the exercise of spiritual gifts (1 Cor. 14). The last type of meeting is a church meeting, for the phrase "in the church" is used repeatedly in the passage which describes it (verses 28,34,35). Of this meeting it is said that all may prophesy. How different from one man preaching and all the others sitting quietly in the pew listening to his sermon! That meeting has no place among the different gatherings of the church, for its nature makes it evident that it is an apostolic meeting, and being an apostolic meeting, it belongs to the sphere of the Work, not of the church. Meetings where activity is one-sided do not come within the scope of the church, for they lack the distinctive feature of all church gatherings; and where any attempt is made to fit them into the church programme, much trouble is sure to result.

To-day, alas! this style of meeting is the chief feature of the churches. No meeting is attended with such regularity as this one. Who is considered a really good Christian? Is it not one who comes to church fifty-two Sunday mornings in the year to hear the minister preach? But this is passivity, and it heralds death. Even he who has attended "church" fifty-two Sundays in the year has not really been once to a church meeting. *He has only gone to a meeting in connection with the Work.* I do not imply that we should never have this kind of meeting, but the point is that such a meeting is part of the Work and is no part of the church. If you have a worker in the locality, then you may have this type of meeting, not otherwise. *The local church, as a church,* has no such meetings. Where they are found in connection with a church, we must discourage them and help believers to see that church meetings are conducted by the church. If apostolic meetings take the place of church meetings, then the church members become passive and indolent, always expecting to be helped, instead of seeking, in dependence upon the Spirit, to be helpful to the other members. It is contrary to the New Testament principles of mutual help and mutual edification. The reason the churches in China are still so weak, after a hundred years of Christian missions, is that God's servants have introduced into the local churches a type of meeting that really belongs to the Work, and the church-members have naturally concluded that if they attend such services and just passively receive all that is taught them there, they have performed the chief part of their Christian duty. Individual responsibility has been lost sight of, and passivity has hindered the development of spiritual life throughout the churches.

Further, to maintain the Sunday-morning preaching, you must have a good preacher. Therefore a worker is not only needed to manage church affairs, but also to maintain the meetings for spiritual uplift. It is only natural, if a good address is to be delivered *every* Sunday, that the churches hope for someone who is better qualified to preach than recently converted local brothers. How could they be expected to produce a good sermon once a week? And who could be expected to preach better than a specially called servant of God? So an apostle settles down to pastor the church, and consequently the churches and the Work both lose their distinctive features. The result is serious loss in both directions. On the one hand, the brethren become lazy and selfish because their thought is only centred on themselves and the help they can receive, and on the other hand, unevangelized territories are left without workers because apostles have settled down to be elders. For lack of activity the spiritual growth of the churches is arrested, and for lack of apostles the extension of the Work is arrested too.

Since so much havoc has been wrought by introducing a feature of the Work into the churches, and thus robbing both of their true nature, we must differentiate clearly between meetings that belong specifically to the Work and those that belong specifically to the church. When God blesses our efforts in any place to the salvation of souls, we must see to it that the saved ones understand, from the outset, that the meetings which resulted in their salvation belong to the Work and not to the church, and that *they are the church* and must therefore have *their own* church meetings. They must meet in their homes or in other places to pray, study the Word, break bread and exercise their spiritual gifts; and in such meetings their object must be mutual helpfulness and mutual edification. Each individual must bear his share of responsibility and pass on to the others what he himself has received from the Lord. The conduct of the meetings should be the burden of no one individual, but all the members should bear the burden together, and they should seek to help one another depending upon the teaching and leading of the Spirit, and depending upon His empowering too. As soon as believers are saved, they should begin to assemble themselves regularly. Such gatherings of local believers are true church meetings.

Meetings connected with the Work are only a temporary institution (unless the object is to maintain a special testimony in a special place). But the assembling of the believers for fellowship and mutual encouragement is something permanent. Even should the believers be very immature, and their meetings seem quite childish, they must learn to content themselves with what help they receive from one another and must not always hope to be able to sit down and listen to a good sermon. They should seek revelation, spiritual gifts, and utterance from God; and if their need casts them upon Him, it will result in the enrichment of the whole church. Meetings of recently saved believers will naturally bear the stamp of immaturity at the beginning, but for the worker to take over the responsibility of such meetings will stunt their growth, not foster it. It is the condition of the church meetings, not of the meetings connected with the Work, that indicates the spiritual state of a church in any locality. When an apostle is preaching a grand sermon, and all the believers are nodding assent and adding their frequent and fervent "Amens," how deeply spiritual the congregation seems! But it is when they meet by themselves that their true spiritual state comes to light.

The apostolic meeting is not an intrinsic part of the church life, it is merely a piece of Work, and it ceases with the departure of the worker; but the church meetings go on uninterrupted, whether the worker be present or absent. It is because the difference has not been realized between meetings for the church and for the Work, that it has ever occurred to the brethren to cease to assemble themselves when the worker goes. One of the fruitful sources of spiritual failure to-day is that the children of God consider the church to be a part of the Work; so when there is a sermon to hear, they constitute a willing audience, but if there is no preacher, the meetings automatically cease, and there is no thought of simply gathering together to help one another.

But how can the local believers be equipped to minister one to the other? In the apostolic days it was taken for granted that the Spirit would come upon all believers as soon as they turned to the Lord, and with the on-coming of the Spirit, spiritual gifts were imparted, through the exercise of which the churches were edified. The usual method which God has ordained for building up the churches is the ordinary church gatherings, not the meetings conducted by the workers. The reason why the churches are so weak nowadays is because workers seek to build them up, through the meetings under their care, instead of leaving it to their own responsibility to edify each other through proper church meetings. Why has it come about that the church meetings of 1 Cor. 14 are no longer a part of church life? Because so many of God's people lack the experience of the Spirit's on-coming, without which a meeting conducted along the lines of 1 Cor. 14 is *a mere empty form*. Unless all those we lead to the Lord have a definite experience of the Holy Spirit coming upon them, it will be of little use instructing them how to conduct their church meetings, for such meetings will be powerless and ineffective. If the Holy Spirit is upon the believers, as in the days of the early Church, He will give gifts to men, and such men will be able to strengthen the saints and to build up the Body of Christ. We see from Paul's first Corinthian epistle that God so equipped believers with spiritual gifts that they were able to carry on the work of building up the churches quite independently of the apostles. (This does not imply that they needed no further apostolic help. They decidedly did.) Alas, that nowadays many of God's people set more store by God's servants than by His Holy Spirit! They are content to be ministered to by the gifts of a worker, instead of seeking for themselves the gifts of the Spirit; so true church meetings have given place to meetings under the auspices of the workers.

In 1 Cor. 14, where a church meeting is in view, apostles have been left out of account altogether! There is *no place* for them in the meetings of a local church! When the members of a church assemble and the spiritual gifts are in use, prophecy and other gifts are exercised, but there is no mention of apostles for the simple reason that apostles are appointed no place in the meetings of the local church; they are appointed to the Work. When the local church meets, it is the gifts that are brought into use; office has no place here, not even that of an apostle. But this does not preclude a *visiting* apostle from speaking at all in a church meeting. This is illustrated by the fact that Paul took part in the Troas meeting. But the point to be noted is that Paul was only passing through Troas, so his speaking there was merely a temporary arrangement in order that the local saints might benefit by his spiritual gifts and knowledge of the Lord; it was not a permanent institution.

Apostles, as apostles, represent an office in the Work, and not any particular gift, therefore they are ignored altogether. Not a mention is made of them in this local church gathering. In the organization of the church they have no place at all, because their ministry, as apostles, was not for the churches but for the Work. As we have already observed, apostles had no say in the management of the business affairs of any church; but from the fact that no part is allotted them even in the local gatherings for mutual edification, it is clear that God did not even intend that they should bear the responsibility of the spiritual ministry in the churches. God gave gifts to the local brethren so that *they* could be prophets, evangelists, pastors and teachers, and, thus equipped, could carry the burden of spiritual ministry in the locality. Apostles do not bear responsibility either for the spiritual or material side of affairs in any church; the elders are responsible for the local management, and the prophets and other ministers for the local ministry.

Then have apostles nothing to do with the local church? Surely! there is still plenty of scope for them to help the churches, but not in the capacity of apostles. On the business side of things they can help indirectly by giving counsel to the elders, who deal directly with the church affairs; and on the spiritual side in the church meetings they can minister with any spiritual gifts they may possess, such as prophecy or teaching.

Their apostolic office is of no account in a church meeting for the exercise of spiritual gifts. As *apostles* they cannot exercise any "apostolic gift," but as *brothers* they can minister to their fellow-believers by the use of any gift with which the Spirit may have endowed them.

Not only apostles, but even elders as such, have no part in the meetings. In this chapter (1 Cor. 14), elders have no place at all. They are not even mentioned. We have already pointed out that elders are for office, not for ministry. They are appointed for church government, and not for ministry. Office is for government, and gifts are for ministry. In the meetings which are for ministry, it is those who have been gifted by God that count, not those who hold office; so in the church meetings it is the prophets, teachers and evangelists who take the lead, not the elders.* They are the gifted ones of the church.

We must differentiate between the work of the elders, and the work of the prophets and teachers. *Their work is different, but they are not necessarily different persons.* It is quite possible for one person to act in both capacities. The elders are those who hold office in a local church; the prophets and teachers are the gifted ministers in a local church. The elders are for church government at all times; the prophets and teachers are for ministry *in church meetings*. Whenever there is a church, the Lord not only appoints elders for its government, but also gives gifts to some brothers to constitute them ministers for the meetings. But this does not mean that elders have nothing to do with the meetings. Whenever government in the meetings is necessary, they can exercise authority there. As to ministry, though they cannot minister as elders, yet, if

*Acts 20.28 ought to be translated: "Take heed to yourselves and to all the flock, wherein the Holy Spirit has set you as overseers, to shepherd the church of God." This shepherding is by oversight: "Shepherd the flock of God . . . exercising oversight" (1 Pet. 5.2).

they are also prophets or teachers, they can minister in that capacity. *It is almost imperative that elders be prophets and teachers, otherwise they cannot rule the church effectively.*

The point to be remembered is, that church meetings are the sphere for the ministry of the Word, not the sphere for the exercise of any office. It is for the exercise of gifts unto edification. Since both apostleship and eldership are offices, one in the Work and one in the church, so both of the officers, as such, are altogether out of the meetings. But God will be gracious to His church to give it gifts for its up-building. The church meetings are the place for the use of these gifts for mutual help.

All meetings on the "round-table" principle are church meetings, and all meetings on the "pulpit-and-pew" principle are meetings belonging to the Work. The latter may be of a passing nature, and not necessarily a permanent institution, whereas the former are a regular feature of church life. A round-table enables you to pass something to me and me to pass something to you. It affords opportunity for an expression of "mutuality," that essential feature of all relationships in the church. In the local churches we must discourage all meetings on the "pulpit-and-pew" principle, so that, on the one hand, God's workers shall be free to travel far and wide proclaiming the Glad Tidings to sinners, and, on the other hand, the new converts shall be cast on the Lord for all needed equipment to serve one another. Thus the churches, having to bear their own responsibility, will develop their own spiritual life and gifts through exercise. It is all right to have an apostolic meeting when a worker visits the locality, but when he goes, meetings of the pulpit-type should be discontinued. Prophets, teachers and evangelists in the local church may also take such meetings from time to time, but they should be regarded as exceptional, for they foster passivity and do not on the whole make for the spiritual development of the churches.

Let us consult the Book of Acts in order to see the example God set for His Church in the beginning. "And they continued stedfastly in the apostles' teaching and fellowship, in the breaking of bread and the prayers. . . . And day by day, continuing stedfastly with one accord in the temple, and breaking bread at home, they did take their food with gladness and singleness of heart" (Acts 2.42,46). Such were conditions in the early days of the Church's history. The Apostles did not establish a central meeting-place for the believers, but these "continued stedfastly in the apostles' teaching and fellowship, in the breaking of bread and the prayers." They moved from house to house having fellowship one with another.

We can now draw our own conclusions from the three points we have considered. (1) Wherever there is a group of believers in any place, a few of the more mature are chosen from their number to care for the others, after which all local responsibility rests upon them. From the very outset it should be made clear to the new converts that it is by Divine appointment that the management of the church is entrusted to local elders and not to any worker from another place. (2) There is no official meeting-place necessary for the church. The members meet in one or more houses, according as their numbers require, and should they be obliged to meet in several houses, it is well for the whole church to congregate from time to time in one place. For such meetings a special place could be procured either for the occasion, or permanently, according to existing church conditions. (3) The church meetings are not the responsibility of the workers. Local believers should learn to use the spiritual gifts with which God has entrusted them to minister to their fellow-believers. The principle on which all church meetings are conducted is that of the "round-table," not of the "pulpit-and-pew." When any apostle visits a place, he could lead a series of meetings for the local church, but such meetings are exceptional. In the usual church gatherings the brethren should all make their special contributions in the power and under the leading of the Spirit. But to make such meetings of definite value it is essential that the believers receive spiritual gifts, revelation and utterance, therefore the workers should make it a matter of real concern that all their converts experience the power of the outpoured Spirit.

If the examples God has shown us in His Word are followed, then no question will ever arise in the churches regarding self-government, self-support and self-propagation. And the churches in the different localities will consequently be saved much unnecessary expenditure, which will enable them to come freely to the help of the poor believers, as the Corinthians did, or to the help of the workers, as did the Philippians. If the churches follow the lines God Himself has laid down for them, His Work will go forward unhindered and His Kingdom be extended on earth.

The Ministry, the Work and the Churches

In the earlier chapters of this book we have already seen what the Ministry, the Work and the local churches are. In this chapter we have seen the connection between the Ministry and the local church, and also the difference between the church and the Work. Now we can consider more minutely the relationship between the Ministry, the Work and the churches, in order to see clearly how they stand, how they function, what their respective spheres are, and how they are interrelated.

In Acts 13 we saw that God had established one of His churches in a certain locality, then He gave gifts to a few individuals in that church to equip them to minister there as prophets and teachers, so that the church might be built up. These prophets and teachers constituted the Ministry in that church. When in life and in gift these ministers had reached a certain stage of spiritual maturity, God sent two of their number to work in other places; and history repeated itself in the churches established by these two apostles.

Do you not see here the relationship between the churches the Ministry and the Work? (1) God establishes a church in a locality. (2) He raises up gifted men in the church for the Ministry. (3) He sends some of these specially equipped men out into the Work. (4) These men establish churches in different places. (5) God raises up other gifted men among these churches for the Ministry of building them up. (6) Some of these in turn are thrust forth to work in other fields. Thus the Work directly produces the churches, and the churches indirectly produce the Work; so the churches and the Work progress, moving in an ever-recurring cycle—the Work always resulting directly in the founding of churches, and the churches always resulting indirectly in further Work.

As to the gifted men raised up of God for the Ministry, they labour both in the churches and in the Work. When they are in their own locality they seek to edify the church: when they are in other places they bear the burden of the Work. When they are in the local church they are prophets and teachers: when they are sent to other places they are apostles. The men are the same, at home or abroad, but their ministries differ according to the sphere of their service. The prophets and teachers (and pastors and evangelists), whose sphere is local, plus the apostles, whose sphere is extra-local, constitute the Ministry. As the former serve the churches, and the latter the Work, the Ministry is designed of God to meet the spiritual need in both spheres. Here again we see the relationship between the churches, the Ministry and the Work. The Work is produced by the churches, the churches are founded as a result of the Work, and the Ministry serves both the churches and the Work.

In the fourth chapter of Ephesians we see that the sphere of the Ministry is the Body of Christ, which may be expressed locally as a church, or extra-locally as the Work. It is for this reason also that apostles, prophets, evangelists and teachers are linked together, though actually the sphere of an apostle's work is quite different from that of the other three. But all belong to the one Ministry, whose sphere of service is the Body of Christ. These two groups of men are responsible for the work of the Ministry, the one being gifted by the Spirit that they may be enabled to serve the local church, the other called from amongst these gifted ones to serve Him in different places and given an office in addition to their gifts. Those who have been gifted use their gifts to serve the Church by serving the church in their locality; those who have both gifts and apostolic commission serve the Church by serving the churches in different localities.

God uses these men to impart His grace to the Church. Their various gifts enable them to transmit grace from the Head to the Body. Spiritual ministry is nothing less than ministering Christ to His people. God's thought in giving these men as a gift to His Church was that a Christ, personally known and experienced by them, might through the gifts of the Spirit, be ministered to His people. They were given to the Church "for the perfecting of the saints, unto the work of ministering, unto the building up of the body of Christ."

Thus in the Ministry we have the prophets and other ministers using their gifts to serve the local church, whilst the apostles, by their office and gifts, serve all the churches. The ministry of these two groups of men is of great importance, because all the work of God—local and extra-local—is in their hands. That is why God's Word declares that the Church of God is built upon the foundation of the apostles and prophets.

And in the offices instituted by God, we have the elders occupying the chief place in the local church, whilst apostles hold no office at all there. Apostles, on the other hand, hold the chief office in the Work, whilst the elders have no place there. Apostles rank foremost in the universal Church and elders rank foremost in the local church. When we see the distinction between the respective offices of apostles and elders, then we shall understand why the two are constantly linked together (Acts

15.2,4,6,22,23). Apostles and elders are the highest representatives of the Church and the churches. Apostles hold the highest office in the Work, but in the local church they—as apostles—hold no office at all; elders, on the other hand, hold the chief office in the local church, but as elders they have no place in the Work.

And in the local church, there are two departments of service, one relating to business management, the other to spiritual ministry. Offices are connected with the management of the church and are held by the elders and deacons: gifts are connected with the Ministry of the church and are exercised by the prophets and teachers (and evangelists). The elders and deacons are responsible for the management of the church, while the prophets and teachers concern themselves chiefly with the meetings of the church. Should the deacons and elders also be prophets and teachers, then they could manage church affairs and at the same time minister to the church in the meetings. We must differentiate between the elders and the ministers. In everyday life, it is the elders who rule the church, but in the meetings for edification the ministers are the ones ordained by God to serve the church. It should be repeated here that elders, *as such*, are appointed for church government, and not for meetings to edify the church. In 1 Cor. 14, where meetings are in view, elders do not come in at all. But elders, in order to be effective, should also have the gift of a prophet, teacher, pastor, or evangelist, but it must be remembered that when they minister in the meetings they do so, not in the capacity of elders, but as prophets, or teachers, or other ministers. It is in the latter capacity that they have part in the Ministry. 1 Tim. 5.17 makes it clear that the usual sphere of their service is to "rule," but some of them (not necessarily all), may also teach and minister.

So the Ministry, the Work and the churches are quite different in function and sphere, but they are really co-ordinated and interrelated. The fourth chapter of Ephesians speaks of the Body of Christ, but no discrimination is made there between the churches, the Work, and the Ministry. The saints of the churches, the apostles of the Work, and the different ministers of the Ministry, are all considered in the light of, and in relation to, the Body of Christ. Because, whether it be the local church, the Ministry, or the Work, all are in the Church. They are really one; so whilst it is necessary to distinguish between them in order to understand them better, we cannot really separate them. Those who are in the different spheres of the Church require to see the reality of the Body of Christ and act relatedly as a body. They should not, because of difference of responsibilities, settle themselves into watertight compartments. "The Church, which is his body" includes the churches, the Ministry, and the Work. The churches are the Body expressed locally, the Ministry is the Body in function, and the Work is the Body seeking increase. All three are different manifestations of the one Body, so they are all interdependent and interrelated. None can move, or even exist, by itself. In fact, their relationship is so intimate and vital that none can be right itself without being rightly adjusted to the others. The church cannot go on without receiving the help of the Ministry and without giving help to the Work; the Work cannot exist without the sympathy of the Ministry and the backing of the church; and the Ministry can only function when there is the church and the Work.

This is most important. In the previous chapters we have sought to show their respective functions and spheres; now the danger is lest, failing to understand the spiritual nature of the things of God, we should not only try to *distinguish* between them, but *sever* them into separate units, thus losing the interrelatedness of the Body. However clear the distinction between them, we must remember that they are all in the Church. Consequently they must move and act as one, for no matter what their specific functions and spheres, they are all in one Body.

So on the one hand we differentiate between them, in order

to understand them, and on the other hand we bear in mind that they are all related as a body. It is not that a few gifted men, recognizing their own ability, take it upon themselves to minister with the gifts they possess; nor that a few persons, conscious of call, form themselves into a working association; nor is it that a number of like-minded believers unite and call themselves a church. All must be on the ground of the Body. The church is the life of the Body in miniature; the Ministry is the functioning of the Body in service; the Work is the reaching out of the Body in growth. Neither church, Ministry, nor Work, can exist as a thing by itself. Each has to derive its existence from, find its place in, and work for the good of the Body. All three are from the Body, in the Body and for the Body. If this principle of relatedness to the Body and inter-relatedness amongst its members is not recognized, there can be no church, no Ministry and no Work. The importance of this principle cannot be over-emphasized, for without it everything is man-made, not God-created. The basic principle of the Ministry is the Body. The basic principle of the Work is the Body. The basic principle of the churches is the Body. The Body is the governing law of the life and work of the children of God to-day.

THE CHURCH

AND THE WORK

III

The Church and the Work

III

Church Affairs

WATCHMAN NEE

Christian Fellowship Publishers, Inc.
New York

THE CHURCH AND THE WORK

(In Three Volumes)

Available from the Publishers at:

11515 Allecingie Parkway
Richmond, Virginia 23235

Printed in the United States of America

TRANSLATOR'S PREFACE

Ten years after the original publication in Chinese of *Rethinking the Work** (1938), there arose in China a need for a further reconsideration of the Work. Yet it was not because the principles or practices of the church laid down in that book proved to be wrong or impracticable, but because light on the parallel subject of the Work was found by that time to be insufficient. Thus in 1948 further instructions concerning the principles and practices of the Work were given during training sessions held at Mount Kuling to the workers who gathered there.

Rethinking the Work had in its day dealt especially with the understanding that *the church is local,* based as that book mainly was on *Acts chapter 13 onwards*; but later, by means of the Kuling talks which now comprise this *Church Affairs* volume, the fact that *the Work was found to be regional* was presented in 1948 on the basis of *Acts chapters 1–12.* And this latter book thus makes more complete the author's treatment of the overall subject of the church and the Work.

The opening chapter of this final volume of the trilogy serves as an introduction,** for it sets forth the complementary concept of the Work as being regional. Following this, twelve different aspects of church affairs are then discussed. Since these talks were originally spoken to younger fellow workers, a

---

*The reader needs to have it brought to his attention again that this Chinese publication of January 1938 appeared in *English* in Great Britain under the title *Concerning Our Missions* (London, 1939), and was much later published in the United States under the more popularly known title of *The Normal Christian Church Life* (Washington, D.C., 1962). For the complete publishing history of the book, see the copyright page of Volume Two of this present trilogy.—*Translator*

**Which is the substance of an address given by the author to fellow workers at Mount Kuling near Foochow, China, on August 19, 1948.—*Translator*

special approach to the subject will be evident to the reader. They were never meant to be a general treatise on behavior in the house of God; instead, they were presented in a form for helping younger workers to know how they were to conduct themselves as they were sent forth by the Lord to establish churches everywhere. It was not unlike the apostle Paul in his giving instructions to young Timothy so that the latter might "know how men ought to behave themselves in the house of God, which is the church of the living God, the pillar and ground of the truth" (1 Tim. 3.15).

These talks are now being offered to the reader as guidelines and not as rules and regulations. The aim in the publication of such a volume today is not towards uniformity of outward appearance, but is only meant to illustrate that these principles can in fact be put into practice. Spiritual principles must be applied spiritually. They will become letters if only applied technically; and, as we know from the Scriptures, "the letter kills" (2 Cor. 3.6). May those who read this volume keep this in mind continually so as not to be tempted to treat this study as a technical manual or some kind of fixed procedure which they must follow, but instead be truly benefited by receiving whatever divine light (or principles) may be found in its pages.

CONTENTS

Scripture quotations are from the
American Standard Version of the Bible
(1901), unless otherwise indicated.

Introduction*

During the disturbed period which has now passed,** we had to acknowledge that we found some practical difficulties in the conduct of the Work of the Lord. This has led us to inquire again of Him and of His word; and accordingly, in recent months, in conferences at Foochow and Shanghai, we have spent considerable time in seeking God's help to solve our problems. What follows is the outcome of those inquiries.

Whereas in the past we had received from the Scriptures much clear light on the church, we confess that we have had insufficient light on the parallel subject of the Work of God. *Rethinking the Work,* which was published in January of 1938 after our 1937 conference for workers at Hankow, presents what we understood at that time on the matter of the church. What we saw then, and stated plainly in that book, is that the question of the churches is one of locality, and that this local character of the church cannot be clearer to us even today. With regard to the Work, however, we have lacked the same clarity, and we now see the reason for this. It was because, in our approach to the matter then, we took as our guide the history which began with the sending forth of Barnabas and Saul, and overlooked what went before. We stressed Antioch

*See the second footnote of the *Translator's Preface* above. — *Translator*

**A reference to the Sino-Japanese War (1937-1945). — *Translator*

and practically ignored Jerusalem. We made Acts 13 our starting point and missed the purpose of Acts 1–12. We did not, at that time, have sufficient light to understand this.

But now God has in mercy come to our aid. The difficulties and trials of the past decade or so have driven us back to those earlier chapters in Acts and shown us their value in a new way. So with humility we can say this, that just as at Hankow in 1937 we confessed that never before had we such clarity concerning the latter part of Acts which deals with the churches, so today, because of the help we have recently received at Foochow and Shanghai, we can thank Him that never till now have the first twelve chapters of the book of Acts been so real to us.

The Work Is Regional

Among several things which have been shown to us, the first is *the important principle of region* or area. Whereas the churches are local, the Work, we have come to see, is regional. To us this is something which has become crystal clear from the Scriptures. To put the matter differently, a church is in one locality, whereas for purposes of the Work, many such localities together form one region. This is evident from the New Testament, although ten, or even five years ago, we did not have the light to see it. It is apparent to us now that the Twelve worked in one region, while Paul, Silas, Timothy and Barnabas worked in another—or in more than one. And if we study the Epistles we shall discern a number of such different regions. Let us note also the words in 2 Corinthians 10, where we find Paul writing of his labors as follows: "Now we will not boast out of measure, but according to the measure of the rule which the God of measure has apportioned to us, to reach to you also" (v.13 Darby). He seems here to allude to the matter of appointed spheres of work, as though God drew a circle for them and drew another circle for another group of His servants, and that within these limits was to be found the sphere of work of a particular company of workers.

This, therefore, is the difference of operation, as we see it, between the church and the Work: that the Work is regional, but the churches are not. No church can exercise jurisdiction over other localities, for its authority is essentially local. The sphere of the Work, on the other hand, is wider and embraces several localities in a single area or field.

At one time we tended to confuse the sphere of the Work with the locality of the church. Today we see clearly that the Work comprises a number of localities, and that its sphere of operation is wide. For example, we find Peter and John cooperating as a team or unit in the Work of one region, while Paul and Timothy labor together as another unit in a different region. The different groups of workers maintain contact and have fellowship with one another, yet they equally have their respective working areas within which they move.

The Region Has a Center

We come now to a *second principle*. Each region, we find, has a center; whereas the churches, of course, have no such center. The church in Jerusalem cannot—as a "central church"—rule the church in Samaria. No local church can control another local church, nor can one church control several churches. The widest scope of a church's authority is its locality; no more. There is no such thing as a regional church or an association of churches. The Church has neither regional council nor headquarters. But with the Work it is otherwise. The Work has a region and the region has a center, and that is why in the book of Acts we see Jerusalem as a center and Antioch as another center.

This will help to explain what may until now have been a problem to some of us. If we have not yet seen that the Work is centralized in this way, then we shall probably have found Jerusalem a difficulty to us rather than a help. We have not understood its special character. While the whole New Testament confirms that the Church—in its practical expression—is local, nevertheless there seems something special to be learned from both Jerusalem and Antioch. What we have come to realize today is that the church in Antioch is one thing, while a Work taking Antioch as its center is another. From the standpoint of the churches, Jerusalem and Antioch are of an equal level with, say, Samaria; but from the standpoint of the Work, Jerusalem is a center and Antioch is also a center.

At the beginning of Acts the Lord's promise is that, when the Spirit is come, they shall witness "in Jerusalem, and in all Judaea and Samaria, and unto the uttermost part of the earth" (1.8). Here Jerusalem is distinctly a working center in the divine plan. Again, in the thirteenth chapter, there emerges a new beginning at Antioch. The Holy Spirit makes a new departure, and from there men arise and go forth to work in other places. Thus Antioch is constituted another center of the Work. It was the Spirit who made a beginning at Jerusalem, and now it is the Spirit who makes a beginning at Antioch.

In Jerusalem Peter, we must remind ourselves, was an elder. Here is something of value we have discovered through reconsidering Jerusalem. In days past we have stressed Peter as apostle, but have overlooked Peter as elder. In Jerusalem he had a double ministry. With regard to that city he was—like James and John—an elder of the church; but with regard to the whole Work that was centered there, he was an apostle and so were they. For this reason, when writing to the church at Antioch they wrote as "apostles and elders" (Acts 15.23). How otherwise could elders in Jerusalem write a letter giving *command* to the church in Antioch? Are they elders who write? But there are also elders among those to whom they write! Going outside their locality as elders, they would automatically become involved in a conflict of authority. If, however, they were not only elders but also apostles, then the letter they sent to Antioch in fact carried the weight of the Spirit's witness, both in the church at Jerusalem and in the Lord's Work through the apostles.

So today we see how the Work of God operates regionally. God would have His Work in an area centered in one place, from which workers go and to which they return. In the local churches it is elders who bear responsibility; but in a regional center of the Work, there are not only elders as such but also workers bearing responsibility jointly with them.

Scripture gives no support for the common practice of assigning a worker to a given locality for work and for government there. Unless he migrates to that locality and becomes a resident elder of the church there, a worker should settle in his Jerusalem. For two thousand years Peter has been blamed for not leaving Jerusalem, and some have even suggested that it was because Peter and John remained there that persecution fell upon the Jerusalem church. There is no basis in the Bible for this view, and the Lord tells us plainly that it is "because ye are not of the world" that "the world hateth you" (John 15.19). No, neither by travel nor by staying at home shall we avoid the persecution which comes when we begin to follow the Lord. That is certain!

But on this question of going and returning, we can be assured that Peter was in his right place. He went to Samaria, for in Samaria was the Work of God; but from there he returned to Jerusalem. He went also to Caesarea; but once again he came back to Jerusalem. All this was because Jerusalem was his center, whereas Samaria was only one of the cities in that region of the Work. Thus it was that the fellow workers, moving from place to place through the region, set out from Jerusalem and returned there repeatedly.

When we come to the choice of a center for the Work, we must be quite clear that this is a matter not for man but for God. Only He can decide the place, and only the Holy Spirit can initiate the Work. Human judgment and initiative have no part in this. We cannot consult together to choose a site for Jerusalem. Only the Jerusalem of the Spirit's choice is Jerusalem indeed.

So Peter moves to and from Jersualem. Later, Paul moves to and from Antioch. They do not settle permanently in other places, but always return to their starting point. Their work is carried on within definite bounds or regions or spheres—call them what you will—and from divinely chosen centers. For each group of workers in any place, it is "according to the measure of the rule which God has apportioned."

We should never appoint a worker from outside as elder of a local church. It was only in Jerusalem that Peter was an elder as well as an apostle. If you are resident in a place, you may be both elder and apostle simultaneously *in that place*, but nowhere else. You may go out as a worker to help other churches, but you must return. It is wrong for you not to return. Like Paul you may take a large circuit and come back, or like Peter you may go out and return directly. Either is correct; but you must return. Paul came back to Antioch, Peter to Jerusalem; this is the Lord's word, and it could not be plainer.

Preaching by Apostles and by Scattered Saints

Now we must ask ourselves, how should the Work of God be carried forward? Here we come to our *third important principle*. We find there are two ways of preaching the gospel and of establishing churches—two distinct methods illustrated respectively by Jerusalem and Antioch. From Antioch apostles go forth; from Jerusalem scattered saints go forth. In the one case, bands of apostles move out—it may be Paul and Barnabas, or Paul and Silas, or Paul and Timothy—to preach the gospel from place to place, to form churches, and to return. In the other case, those who believe emigrate to new cities and new lands, preaching and telling of the Lord Jesus wherever they go; and wherever these who migrate are found, churches spring up. Whether they are distributed abroad by peaceful means or by persecution matters not; the fact is that by the scattering of the saints, the gospel itself is scattered abroad.

Here, I think, the Lord has left us unmistakable footprints in which to tread. Never let us regard these early chapters of Acts as inapplicable today. Like the book of Genesis, the Acts of the Apostles reveals the beginnings of God's ways, and what He did then sets a pattern for His Work always.

In Jerusalem it was persecution which God used to scatter His saints. They were compelled to emigrate. At that time there must have been many thousands of believers in the Jerusalem church. From that city there was a great outward movement; and yet, when Paul returned there after many years, there were still the same large numbers (Acts 21.20—"Thou seest, brother [Paul], how many thousands [Gr. *myriads*] there are among the Jews of them that have believed").

Here is an important secret of God's working: that after this year's harvest, wheat will grow again just as richly next year. You must not remain stationary, but must move on and make room for other believers; for it is the measure of the outgoing that determines the increase. As many more will be added as moved out, and if there is no moving out there is no adding. The way of God is to send out group after group of Christians, and so to scatter the seed in new fields.

Hence we have discovered three things: that the work is regional, that it operates from divinely chosen centers, and that the movement out is two-fold, by workers who go and return, and by the migration of scattered saints. Let us on no account let go these new lessons, for it is through years of opposition and many difficulties that we have learned them. For many of us, at least half of our time is gone; for the remaining half, let us steer a straight course. For my part, I believe that the light we have now been given is both clear and timely. Throughout these two thousand years the Church has sought in vain to fit Jerusalem into its place; and today, for us at least, God has graciously fitted it in. Just as at Hankow we saw the local responsibilities of the churches, so currently we see the regional character of the Work based upon a strong testimony at the center. If we should still hold on to the traditional idea of one worker per church, we would soon reach an impasse, for in the region of Pin Yang alone there are more than a hundred assemblies of believers, and these in themselves would devour more workers than we now have. How could we ever hope to meet the need of all China?

But if a strong testimony is preserved at the center, and if workers move to and fro, always returning to that center, but leaving the affairs of each assembly in the care of local brothers, then there is no such difficulty. Even the Twelve might have been hard put to it to preserve on their own a permanent preaching ministry throughout all Judea and Samaria, but for them to preserve such a ministry in Jerusalem was no problem at all.

And this is what is needed today. Let us take Shanghai as an example. In the purpose of God, it has served as a center for work that has grown up along the railroads to Nanking and Hangchow and in the region of the Kiangsu-Chekiang border. A strong testimony should therefore be maintained in Shanghai, reinforced by the presence of workers who move about the region from that city as their center. But all other churches in the area should be maintained by their own local brethren, not by workers posted there from Shanghai as "ministers" or "pastors." And at the same time some of the many believers now in Shanghai should be encouraged to migrate to fresh places—group after group going forth with the gospel. For the principle of Jerusalem is the principle of emigration, even if in our day it may not be persecution which sends us out preaching the Lord Jesus, as it did them.

Or take again Foochow. If Fukien Province and Taiwan

Island together represent a region of the Work, then according to our present understanding, Foochow may be regarded as its center. It is the brethren's responsibility, therefore, to maintain a strong testimony in that city, as they move from thence back and forth throughout the area. In such a center there will be apostles and elders ministering God's word, and from time to time two or three from among them will go out to one place and another to strengthen and help forward the Work. But that is not all; for the Work of the gospel in that area does not depend on these alone. The many brothers and sisters who have been brought to the Lord in Foochow we should now exhort to move out to other places. Encourage a score of believers to go to Nanping and settle there for the Lord's sake; let thirty go to Putien, thirty to Amoy; exhort other groups to cross over to Taipei and Tainan in Taiwan. As they move forth they carry the gospel with them. That is the right way. Should you instead attempt to send out so many evangelists within a number of years, you would be severely burdened with their financial support, you might have difficulty in finding enough suitable candidates, and the end results would probably be insignificant. No, it is the Church as a whole that must go forth with the message—band after band of believers moving out for the gospel's sake and penetrating even into the interior villages.

Need for Basic Training

It will be apparent from what we have said that the state of things at the center of such a field of Work comes to take on a new significance. Not only must a strong preaching ministry be maintained there in the face of a continual drain away of believers by emigration, but also the many who are sent out must go forth properly instructed if they are to become a source of strength and not of weakness in the places to which they go. Be they peddlers, ricksha men, domestic servants, or people of whatever trade or profession, they must know how to preach the gospel and win others to the Lord, and to be a definite help towards building up the local church in the areas to which they emigrate. All this calls for concentration of effort at the center. The labors of the workers must not be dissipated by scattering, but each center should be fully cared for, and provision made there for the saints to be instructed and prepared for the tasks ahead of them.

For it should be clear to us how important a matter is this training of the believers in the fundamentals of Christian life and witness. In order to prepare them for such adventuring forth as we have outlined above, all brothers and sisters need to be given a basic training. In Foochow and Shanghai we have already made some beginning in this. What are needed in all such centers of the Work are special instruction classes alongside the other ministries in the church. Such special meetings should continue weekly throughout the year, following a planned yearly curriculum. These meetings should not aim to progress too far, but should rather be repeated annually, so that no matter when a person joins them, after fifty-two weeks' instruction he will have completed the course. Thus those who move out and have opportunity to carry the gospel further afield will at least have completed this series of basic lessons.*

Only in this way will the tremendous task be completed, for if the preaching is to be left only to fully-trained evangelists, what impression will be made upon the whole of China? Today

---

*Published subsequently in Chinese and delivered originally by the author as messages during the same 1948 training sessions for workers (held at Kuling Mountain near Foochow, China) at which this present address was also delivered. Much later they were translated into English, re-arranged and variously grouped together into six volumes, and published under the general title of the *Basic Lesson Series* (New York, Christian Fellowship Publishers, Inc., 1972-75). The six individual volume titles in this series are as follows: *A Living Sacrifice* (1972), *The Good Confession* (1973), *Assembling Together* (1973), *Not I But Christ* (1974), *Do All to the Glory of God* (1974), and *Love One Another* (1975).—*Translator*

this country has 450 million inhabitants, only one million of whom are Christians.* But give all these Christians the sam . fundamental training and then send them forth, and very soon you will see the Church proclaiming the gospel to the farthest limits. They need not wait for tribulation. Whether persecuted or not, go forth they must. They can move out today, a few at a time, to different kinds of employment; and when they have led others to the Lord in the places where they are found, workers from the center may perhaps visit them; but already a church will have come into being in each new place.

Few will deny the superiority of this method of preaching the gospel, for when it is the Church that witnesses like this, God begins to work and people get saved. Even if in some localities the platform ministry may, we feel, leave something to be desired, by this method of spontaneous personal witness by the whole Church, the gospel at least is scattered widespread in every new area where believers are found, and where it is scattered the seed springs up and fruit is borne.

Workers Together

Furthermore, we see now, do we not, the supreme value of coordination in the Work? Without some true coordination, the sure result of all our labors will only be failure. In days past, perhaps, fellowship among some of us has been too weak. You have gone your way and he has gone his, and too often there has been loss as a result. From now on there must be among us all a new relatedness, if the great needs we have spoken of are to be met. No one can afford any longer just to be independent and make his own plans.

For here is the challenge. Since we have been shown the way, everything turns now upon the human vessels. True, until we saw the principle of Jerusalem, we could not but feel there

---

*The author's figures as of 1948.—*Translator*

was something wrong with our *way* of working, and this we have just reviewed at length. But today, as I read the book of Acts I look at Peter, the servant of God, and , observe how he conducted himself in those early days and learn a lesson from him. He might easily have gone off on his own and settled in, say, Joppa or Caesarea. But he did not, and I cannot but sympathize with him for the centuries-old misunderstanding of his motives in not doing so; for I now see clearly that he was right in coming back each time to Jerusalem and to the other apostles. The Work of God in any field does have a center, and that center implies fellowship.

Now, with new meaning, the way has been shown to us—the way of relatedness. God has made plain the need for coordination among the workers in any region, and the need too for coordination of the different responsibilities. If today, as brethren working from various centers, we will be faithful in this, and if the Lord is merciful, I believe it will not be many years before the whole of China is won to the gospel. And what a great prospect, to win the whole nation to Christ!

But if we should fail the Lord, I do assure you that in fifty years' time we shall be no further forward than we are today. Oh, I acknowledge that there has been much blessing from God upon us. For God desires to save souls, and in His mercy He has graciously saved quite a number among us. Yet I have not felt satisfied with the progress we have seen; and during recent days I have gone back to God's word again and again for light. It is true, I agree, that at Hankow eleven years ago we saw very clearly His way for the church; yet it is equally true that the gospel has been hindered, and even the churches have suffered, because we did not also see His way for the Work. Today, thank God, after many trials and sufferings, He has made known to us more clearly His way of working.

The opening chapters of Acts have a special lesson for the Church of God in every age. Just as the Jerusalem above is a figure of the Church in heaven, so Jerusalem on earth sets an example to the Church down here. Peter first worked there; and then, from there as his center, he went out to preach the gospel and returned. From there, too, the saints were driven forth by persecution; but, praise God, they could not flee Jerusalem without, in doing so, carrying everywhere the gospel with them. How glorious it is!

Today the question is not merely one of methods but of men. Will we be faithful to the Lord? If we will not, I say most solemnly that He may be compelled to set us aside, and to choose, perhaps ten or twenty years hence, others who will press on in His way. But I ask myself, need twenty years be thus thrown away? Surely they need not. Let me do my part and you do yours. As we go forth in His Name, let us go in fellowship, speaking of Him everywhere. And before long we shall see the Church's testimony established in many more places yet, until this whole land has heard the good news of the gospel. What tribulation we have been through to discover this road! May we not lose it.

1 The Order of Church Offices

In the church, there are only two offices: one is the office of the deacon, and the other is that of the elders or bishops.

(1) THE DEACONS

According to the Scriptures, the work of the deacons is to serve. They have no other duty. God has not set up deacons as authorities. Their function lies exclusively in the area of serving or waiting upon others. The word for "deacon" in the Greek is the same as that which is translated "minister," as in the case of "the minister of the word." It means to serve or to manage affairs. One may call it either service or ministry, yet they are the same. Among the Protestants, for example, the Anglican Church prefers to use the English word "ministry," whereas the Wesleyans prefer the word "service." Since the Wesleyans have come out of the Anglican Church, they consider the word used by the Anglicans as sounding too official; hence they prefer to use a comparatively more common word. Nevertheless, whether ministry or service, they mean the same thing.

For Those with Spiritual Understanding

Since this office of deacon is set up in the Church exclusively for the purpose of service, it is well from the inception of a local church's existence to allow all the brothers and sisters to serve. Some of them will be steady and dependable, and will therefore have spiritual weight. These brethren the church may set apart as deacons (or deaconesses). Accordingly, all the brothers and sisters serve, but only the trustworthy with spiritual weight should formally be made deacons (or deaconesses). The work is performed generally; but the office is for the trustworthy and spiritual only, for we do not wish to see the constant changing of deacons.

In this regard, let us be careful in the choosing of deacons that we do not select those who, though they may be long on the ability to do things, are short on spiritual understanding. This is a great danger as well as a great temptation to the workers. Some brothers and sisters are very capable, and how we like to make such ones deacons. Capable though they are, however, they tend to inject their worldly wisdom and worldly ways into the church. Consequently, in the selection of deacons, we must seek for brethren who know the way of the Lord as well as know how to do things. We must look for a person who has spiritual understanding before the Lord as well as spiritual worth; otherwise, worldly maneuverings and worldly ways and means will all be brought into the church. For although things may be successfully accomplished, the church will, by such a one, be changed into a society. This is completely out of order.

Keep in mind that we must maintain the spiritual standard of the church. On the one hand, we should not despise talent; on the other hand, we must not indulge too much in it. We cannot permit people to bring worldly ability and wisdom into the church, because a slight carelessness in this area will invite worldly maneuvers into the church. And the problem thus created for the future will not only be great but will also be a difficult one to solve.

As to the rest, I think the Bible has given clear instructions on the qualifications of the deacons. Here I would wish to emphasize only two things: that (1) a deacon be one who not only is able to serve but will do so diligently; and that (2) he have spiritual understanding. Such kind of person may then be made a deacon.

(2) THE ELDERS

The Scripture also speaks much concerning the office of elder. This office is for the purpose of managing or governing the church.

May Not Be Simultaneously Ministers of God's Word

An elder may not necessarily be a minister of God's word. It is of course more commendable if he is also such a minister. According to the Bible, a minister of God's word is different from an office in the church. And it is clear that elders fill a church office—an office that was established for the purpose of executing, governing and supervising the whole church. Yet an elder may or may not at the same time be a minister of God's word. "Let the elders that rule well be counted worthy of double honor," wrote Paul, "especially those who labor in the word and in teaching" (1 Tim. 5.17).

Basic Qualification Is Spirituality

The Bible has clear instructions on elders. Here I wish to remind brethren of the basic qualification for an elder—that such a person must have spiritual worth: that he knows spiritual things and possesses spiritual understanding, that he is familiar with God's ways. In other words, an elder must be experienced in spiritual matters and be able to discern the spiritual conditions of God's children so that he may manage the affairs of the church. This spiritual foundation he must have to begin with. And with the gift and ability which God has added to him, he is then able to take care of the church. Only such persons can become elders in the church.

I hope you brethren will not choose one to be an elder simply because he is capable—simply because he can manage things, but at the same time he has no spiritual understanding before God. I am aware of the problems which have arisen in a number of places, and this is due, in my opinion, to selecting people to be elders who are well known in society, who have position and ability, and who have depth of worldly experience. Please recognize that a person may be able to manage a society or a home, but he is not necessarily capable of governing the church. And why is this so? It is simply because the basic requirement for governing the church is one of spirituality.

Executive Experience Is Useless

Once there was a brother who had had twenty years of executive experience. Many brothers asked me why he had not been invited to be an elder. My reply was this: twenty years of executive experiences in the world does not count for even one single year in the church, that although he was a good Christian, his understanding of spiritual things proved to be insufficient. The Church is something spiritual, and therefore only the one who has spiritual measure before God and who knows spiritual ways and is spiritual can be an elder. Otherwise, you will have a problem on your hands immediately.

We would rather choose people to be elders who have spiritual measure but without much or any working ability rather than those who have the latter but not the former. Of course, it is better to have elders who possess both qualities—who understand spiritual things and are also capable of managing affairs. For how can a person take care of the house of God if he is not able to manage his own household? Yet does this imply that whoever can govern his own house can equally govern God's church? Not at all, for if spirituality is the basic requirement in being an elder, then one can reason that not all who are able to manage households can necessarily manage the house of God. Quite a few, including unsaved people, can govern their houses well; nevertheless, can we on that basis alone ask them to govern the church? No, only a person who knows the spiritual way and is successful in his home management may govern the church of God.

Hence in selecting responsible brothers, we must choose those men with spiritual measure, who are acquainted with the spiritual way, who are not prone to pride, vaunting, and self-importance. Their life before God must be steadfast. Choose only those whose life is trustworthy; do not pick the proud. Do not select as elders the so-called genius among you, but choose the reliable. Such ones must be steady and trustworthy, who possess spiritual weight, knowledge and understanding. These and these alone may be chosen as elders.

Rule Well His Own House

Yet even finding a few men such as these, attention then must be turned to their ability to rule their own households. Those who rule their own houses well can be made elders, but anyone who cannot govern their own houses cannot at all govern the church.

If the Church were a worldly institution, we would only need to choose capable people. But the Church is a spiritual organism, and therefore the first qualification to be raised is the one of spirituality, and *then* ability, and so forth. Moreover, an elder must be dependable. He cannot be a person who changes every so often like the swaying of a drunkard this way and that way. Such a man cannot possibly rule the church. To govern the church, an elder must be one who is steadfast and reliable. At the same time, he must know how to rule his family well. Many problems in the church can be eliminated if those chosen as elders have spiritual understanding as well as an ability to rule well; otherwise, the spiritual side of the church will be damaged even if various matters are successfully being managed. Hence do not reverse the order between the foundation and its superstructure—that is to say, do not choose a man who is only capable of management. Such a person may at most be a deacon, but never an elder: he may *receive* orders but not *give* them in the church.

An Example

There was once a brother, now dead, who was at one time an elder in a church. During our early Shanghai days, he frequently visited me and conversed with me. He was a good brother, capable and zealous, but with little or no spiritual understanding. He was very much lacking in spiritual experience. Once during a conversation with me he said: "There was a sister among us. She wept in the meeting because she had committed sin. Mr. Nee, do you not think this laughable?" When he had finished speaking, he just sat there and laughed aloud. A church elder had considered the weeping confession of a sister to be laughable! You can see by this, can you not, where he stood spiritually? Without a doubt he would be reckoned as top management in any worldly institution, but how poorly he bore responsibility in the church. And why? Because he himself had never cried over his own sins, and consequently, as an elder who witnessed someone else crying, he treated it only as a joke! What spiritual insensitivity! To cry over sin is the most elementary of spiritual experience, and yet he was totally ignorant of it. He looked at spiritual matters in a bizarre fashion, even viewing them as quite laughable. He had no spiritual understanding. I only mention this as an illustration. Similiar incidents occur throughout the Church in large numbers. If these such as this man become elders it will spell the end of the spiritual life of the church.

The Church Specializes in Spiritual Things

Let me use another illustration. Suppose you meet a most clever and capable person today. If he were to be invited to join a hospital, he could at most be asked to serve as the general manager of the hospital, he could not be asked to serve as a resident physician. This is because he might be able to look after business affairs but he most certainly could not attend to patients' sicknesses, since a hospital is basically a medical and technical institution and not a business corporation. Or if he were asked to join a commercial school, he could be the business manager of the school, perhaps, but not the dean or principal of the school; for to fill these latter posts requires special technological background and knowledge. Now just as a hospital is particularly specialized in healing the sick, and just as a commercial school is specialized in teaching commerce and finance, so a church exists in a special way for performing spiritual functions; and therefore, only those with spirituality can govern its affairs.

Let it be known that the Church is first and foremost spiritual in nature, its business or administrative aspect being only secondary. Hence in your choosing elders in various localities, spirituality must be the first thing you look for, and only then is the ability to direct, supervise and lead to be a consideration. To have the ability to lead is not enough to be an elder; he must also have spiritual experience and understanding. Having experience in spiritual things and an ability in managing affairs are the criteria for eldership. Yet spirituality is the predominant qualification for the choice of any elder.

Train the Elders

As you may recall, Paul himself lived in Ephesus for a time

and there were elders in the Ephesian church. While there, he gave these elders sufficient training. So that he could say to them at his farewell: "I shrank not from declaring unto you anything that was profitable, and teaching you publicly, and from house to house, . . . among whom I went about preaching the kingdom . . . For I shrank not from declaring unto you the whole counsel of God. Take heed unto yourselves, and to all the flock, in which the Holy Spirit hath made you overseers, to feed the church of the Lord which he purchased with his own blood. . . . Wherefore watch ye, remembering that by the space of three years I ceased not to admonish every one night and day with tears" (Acts 20.20-31 mg.). He by the Holy Spirit had not only appointed them as elders but had also trained them. He did not merely commit the church into their care and let them try their best; he in addition helped them and instructed them how to function as elders.

Later on, Paul left Timothy at Ephesus and Titus in Crete so that they themselves should appoint elders. By reading Paul's letter to Timothy and his letter to Titus we can readily see that it is not enough simply to appoint elders, but additionally they must be helped to serve together. In these letters Paul advised the two young apostles that they must *train* the elders whom they appointed in the churches. There are many charges in these two letters, and these charges pertain to instructions as to how to work together with the elders in the church: "These things write I unto thee, hoping to come unto thee shortly; but if I tarry long, that thou mayest know how men ought to behave themselves in the house of God, which is the church of the living God, the pillar and ground of the truth" (1 Tim. 3.14,15).

What is the relationship between the apostolic worker and the elders? In appointing elders in a certain locality, the worker does not merely appoint them—committing all authority into their hands—and then let them carry on (even as it were, let them go wrong). Not at all. After the elders are chosen, you as a worker must continue to observe how they operate, and train them to do things. Only then may you go to another place to appoint and to train. Otherwise, shortly after a local assembly is established and the elders are appointed, it will cease to grow. For here is a group of men who have never managed church affairs before. True, they may have a *little* spiritual experience; nevertheless, they do not know how to govern in the church. How can you expect them not to go wrong?

Today your responsibility as workers is rather weighty. You should seek opportunity to train elders to be such. Many people are by habit somewhat frivolous. And if later they are the ones who come to manage the affairs in the church, they may be frivolous and careless as before. You must therefore help them. Whenever their attitude displays itself as being loose and flippant, they should be reminded that they are dealing with spiritual matters before God; and consequently they cannot afford to be so light and playful. Some people are used to speaking and criticizing in a thoughtless manner when managing worldly affairs. And more likely than not they may bring this very same habit into the church. Now if you hear such critical and careless words fall from their lips, you should immediately let it be known that in the church it is submission and not opinion which is important. We need to learn obedience and not be so opinionated.

Perhaps some people will manipulate spiritual things. You need to remind them that among God's children there is no place for manipulation. We must *deal* with situations in the church, not try to avoid them. Those who can deal with situations are truly qualified to be elders, not those who attempt to avoid matters.

Some others may be so accustomed to being heads of their families or their firms that their attitude tends to be forceful, their speech tough, and their spirit hard. You must help them to speak firmly yet in a tender spirit. It is the combination of these two that will accomplish things.

Although all these facets of being an elder may seem small, they nonetheless are basic. How terrible it will be if the elders of a church are afraid of anything happening and so they let things slide without dealing with them. Such persons cannot be elders. Yet neither should elders always be seeking opportunity to breathe out anger and disapproval. Their spirit must be broken before God. They have to be smitten by the Lord so that they are delivered from any personal feelings. They must be tender before God, yet firm in dealing with the matters that confront them.

As you train the brothers in so conducting themselves, then quite naturally, when they approach the church in terms of managing its affairs, they will not be careless nor will they bring their hardness into it. Remind them continually that they are in the church, not in their homes or offices. You must help them by means of spiritual admonitions, and after some days they will be able to rule the church well.

The Elders Meeting

I believe all the responsible brothers who serve as elders in various localities must meet together once a week. You may call such a time the elders meeting or caring meeting. This is the time when the responsible brothers pray together. This is also the time when they see brothers and sisters.

I know of a local assembly (not in China) where on a certain day of the week the responsible brothers gather themselves together. In the morning those brothers will come with their lunch, and there they engage in the management of the affairs of the church. They pray over every item which needs to be considered. Although we may not be able to spend an entire day, we can at least set aside half a day or a few hours each week for the responsible brothers to meet.

Using Half the Time Considering Affairs Before God

During the first half of the appointed time, the responsible brothers should close the door to everything else except the consideration of church affairs before God. They should reverently and carefully consider every item in the presence of the Lord. They can discuss these matters, and fellowship on the light they receive. Yet things are not to be settled by discussion. The Bible shows us that one facet to dealing with church matters is discussion; even so, discussion is for the sake of finding light and not necessarily for making any decision. Discussion is for finding out the facts—to lay the matter out; it is not for making the decision.

Using Latter Half of Time Receiving Brethren

Set apart the latter part of the elders' time to receive the brethren. Whether there will be brothers or sisters actually seeking an interview, the responsible brothers must nonetheless be there and available. Time must be set aside for this purpose, for it will greatly help in the governing of the church.

The Worker Should Meet with Responsible Brothers

The worker or workers should stand by and observe how these responsible brothers function. There are certain things which need to be exposed and communicated to these responsible brothers. For example, their frivolity needs to be corrected, their attitude and spirit must be adjusted. Remind them also that they are dealing with spiritual affairs. Sometimes they need to be taught how to answer questions or how to explain things. At the beginning, perhaps the worker should answer the questions which are asked, and should afterwards explain to the responsible brothers why the questions are answered in such ways, explain what is the scriptural basis for such answers, and identify what the inner feelings are. Moreover, when some brother comes for an interview, he may need to be reprimanded. Then after that brother leaves, an explanation for such an action should be given to the responsible brothers. Later on, the worker may sit by the responsible brothers and let them answer.

Train Some Trustworthy Responsible Brothers

We believe in the ministry of the body—that is to say, the entire church is to serve. It is not two to three persons serving; rather, the whole church must serve. Hence it is a serious mistake if the Work does not cause more brethren to serve. Yet even with many people being saved and many serving, the Work is still a complete failure if it does not produce some trustworthy brethren to bear responsibility in the church. I hope as you go forth to work that you will be very busy and not just generally busy, because there are many works you will have to commence from the beginning.

Do see that much work awaits you, not least of which is the matter of training some responsible brothers. Do not so labor that you end up bearing all the responsibilities, thus leaving no strength in yourselves to train others for responsibility.

The principle of the church is seen in our Lord Jesus putting himself in the midst of the twelve disciples, then the Twelve putting themselves among the three thousand, and the three thousand then placing themselves among the millions. Accordingly, as workers, place yourselves in the midst of a few responsible brothers, and these responsible brothers shall in turn put themselves in the midst of the brothers and sisters, who in turn again shall place themselves in the midst of a number of sinners: with the result that the circle grows ever wider and wider. Unless this is done, I will consider our ministry to be a huge failure.

You must therefore train the elders at various localities to be able to take responsibility. Paul did not leave Titus at Crete and Timothy at Ephesus merely to appoint elders and then to depart. He instructed them to train those whom they appointed as elders until the latter themselves could know and handle responsibility. Such is the way for the church.

Hence I hope hereafter that you all will be busy, very busy. May there be no one who is lazy, for the lazy are of no use to the Lord. Do realize that for you to put yourselves in the midst of the responsible brothers, your spiritual condition must be superior to theirs; otherwise, you will not be able to help them.

Show Them How to Do Things

Concerning the training of responsible brothers, each time you gather with them, you should show them how to do things. Suppose you stay in one locality for three months. During that period you should arrange a time to gather the responsible brothers and train them how to manage church affairs. Talk with them about all the matters of the week ahead which concern the church and pray with them. During the first half of that time do not see anyone, but shut yourselves in to God alone, because this part of the time is devoted to taking care of things before the Lord. It is not unlike the time when Moses and Joshua were up on the mountain.

After you have settled these affairs, you go out and notify the deacons as to what needs to be done in the week. There are things which all the brethren should be notified about by the deacons, and there are also things which need to be distributed by them to the brethren to do.

In managing church affairs, the first thing is in knowing how in fact to manage, but the second is in knowing how to supervise. Here you must never be passive. In the early stage you have to be more active, taking the lead and superintending. Only when the brothers and sisters have been built up must you let them go ahead and do the work. This is the church. At the beginning you cannot let the brothers and sisters do things by themselves. You must give yourself to the responsible brothers and then the responsible brothers must give themselves to all the local brothers and sisters.

The elders meeting must be very solemn. During those few hours they are shut in with God. They will place everything concerning the church before Him and seek to know how to deal with each item. Decisions should then be made known to the brethren or to the deacons. And later on have a few hours set aside in which to receive the local brothers and sisters who seek help. And make sure that at that time brothers and sisters can find *all* of the elders there, not just one of them.

The Church Is All Brothers and Sisters Serving

You workers must work until one day all the brothers and sisters start to serve. That is to say, everyone is to be serving God, everyone is to be functioning as a priest. Then you will really see what the church is.

I wonder if you have truly seen this way or not? You must understand this way. And the way is to give yourself to some brothers, and these brothers in turn are to give themselves to all the brothers and sisters. And as all the brothers and sisters are serving, you shall witness the church. If in the church only one ministry (that of the elders) is active and all the brothers and sisters are passive, at that point it is not a church but a denomination. Let me reiterate that if you cannot arrive at the ultimate goal of getting all the brothers and sisters to rise up and serve, your work is a total failure because there is not the reality of the church. Be ever mindful that this we have been saying here is your way—that you give yourself to the elders and that you show them they are not to monopolize all the church affairs. They are overseers, not monopolizers. They are not to be a substitute for the whole church in its work, but rather they are to supervise the whole church itself in working. The elders do not do all the works themselves; on the contrary, they encourage and teach all the brothers and sisters in the church to perform its work. And when that point is reached, you do have the reality of the church.

Elders Meeting Is Source of Activities

The elders meeting is the source of all activities. Many things originate from it and many problems find their solutions there. When the brothers and sisters notice how the responsible brothers deal with various affairs before God, they realize these are not casual and nonessential matters, and therefore the brethren must walk softly before the Lord. If the elders meeting is conducted in this matter, all the brothers and sisters will be helped.

Read More of Timothy and Titus

More and more people need to read Paul's letters to Timothy and his one letter to Titus. Observe how God through Paul instructs them to train and to lead. Learn from these letters how to help the responsible brothers place themselves among all the brothers and sisters and lead the whole church into service.

Appointment of the Responsible Brothers

Someone asks how the dilemma can be solved when in appointing people to be responsible brothers there is still a little reservation about them and yet the need is obviously there to appoint them? The answer is as follows: gather together some whom you sense are promising, and tell them to first come and learn to take responsibility. You should train them how to bear responsibility. Some might be made deacons first before they are made elders. So that in choosing them and gathering them together, be careful as to what you say to them. Tell them you are readying them for the work of deacons. Do not tell them at the outset that they have been chosen to be elders. By so doing you will be in a position to observe which of them are fit to be deacons, and which of them are more advanced than the rest. Then, after a certain time has elapsed, you can put them either in the position of elder or in that of deacon. But if you were to make them elders at the very beginning, it would be very, very difficult to change their position afterwards. To change the position of a deacon is comparatively easy, but to change that of an elder is extremely difficult.

Observe Spiritual Future

Especially in the choosing of elders, eyes need to be wide open to perceive what is the spiritual future of this or that person. This is not said to suggest that we cannot be mistaken, since we do indeed often make mistakes. It is only meant to convey that the issue is one of spirituality. You should be very careful before God in bringing these brothers into such a realm. For in the event an elder is unfit and needs his position to be changed, he no doubt will be hurt by it. It is a hard thing to set up authority and then attempt to overturn it. We must therefore learn to discern before God the current spiritual condition of these brothers and also their spiritual future.

Many people are good material. Do not spoil them but train them well. Do not be hasty about setting in people as elders. Whether or not you have confidence in these brothers, it is best if at the outset you tell them you are asking them, as the more promising ones among the flock, to come and learn how to manage church affairs, and that you will show them how.

Helping Responsible Brothers in a District

In the future, where a local assembly is also a Work center, the following can be done. Suppose the center is in Peking.

You notice that there are three brothers in the region of Suiyuan and also two brothers in the assembly at Taiyuan who are very promising. You can invite them to Peking and ask them to attend the responsible brothers meeting there.

However, such a meeting is not open to everyone. It is a holy time, a privilege given only to those for learning. At first, let such brothers sit in on the meeting to observe how spiritual affairs are handled before God, how problems are solved, how questions are discussed, how prayers are offered, and how decisions are made. Also, they can be shown how brothers and sisters are received, how fellowship is extended to brethren who come from abroad, and how requests for baptism and the breaking of bread are answered. Set an example before them. After a while, you may even ask them to answer some of the questions that confront you in order for you to see how well they conduct themselves.

After some time, they may be sent back to their original localities to allow them to try it out but without giving them any position. A few days later you may visit their places and hear what the brethren there say about them. Of course all criticisms are not necessarily correct, but at least you will know the things which they have done. The criticisms of some people are untrustworthy because such ones never submit to authority. But if a brother is really wrong, you should try to find out where the root of the problem lies. And then on your next visit, you will be clear as to the fitness of that person to take responsibility.

Must Be Solemn

At the elders meeting, you must hold the reins but you must let the local responsible brothers also hold the reins. Show them that such a time is even more solemn than was the time when Moses was on the mountain, for he merely passed on the Law, but we today govern the church. I truly consider the management of the church as far exceeding in seriousness the receiving of the two tables of the Law of Moses at Mount Sinai.

During this time, let the whole atmosphere be solemn. No flippancy is to be allowed. As soon as people come to such a meeting, let them see that we have come to manage the things of the church in God's very presence, and therefore we cannot afford to be careless. This is similar to the time when the high priest entered the holiest place of all. It is the time when we serve our God. Let there be few idle words, for if there are many such words, the time will be wasted.

Speak Nothing Behind the Back

Anyone attending the elders meeting who fails to voice his opinion in the meeting and yet speaks his view to brothers and sisters afterwards should be reprimanded at the next session. Such a person is not fit to be a responsible brother. If anyone has feelings on a matter and has words to say about it, he ought to express them when the responsible brothers are gathered together. Silence in the elders meeting but talkativeness outside its precincts is being double-tongued. Such a person should not be in the elders meeting, for such conduct is unchristianly. If anyone has any feeling about a matter, he should express it in the elders meeting; otherwise, he should keep his mouth closed anywhere else.

Please realize that in the early church, the very life of a local assembly lay in the elders meeting. If the elders meeting becomes something loose and careless, if matters are decided without prayer, God's work is finished in that locality and there is no spiritual weight there.

I hope all the responsible brothers know that they are all wholly responsible for anything said behind the back of the elders meeting. There should be no personal consideration shown towards any elder, but on the contrary, the one who conducts himself in such a fashion must be strictly admonished by saying to him: "Brother, this was *not* true Christian behavior. If you have something to say, say it before the other responsible brothers. For you destroy the oneness of the body if you talk behind the back of the other elders."

Cannot Tell One's Wife

Another thing to be noticed here is that whatever happens in an elders meeting should not be told to any other brother or to any sister—not even to one's own wife. This is a sacred trust which all must maintain. Nothing in the elders meeting can be carelessly spread. There must not be any leak of information. The brothers must be strictly trained in this respect. Unless all agree otherwise, nothing should be told outside the meeting. There is no need, however, for the elders assembled to be reminded of this each time they meet, since not to tell anyone on the outside is the understood rule among those elders.

How Decision Is Made Need Not Be Told

As the responsible brothers make things public, they have no need to tell how the decision was arrived at in the elders meeting. It is best to leave this information buried.

All Meetings Must Be Brought High

If the elders meeting is strong, all the other meetings of the church will naturally be lifted to a higher level. For this meeting is the center of everything. Much spiritual energy must be spent on this meeting. All the brothers who attend must concentrate themselves in weighing every matter before God.

"Watchtower" of the Church

This elders meeting is "the watchtower" of the church.

Many things yet unknown to the brethren are known by the responsible brothers. Many things still unseen by the brethren are already seen by the responsible brothers. Oftentimes the responsible brothers sense things before the other brethren do. The fact of the matter is that everything concerning the church must be first sensed in this meeting. Before problems arise, they are already known there. And therefore, certain things may be done before the problems even rear their heads. Learn to perceive things in advance.

I do not say that there is no need to pray individually or to wait. I only say that at the elders meeting it is time to deal with matters collectively. Naturally, each one must have preparation beforehand. For without being prepared there will be nothing to say and to decide in the elders meeting. If there is nothing to discuss or implement in the elders meeting, it is a positive proof that the responsible brothers are lazy before God. If some of them are strong and have their eyes open, there will doubtless be many things to deal with at the meeting. The high priest wore the breastplate with the names of the Twelve Tribes inscribed on it. Each time he went into the presence of God he wore this breastplate. Not on a single day could he put aside the breastplate. Similarly, you should learn to bear the assembly before God daily, and daily some concerns for the brethren will be found. And as a result, you will discover that normally there will not be enough time in the elders meeting to handle all such concerns. Several hours can so quickly pass away that sometimes words have to be cut short because there is no time left.

If the elders meeting is strong, whatever follows will be easy. All the other meetings in the church are to be watched over in the elders meeting. If, for example, the gospel meeting happens to be weak today, the elders will focus their strength on it and mobilize the strength of the whole assembly towards it. The elders meeting is therefore "the watchtower" of the church.

Respected by All

The elders meeting should be so conducted that it draws respect from all the brothers and sisters. All know that this is a time when the responsible brothers are managing the affairs of the church before God. I often view the elders meeting as being somewhat similar to the prayer room of John G. Paton's father. His house was not large: a bedroom on one side, a kitchen on the other, and in between a small study. But when the door of the study room was closed, all his sons knew that their father was engaged in business with God. Every child tiptoed around the house and dared not make any noise. They could never forget the groanings in the study even after five decades. John himself commented that "even today I can still hear my father praying for me in that room." Let all the brothers and sisters know that this is the time when the responsible brothers are doing business with God as they give their all for the church.

Two Different Situations

Today we need two different situations before God. One is the need of *fellowship* among brothers and sisters. I believe that after working on this problem for the past twenty years, there has been gradual progress. Thank God that today brothers and sisters have at least some consciousness and feeling towards other brothers and sisters. The other situation is the need to recognize God's *authority*. Brotherly love is one thing, to be servants before the Lord is another. We must learn to obey God's orders. As we go out to serve, we need to hear His word before we go out. This we must learn together today

The Most Solemn Hour

This hour among the elders is most solemn. It is a time when we learn to wait on the Lord with single-mindedness and to know how to manage things before God. There should be no hindrance, and everything must be done well with godliness and assurance. I tell you, the church has a future.

We may become very familiar and easy at other times, but when we come to the hour of the elders meeting, familiarity is out of the question, for we are truly approaching the presence of God. During ordinary times we focus on brotherly love, but at this hour we draw near to God together as His servants in order to receive orders and to implement His will. Let us learn to be still before God and hear Him. And if we are not clear concerning His will, we will inquire and search before Him. Learn before the Lord and pray.

2 Priestly Ministry

Concerning priestly ministry, I believe the first thing to do is to set forth the basic underlying principle, which is, that all God's children are priests and all should therefore serve God. If we are governed by this principle, we shall see how to help all the brothers and sisters to function as priests in their local assemblies. In other words, we shall seek how to arrange spiritual activities so that the entire body of believers—both beginners and those who have trusted the Lord for a number of years—may participate. We will now spend a little time together finding out what are the various spiritual endeavors in a local assembly the brothers and sisters can all take part in.

Several Spiritual Activities All Believers Should Do

A few things to begin with which all the local brothers and sisters can participate in are the following:

(1) Preach the gospel.

(2) Visit those who profess to have received the gospel they have heard, and lead them into the right path of being Christians.

(3) Visit new Christians. They have believed, and have been led into the right path; now they need to be helped to go on.

(4) Take care of special needs. In the church there are many such needs. Some have family problems, some are sick. Some experience distress, some have funerals, and some have

weddings. All these should have the help of the church. We may put all such activities under the general heading of "care visitation." This is a kind of work in which all the brothers and sisters can be involved.

(5) Care for saints who go abroad or come from abroad. I look upon this kind of service as being a very important one. For after we issue letters of recommendation to brothers and sisters who go to other localities, we still need to look after them. And with regard to people who come from outside, we must provide them special care as well.

Let us take up each of these various works one at a time.

(1) *Preaching the gospel.* Let us notice that among the ministers of God's word whom the Lord sets up in the Church is the evangelist (Eph. 4.11). But Paul exhorts Timothy to "do the work of an evangelist" (2 Tim. 4.5). By comparing these two passages, we shall see that some people are called by God to be evangelists whereas some may not be evangelists and yet they are to do the work of an evangelist. In other words, the evangelist must preach the gospel, but whoever is not an evangelist should nevertheless do the work of an evangelist. An evangelist is a special "gift-person" from God given to the Church. If God calls you to be an evangelist, you should preach the gospel with singleness of heart and bring people to the Church. If God has not appointed you as an evangelist, you and all God's other children should nonetheless "do the work of an evangelist"—even as the word of the Lord has indicated.

To put it another way, "the work of an evangelist" is to be done by those who cannot do it as well as by those who can. This work must be carried on universally. Young people like Timothy should do it. Everybody else should do it.

For this reason, encourage the entire assembly of brothers and sisters to spend time in doing the work of an evangelist. We should never be lazy and forget the sinners, nor should we simply let a few carry on this work alone. Let all the brothers and sisters be reminded that they all are priests and all must therefore serve God.

(2) *Gospel care.* This is also what we ought to do before God. We expect all the brothers and sisters to learn responsibility in this area too.

This responsibility starts with bringing unbelievers to the meeting and does not cease until they are baptized. The work of gospel visitation includes bringing people from home, school, hospital or office to the meeting, and looking after them until they know the Lord themselves and are baptized.

Bring People to Gospel Meeting

Have the brothers and sisters bring people to gospel meetings. Do not have them bring too many at one time. Though it is good to bring more, yet in order to take care of them properly it is better that only three or four persons be brought each time. This is not a rule, but probably four is a good maximum number. This does not mean that if there is opportunity to bring more, people cannot bring them. In case they wish to bring more, have them seek out the responsible brothers and ask them to arrange some other brothers and sisters to share their responsibility.

Sit with Them

Let us discuss how we should take care of the friends in a gospel meeting. If you bring four people, seat two of them on each of your two sides. When the Bible is read, find the place in the Scriptures for them. When singing, find the hymn for them also. Do not treat them as geniuses. Since they may never have sung hymns or read the Bible before, you must help them.

During the preaching, if someone does not understand, explain it in a whisper. When G. Paget Wilkes was preaching in

Shanghai, he told the following joke. An Englishman went to Japan and preached the gospel in a large public auditorium. Many people were there that day. At one point the English preacher said to his audience, "You all know, of course, how the children of Israel came out of Egypt." Paget Wilkes hurriedly went up to him and whispered that he might have to spend two hours to explain to the people who these Israelites were and what the exodus was all about! From this story we should realize that there are many things our unbelieving friends may not understand. Although we cannot spend two hours as humorously suggested by Paget Wilkes to explain, we may at least use two or three sentences to do so.

Strengthen and Help the Preaching with Prayer

The greatest work any of the brethren can do is to support the gospel preaching. For the preaching of the gospel is not for believers to hear or to criticize. It is aimed at the sinners. So that while you sit by the people you have invited, and as you sense that certain words spoken carry a great impact, or that the spirit of the preacher is being released, you should silently pray, saying something like the following: "O Lord, send this word into people's hearts. Use this word to save this person. Lord, use this word to save even these two people." Thus you add weight to the word preached with such prayer. And you also pray for the people in your care.

Accept Seating Arrangement

Some who have not brought anyone to the gospel meeting may help by taking care of those who have brought more. It will be good if all the brothers and sisters sit either on one side or at the back, or stand near the door so that the brothers in charge of care that day may make the necessary arrangements. The friends from outside who attend need to be escorted. They are coming to hear the gospel, hence we can keep them company. Even if they are not brought in by you, you can still be one of those who sit with them. Gospel care is therefore twofold in nature: one is to bring people in, the other is to take care of them in the meeting. We who are responsible for the management of the church must so work until all the brothers and sisters are serving in the assembly.

At Time of Drawing Net

At each gospel meeting, there should be "the drawing of the net" so to speak. To *cast* a net is one thing, to *draw* a net is another. When the gospel net begins to be drawn in either by asking people to raise their hands or to accept the Lord, brothers and sisters need to join in and help. The ways of drawing in the net are varied. There is much liberty as to the ways, so long as the net is eventually drawn. At that time, there are many things one can do. Some hitherto unconverted ones need a little nudging and then they will come in. Others need to be pushed and then they fall in. Brethren should pray on the one hand and persuade on the other. If you know for sure that your friend's refusal to stand up is due to pride, then you should exhort him to humble himself. Or if you know it is the love of the world that hinders him from standing up, you can plead with him by saying, "Why do you still long for the world? Why will you wait until the next time? If you feel you are ready, do not wait."

Do Not Wait Till Four Months Later

One matter which is of great importance in the preaching of the gospel is this: do not wait till four months later. Many people involved in gospel preaching have the wrong concept of waiting four months; but the Lord Jesus declares this to us: "Say not ye, There are yet four months, and then cometh the harvest? behold, I say unto you, Lift up your eyes, and look on the fields, that they are white already unto harvest" (John 4.35). How very strange is the Lord's answer here. We need to see that the harvest of the gospel far exceeds human expectation. Do not be so foolish as to imagine that there must necessarily be four months until harvest once the seed is sown. The Lord Jesus views it differently here, for He says that whenever you sow, you may harvest immediately! There is no such "four months' principle" in His thinking!

Some people may appear to be totally ignorant. Yet keep in mind that whether their understanding is opened or not does not depend on you but on the enlightening of the Holy Spirit. I know of at least a few brothers who pretended to believe but who nonetheless ended up being really saved. We therefore must encourage them in season and out.

After the Meeting

After the meeting is over, brethren can stay with their friends, praying with them and conversing with them. Bring them to the Lord, lead them in prayer, and help them to accept Christ. Then you can obtain from them their names and addresses. Be sure the address is correct, since this will save the time of those who do gospel visitation. If possible, ask them when they will be free and what will be the most convenient time to visit them. Write all this information down quickly lest they get bored. Then give the record to the responsible brothers as reference for future visitation.

Instill Need and Knowledge

Some people accept Christ out of felt needs, but they do not have any gospel knowledge. Other people *have* gospel knowledge but they do not sense need. Still others have both need and knowledge, yet they cannot make a decision at once. All these people must be helped. Create need for those who feel no need, supply knowledge to those who have no knowledge, and help the hesitant ones in making a decision.

Tell Them of Baptism

After people have been brought clearly to the Lord, they should be informed immediately of baptism. Look after them, seek them out many times until they are brought to the place where they are ready to be baptized.

Before Meeting Begins

Another thing to be added here is that sometimes it may be embarrassing for people in a gospel meeting. For example, long before the gospel meeting has ever started people may already be sitting there. Some of them may come as much as an hour early. I can assure you that there are two places where time seems unbearably long: one is in hell, the other is in the church. For the one who goes to hell, he finds time intolerably long there. But to the unsaved who come to church, he too feels that time is terribly long. If these people come early and the gospel is not being preached yet, they may go away or they may sit there wondering what it is all about. At times I have a deep feeling inside me as I have looked out at the faces of the people sitting there waiting: they have always appeared to me to be like sheep without a shepherd. They surely need to be taken care of before the meeting starts.

One of the ways they can be taken care of is to not let the unbelievers sit together. Instead, try to arrange at the beginning to have one or two believers sitting on either side of them. All who participate in such work must be fully equipped with tracts, gospel messages, and a Bible. If because of our neglect these unbelievers just sit there unattended, even the most enthusiastic among them will turn cold.

All Function As Priests

None of the work already described can at all be accomplished without the entire body of believers participating in it. Show the brethern they *all* are priests, and that accordingly everyone has something to do. This will make the gospel meeting strong, for this will be the entire church preaching the gospel rather than just the few. Unless all are involved, where is the church?

As Many As Are Priests

Let me underscore what we have said before, that as many as are the people who serve, so that many are the people in the church—as many as are priests, so that many are the people of God. Do not invert the order and say that as many as are the people of God so that many are priests. That is the wrong order. It should instead be: as many there are who serve, so just that many are the people of God.

Functionless Members

When I was in England, a brother once said to me: "Many in the body are functioning members, but many others are functionless members." To this I replied, "According to the Bible, all are functioning members, there is none functionless. If there *is* any who is functionless, that one probably is the appendix." My response caused that brother to laugh. But is it not true that in the thinking of many brethren some members in the body of Christ have functions while some other members have no function at all? But may I ask this, Where in the physical body is there a functionless member? Where can you find any? Let me answer that in the whole body, the only functionless member to be found is probably the appendix. Can it be that in the spiritual body the appendix happens to be you? Let me remind you that all members have functions. And so it follows that as many as are *functioning* members, that many are the members in the body of Christ.

We Are a Priesthood

Let us correct our thinking here. Today we must see that service pertains to the *whole* church. It is the *church* preaching the gospel and not just a few brethren. Priesthood includes all the brothers and sisters. As many brethren as are serving, just that many are there who are brethren in the church. Let it be that the number of those who serve determines the number of brethren who are in the church. We cannot let it be that only a few serve among five thousand brethren or even among just a thousand brethren. We cannot allow any non-functioning members. All are members of the body of Christ; and therefore each of the brethren must be reminded that he or she has his or her function; none can be functionless. This fundamental principle must be seen and maintained. Otherwise, this work that we are about is not New Testament work. It is but a modified form of Catholicism—a system of limited priesthood. Since all are priests, we all belong to the priesthood.

(3) *Care for the beginners.*

Meeting for Beginners

After a person has believed and been baptized, he should be brought into a series of meetings for beginners. In such meetings, a special subject involving one single aspect of basic truth and conduct will be presented every week.

Help and Care

After a person starts to come to the beginners meetings, he should be assigned a more advanced brother to take care of him. How will that brother take care of him? By helping him to enter into every subject lesson experientially.

In case of absence, the advanced brother should go and give him the lesson(s) he missed. Whenever he attends the beginners meeting, the advanced one should find out afterwards if he understands what has been taught. On this point, let me share my feeling with you workers, especially with those of you who are ministers of God's word. I think we all have had that painful, shameful, and even indignant experience of having preached a rather deep message in a meeting, but later as you made contact with the brethren you discovered that your message had been like the wind which blows over the roof—it did not touch the ears of the audience. If you do not believe this is true, then you should try to encourage them to ask questions after you have finished speaking. I have often observed that asking questions reflects the condition of the hearer, while giving a message reflects the condition of the preacher. How frequently it is that when a most spiritual message has been given it has fallen a thousand miles distant from the mind of the hearers.

For this reason, do not assume that people understand what they hear. These beginners must be visited and helped until they clearly understand these words.

Beginners to Look After Unbelievers

All the beginners should be engaged in looking after unbelievers. Put a few stronger saints in their midst to help them do the work. Show them that since they have believed in the Lord, they are now priests of God, and all priests are to serve. How well these beginners shall serve will depend on how well they are helped.

Be a Foreman

Today it is no longer the workers who go out to work, it is instead the workers who help others to work. If the worker always does the work, he can never finish the work. I repeat, if you go out to work, if you yourself only work, you are a failure. Paul not only works with his hands, he also is a foreman. Learn to work and learn to be a foreman. Learn to train other brothers and sisters to work.

(4) *Care for special needs*. In this regard do not have too many brothers and sisters involved. In gospel work, in gospel care, in care for beginners—almost all the brethren should be mobilized. But caring for special needs is a different matter. It should be done by a few brothers and sisters who carry spiritual weight before the Lord.

When a brother encounters difficulty, let him be helped by these few. In case of joy or sorrow, again let these few help and pray with such ones. Or if there is a family problem, let these few pray and comfort them. Or if there is need for relief, let it be done through these few brothers and sisters.

As soon as brothers and sisters hear of anything of this nature, notify those who are responsible for special needs. They will distribute money to the poor, send food to the hungry, give clothes to the naked, render comfort to the troubled. They will visit prisons, pray for the sick, and help solve problems for the family.

A Foolish Concept

I do not know when this foolish concept commenced, but many seem to have the thought that the church ought not to have any problems. But do not forget that from the time of the early apostles the Church of God has encountered *many* difficulties. Do not fancy such difficulties as being abnormal for the local church. The Church since the apostolic days has been marked by many, not a few, tight situations.

Let us recall that not long after the day of Pentecost, there occurred the affair of Ananias and Sapphira. This was followed closely by the matter regarding the Hellenistic widows. Not many days after that, Stephen was martyred; and then Peter was jailed. Such problems have continued on without ceasing. So that from ancient times till now, the history of the Church has been full of obstacles and problems.

In this regard, we need to look more closely at the seven Asian churches mentioned in Revelation: five of these local churches were corrupted and seemed to have no difficulty; yet one of them received no reprimand—even the church in Smyrna, but it was a suffering, "martyr" church; and there was one church among them that was praised by God—Philadelphia; but interestingly, the Lord said to it, "Thou didst keep the word of my patience" (Rev. 3.10). *That* is the word of the Lord the Church of God is always to keep—not the word of *success*, but the word of *patience and "steadfastness"* (margin). A local church must pass through many difficult times requiring patience in the face of many problems and hardships. Only a worldly church will meet with less hardship. A true church will encounter many problems and some defeats.

So never say if a local church is always peaceful and uneventful that that is the sole evidence of the blessing of the Lord. What usually happens is that it is blessed on the one hand and encounters difficulties on the other. A church may undergo many hardships, yet still have the Lord's blessing.

(5) *Care for those who move and for the brethren from abroad.* When a brother has departed for another locality, the writing of a letter of recommendation on his behalf is not the

last responsibility of the church. At the very least, there should be some people responsible for corresponding with him to keep him informed on the condition of the local assembly as well as to supply him with the gist of the messages spoken during his absence. For quite a long period of time I felt ashamed and as though I had sinned, as I thought of the many brothers and sisters who over the past five years had gone to other places without anyone having corresponded with them. We could not and did not know how they had fared.

Let us today see that whenever a brother or sister goes out from us, there should be one or several of the brethren taking up responsibility to do some correspondence: a letter a week or a letter every other week or at least a letter a month. In that letter inform the brother or sister of the condition of the church and of the other brothers and sisters. If we send out ten letters of recommendation today, we must find two or three people to take up the responsibility of corresponding with those ten or so who go out. No matter how busy we are, we must correspond; for this is a service unto the Lord. And in writing such letters, they should not be just chit-chat, but a summary of the spiritual condition of the church. And in so doing, we will be blessed by God, and all the brethren who go out may perhaps stand even more firmly in the Lord.

Another thing which can be done is to send to them the gist of any special message given during the week. It is not necessary to relay the whole message but simply give the central thought. Nor is it needful to record all the messages spoken during the month but to share merely the essential points. This will at least supply the needs of the absentees. Some may have gone to places where they have no fellowship or perhaps they are lonely and in precarious situations. Except they are kept by God, they have no way to grow. How can they grow if they receive no supply? Therefore, such sharing of the principal thoughts of messages will help stabilize the spiritual condition of these brethren.

Write to Local Assembly As Follow-Up

I often consider the writing of a letter of recommendation as not being the last thing for us to do. So far as the church is concerned, after a month or two a letter should be written to that local assembly where the brother or sister goes, making an inquiry about him or her and asking for a reply. In the letter, such questions as the following should be included: What is the current spiritual condition of that particular brother or sister? How do you help him or her to grow? How do you take care of the person? Let me say that the lazy church will find itself unable to answer such questions as these. Frequently people are lazy, and sometimes churches may be lazy too. Laziness is what we are fearful of. Let me say, in addition, however, that such letters as the above will awaken some of the churches from their laziness, for they must answer them.

Take Care of Brethren Coming from Outside

Brethren from abroad need to be taken care of too. I hope there will be many people in the assembly serving in this area, for this also is to be included in the various priestly functions of the church.

Let those who are responsible for taking care of the absentees take care of the brethren from abroad as well. And why? Because they read the reply letters from other assemblies, and this thus enables them to know the problems of those who have gone out from those same assemblies. It is therefore most convenient for them to take care of the brethren from abroad.

Such care does not need to be prolonged beyond two or three months since by that time these brethren from abroad will have now become local brethren. As local brothers and sisters, they should by that time have begun to fulfill their local functions.

I wonder if you have now seen what is the ministry of the church? The local church is to serve in all of these areas. These five areas which we have just discussed pertain to the spiritual side of the church. There are many other miscellaneous things which can be added to this list, but these that have been mentioned already are only meant to serve as a suggestive outline, but even these few need to be done well.

THE WAY OF SERVICE

Rather Not Have Sunday Morning Preaching

I do not know if you have ever thought about what I am going to say next, but I would like to have a heart-to-heart talk with you all. Are you able to see that perhaps the Protestant churches currently put too great an emphasis on Sunday preaching? I for one consider this emphasis as contributing to today's problem. I hope you will think very carefully on whether you would like to maintain such Sunday preaching. I myself would rather have *no* Sunday preaching if I could witness the fact of every brother and sister busily serving: if I could see everybody involved at the time when the gospel is preached; if I could see everyone engaged in gospel care, if I could see everyone taking part in harvesting, and after harvesting, everyone participating in gospel visitation; and if I could see that the various kinds of needs were being met by brothers and sisters assuming their responsibilities to meet them. This that I have just described is the church. Let me illustrate it in this way. Suppose in a certain locality, the Sunday preaching is very strong but not all the body is serving. That is Protestantism. If only four or five brothers are active there and the rest of the body is passive, that is the priestly system of the Roman Catholic Church or the pastoral system of the Protestant churches. It is certainly not the church as God would have it.

No Non-functioning Member

Our future lies in the *whole* church serving. I hope all the brethren will pay special attention to this rule. Although this vision may easily be forgotten because of much activity, we must put it before ourselves each time we go out to work. With vision we can work. Without vision we cannot work. Brothers and sisters must rise up and serve. We need not be anxious about the greatness of outward difficulties or the amount of people's resistance. The real issue lies in whether we have truly seen the way of service. If we are clear, let us focus our entire strength on it. And never mind the number of people, as long as all of them serve; for it is bewildering if in an assembly of, say, two thousand people, only five hundred serve and the rest do not. Let us see that if there are five hundred brethren in a local church, all five hundred of them must serve.

3 Levitical Ministry

Concerning Levitical ministry, not much needs to be said because it is so simple. The work of the Levites was different from that of the priests in Old Testament times. The priests ministered to God as well as in the tabernacle; the Levites, on the other hand, ministered to the priests and assisted them. In other words, what the priestly ministry represented in the Old Testament was spiritual service; but the Levitical ministry, mundane service. The Levites washed the sacrifice, poured out its blood, cast away its dung, and helped in stripping its skin, as well as bore upon their shoulders the things of the tabernacle. For as God's pillar of cloud was taken up from over the tabernacle and the latter commenced to be moved, the Levites stepped forward to bear the things of the tabernacle. Such was the Levitical ministry.

Temporal Yet Not in the World

What the Levites did was of course related to God. It was not spiritual and yet was closely related to the spiritual side of things. It was temporal, and yet was not in the world but in the church. We can therefore conclude from this that the work of the deacons in the New Testament period is of this Levitical nature. It is parallel to the ministry of the Levites of old.

There are deacons in a local assembly; and even though

their work is to manage business affairs, these affairs are related to the church nonetheless.

All Must Learn

All brothers and sisters should have a concern for, and be clear about, the affairs of the church. All must be actively involved. Cleaning the meeting place, taking care of guest rooms, keeping in order the towels, blankets, sheets, and so forth—all these are Levitical-type services. Taking care of the poor saints in the midst is also a work of the Levites. To meet or to send off brothers and sisters who are from abroad is likewise a Levitical-type work. Many works in the church office also belong to those who perform like the Levites did.

So, when a person serves God, he may on the one hand do the work of the priest and on the other hand do the work of the Levite. He must do both. He takes part both in spiritual service and in mundane work. Recall the example of Stephen and the other six: they had served the tables. Such was Levitical work—the work of deacons. Recall, too, how the disciples had distributed the loaves and the fish to the five thousand and the four thousand, as well as gathered the left-overs in twelve baskets and seven baskets, respectively. These were works of deacons. Take as another example that of Judas, who took care of the purse among Jesus and the Twelve. That had been especially what would be termed a deacon's work today. Furthermore, the disciples had been sent by the Lord Jesus from the well at Sychar to buy bread in the nearby town. Was not this also a kind of deacon's work? As a matter of fact, much Christian activity today belongs to this category. And the entire body of believers needs to learn to serve in this capacity.

Home Helps

I would like to make a suggestion for brothers and sisters to consider. Many of you have leisure time, whereas many others —particularly the sisters—do not have any time for leisure at home. They must cook and take care of the children. Why cannot some arrangement be made to send brothers and sisters to these homes to help? Whoever is responsible for such service could tell a needy sister, "We have two sisters who will help you in washing for two hours every week." This is another example of Levitical work. In the instance in the book of the Acts when the supplying of the Hellenist widows had been overlooked, there had been murmurings. And why? Because this was the church, and if there was a need, it had to be met. And although it was mundane and not spiritual in nature, it must nevertheless be done, because this is the expected thing.

Twelve Mundane Affairs

We ought to mention a number of things before the Lord for you to consider as mundane matters of a deacon nature: (1) Cleaning jobs. (2) The arrangement of furniture and such like, as well as the ushering work in the church. (3) Special care for the Lord's table and for baptism. Some must be responsible for preparing the loaf and the cup. Some trained persons should take care of baptism in such aspects as helping those to be baptized in the going down and coming up out of the water, in the changing of their clothes, etc. (4) Distribution of relief to the unbelieving poor. (5) Sending relief to flood and fire victims. (6) Sending off and meeting those brothers and sisters who travel from one place to another. (7) The management of church finance. (8) The management of the kitchen. (9) The management of the church office. (10) The management of transportation, and making the means of transportation available. (11) The management of correspondence and documents. (12) Assisting in needy homes.

I trust that every brother and sister will bear some burden in such church affairs as these. Do not let some brethren work while others do no work at all. The service of the church must involve the entire body.

Principle of Body Ministry

Let all be clear on this principle. The entire body of believers must engage in Levitical as well as in priestly ministry. All must work, whether little or much; and all must work heartily. We have a natural tendency to use those people who have the two talents. Church history bears this statement out. On the one hand, the five-talents people know how to exercise themselves; they do not need any encouragement to serve. The one-talent person, on the other hand, tends to bury the talent he has, and once done, it is difficult to stir him to action. Yet the two-talents individuals are most available. They have a little ability but they will not bury it. They will put themselves to work. Nevertheless, if only the two-talents brethren are used and the one-talent brethren are left unused—that is a total failure.

What is the church? The church is that in which all the one-talent people engage in temporal as well as spiritual services. You who are assembled here at these training sessions, do not shake your heads and sigh, "This person is useless or that person is useless." I tell you, if such attitude exists among you, the church is finished. For if you *treat* him as useless, he *will* be useless. You can of course tell him that he is useless *in himself*, but you are to also tell him that *the Lord has given him one talent* and *commanded* him to *trade* with it. *The Lord* will use him. Now if you do not know how to use the single-talented ones, by this very fact you are proven to be lacking in leadership ability before the Lord. You who are leaders are to use all the so-called useless brothers and sisters, for this is the work of a worker. A worker will use all the useful brothers and sisters and he will also transform all "the useless" into usefulness.

The basic principle to recognize is that the Lord never gives anyone less than one talent. In the Lord's house, no servant is without any gift. He has at least one talent. And hence none can make excuse, saying, "The Lord has not given me anything." I want you to know that all God's children are servants. We all are servants as well as children. In other words, being members one of another in God's house, we all have ministries. If we consider anyone to be useless to the Lord, we do not know what the grace of God is. We ought to understand His grace fully, seeing that if He has said that this person or that person is His servant, can anyone of us stand up and say that that person is not? If it were left up to us to choose, more often that not, we would consider only three or five in the entire assembly as being useful and choose only them; yet God declares that *all* are His servants. Accordingly, we must let all serve.

Whether or not we shall succeed in our work hereafter will depend very much on how we see the work done. Will it be done by a few especially gifted persons, or will it be done by all the servants of the Lord? Is the entire church working? That is the critical question.

Body of Christ Is Living Organism

The body of Christ is not a doctrine; it is a living organism. If such is so, then we must be sure to learn this one thing: that only when all the members are functioning do we have the reality of the body of Christ. Only then can we see the church.

Today's problem lies too much in us, for we have inherited the priestly system of the Roman Catholic Church and the pastoral system of the Protestant churches. And if we become just a little careless, we may end up monopolizing among ourselves as elders and workers all the services of God. It is futile to only *preach* the message of the body of Christ; we must also be bent on seeing that it *operates*. If we believe in the concept of the body of Christ, we need not be afraid of its functioning. We should believe that the Lord will call all the members to function.

God Has Walked Before Us

I do not expect any brother who is going out, to work by substituting certain people for others instead of leading them *all* to serve. When you arrive at a certain place, you may at the beginning lead eight or ten people to serve. But after a certain period has elapsed they will lead sixty, eighty, or a hundred more to serve. If you must use those with five talents to suppress the one-talent person, you are not a wise and faithful servant of the Lord. You should indeed get the five-talents and the two-talents brethren to serve, but you should also get all the one-talent people to serve. Those whom you may look upon as useless should all be serving as well. Then you shall see the glory of the church.

I desire to see all the simple people serving; I do not want only a few prominent ones preaching. I have no more admiration for the highly gifted than I do for the one-talent people.

Let Philadelphia Appear

If through God's dealings with us and our work we are able to open the way of service to the one-talent persons, we shall see for the first time what brotherly love actually is: Philadelphia shall appear. Today we must have brotherly love as well as government. I believe in authority, but I also believe in brotherly love. Without authority, the church can make no progress. "Didst keep my word"—this is a statement that reflects authority. "And didst not deny my name"—this too is a statement that reflects authority (Rev. 3.8). So that Philadelphia is identified by these two authorities; yet Philadelphia itself is brotherly love. All the brethren serve in love. And when this appears in our day we shall know what the church truly is; otherwise, we will simply follow in the train of the Roman Catholic and the Protestant systems. We will not know what the brotherly love and the authority of Philadelphia are.

Two Ways—Gift and Authority

Cannot Be Left Unused

First, you should not use a brother because you see he is useful and leave another brother unused because to you he seems useless. In the church there cannot be any member left out. To recover the testimony of the Lord Jesus, all the one-talented must rise up. All who belong to the Lord are members of the body. Everyone must rise up and exercise his gift. And then you shall see the church. Do not despise the one-talented. Do not substitute others for them or suppress them. Believe in God and put them to work. Since God has confidence in calling them servants you must have faith to cause them to work.

Authority Solves Problem of the Flesh

Second, in the church we need have no fear of the activities of the flesh. For two things must be established in the church: one is authority, the other is gift. All the one-talent people should come forth to serve, to work, and to bear fruits. What if the one-talented come with their flesh? Let me say to you that their flesh must be dealt with. The solution to this lies in authority, for authority represents God.

Gift is gift, and authority is authority. They are two different things. All the one-talented people must exercise their gifts, and the problem of their flesh is to be solved by authority. Suppose a brother is serving, and his flesh is brought in. Tell him this: "Brother, you cannot do that, you cannot bring in your flesh." Or say to him, "This attitude of yours is not right, we will not permit such an attitude." When he hears this, he probably will go home tomorrow and refuse to do anything. If so, you must seek him out and say to him, "You cannot quit, you must do the work." Although he has brought his flesh in, he should still be allowed to do the work; only he must be told what he can do and what he cannot do. Deal with him with authority.

This that has just been discussed looms as a very great temptation. As soon as the one-talent person is used by the Lord, his flesh immediately comes in. The flesh of the person and his one talent appear to be joined together. We must resist the flesh but use the one talent. Today's practice is that we too often bury the one talent as well as bury the flesh. Where, then, is the reality of the church in all this? No, we must do differently! Use authority to deal with the flesh, but also encourage the one-talent people to function. Perhaps they will say, "To do is wrong, and not to do is also wrong; what, then, should I do?" The answer is, "To do is indeed wrong, because the flesh has come in; yet not to do is also wrong, because the talent is buried. The one talent you have must come in, but the flesh must go out."

If authority can be maintained and all the functions of the members of the body can be brought in, you will behold on earth a glorious church. The way to recovery is then made easy. I do not know how long a time our Lord will grant us in the future. I believe, however, our way is becoming clearer and clearer. We must concentrate all our thinking and galvanize all our energy on helping brothers and sisters to serve together as a body. And thus will the life of the church truly begin, and the Lord will surely come soon.

4 The Minister of God's Word in the Church

Let us spend a little time together looking into the matter of the minister of God's word in a local assembly.

NO NEED TO MAINTAIN SUNDAY PULPIT

According to past custom, we used to maintain a Sunday pulpit in all the local assemblies. Yet even in *Rethinking the Work,** we had already come to see that a local assembly has no need to maintain such a Sunday pulpit. For this kind of meeting is not strictly a church meeting. A prayer meeting is a church meeting. The kind of meeting described in 1 Corinthians 14 where gifts are exercised for the edification of the body is also a church meeting. The breaking of bread is a church meeting too. But the Sunday morning preaching is the product of the Roman Catholic, as well as the Protestant, Church. It is not a church meeting, but as a matter of fact it is a ministry meeting.

Reason for Its Retention: "Like all the Nations"

Although there is no need to maintain a Sunday pulpit in a

*The book written by the author which forms Volume Two of this present trilogy and which was published in China in early 1938.—*Translator*

local assembly, what has been our experience? It has been retained these many years. It has made us to be "like all the nations" (1 Sam. 8.5). We are reluctant to give it up because all the "nations" around us have this Sunday preaching. Why can we not be delivered from it? Wherein lies the problem?

I think one of the big reasons is that if the Sunday preaching were taken away there would be nothing to fill in the gap. Since all the nations around us are doing it, we find it extremely difficult to maintain a local assembly if we do not have such preaching on Sunday. It appears to be very hard for people to come into our midst and be treated to no sermon, whereas the opposite case is true elsewhere in the denominations.

Difficulties of Its Retention: an Outside and an Inside One

In our past experience we have not followed through on what we had earlier seen because of both an inward as well as outward reason. The outward reason has been that since all the nations around us have practiced it, we felt that many brothers and sisters would go elsewhere to hear preaching if we did not ourselves have Sunday preaching. This has revealed to us, however, just how few have really been priests among us. Too many among us have had to be served instead of their serving. To be a priest is not to be served but to serve. And listeners, as we know, are to be served; they far too often do not serve. Thus this, as you can see, has been an outside difficulty.

In addition, without any Sunday preaching, there would have also been an inside difficulty. Many brothers and sisters among us, who had already been Christians for ten or twenty years, would have felt uneasy because this would have been so different from their former habit and customary expectation.

See Accurately

I wish to consult with you on this matter. Here I am not

preaching, I am merely suggesting. But we do need to see very accurately.

Up till now I have not been able to read from the Bible anything regarding a Sunday pulpit. Especially in a local assembly, there is no biblical justification for maintaining a Sunday pulpit. In order to strengthen any such pulpit, you will probably need to have a worker stationed there. You may call him a worker, a priest, or a pastor, but the fact is that someone is needed there if the Sunday pulpit is to be maintained.

We do not believe in a restricted system of priests, because *all* of us are priests. Can we accept a modified form of the pastoral system resulting in something such as a worker system? We cannot. We must instead learn to help all the brothers and sisters to be priests. As they all come forth to serve, the number of those waiting to be served will automatically be decreased among us. We must eliminate the number of those to be served. As long as the served are there, all will expect others to be priests and themselves to simply be God's people. And if so, then there will be no way to eliminate the Sunday pulpit and there will never be a true reflection of the body in that locality, for there will be too many people who are passive in behavior—they waiting to hear but not prepared to speak. If ever the Church is going to be the Church in reality and if ever Christ is going to have a true expression of the body in a locality, all the brothers and sisters must serve—the one-talented person as well as the two- and five-talented persons. Only this can be the condition in which a group can truly be said to be the body of Christ.

The Way of the Church: Working Instead of Listening

I think the way through the problem is this—that just as soon as people are saved and brought in, they are immediately to be put into the work of the assembly so as to turn us from the habit of listening to Sunday preaching to the habit of working and serving on Sunday. In the past we had correctly taught that the habit of listening to Sunday preaching was wrong and yet we had nothing to fill the void which would have been created had we ceased such preaching. We had not perceived the concept of Sunday serving and working as a substitute for Sunday listening. Today, we realize that Sunday working is right and proper.

If all the one-talent people everywhere would rise up and work, we could quickly restore to the body of Christ the condition of the early church. Let us imagine that on the Lord's Day morning, we preach the gospel. On that day the entire body will be mobilized to save souls. Accordingly, everyone will be busy on Sunday, because on that day we shall all be preaching the gospel together.

No doubt the Church on earth needs to be fed. I believe in feeding, but I also confess that the mission of the Church on earth is not only feeding, it is preaching the gospel as well. All the brothers and sisters should go out to bring in people. We advocate that each one bring in two or four more. And thus, the entire body will be busy. All will be preaching the gospel, all will be saving souls.

If every Sunday we can bring in people and lead them to Christ, then I assure you that after a time the habit of listening to a sermon will pass away, and the reality of the church will appear. Who today are the church members? Those who merely listen to a Sunday sermon. But a Christian is one who goes out to save souls.

All Are Priests

The universal priesthood of believers is a subject which has been preached for over a hundred and twenty years, from 1828* till now. Yet even in our day priestly function is still not

*This specific year marked the beginning of the so-called Brethren movement, which has asserted a tremendous influence on the course of Church history ever since. —*Translator*

a universal fact in the Church. The Church as the body of Christ has been a truth which has been recovered since over a century ago; and especially during the last decade, some have come to a clear understanding of its spiritual value and worth. Nevertheless, it is possible for this truth concerning the body of Christ to remain but a teaching in the Church and for the reality of church life to still be very much lacking.

May God open our eyes to see what the body truly is. The concept of body life means that every member of a local expression is functioning—just as in the physical body, there is no member that is without any function. In like manner, therefore, no one who belongs to Christ is to refrain from being a serving priest. All the members must function, and all the priests must serve.

Serve Men in Morning, Serve God in Evening

I do not know if you have caught this vision. If one day the habit of listening to a sermon is ruled out of the mind of God's people, the whole church will be serving according to the word of God. On Sunday morning the entire body of priests will serve men in preaching the gospel, and on Sunday evening the entire priesthood will again be serving—except that at this time they shall be serving God in the breaking of the bread. How good this will be.

Hereafter there is not to be much difference between the workers and the brethren. The former may merely be spiritually stronger before the Lord than the latter. So far as the Work is concerned, there is no difference, because all are fellow workmen. Only when we enter into the *practice* of this will we understand the New Testament, since the Scriptures consider all the children of God to be fellow workers because everyone is working. The only difference lies in the fact that the so-called workers are sent out in order that they may devote all their time and energy to the Work.

THE SUPPLY OF THE WORD

Let us turn for a while to this matter of the supply of God's word before we return again to a further discussion of the way of the Church.

The Supply of the Word for Beginners

If the preaching of the gospel is strong, many people will be saved. As the saved people increase, the church will naturally have more problems. This is because all kinds of people will come in, just as in the drawing of nets all kinds of fishes will be gathered to the boat. And accordingly, we need to take care of them and give them some help in the word of God each week.

To this end we have prepared fifty-two basic subjects or lessons.* We desire that once a week all the new believers will be gathered to hear God's word. At least a year's time will be spent in presenting them with all the principal subjects in the Scriptures which are concerned with the Christian walk. Thus will they be amply supplied with the word of Christ.

God's word may be repeated even as God's anointing may be repeated. Of course, if we are not living before the Lord, these messages will become dead. But if we *are* living before Him, the repeated sharing of the fifty-two lessons can continue to be living. Year after year these topical lessons may be delivered. And as the word of God is repeated, the anointing is repeated, and life is also freshly quickened again.

We have now seen two kinds of meetings: one is the Sunday morning meeting when the gospel is preached that people may be saved. And after people are saved and brought in, they can be given good care through these basic lessons. The word of

*These basic lessons, published subsequently in Chinese, were eventually translated and published in English in six volumes. See the fuller explanatory footnote on this in the "Introduction" chapter to this present volume, at the sub-head in that chapter entitled, "Need for Basic Training." Complete bibliographic information is therein given. — *Translator*

God supplied on Sunday morning pertains to the gospel; God's word supplied during the week pertains to the edification of new believers.

The Supply of God's Word According to 1 Corinthians 14

Some may ask this: if we have older brothers and sisters in our midst—the many brethren who are not beginners—how do we supply *their* need in God's word? Let me mention that this can be supplied by means of the fellowship meeting according to 1 Corinthians 14. At that meeting time, some may have the word of the Lord, some may have revelation, some may have a song, and some may have prayer. Let those who have the burden of God's word receive the burden from the Lord and not be passive. They should speak at such a gathering.

Today, such a meeting is often weak because many gifted brothers with ministry are too passive. Unless a burden is impressed upon them such as for speaking on Sunday morning, they will not go to God and seek for His word. They just breathe a sigh of relief at a fellowship meeting. Yet if *they* do not have a sense of responsibility, how can the meeting be strong? If all are passive, who will be active in the meeting? And hence the meeting according to 1 Corinthians 14 is not the kind of gathering where all come without responsibility. It is a meeting in which all are responsible. Let us understand that it is wrong for one to take upon himself *all* the responsibility, but it is equally wrong for all not to take *any* responsibility.

How should such a fellowship meeting be prepared? Just as in the other meetings, the responsible brothers should come together and pray at least half an hour before the gathering begins. They should have assurance from the Lord before they enter the meeting. None of them can rush into it at the last hour. Every one of the responsible brothers must be prepared beforehand in order that only those with a real burden and who are fearful of hurting the meeting if not properly prepared will come to share, instead of it being people unspiritual but ambitious who end up sharing. First, you need to pray that the Lord will control the fellowship meeting according to His will. And second of all, the responsible brothers should not be pas sive in such a gathering.

I often wonder why some brothers who are ministers of God's word sit back and let other brothers speak, and when the meeting proves to be weak, they then shake their heads! It is strange to me that people who *can* take responsibility end up doing nothing at a fellowship meeting.

The Supply of God's Word by Apostles

The supply of God's word by the apostles is the supply through the ministers of God's word. Preaching of the gospel and the edification of beginners should be adequate in ordinary days. And this will help form the habit of serving among the brethren. As a further aid and in order to strengthen the supply of God's word, we can also have the meeting according to 1 Corinthians 14. All this, then, is the arrangement for a local assembly.

What, though, is the responsibility of an apostle? When such a brother passes through a certain place, he may stay for a few days, even as did Paul when he passed through Troas and spent seven days there. He may give the local assembly or a combination of several assemblies some special time in the ministry of God's word.

MUST GO THE WAY OF RECOVERY

Permit me to say that the condition of the Church today is too far from New Testament order! We must therefore correct the situation. God walks in the way of recovery. And we too must walk that way. We must help the brothers and sisters into service. They should serve new believers as well as sinners. They should learn to edify one another with the work of God according to 1 Corinthians 14.

For the church as a whole to preach the gospel—that is truly a tremendous thing. It is a glorious work. There is no need to have some greatly gifted persons such as a Charles Finney, a Charles Stanley, a George Whitefield or a John Wesley. Let me tell you that the power of all the brethren in preaching the gospel far exceeds the power of these great men.

We may have to wait twenty or even fifty years for a person with five talents to appear on the scene. How rare it is to have such a man. But by putting forth five of the one-talent brethren, you *have* the five-talents person. As you put the most untalented five together, you get the five talents. The church does not have many five-talents people; but when it as a whole begins to preach the gospel, you have five-talents brethren many times over! And they are always there, and they are everywhere. Whether or not the gospel can reach the world depends not on the workers but on the Church.

Hence today the vision must be clear, the revelation from the Lord must be thorough. O Lord, I pray that You put the burden of work upon the Church. In the physical realm, what the head directs is the body and not just the individual members of the body. It takes the entire body to manifest the full strength and power of the head. So too is it in the spiritual realm of the Church as the body of Christ. I therefore desire that there be true local representations of the body of Christ in China. Do not think of the body of Christ as only a heavenly concept. It is too idealistic for anyone to try to find a local assembly in heaven. The body of Christ must and will be manifested on the earth. For even though it is so spiritual, it can still be manifested on earth.

MIGRATION—ANOTHER WAY OF PREACHING THE GOSPEL

In the book of Acts, we see two different ways of preaching

the gospel: (1) one of them is found in Antioch, from where the apostles go forth to preach the gospel; and this has been the way which the Church has emphasized these many many years. But (2) let us today recognize that Jerusalem symbolizes another way of preaching the gospel—one that is quite different from that of Antioch. The way of Jerusalem is, that after a number of people are saved, they migrate to other places to preach the gospel. By reading carefully Acts chapters 8, 10, 11 and 12, we see that it is right to migrate for the gospel's sake, whether it come through persecution or by other means. If many people are saved in one place, as happened in Jerusalem, they should be sent out; or else, persecution will eventually come to disperse them.

As people migrate to other places, they go out to preach the gospel. Workers must never entertain the thought that they are the only ones who go out to win souls. At times it will be the apostolic workers who venture forth to gain souls, but at other times it will be the ordinary saved ones who are sent out to gain souls. These two ways must both be adopted.

During the days of the early apostles, preaching the gospel had a definite priority over listening to a sermon. As we read through the Acts of the Apostles, we can perceive that at that time there were not as many ministers of God's word as we have today. For then the children of God paid more attention to the preaching of the gospel than to listening to a sermon. Today, though, it seems as if the basic thing for a Christian to do is to listen to the Sunday sermon rather than to preach the gospel. Hence we must see clearly and accurately the way which lies before us. We must help brothers and sisters along this new way so that they will put the preaching of the gospel first before they do something else. And the result will be that more people will be saved, there will be no need to maintain at different places so many workers, and we shall see the local church being raised up.

I thank God for what Romans 12 says: "he that teacheth, to

his teaching; or he that exhorteth, to his exhorting" (vv.7b, 8). It does not say: "he that heareth, to his hearing." Had there been such a word as that, the Church would have disappeared. Do keep in mind that there is to be no such thing as only listening to a sermon. This is *not* what is meant by body functioning. May God be gracious to us that we may all rise up to serve and to preach the gospel.

THE VISION OF THE WORK

This vision is now put before us. Henceforth, let us work daily according to this vision. So long as all the brothers and sisters do not have the vision to serve, we who are workers will need to work on. Yet they all must eventually rise up to work—to preach the gospel. The whole church locally must serve, the whole church locally must preach the gospel. Only in this way shall we have the New Testament church.

According to many Bible scholars, the Roman Catholic Church is the church in Babylonian captivity. Just as the children of Israel had been taken captive into Babylon, so the Church generally has also been taken captive. The Protestant Church came back from Babylon, but she has not built the temple. Although many have returned from Babylon, the holy temple has not yet been rebuilt. Today you and I, in the current history of the Church, are those people who must rise up to rebuild the temple. Like Zerubbabel, Ezra, Nehemiah and the remnant who rose up and rebuilt the temple and the city of Jerusalem, we too must learn to bring forth again God's Church and its testimony in our time. Many have come out of Babylon, but they still carry with them many Babylonian traits and manners. Up to this present moment, the Church is not as it ought to be. The Catholic Church may be stricter than the Protestant churches, yet neither comes close to the Church that is on God's heart. If there is a local assembly, it must collectively preach the gospel and it must collectively serve within these years. Oh, how I hope that these two words will be repeated a million times over: the local assembly must preach the gospel, the local assembly must serve. When this happens we shall then have the local church as it ought to be; otherwise, it becomes a mystifying group, with nothing about it approaching any resemblance to the church on God's heart.

Now I know that it will certainly be difficult at the beginning. Nevertheless, the vision must be seen clearly and accurately. The responsible brethren should come together to inquire of God—to pray and to take counsel: O Lord, how should all the brothers and sisters rise up to serve? This is therefore our way: not that the few work all the time, but that all come to work. It will not do if a few of you do everything and the rest do nothing. *You* must work, but *they too* must work: you work in order to bring *them* into working.

CHURCH MUST BE IN LIBERTY OF HOLY SPIRIT

We have said enough on the ministry of God's word in a local assembly. Concerning the mutual edification that is in accordance with the fellowship meeting described in 1 Corinthians 14, it really depends on the spiritual condition of the local brethren. I think most would agree that the strongest supply of God's word happened among the Brethren during the last century. Yet why was this? Because they followed the principle of 1 Corinthians 14 by letting the Holy Spirit have His liberty. Though there were many *weak* words, there were also many *strong* words being released. So that in such a meeting, even if many who should not have spoken did speak, those who should have spoken were given the opportunity to speak. As the Holy Spirit has His freedom, we may expect Him to speak in the assembly as well as to order things in the assembly. Let the church be in the liberty of the Holy Spirit.

5 Various Meetings in the Church

Let us take up the various meetings of the church, one by one, and discuss them in some detail.

(1) The Gospel Meeting

The local brothers should set apart a special time, possibly on Sunday morning, when all the brethren in the church work together in the preaching of the gospel. Or, the gospel may be preached in different districts of the city. It needs to be preached with all our strength.

At the time of preaching, we need to bring people in, to sit among them and talk with them. After the meeting is over, send them home. But continue relating to them until they are baptized.

The gospel messages may be presented strongly. At the same time it is essential that the attitude of the brethren must be right in a gospel meeting. Frequently it is the brethren who ruin the meeting. We need to remember that the gospel is not preached for us to hear. We must help the meeting instead of weakening it. Learn to lead the people who sit by our sides to believe in the gospel. Naturally, *we* do not need the gospel, but the *friends* do. If the attitude of all the brethren is right, it is much easier for the brother who preaches the gospel to do so.

Otherwise, he has to cope with the reaction of the brethren as well as with that of the sinners. Remember that he is not there to pass the test of preaching the gospel but to lead people to Christ. Let us therefore work together, and then there will not be much of a problem in a gospel meeting.

Do not let a gospel meeting be too long or too short. Two thirds of the time may be spent in casting the net, the other third of the time in gathering the net.

(2) The Beginners Meeting

Since the topics of this series of meetings are prescribed in advance, the delivery of them must be definite. In each local assembly find two or three brothers who are able to deliver these messages. In case one brother is absent or sick, the other may stand in. In a large assembly, this can be done according to districts and can have more brothers involved in the delivery of these messages.

Hopefully, these lessons for the beginners will not be subject to change so that they can be covered once a year. And if these lessons are given according to order in various localities, people who travel elsewhere will hear the same message. Thus they will be edified in many subjects. Due to the fact that many brethren have not learned these basic lessons of the Christian life, we have encountered numerous difficulties. Hence we hope hereafter that this meeting for beginners will be effectively done so that all new believers will learn these basic lessons* well.

---

*Again it should be pointed out that these basic lessons, published subsequently in Chinese, were eventually translated and published in English in six volumes. See the fuller explanatory footnote on this in the "Introduction" chapter to this present volume, at the sub-head in that chapter entitled, "Need for Basic Training." Complete bibliographic information is therein given. — *Translator*

Make-Up Lessons Must Be Carefully Given

One point which needs to be emphasized is that those who are responsible for visiting the beginners must themselves learn these lessons well. Otherwise, they will not be able to supply the beginners with the lessons missed due to their absence. I hope the brethren will realize this problem. Perhaps a basic lesson may have been given in one and a half hours, but in giving a make-up lesson on it, it was done in two minutes! It was presented not just as an outline, it ended up as an outline of the outline! I remember one brother, in giving a make-up lesson, merely said a single word: "The topic for today is, to read the Bible daily." And that was it! If you go to a person's home to give him lessons he has missed, you cannot say only this word! Unless the Holy Spirit works in a special way, one word like this is not enough. There needs to be detailed explanations presented by means of different sub-headings so that the hearer may feel as though he had personally attended the beginners meeting himself. If not, the loss is great.

Remember that once the gospel is preached, the future of the assembly will depend much on how effectively the beginners meeting with its program is carried on. This meeting can very largely decide whether the next generation is going to be strong or weak. If this meeting is weak, how can the next generation be strong? Yes, people have believed in the gospel and are saved; but where is the church?

The Teaching and Fellowship of the Apostles

I hope you will remember especially what the book of Acts says: "And they continued stedfastly in the apostles' teaching and fellowship, in the breaking of bread and the prayers" (2.42). The verse preceding this one spoke of baptism, and it is followed immediately by the apostles' teaching and fellowship. So that after three thousand were saved and added to the

Jerusalem church, they were given teaching and fellowship by the apostles immediately. How very important is the building up of the new believers. Our so-called edifying of the beginners in our midst is to be none other than the apostles' teaching and fellowship.

Once the gospel meeting has brought people in, the work of nurturing them must follow. If not, many shall be born but few shall be nurtured. How can the local assembly ever be strong if this is the case? Therefore, on the one hand the preaching of the gospel must be strong, and on the other hand the edifying of the beginners must be strong too. If both are strong, we shall have a promising future.

(3) The Fellowship Meeting According to 1 Corinthians 14

I believe we have to look to God and learn much before Him concerning this meeting. In this particular gathering of the saints, the entire body of brothers and sisters assemble together to be led by God to rise up and serve. Many are there serving, and so it provides much help to the church there. Here, personal testimonies as well as God's word may also be given.

Responsible Brothers Must Supervise This Meeting

Find out a few brothers and sisters who are gifted in helping people. Ask them to share more at such a meeting. Some brothers and sisters do not have much to share. It is evident they possess less gifts, and also less grace. The responsible brothers can inform them privately not to speak too often. With respect to some brothers, they may be given a limited time in sharing, but be careful not to offend the Holy Spirit. For some of them may stand up and share two minutes with great profit, but they like to extend their sharing too long. It needs to be understood that if all who stand up to share have received deep dealings from the Lord, such a meeting is bound to be strong.

Many think they can help people. They are so self-confident; yet they do not know how to touch peoples' spirits. Such will never realize their weakness if they are not told. So the responsible brothers must tell them that when they get up to speak before God, they should speak briefly, since any prolonged speech of theirs will not help the people. On the other hand, if someone speaks and people are edified, the responsible brothers should encourage him to speak again. Although the responsible brothers may not be ministers of God's word, they nevertheless govern the church. And as such, they cannot be lax. Some brothers may need to be *en*couraged to speak more so that the church may be edified; whereas some other brothers may need to be *dis*couraged from speaking too long since only as they speak briefly will the church be edified.

If the resposible brothers are not passive but can give a little supervision to the meeting, I believe the 1 Corinthians 14-type fellowship meeting may produce rich supplies to the church.

What is extremely important is that the responsible brothers must not speak to, or deal with, people casually, since a little carelessness may result in offending against the Holy Spirit. What the elders of the church should fear most is offending against the Holy Spirit. For the Holy Spirit is the true representative of Christ. He represents Him in exercising authority on earth. Elders can speak only when they understand the thought of Christ. Not knowing the mind of Christ, they must not speak.

Can a sister give her testimony in such a meeting? I personally think she may.

(4) The Prayer Meeting

There are a few points which brethren should remember concerning a prayer meeting.

Brevity—The first point for all the brethren to learn is to be brief in prayer. All prayer meetings are ruined by lengthy prayers. Learn to pray short ones. New believers should pray briefly at the beginning; the more advanced brethren may pray longer. I believe for a prayer meeting to be strong and powerful, the prayers must be short. Lengthy ones are frequently filled with empty words.

Realness—The second point the brethren must be reminded of is that the prayers in a prayer meeting are to be real. The brethren should be warned not to see too much difference between private prayer and public prayer. This means they must learn to be real. It is true that in a prayer meeting the words uttered need to be clear. Frequently in private prayer, the words need only be half-uttered. Nevertheless, it is a fact that many words *not* used in private prayers *are* used in public prayers—and for ulterior reasons. Such prayers are false. Sometimes at a prayer meeting you wonder whether the brother is praying for *you* to hear or for *God* to hear. The brethren must be taught to pray out of their hearts and to pray for *God* to hear. Do not ever allow any brother or sister to make prayer a kind of preaching, or to make it a kind of report to God. Teach them to pray briefly and genuinely. These are the two basic conditions for a good prayer meeting: to say only as much as is in the heart, and to not stretch what you do pray beyond reality.

Concentration—Finally, the third matter to be noticed is for the brethren to decide on the subjects to be prayed for. We must learn not to pray for whatever each of us deems fitting. If a prayer meeting has presented to it twenty or thirty matters to pray for, and with everyone praying for his/her subject, the agreement spoken of in Matthew 18 evaporates. Where there is not one mind and one heart, how can we expect God to hear?

Accordingly, the matters for prayer must be decided upon. They should be mentioned. Perhaps at a given prayer meeting only one thing is to be prayed for. Suppose, for example, there is a problem in one locality, and so we decide to pray for that locality. At the time of prayer, all the brothers and sisters lay aside other matters and concentrate on praying for just this one item. From start to finish, the church prays for only this one thing, with all present bringing merely this one matter before God. Such a situation as this sounds more like a prayer meeting.

A prayer meeting is not when everybody brings in his own personal prayer and prays for it. Such a meeting must be concentrated, and its prayer must be with one accord Hence the responsible brothers may mention but just this one subject for prayer and all will pray for it and not for anything else.

But if there are five or six matters to be prayed for, then when the announcement is made, make it one at a time. Let one subject be prayed through first until the burden seems to be lifted through prayers, and only then is the second matter to be mentioned. And thus, even in the case of many matters for prayer, the prayer offered up is concentrated, since they are mentioned one at a time.

In view of this, the responsible brothers must learn how to lead the meeting before God. Their spirits need to be opened so as to be highly sensitive. For example, a certain matter has been prayed for, and it may now have arrived at the point when either stopping the prayer or continuing with it may be called for. If the burden is thus discharged, the next matter should be mentioned and prayed for.

Keep in mind that many prayer meetings fail because there are too many subjects to pray for.

(5) The Breaking of Bread Meeting

This is the time of true worship. It can be divided into two parts of worship: the first part is towards the Lord Jesus, the second is towards God. In the first part, we see the One who was sent; in the second, we come to the One who sent Christ. In the first part, we meet the Lord; in the second, we meet God.

Brothers and sisters should learn to enter into the first part quickly. If the feeling towards the Lord be slow, there will not be time for the second part. In the first part let the Lord be touched quickly. It should not take too much time or too many prayers before He is touched. As soon as we touch the Lord, we should begin to break the bread. After the bread is broken, we should go immediately to the Father.

Most likely our problem today centers upon a weakness which we have at the beginning of the breaking of bread. Or it may be that oftentimes the feeling of the brethren towards the Lord has definitely reached its height, and the bread lies on the table unbroken; and thus the spirit of worship ebbs away. With the result that it may take two or three peaks before the breaking of the bread finally occurs. The best is at the first peak, when immediately thereafter, the bread should be broken. If so, this will allow time for worshiping the Father. During this latter time, the Lord Jesus will lead us to worship the Father, He now taking a different position in that He is now leading us in singing. The Lord Jesus leads us to draw near to the Father and to sing praises together. The Son and the many sons join together in praise.

(6) The Sisters Meeting

The sisters meeting is also a helpful one to the church. In some localities, there *is* such a need for the sisters to meet; in some other places there *may not* be such a need.

If one or two sisters who are entrusted by the Lord with His word come to a local assembly, we should arrange to have a sisters meeting for them so that they may have the opportunity to exercise their gifts. Or if there are sisters already in the locality who are being used by the Lord, such a sisters meeting is in order. For this meeting enables these sisters who are used by God to have opportunity to give other sisters some spiritual assistance. But if there is not such a sister around, then such a meeting is not necessary.

(7) The Children's Meeting

The children's meeting is also needed. It is one of the works of the local assembly. Some brothers and sisters, especially the sisters, should undertake this work. The children may be taught to learn and to memorize Bible verses. They may learn to sing songs whose words consist of Scripture verses. They may be helped with visual aids.

If the children's meeting is well conducted, it has a good chance of adding to the number of believers. As more and more people are saved, the importance of the children's meeting increases accordingly, since the future of the church is to be found in the next generation.

6 The Deacons Office

And they sold their possessions and goods, and parted them to all, according as any man had need. (Acts 2.45)

For neither was there among them any that lacked: for as many as were possessors of lands or houses sold them, and brought the prices of the things that were sold, and laid them at the apostles' feet: and distribution was made unto each, according as any one had need. (Acts 4.34,35)

Now in these days, when the number of the disciples was multiplying, there arose a murmuring of the Grecian Jews against the Hebrews, because their widows were neglected in the daily ministration. (Acts 6.1)

Let none be enrolled as a widow under threescore years old, having been the wife of one man. (1 Tim. 5.9)

The Bible records in detail the spiritual—but not the physical arrangements—of the church. This is a most amazing thing. In the New Testament, the spiritual arrangements are shown us in great detail and perfection, but its physical arrangements are simply mentioned without any elaboration. The Bible tells us clearly how to exercise spiritual gifts, how to meet, and what the purpose of gathering together is (which is that of edification). It reveals to us distinctly how the church is local in practice—with the brethren, deacons and elders—and also how the elders are bishops or overseers. It plainly discloses to us as well how the Work is regional—with apostles being sent out and they then returning to their center. So that the Bible does indeed give us very clear guidance on the spiritual arrangements of the church. Anyone who is simple, pure and attentive enough before God, as well as being willing to learn, will find no great difficulty in this area. He will be able to receive clear light.

We may perhaps find it rather puzzling, however, that even though the New Testament *mentions* a goodly number of physical arrangements, they are not recorded in any great detail—as though the Bible shies away from doing so.

We have purposely quoted three passages from Acts. In two of them we are told that distribution was made according to the need of each person; and in one passage the Grecian widows were being neglected in their daily ministrations. At that time there were tens of thousands of believers in the church at Jerusalem. Today as we read these passages, the phrase "according as any one had need" may appear to be a very simple statement. But in what manner did the apostles actually make distribution according to each need among the tens of thousands of believers who had been saved not too long before? Let us understand that such activity had to involve much work with many and varied arrangements. It was not done in one or two days nor by just one or two persons. It was not merely a matter of serving one or two meals; it involved a tremendous undertaking to distribute according to each person's need.

I think all who have ever managed any substantial affair know how difficult this must have been. Here on Kuling Mountain there are presently only about one hundred people, but we have nonetheless felt the problem of supply. You should know that there are three or four brothers in the city (Foochow) and two or three brothers here on the mountain who are busy with supplying the need of all one hundred of us. And even in this current case, the task undertaken has not been a perfect one. If that be the case here with just a few of us, then how about tens of thousands of people?!? Yet the Bible simply records one descriptive word to summarize that gigantic undertaking: "According as any one had need"! To determine how many "any man's" there were there is difficult enough; to learn how they distributed "according as any one had need" is even more difficult. Yet even though the Scriptures use but a few words to describe what was done, we can begin to understand that those few words had to have represented an enormous amount of work. It must have required a great deal of organization and calculation and have involved many many people. Yet in an amazing way, the Bible treats in only a few words that which must have surely required weeks and months to do as though it could have been done in half an hour. What happened on the Day of Pentecost was recorded in great detail in Acts 2, but the kind of physical arrangement whereby distribution among the saints according to every man's need was made was not revealed here in any particular.

Learn Both Sides

(1) Church Affairs Must Be Arranged

We desire the brethren to learn a basic principle, which is, to see both sides of a matter. On the one hand, the Bible shows us distinctly that church affairs must be arranged. Perhaps some brothers entertain the erroneous concept that church affairs need not be ordered, as though they will just spontaneously be done. But the Scripture says plainly that distribution was made in those early days according to the need of each believer. Nothing was distributed casually, but all was given according to need. Hence, there *is* arrangement.

(2) Man, Not Method, Should Be Emphasized

On the other hand, we wish the brethren to notice that God does not *stress* arrangement. God does indeed order things, but He does not record such ordering in the Bible. The *fact* of arrangment is recorded, but the *method* of arrangement is not disclosed in the Scriptures. For God does not consider the method of arrangement so important as to deserve to be written up in His word. You may ask why. Simply because what God needs in the body of Christ are men of wisdom and spiritual understanding. If God's grace is upon them, His grace will also be manifested in the mundane affairs of the church. A person who is full of the Holy Spirit will know how to manage spiritual things. He may also be a skillful artisan to make the tabernacle of God. This too is spiritual work. So that God wants us to learn in spiritual things. In the Bible, from beginning to end you see spiritual arrangements—spiritual things and spiritual principles—but you see very little, if any, of physical arrangements. The facts are there, but not the detailed methods.

Danger of Recording the Methods

God knows human temptations and perils. After a while, all the spiritual principles will be lost, with only the physical affairs remaining. People may use methods which originate from God, but they may not necessarily be spiritual persons. Had the rules and regulations which the apostles adopted in managing the church affairs been recorded in detail, let me tell you that all who would read the Bible would be intent on learning these methods before they would try learning to be spiritual. For men are just naturally carnal, and therefore they can learn fleshly things far faster than spiritual things. Many brethren, when they learn about baptism, first argue about immersion or sprinkling before they notice its spiritual meaning. Instead of learning the meaning of baptism, they quarrel over the outward way of baptism. If there had been one book in the Bible which as a kind of manual had dealt exclusively with managing the mundane affairs of the Church, let me assure you that people would probably have thrown away the present twenty-seven books of the New Testament and would have made this one book a "must" reading for everybody. And thus this manual would have caught the attention of the entire Church and become the attraction of all Christians throughout the generations. It is for this very reason, therefore, that the Bible exhibits the characteristic of showing us only the grace of God without giving us His managerial techniques.

In many churches, there *is* such kind of manual. From Church history we learn that each time after God had given a revival in which many souls had been awakened and some servant or servants of the Lord had been used, people said that the church was now in need of arrangements—both in her spiritual and physical aspects. With the result that they devised many arrangements and wrote them down in a manual lest these arrangements would later be forgotten. Such record-keeping served as operating procedures for the later generations to follow. But let us be reminded once again from Church history that as time went by, the spiritual blessing began to ebb away, the living water was lost, and the power evaporated. The second generation became weaker than the first, and the third generation became even weaker than the second. So that while the spiritual blessings almost all ebbed away, the operating procedures were left intact. Now this describes in general terms the present-day condition of Protestantism.

It is for this reason that God refuses to show us in the Bible His methods for managing affairs; instead, He leaves them to the leading of the Holy Spirit. As the Holy Spirit fills the people, He gives them wisdom to manage things, thus avoiding the danger of one day having the shell, the method and the procedure in hand but the blessing, the living water and the spiritual power totally gone.

Is not this the basic problem with the Church? For in its long history, whenever a group of people have been raised up by God, there came forth a method or procedure which after one or two generations was the only thing left.

In view of this, we have tried for many years to avoid developing a fixed method or procedure. We do not want to have any method among us. If there is spiritual power and life, if the Lord's blessing continues, the maintenance of such a method may be convenient. But if one day these spiritual things are forfeited and only a method is left behind, we will simply be following in the footsteps of the Protestant churches. Only a shell will be left, with the inward spiritual reality gone.

Nevertheless, we must be careful not to fall to the other extreme as many others have done; for they contend that the church should have no method whatsoever. I wish all to pay attention to this point. Anyone who reads the Bible carefully knows that there *are* methods or procedures spoken of in the Scriptures. If we look at the physical care that was needed after Pentecost, I am sure we will be convinced that there *must* be operating procedures. And even though the Bible—as we have seen already in the case of the Jerusalem church—seems to touch on this matter lightly in just a few words, much attention to management methods and operating procedures lie behind those simple words. For it would have been terribly chaotic for the early apostles had there been no arrangements at all. So I would have all the brethren see that in the apostolic church of yesteryear there was indeed a working procedure.

Even so, God does not wish such procedure to remain to be copied by later generations. In a given period when the Spirit of God is working in a certain place, a method will just naturally be produced. But whenever the spiritual blessing which came expires, let such a method expire with it. We do not expect the method or procedure to linger even a day longer than does the spiritual blessing.

Oh, do let us find a way out of these two extremes. Some people are like the Protestants, always looking for a method or procedure. Yet the less water there is in a cup, the more attention there will be given to the outward appearance of the cup. For the day when finally a cup is not used to contain water at all, it will be hung up on a wall to be admired as an antique. Then will the people really stress the outside when that happens! But we know that God does not approve of such an emphasis on the outward. On the other hand, however, it is not entirely without external method. This is clearly demonstrated for us in Acts chapters 2, 4 and 6. As long as the problem with the widows of the Grecian Jews remained unsettled, the apostles considered the matter of the physical needs of the entire Jerusalem assembly to still be unsatisfactory. Out of the tens of thousands of believers who had been in need, only some widows still had problems unsolved, and yet the apostles were not satisfied, and felt bad about it until a solution was finally found.

Let us also recall Paul's word to Timothy (1 Tim. 5.9). It would appear as though Timothy had been keeping the names of widows in a book, yet we do not find a record of such a book of widows anywhere else in the Bible. Once again, a method or arrangement is but casually recorded in Scripture. And although we can safely infer that Timothy was familiar with such a book, Paul did not specify how big a book it should be nor how the names should be recorded in it. He only mentioned the matter of widows being enrolled, since he treated this subject as being something commonly known. He did advise that none was to be enrolled as a widow under sixty years of age. Even so, he did not state where this book came from and where it went afterwards.

Pray for the Method

I wonder if you are beginning to recognize God's way from

all this that has been shared? The Bible cites the fact of an arrangement and of a book, but it does not place much emphasis on the matter. God will not spend more than a few words on it. Yet is there not already enough in the Bible to enable us to manage church affairs? The principle is already given: there is a book! The principle of a book is there, but as to the how and the what and the where and so on *about* that book as it may pertain to us today—that must be carefully prayed over. We know the early church had a book, but we do not know how they kept the book. And hence, we must ask the Lord to show us how. He refuses to describe for us the details concerning this book lest we could conveniently come to know the how without there being any need for prayer. On the one hand, then, the Bible makes plain that the Church is to have methods and arrangements; but on the other hand, it must find the way through from God for itself.

Therefore, I wish the brethren assembled here could see this before God: Do not stress method or procedure, for that will be death. As soon as your attention focuses itself on method, it will kill. For when the spiritual blessing goes, the corpse will remain. Yet neither do I wish brothers and sisters to become careless about searching out ways to manage church affairs. This too would not be right. Though the Bible never tells us how, it does give us a principle for managing affairs. For God always has a way. It behooves us today, through prayer, to find out that way. Do not be so spiritual as to be methodless. There is a method, there is a book. Things will need to be done "according as any man has need."

The Method for Today

(1) A Deacons Office

If there are only a *few* believers in a local assembly, then naturally there is no need for a deacons office. But if there are *hundreds* of people, confusion will set in without there being a deacons office. Accordingly, this will be the first arrangement to be made.

(2) The Principle of a Book

The second thing to consider will be the principle of a book—that is to say, the principle of having records kept. Now if the book had been an action and not a principle, then God would have no doubt told us how thick and how wide the book was to be and how things were to be recorded in it. But He merely mentioned it in passing, thus indicating that this book actually represents a principle. Whenever something is merely mentioned in the Bible without giving any pertinent details, we can be assured that this thing is a principle, not a particular concrete action or activity to be undertaken.

Why do we need a book? Because human memory is so undependable. If things are to be done from memory, many will be left undone. For sometimes we remember, but sometimes we forget. Of course, there are some brothers and sisters who have wonderful memories. Yet even with them, something may be forgotten. What, then, can you do? Well, if things are recorded in a book, they will not be so easily forgotten as is the case when depending on one's memory.

Furthermore, even if one's memory is good, it will not always be available. If the one who can more easily remember is absent, what will happen to the matter which is to be done? If, however, the matter is recorded, anyone who opens the book can know it. Timothy must instruct the church at Ephesus as well as the churches in the surrounding areas. Titus must look after the different assemblies in Crete and to appoint elders in those cities. Suppose Timothy went to Rome and Titus returned to Jerusalem, what might happen to the widows if there were no books kept? Must people be sent to Rome to ask Timothy? And even should that happen, what if Timothy could not remember?

Thus we see the necessity of having church records. And that is what is to be derived from this principle of a book. Nothing is to be dependent upon memory. As days go by, even the best memory will fail. I cannot suppose that after so many years very many people can still remember everything. And even if someone can still remember, what will happen if he is not available at the critical moment of need? The principle of a book is therefore introduced to us in God's word. In the New Testament the Lord does show us that such recording is a principle. And hence we should record the things of the church.

For this reason, we sense the need of having a deacons office in any assembly with a considerable number of people in it. If you do not feel like using the name "deacons office," you may use whatever name is comfortable for you. We will not stress the name, we only wish to follow the principle.

(3) Things Done in Deacons Office

(a) For Maintaining Communications

The principal works of a deacons office are two in number The first is to maintain communication among the brethren. When there are hundreds or perhaps thousands of brothers and sisters in a local assembly, it will be difficult to find one or two particular persons. Visitors coming from abroad will not know whom to seek. People working in the deacons office can help them make the necessary arrangements.

In order to distribute to each according as any one has need, it will be necessary to have a local record which tells the kinds and degrees of need, the number of people in the families, and so forth. A few people must be there taking care of the distribution. In order to fulfill such a function, the deacons office can be the center of communication.

(b) For Keeping Records

The second use of a deacons office is to keep many records. The church conducts many affairs. Within a given week, many letters of recommendation may have to be sent out, many announcements made, many prayer requests taken up, many people received to the breaking of bread, and many baptized. All these matters need to be recorded. Moreover, some brothers and sisters may change their addresses, some may be sick, and some may have family problems. These too must be recorded so that proper help can be rendered.

I do not say these things must be kept forever. I rather expect them to fade away when spiritual reality fails. In the days of blessing, these things are needed, method is useful. But when the blessing disappears, these procedures should not be preserved.

(4) The Needs in the Deacons Office

Here we require some training and some knowledge. I do not expect every place to adopt exactly the same measure Since our needs are somewhat similar, however, the steps taken will probably not be too far apart from one place to another. Please keep in mind that we wish to follow the principles given in Acts chapters 2, 4 and 6. We will use the principle of a book. We need to ask God to give us a method which suits our special need. The Bible does contain methods, but it does not propagate them. Accordingly, we too will use methods, but we do not expect the methods adopted to be passed on. At the beginning, there is a need, and so we search out a way to meet that need. But after five or ten years, it may be necessary to adopt a new method for the need of that hour.

(a) Need a Place to Receive People

Because of the need, there must be a place where people can be received and matters can be transacted. At least a place where a few desks and shelves can be placed, and where people may have room to stand. You can call this place the deacons office if you wish. Such a place should be near or within the meeting place.

(b) Need People Working There

There need to be people working there to receive others. Such people are deacons or whoever else may desire to help.

Now I realize that it is easy for the church to hire people to manage its daily affairs, but I feel this is very much unlike a church. If a church can hire Levites by paying them salaries, why not hire priests as well? In so doing, however, a salary system will be restored. I would hope that the works of the Levites and the priests would not be accomplished by hiring people but by the brothers and sisters themselves performing these tasks in rotation. It is best if some brothers and sisters can set apart a day or an hour in a week to take care of the various church affairs.

To notify and to Inquire

If a certain brother is sick, the deacons office can be notified. Immediately the deacons can notify the responsible brothers or others concerned; moreover, as soon as something happens, notice may be sent from the deacons office so that within a short time all the brothers and sisters in the locality will know about it.

Or if any brother or sister wants to contact another brother or sister, he or she can call the deacons office. The person on duty can look at the record and give the address or telephone number.

Or another assembly elsewhere may write to ask if a certain person was baptized in your assembly. What if the elders cannot remember? As the number of those to be baptized increases, there will be a need for a record to be kept. By examining the record, the answer can readily be ascertained. Another matter which can be solved in the deacons office need not go to the responsible brothers. Only those things which it cannot handle should go to the responsible brothers. Otherwise, the latter will be so busy receiving people or whatever else, that they will have no time to take care of the church.

I thank God for the way things were managed during the time of the early apostles. For when there were murmurings among the Grecian Jews concerning their widows, the apostles were able to hear them. This is actually the work of the deacons. Their eyes must be open. As soon as something develops, they should notify the responsible brothers. Consequently, let us remember that a church is not as complicated as is a group in Protestantism, yet neither is it so simple as we sometimes tend to think. Protestantism has tended to over-organize itself, but *we* have tended to overturn the organization that *is* mentioned in the Bible. Both tendencies are wrong. What we need is a place in which to take care of the necessary business of the church.

To Receive and to Care

There need to be people in the deacons office to receive all who come in. From morning till evening, whenever there is any inquiry, it can be readily answered. Local brothers and sisters must not only serve in other capacities but also serve in the deacons office. The deacons office can help the church in many ways.

Some may look at such an office as being unspiritual. Our reply would be this: Does not David say, "I had rather be a doorkeeper in the house of my God" (Ps. 84.10)? Let us not become so spiritual that we cannot even keep the door of the house of God well. Do not assume that there is a great deal of difference between the Levites and the priests. They are *equally* important. Without the service of the Levites, there can be no local church.

May we all have the desire to spend two or three hours of each week working in the assembly. We are taking care of God's affairs. We are serving Him and serving His people so that all may grow. Never make this a personal work. Let the entire body serve in the many church affairs which need to be taken care of, such as arranging to meet brothers or sisters who come from abroad, taking care of orphans and widows, helping people to locate brothers or sisters, or assisting when accidents occur or family troubles arise. Then, too, someone may come to the church to inquire about the gospel. As more and more tracts are distributed, there will naturally be more inquirers who will knock on the door of the meeting place. The brothers or sisters who are in the deacons office can themselves talk to them or they can find other people to talk with them. This is why we need a place and people to staff such an office. Those brethren who do such deacons work can immediately render helps of all kinds when needed.

To Record Works

Always remember the principle of the book. Except for emergencies and unsettled matters, the brothers or sisters on duty should record all the works done. This will serve as a reference in future days. These records are very important. An assembly should keep a record of all who have been baptized; it should also keep a record of all who have been received to the Lord's table. It should have a record of all the letters of recommendation written as well as a copy of each letter. It should also have a record of the names and addresses of, and important information concerning, all the brothers and sisters. It should keep a record of all who have signed their names at the gospel meetings, and also keep a record of visitation—gospel, beginners, and elderly saints respectively. The works of the priests require a record too—how many people are put into what work.

The greatest use of record-keeping lies not in preservation but rather in inducement. Through such record-keeping, the responsible brothers are able to ascertain if certain matters are well taken care of by certain brothers and sisters. The responsible brothers are overseers, and they can be helped in their oversight of the church through these records.

To sum up, at the very beginning tell the brothers and sisters in the deacons office that when people come in they must be received politely but not in too businesslike a fashion. All the records must be kept neatly and accurately. Nothing should be done carelessly, for this is God's work. Let me tell you that all the lazy people will soon resign. Let us mean business before God. Even only an hour put in will help the church to be built a day earlier.

The Way Today Is All Serving

Please understand that responsible brothers do not speak from the platform once and then their responsibility is finished. Their duty is to get all the brothers and sisters to work. Without accomplishing this, we have no future. If all is dependent upon the Sunday preaching, then let us all be preachers. We rest six days and work one day, whereas God worked six days and rested one day. No wonder preachers have become lazy. No, we must work every day and cause all the brothers and sisters to work. The question is not whether *you* have done it, but whether the *others* as well as yourselves have done it.

Hence your work is, on the one hand, that *you* work, but on the other hand that you get *other* people to work too. You must lead them to work. Do not give them works and leave them alone. Follow up on them and see how the works have been done. Ask if there is any problem which you may help to solve. Thus shall the church be truly brought forth.

For the church to indeed appear, people must come forward. One day you shall see the whole church serving, the whole church preaching the gospel. In this way shall God's endeavor of recovery begin on earth, and God will have His Church. Otherwise, Christianity—which was taken captive into Babylon—will not have returned today. For currently people are still passive and there is still the intermediate class: on one side is God, on the other side are men, and in between is the intermediate class through whom men approach God. I wonder if you have recognized this problem.

So we see that the deacons office is instrumental in managing affairs. Recognize it for what it is—the instrument by which the brethren manage church affairs. By such records as are kept, the actual condition of the church may be known. Do you now see what God's Work is? It is not only preaching from the pulpit. We acknowledge the importance of the ministers of God's word. It is a very precious ministry. Even so, we want everybody else to serve.

Starting from Consecration

Someone may ask the question, How do we activate the entire body to work? I think the way to do this begins with the matter of consecration. This is a new way, and therefore it needs to be well ordered. *First of all,* all the brothers and sisters must be shown that service belongs to the whole church and that every member in the body has his or her function. The universal priesthood of all believers needs to be affirmed and underscored repeatedly. The truth about authority must also be told. *Second,* we must pay special attention to this principle of consecration—of selling all. Unless people sell all, their service will be false and unsuccessful. They must put everything on the altar for the sake of serving God. Hence the basic thought is that all must offer everything for the service of God. Today the Lord calls all who belong to Him to serve. Otherwise, all that we have seen and suggested will become merely dead method which will end in nothing. It is not a mere method, it is a way given by God.

When this that we have just now said is presented to the brothers and sisters, it must be presented strongly. Do not deliver it in such a way as though asking for their help or asking them to help God. Such a position is totally wrong. We must let them see how noble and glorious it is to serve God. Tell them that their vocation today is to serve the Lord, that their professions are but avocations. The main purpose is to learn to serve God, the other professions are mere sidelines. Do not fall so low as to *beg* people for God. No, we cannot beg them to serve Him. They must come to be accepted by God. If He wants them to serve, they must come and serve. The entire body of believers must serve; but if not, there will be no church. All the brothers and sisters must prostrate themselves before God and then rise up and serve.

Use Whomever God Has Apprehended

Some may further ask this: How are we to deal with a situation wherein some of the brethren do give themselves to God but others do not? The answer is that we can only use those whom God has apprehended. As many as have been apprehended by Him, just that many will we draw in. Nevertheless, we must be careful to get the rest to also be committed to God.

Work Till Everyone Serves

This is the way we wish to establish this: Let all the workers put everything they have into the Work, and let us call all the brothers and sisters to put their all in too. This is not something which a few can accomplish. It requires each and every one to be in the Work. All our strength, life and wealth must be put in. The higher we climb the more blessing God gives. The lower the note sounded, the fewer the number of people who will come. The more we are fearful, the less the number of people who will join in the Work.

Let us clearly understand that to be God's servants today is a great honor conferred upon us by the Lord. It is not *we* who favor *God*. Otherwise, how can we ever serve Him? If someone asks you to do an earthly work, *you* will thank *him* for the privilege, will you not? Then why should you think that God ought to thank you because you come to serve Him? Pardon me for having little patience with such thinking. If I hear someone say, "God loves you, therefore you ought to serve Him"—as though God should be very pleased to have that person's service—then let me tell you that I have no patience with such words. What you *should* say to that one is this: "You should be most pleased to be allowed to serve God, for shouldn't all people be pleased when they realize that a person such as they may serve the true and living God?"

Serving God Is My Glory

I need to see that if in my life I could serve God by crawling, that that would be my glory. If God would want me, then that is my greatest honor. How utterly foolish any of you are who think God needs to use such as you are. If He is willing to accept you, then this ought to be viewed as the *highest grace*. How odd for people to think they favor God or grant Him honor when they serve Him. I deem this to be most strange. I therefore hope that you all will see before God that there is no glory greater than that of serving Him. If I may stand at the gate and beg to serve God, that will be glory for me. For the Lord to be willing to accept me, that is most amazing. Does not God say, "I will have mercy on whom I have mercy, and I will have compassion on whom I have compassion" (Rom. 9.15)? Such is His mercy that He wants *me* to be *His* servant. How totally wrong you are if you consider yourself cleverer, higher, richer, or wiser than other people by your coming to serve the Lord.

Hence do not persuade people to serve God. Instead, convey this attitude to them: If people reckon it glory to serve a president, how much more is the distance between that president and God! If I am able to serve the Lord, *that* will be my greatest glory. When people offer things to God, it is not a question of how painful is the sacrifice but whether the Lord will accept them. For how do you know what He will accept? Do realize that this is more than even a matter of consecration, it is a matter of divine acceptance. Tell the people that whether or not God will accept them is really the central question. If He is willing to accept them, then that will be their glory. Consequently, it is really not a question of whether men are willing to offer, but a question of whether God will accept. Let the way be straight and the position high. Speak from His ground and from His perspective.

How dare people be arrogant before God. How pitiful if anyone should think about himself when he comes to serve. Will the Lord ever use such a person? Never! For man to be allowed to serve the Lord of Lords, that is the utmost glory! May God be gracious to us that we may walk straight in His way and manage the church affairs well.

7 District Meetings

If a locality is too large and the people are too many, district meetings become a necessary arrangement. We do not believe in the congregational church system which makes each congregation a separate unit. For the Bible teaches locality, not a congregation, as the unit—such as Corinth or Rome. So that when there are multitudes of brethren in one locality, such as Jerusalem which had tens of thousands of people, you realize immediately how impossible it was for them all to meet in one place. Even during the first few days, what with three thousand and then five thousand believers added, it was quite impossible for them all to meet together in one place. One can readily see, therefore, the need for some arrangement.

"By Hundreds, and by Fifties"

We do not use the particula portion of Scripture found in Mark 6.34-44 as *evidence*; we only take it as a *guide*. Recall how at the time our Lord Jesus multiplied th loaves, there were five thousand men present—besides the women and children. How, then, will you distribute loaves to such a multi tude? Quite naturally, the Lord ordered them to sit in companies of hundreds and fifties. Today we would accept the Lord's principle of such an arrangement. As the brothers and sisters increase in larger number, we can adopt the Lord's way by dividing them into hundreds and fifties.

Please notice that our Lord did not divide the multitude into either *all* fifties or *all* hundreds. He divided them both by hundreds *and* by fifties. This means that the dividing was by convenient numbers. So that today as the brethren in a church increase, we can divide them in convenient, not in fixed, numbers. According to convenience and geography fifty or a hundred people may meet separately. Since the difference between these two numbers was double, the Lord merely gives us a convenient number.

According to this principle, I think responsible brothers in various localities should learn to make such an arrangement. As people increase, divide into districts. The number of people meeting in one place or another will vary somewhere between these two numbers. Such kind of dividing will be most convenient because there will be fewer people and they will be easier to look after. Furthermore, with fewer people in a given meeting, there will be more opportunity for all to participate.

Meeting Separately

The gospel meeting, the prayer meeting, and the beginners meeting may all be held according to the individual districts. Even the ministry meetings and the breaking of bread meetings may be conducted in the individual districts. However, if a worker is in the region, and some special ministry of God's word is to be given, it will be more expedient to hold joint sessions.

District Care

Care may be performed according to district. The responsible brothers should learn to so arrange themselves that there will be one or more of them in each district. Thus they can take up responsibility and take care of the spiritual situation of the district.

Possibility of Balanced Growth

If the districts are properly divided and district needs are well met, we can expect a general and balanced growth in the meeting. For people may all pray and share together before God.

Church at Jerusalem Met in Districts

The Bible has not shown us how Jerusalem was divided into districts, but as we read the book of Acts we nonetheless know that the church did meet in various district settings. We find, for example, that their prayer meetings were held in different homes. Recall the story of Rhoda the maid after Peter had been delivered by God from jail (see Acts 12.3-17). In that home a prayer meeting was in progress when Peter knocked at the door. Let me reiterate the point made earlier that the Bible does not tend to describe *in detail* those matters which pertain to church affairs, since God is not willing to let us have a framework. But it does contain a *shadow* of things arranged. Only *shadows* are found in the Bible in order that the Church throughout the generations to come might learn something from God when a similar circumstance arises requiring an arrangement to be worked out for the management of a church matter.

As a matter of fact, it was impossible for all the brothers and sisters to assemble together to break bread either. This was a physical impossibility. If there was but one cup, how big must that cup have been! If but one loaf, how could it have been passed? How long a time must have been consumed in passing the loaf and the cup to a group of a thousand people which later on grew to tens of thousands of people! This obviously became absolutely impossible. Even if all seven days in the week had been used for the breaking of bread meeting, the passing of one loaf and one cup could hardly have been well distributed. Thus we can see clearly that there must have been district-type meetings held at that time. The house where Rhoda answered the door (in this case the home of Mary the mother of John Mark) was but one of the many houses for meeting.

Let Us Maintain This Principle

I trust we will be able to maintain this principle before God: on the one hand, we confess that the Bible does make some arrangements; on the other hand, we concede that it does not give us the detailed rules and regulations concerning these arrangements.

The Bible mentions, for example, letters of commendation, yet it never tells us how such letters should be written. You will remember that Paul said he did not need such a letter: "Are we beginning again to commend ourselves? or need we, as do some, epistles of commendation to you or from you?" (2 Cor. 3.1) This implies that there *were* letters of commendation. But Paul did not describe at all how these letters were written. So that as we write our own letters of commendation today, we must learn to write them well. There is no form which we can fill in. We must instead learn to write them continuously.

As God touches upon various church affairs in His word, He always gives us a principle. He merely shows us there is something He does, for He never takes into consideration that the Holy Spirit will ever leave the Church. From God's viewpoint the Holy Spirit is Christ's representative in the Church. The Holy Spirit dwells in the Church. And consequently, if we truly submit ourselves to the Head of the Church, we will be taught by the Holy Spirit how to act according to the particular principle given.

I hope you will be able to understand this matter of the district meeting. Though we do not have any Scriptural evidence of rule telling us what to do, we nonetheless recognize that the district meeting is a must—physically speaking. In the book of Acts, we notice it was definitely created: "from house to house" (Acts 2.46 AV, literal Greek). And the house where Rhoda was present was one of these very houses. These passages disclose the principle of having district meetings.

I therefore hope you will keep this principle ever in mind: that regarding spiritual things, the Bible gives us great details so that nothing significant is left untold; but that regarding physical things (Levitical service) it only gives us hints but no rules and regulations. It shows us something, but without revealing how. Yet as we do it, we realize that the Holy Spirit has not left us. The Holy Spirit is in the Church; He is the Head of the Church. We can wait and pray and receive light as to how to meet in districts.

8 The Local Assembly That Is Also a Work Center

Another matter to be considered: a local assembly where the Work center is. There are two kinds of local assemblies: one is the ordinary local assembly, the other is the local assembly where a Work center is located. These two are actually not much different from each other, the only distinction being what place the apostles have in a local assembly.

Elders, Deacons, and Brethren in a Local Assembly

Let us look at the church at Philippi. The church there had the saints, the elders, and the deacons: "To all the saints in Christ Jesus that are at Philippi, with the overseers and deacons" (Phil. 1.1 mg.). This statement of greeting makes it very clear that the letter was written to all the believers in the church there with its elders and deacons. This is the arrangement for an ordinary local assembly.

Apostles in a Work Center

In a local assembly where a Work center was located, apostles were being added. Ordinarily, in a local assembly the elders form the governing body; but in a local assembly that is additionally a Work center, apostles also reside there.

Apostles Who Are Also Elders

Apostles are responsibile for the Work in a given region; they are there specifically for the Work. But at the same time some of these apostles may also be involved in the affairs of the local assembly. So that in the place where the local assembly and the Work center co-exist, some apostles act in a dual capacity both as apostles *and* as elders. So far as the Work is concerned, the apostles take care of it in this region. But since this is where the local assembly is, they also take care of the church. However, they cannot govern the local assembly as apostles, but these apostles must also become elders.

The Bible shows us how things were done in a church council (the only instance of it, incidentally, recorded in the Scriptures). When a letter sent from this council was written, it was written by "the apostles and the elders, brethren" in Jerusalem (Acts 15.23).

I wish to point out here that Peter was an apostle, perhaps even the chief among the apostles. But in Jerusalem, he was also an elder (as his First Epistle in the New Testament would indicate: "The elders therefore among you I exhort, who am a fellow elder"—5.1). So that Peter not only was an apostle but also an elder. Likewise with John: "The elder unto . . ." (2 John 1), "The elder unto . . . " (3 John 1). Hence John, one of the original twelve apostles, was an elder as well.

In 1 Peter 1.1, Peter tells us that he is an apostle. And he *writes* the letter as an apostle. But in 5.1 of the same letter, he further reveals to us that he is also an elder. 2 and 3 John both begin with the same greeting: "The elder unto . . ." John, however, does not mention that he is an apostle. This is rather unusual. He is neither like Paul nor Peter, in that these two always wrote as apostles.

In any case, the two great apostles in Jerusalem (Peter and John) were also elders in Jerusalem. They were noteworthy among all the apostles who were in that city, and they were also elders there at the same time. Except for James, the other original twelve apostles were not identified by name at all. Of the twelve, these three apostles—Peter, John and James—were the only ones noted in the book of Acts. But two of these three, from the record of the New Testament epistles, are singled out as also being elders.

Now there was another James—brother to our Lord Jesus—who also being an apostle (Gal. 1.19) seems to have made the final decision at the church council in question. Both from the word of the Bible and from Church history, we can be certain that at the time of this council, he too was an elder in Jerusalem. And it would appear as though he had surpassed even Peter in leadership, for it was he who made the final decision of the council.

Apostles Cannot Deal with Affairs in Local Assemblies Directly

From all of this, then, it becomes clear that if you are an elder of a local assembly, you cannot rule over things in other assemblies elsewhere. If you are an elder of the church at Jerusalem, you cannot manage local affairs in the local assembly at Samaria. For the elders in the Bible are all local in character. You cannot transcend the scope of a local assembly and control other local assemblies. As apostles, you cannot touch matters in a local assembly directly. You may deal with the elders, but you cannot deal directly with local affairs.

Take as an example the labors at Corinth done by Paul. It is quite plain in the book of Acts that Paul visited Corinth and labored there. The relationship between him and the church at Corinth was indeed very deep and strong. He even wrote at least two letters to the believers there; not only *he* visited Corinth, but he sent Timothy and Titus on visits there as well. All this represents Paul's work. Even so, when in the church at Corinth a person had sinned, Paul himself had no way to cast him out, simply because he was an apostle and not an elder in the church at Corinth. He had no authority to post an announcement that said: "I have excommunicated so-and-so." He must instead write to the church at Corinth, saying, "(You) put away the wicked man from among yourselves" (1 Cor. 5.13b). *He* could not excommunicate that person *for* the church, for Paul was not an elder; he was only an apostle. Nowhere in the Scriptures are we shown that Paul ever became an elder in some local assembly. He was strictly an apostle, an apostle to the Gentiles. He thus could not control any local assemblies. As elders cannot control other assemblies but can only manage their own local assemblies, so apostles cannot touch directly the government of any local assembly but can only govern the regional Work. And hence affairs in the church at Corinth must be handled by the Corinthians themselves; Paul cannot manage for them.

So what did Paul end up doing? He wrote: "In the name of our Lord Jesus, ye being gathered together and my spirit, with the power of our Lord Jesus, to deliver such a one unto Satan for the destruction of the flesh, that the spirit may be saved in the day of the Lord Jesus" (1 Cor. 5.4,5). As an apostle, he could exercise spiritual authority to deliver to Satan the brother who had sinned, but he had no way to excommunicate the brother. And this is the way the Bible prescribes for handling church affairs.

Peter Bears Double Responsibility

In a local assembly, such as in Jerusalem, where there was also a Work center, the apostle Peter bore a double responsibility. He had authority to take care of the Work in the region surrounding Jerusalem, but at the same time he also acted as an elder in the local assembly there. If you are not an elder in Jerusalem, you cannot directly control the affairs of Jerusalem. So that Peter and John were both elders in Jerusalem, and James was an elder there too. But Peter must additionally handle the Work in Samaria because he was also an apostle. He managed the Work in that region in the capacity of an apostle and managed the affairs of the church at Jerusalem in the capacity of an elder. This is quite clear in Scripture.

This is why one day when there was a problem in Antioch and people were sent to Jerusalem to make inquiry, the letter written by the brethren in Jerusalem could say, "The apostles and the elders, brethren . . . For it seemed good to the Holy Spirit, and to us" (Acts 15.23,28). The apostles in Jerusalem were in relation to the region; the elders in Jerusalem were in relation to the local assembly. Such decisions were thus made by both the apostles and the elders.

I feel good about all this, for in spiritual matters pertaining to the local church, God has not left anything for us to fill in but has given detailed direction. The apostles are responsible for the Work while the elders are responsible for the local assembly. In this case, however, Peter held a double responsibility.

Some Apostles Were Not Elders

Some apostles were not elders, such as Paul and Barnabas. In reading the New Testament carefully, we cannot find any place where Paul was also an elder. In the church at Antioch, Paul and Barnabas had part in the ministry of God's word but no part in any local office. They had ministry but occupied no governmental office. They were neither deacons nor elders. They were instead prophets and teachers. Accordingly, in Antioch these two apostles belonged to ministry and not to government.

Antioch, Another Beginning of the Holy Spirit

Let us take note that just as Jerusalem was begun by the Holy Spirit so Antioch was begun by the Holy Spirit too. Antioch did not conceive a new way of work by itself; it was simply another beginning of God's Work by the Holy Spirit.

Antioch—Fatal to Roman Catholicism

Please be aware that this new beginning of the Work in Antioch has tremendous significance for the Church. If we know God, we will bow our heads and worship Him each time we come to Acts chapters 13 and 14. I often thank Him for these two chapters. Chapter 13 serves as a fatal blow to Roman Catholicism. Without that chapter, we would have had to return to Rome—whether Rome was right or wrong. And why? Because the Holy Spirit had commenced in Jerusalem, and Jerusalem had then become a center of the Work. And had the Holy Spirit not made a new beginning in Antioch, we would have had to confess that God had but one center on the earth.

Do you now perceive this significance? If you do not have the Work in your mind, you will not sense the immensity of what happened at the time of Acts 13. But if you have the Work on your heart, you can see that this was a great step—a most strategic step—taken by the Holy Spirit. For up through the time of chapter 12, all you could see was the Work of Jerusalem—that even the Work done at Antioch was also that of Jerusalem; for in reading from chapter 11 onwards you will notice that the Work in Antioch had been done by the brethren coming out of Jerusalem. If only this evidence were available, you would just naturally have to confess that God's Work has a single center on earth, which center was Jerusalem. At some future time in Church history it might have been removed to another place—this we cannot be sure about—but nevertheless there was a center. In other words, you would have to acknowledge, on the basis of only *this* amount of evidence from the Bible that Christianity was to have but a single capital. Jerusalem would become the capital of Christianity just as Mecca became the capital of Islam and Chufoo, the capital of Confucianism. But thank God that the Holy Spirit made *another* beginning in the Work—this time at Antioch. Because out from Antioch the Holy Spirit sent apostles also.

Paul and Barnabas Become Apostles Too

How did Paul dare to take up the "title" of apostle? Barnabas was a good brother, but in Jerusalem he was just an ordinary saint and not an apostle. And Paul himself was certainly not an apostle originally. However, after the Holy Spirit singled them out by name in Antioch, then set them apart and sent them out, we will notice that Luke in his narrative described them as apostles. Later in his account, Luke wrote: "The multitude of the city was divided; and part held with the Jews, and part with the apostles [Barnabas and Paul]" (Acts 14.4). The Holy Spirit, through Luke here, did not declare that He had ordained them as apostles or had set them up as apostles; it was simply recorded that they *were* apostles. In other words, God himself made a new start by His own Spirit. It was not begun by Paul and Barnabas themselves. Had this new adventure been started by them, we could disavow it. But the Holy Spirit was the one who had commenced anew at Antioch. *He* appointed apostles and sent them out to the Work. And immediately we come to realize from the *additional* evidence that there is *more* than one Work center. For now there are at least *two* regional areas of God's Work in existence. And the concept of one single center on earth is thus forever destroyed. Christianity has *no* capital.

Let us thank God that wherever the *Holy Spirit* commences a Work, there is the capital of Christianity, and against such there is no human restriction. After all, the *Lord* is the Head of the Church, and the Holy Spirit is *still* His representative on earth. Oftentimes He uses us, but many other times He works outside of us. For Jerusalem and its saints had no way of monopolizing the Work of the Lord! We observe on the one hand that God had already set up Jerusalem as a center; but we observe on the other hand that He could also set up Antioch as a center too. He can therefore set up Shanghai as a center, and in addition set up Foochow as a center. Let us clearly see, then, that there is not just one center of God's Work. If there be but one single center, then the principle of Rome would be right.

May Have Third Or More Regions

This that we have been speaking about is a matter of great consequence. Acts chapter 13 is a foundation stone of Christianity. Without it, we would be confronted with many monumental problems. Without it, the idea of a pope would be all right. Without it, the Roman concept of a capital for Christianity would undoubedly be correct. But we now know that before God there is not just one center, but two centers; not only one regional area of God's Work but two regional areas. As a matter of fact, as it pleases the Holy Spirit, He can set up the third, the tenth, the hundredth, the thousandth or even the ten thousandth region on earth. Everything is according to the thought of the Holy Spirit in His labor on earth, for nothing is to be according to man's idea.

Apostles Not Being Elders May Go Out Continuously

The uniqueness about these two apostles who were sent out from Antioch is that they were not elders in the church at Antioch. Thus as they went out to work, they traveled as itinerants from place to place. Paul and Barnabas did return to Antioch, but they did not return quickly. Paul, for example, stayed in Ephesus for three years. Had they been elders in Jerusalem, they would probably have been in Ephesus for three weeks and then would have returned to Jerusalem. They could have ventured out from Jerusalem, but they would then have had to return quickly. They would have gone out because they were apostles; they would have returned within a reasonably short time because they were elders.

Paul and Barnabas being apostles but not elders could go out for many years without their absence creating any problem in Antioch whatsoever. They could go wherever the Holy Spirit led them. For they were only apostles, not elders as well. Peter and John, on the other hand, were *both* apostles *and* elders. So they went out for a short while and returned quickly to Jerusalem; otherwise how could they have ever taken care of their responsibility back in Jerusalem? They could not but go out because they were apostles, yet they could not but come back—and that quickly—because they were elders. This is truly something remarkable. They were apostles, so they frequently went out; but they were also elders, and therefore they always came back. They had to take care of their responsibility in Jerusalem, hence they could not travel too far away.

Need Strong Meeting

Why do we spend so much time these days together in explaining this matter? Because this has much to do with your future work. This is a principle you must accept. If you are responsible for the Work in a region as well as responsible in establishing a local assembly, you will need to learn to be apostles as well as elders. And this will also require you to have a strong meeting in the locality. A number of Bible commentators tell us that the church at Antioch was the strongest one of that time. Many tell us that it was a model church. In fact, I recall in my youth having read a book called *The Model Church,* and it spoke at length of this very church at Antioch.

Now if anyone is not in responsibility for the local assembly, he should devote himself to apostolic work—that is to say, he should always go out to work and later return. Even if he should stay longer on the outside, he will create no problems by his lengthy absence. Yet there will be other people who shall return shortly after they go forth, such as Peter did in going out to Samaria and to Caesarea but very soon thereafter coming back to Jerusalem because he also was an elder there.

Henceforth, those brethren who act as apostles must go out and those who act as both apostles *and* elders must return. The way is neat and clean.

Only Difference Is in Platform

A local assembly which is also a Work center is not different from any other local assembly except in one respect; in a local assembly that is also a regional center live the apostles as well as the local elders; moreover, some of the apostles may also be elders. So that probably there will be some difference in the platform, for due to the presence of apostles and their willingness to share, there will undoubtedly be a special ministry of God's word. And this is something which an ordinary local assembly would not have.

9 The Relation between a Local Assembly and the Work

What is the relationship between a local assembly and the Work? What is the relationship between a local assembly and the apostles? We wish to look into this matter. Local assemblies such as Jerusalem and Antioch were special and exceptional because they were Work centers as well as local assemblies. So far as being a local assembly was concerned, they were no different from any other local assembly of that day. But so far as the Work was concerned, they at the same time were Work centers. And therefore we do acknowledge Jerusalem and Antioch as having been somewhat different from other assemblies. So the question now comes down to what the relationship of the *other* assemblies was to the Work?

In our book, *Rethinking the Work*,* we attempted at some length to show brothers and sisters that the local assembly is the highest church authority on earth. And why? Because apart from the individual local assemblies, our Lord has not established any union of churches on earth whatsoever. The Scriptures do not contain any idea of a mother church; it only confesses a local assembly as a unit. The local assembly is the only unit, above which there is no other church authority.

Highest Authority in Local Assembly Rests upon Elders

The highest authority in a local assembly is represented by

*See footnote on opening page of Chapter 4 above. — *Translator*

the elders. Everything in the church is governed directly by them. An apostle cannot touch a local assembly directly—that is to say, he cannot directly deal with local affairs. A person in Corinth needed to be excommunicated, but Paul himself could not cast him out. This is a very revealing case. For here is shown the relationship between a given local assembly and the Work or between a local assembly and an apostle. In other words, the apostle cannot intervene directly; he must do it through the elders. For God has not ordered the local assembly to obey the command of the apostle directly, He only calls for all the brothers and sisters in a local assembly to accept an order of its eldership. If the spiritual condition of the elders is right, they themselves should receive the apostle's word.

Elders Are Appointed by Apostles

Let us note again that elders are appointed by apostles. Timothy and Titus were also apostles; they were especially sent by Paul. One was in Ephesus, the other was in Crete. They appointed elders in different cities. Do not forget that the authority of the elders does not come from the church. No elder is elected by the local assembly. Elders are not chosen by the local brethren; they are set up by the apostles. A local assembly has no right to choose its elders, and therefore should not do so. God shows us that it was Paul, Timothy, and Titus who appointed elders; that is to say, the apostolic workers appointed them.

Church Must Learn to Obey Elders, Elders Learn to Listen to Apostles

A local assembly that has elders established must listen to the words of its elders, and not to the words of a Timothy or a Titus. For elders are the bishops or overseers of the church. The highest authority of a local assembly is vested in them. But elders do receive their authority from apostles. The apostles give elders authority to govern the local church's affairs directly. So hence it behooves the elders to learn to listen to the words of the apostles. They must not despise the counsel of the apostles. It is possible for the church not to obey the apostle's order directly, but it is not permitted for the church not to accept the order of the elders. This is God's way with local assemblies.

Apostles Responsible for Work, Elders Responsible for Church

The apostles are responsible for the advancement of the Work; they are not involved in the care of local church affairs, which is the responsibility of the elders. The apostles are concerned with the promotion of the Work of the entire body of Christ. Thus the Bible gives us clear arrangements for workers, the local assembly, and the elders.

How the Church Decides on Issues

I believe all workers and elders share a common notion: a preaching meeting can easily be handled, but a business meeting is rather difficult to conduct. There does not appear to be much problem in spiritual things; the biggest headache is tending to the church's affairs. For in such situation it is quite easy for each one to have his own idea. Many things cannot be settled because of differing opinions.

Acts 15: the Pattern for Church Council

Acts 15 is the only place in the entire New Testament where there is a record of the church having met for business. As you know, the Roman Catholic Church has had many councils, but in Jerusalem there was only one council held. Let us keep in mind that God puts this in the Bible as a pattern for all church councils. Do not incorrectly interpret Acts 15 as being a bad experience. On the contrary, it is a most precious chapter in the book of Acts. Without it we would be at a loss when we today try to manage church affairs. Acts 15 provides the pattern given by God for the Church to follow during these two thousand years ever since.

A Problem Arises

Here in Jerusalem a problem arose. Many foolishly assume that having no problem is a sign of spirituality in a church. Let it be known that a sign of spirituality in a church is not that it is without any problem but that it has the means to solve problems. If a church is spiritual, it will have many difficulties because it has to consider many things. A church that is not spiritual is so permissive that it can do anything in any way. The more it is under the hold of a "strong man" (see Matt. 12.29), the more uneventful it will be; whereas the more spiritual it is, the more matters it will have that need to be solved.

Jerusalem has a problem. Where did this problem originate? Many who were formerly zealous in Judaism traveled widely to many places, even to Antioch. They told the believers there that they must be circumcised according to the Mosaic Law. Under such a circumstance, Paul and Barnabas felt it necessary to go to Jerusalem, and some other brothers in the church at Antioch went with them.

Apostles and Elders Meet, but Brethren Allowed to Speak

They went to Jerusalem to see the apostles and the elders: "Go up to Jerusalem unto the apostles and elders about this question" (Acts 15.2). "And when they were come to Jerusalem, they were received of the church and the apostles and elders" (v.4). The church received them, the apostles received them, and the elders received them. All three received Paul and his party.

But there were believers present who had been Pharisees before. With their Pharisaic background, they rose up and declared: "It is needful to circumcise them [the Gentile believers], and to charge them to keep the law of Moses" (v.5). I trust that all brothers and sisters can begin to perceive from the Bible how a council on business is to be held. The Jerusalem council was one consisting of the apostles and the elders. It was not a council of the local church. Its responsibility fell on the apostles and the elders.

Now there was no difficulty over this matter of circumcision and the Mosaic Law among the apostles and the elders themselves. But some believers with a Pharisaic background were strongly advocating that the Gentile believers be circumcised and that they keep the Law of Moses. Let it be understood right here that the main body which was discussing these Church matters were the apostles and the elders. They also were the ones to make the final decision. But before they made any decision, they felt they must hear what some opposing brothers had to say. It was a meeting of the apostles and the elders in Jerusalem, yet they allowed these brothers to come in and present their view. Those who opposed the matter of grace alone had their reason, and they were given opportunity to voice it. Do not interpret this as being unspiritual, for God desires the responsible brothers—those with authority—to be persons who can listen. They should be able to sit there and listen to contrary views. Anyone who cannot listen to an opposing view is not fit to be a leader in the Church.

"And the apostles and the elders were gathered together to consider of this matter. And when there had been much questioning . . . " (vv.6,7a). Many words had been said, all sorts of arguments had been offered, and many opinions had been raised. Many brothers agreed and many brothers disagreed. The apostles and the elders allowed all who had opinions and who wished to express them to come forward and speak. Although the meeting belonged to the apostles and the elders, they permitted anyone and everyone from the entire body of believers to come and express himself as he wished. Let me tell you that this is the principle for managing such affairs to be found in the Bible. It certainly is not by suppressing or by refusing to hear what people have to say. Even words which appear weak and nonsensical have to be heard out. By so doing, the responsible brothers whose spiritual condition is right may, in the process, come to know how to decide as they sit and listen. Many responsible brothers in the Church lack this habit of listening. Or if they do listen, they may simply listen to one or a few, rather than all the brethren who may wish to speak. The Church is not like the Roman Catholic Church—which is as dictatorial as Thyatira was (Rev. 2.18ff.), nor is it democratic as was Laodicea (Rev. 3.14ff.). The Church follows the Jerusalem principle: let all the brethren speak, but let the responsible brothers decide. The people themselves are not to make any decisions.

Apostles and Elders Decide, Church and Holy Spirit Approve

How was the matter ultimately settled? It was really amazing. The brethren had spoken, and now the apostles and the elders spoke. The first one among them who stood up to speak was Peter. He rose up to tell his experience and to offer his own opinion: "Brethren, ye know that a good while ago God made choice among you, that by my mouth the Gentiles should hear the word of the gospel, and believe. And God, who knoweth the heart, bare them witness, giving them the Holy Spirit, even as he did unto us; and he made no distinction between us and them, cleansing their hearts by faith. Now therefore why make ye trial of God, that ye should put a yoke upon the necks of the disciples which neither our fathers nor we were able to bear?" (Acts 15.7b-10)

Next Barnabas was invited to speak since he had originally been a part of the church at Jerusalem before moving to Antioch. He was followed up by Paul.

Here we see that Peter spoke, Barnabas spoke, and Paul spoke. Finally, James rose up to speak. How beautiful verse 13 is: "And after they had held their peace, James answered, saying, Brethren, hearken unto me." He stood foremost among the brethren in Jerusalem. After Peter and Barnabas and Paul had all testified to the same effect, we now observe what James had to say: "Brethren, hearken unto me: Symeon hath rehearsed how first God visited the Gentiles . . . Wherefore my judgment is [this is a word of authority], that we trouble not them that from among the Gentiles turn to God; but that we write unto them, that they abstain from the pollutions of idols, and from fornication, and from what is strangled, and from blood. For Moses from generations of old hath in every city them that preach him, being read in the synagogues every sabbath. Then it seemed good to the apostles and the elders, with the whole church . . ." (vv.13-22). Thus was this matter settled. This was the first church council ever recorded in the Bible and it was also the last one!

I wish you to see that *this* is the way the *church* should decide on issues. It is different from the ways the *world* practices. In the world either the majority of the people rules (as at Laodicea) or one or two at the top make the decision (as at Thyatira). In the church, all the brethren have the opportunity to speak and to argue. Everyone who wishes to speak may speak. But this is *not* for the purpose of deciding there and then accordingly; rather, it gives the church time to wait upon the Lord, for a simple brother in the midst may quite possibly speak out the mind of God. And hence each may speak and argue, but the arguing does not continue endlessly. After much questioning and discussion, let the responsible brothers—those with spiritual stature before God, and whether apostles or elders—express their thoughts. Finally, through the one with the highest authority, God discloses His mind. And you see that the opinions of all the responsible brothers are the same. After hearing the same from them, the decision is at last made. And all the other brethren learn to accept this decision: "Then it seemed good to the apostles and the elders, with the whole church." This is the way the church manages its affairs.

In managing its affairs, the church does not resort to casting a vote. It leaves the final decision to those with spiritual weight. All the arguments must be heard; we must learn to allow all the brethren to speak, and to learn to listen to their arguments. Do not view this as wrong. Let them speak indeed; but on the other hand, ask God to give you a right decision.

Subsequently, we find that this was not only the decision made by the apostles, the elders and the whole church, it was also made by God. How marvelous is the word which follows: "It seemed good to the Holy Spirit and to us" (v.28a). The anointing of the Holy Spirit was there. This matter was decided by "the Holy Spirit and us," who then direct the apostles and the elders to write a letter.

I expect all the brethren to see that the way the church manages affairs is neither dictatorial nor democratic. In the church there is no such thing as the majority listening to the minority or the minority listening to the majority. It is neither one man's opinion nor a majority opinion. There is only the brothers and sisters speaking their minds and those who are spiritual deciding for them. The final decision in church matters is indeed to be in the hands of those with spiritual authority; nevertheless, they must let all who wish have an opportunity to speak. And as those with authority are listening, they must try to touch the Spirit. And ultimately they may rise up and say that a few of us brothers make such and such a decision. And after a decision has been made, the whole church follows it with one accord. How different is this way from that of the world.

Touch the Spirit of Scripture

The most important thing in reading the Bible is for us to touch the spirit of the Scriptures. I hope you will take Acts chapter 15 and try to touch its spirit. There was "much questioning" from the brethren (v.7). When the Bible records "much" it must have been much. Possibly those believers who had formerly been Pharisees probably still had many foolish things to say.

Peter Untouched by Much Questioning

The spirit of the man we first wish to touch is Peter's. When Peter rose up, what did he say? Evidently he was untouched by the arguments of these men. As he stood up and spoke, he was like a newborn baby without any outward feeling, and in no way was he touched by the spirit of argument just manifested in these brothers. This must be the condition of the responsible brothers. Each time when the church convenes for business, a responsible brother whose inside is touched by outside discussion is unfit to take responsibility. When Peter stood up, he did not have any spirit of questioning. If anyone in responsibility joins in the argument, he is not fit to lead or to exercise authority. For authority never argues. In arguing, the position is lost.

How beautiful it was that when Peter got up, he had not a word of questioning. How lovely when he said: "Brethren, ye know that a good while ago God made choice among you, that by my mouth the Gentiles should hear the word of the gospel, and believe" (Acts 15.7). It is not just today that I speak thus; I speak today what I have spoken before. And that was a good while ago. "And God, who knoweth the heart, bare them witness, giving them the Holy Spirit, even as he did unto us" (v.8). Peter had neither laid hands on them nor baptized them. If I myself had laid hands on them, Peter might have said, then you might be able to argue that it was because I was the one who had given them the Holy Spirit. If I myself had baptized them, you might be able to argue that this is what I have done. No, I neither laid hands on them nor baptized them nor even prayed for them. It was the Holy Spirit himself who came upon them. Therefore, you cannot blame me for this thing having been done. "And he made no distinction between us and them, cleansing their hearts by faith. Now therefore why make ye trial of God, that ye should put a yoke upon the neck of the disciples which neither our fathers nor we were able to bear? But we believe that we shall be saved through the grace of the Lord Jesus, in like manner as they" (vv.9-11). So clear, so simple, and without any argument or spirit of questioning.

Let me declare to you that the Bible has a spirit behind its words. And as you touch this spirit, you will be touching the Book. Peter put forth his case simply, without being affected by much questioning and debate. He maintained his dignity and spoke as one with authority. Hence I do hope that at a church council none of you falls into argument, for once you do, you are not fit to make decisions.

Barnabas and Paul Brought in Presence of God

Let us next focus on Barnabas and Paul who rose to speak in succession. Please notice especially the solemnity before God when these two brothers testified. They did not stand up to deliver some stirring but careless words. They did not utter any trivial statement. This was the time to stop arguing, not a time to inflame the passions of argument. The best way to put argument to an end is to bring in the presence of God. In such a meeting, idle words must cease. *Your* words cannot stop any *idle* words, only the presence of the Lord will stop them. You need to be a person who brings in the Lord's presence. After Peter finished speaking, "all the multitude kept silence" (Acts 15.12a) and listened to Barnabas and Paul. These two could then bring the people to the Lord. Though the people present were their seniors, they nevertheless brought them to the Lord and brought the presence of God to the meeting. All the noise of argument ceased, and everyone was listening quietly to what God had wrought through them.

Every servant of the Lord should be able to bring the presence of God to His church. For when the Lord's presence is brought in, all will keep silent. I hope you can discern this fundamental principle. Never use words against words, opinion against opinion, reason against reason, and strife against strife. It will be total failure if you resort to such tactics.

As we saw earlier, Peter began first. As he rose, his spirit was not affected at all by the much questioning of the brethren. He showed the brethren his condition before the Lord. He stood there and spoke as one who knew the authority of God. Thus he had opened a way for Barnabas and Paul to speak next. When they spoke, they brought in the presence of God, so that all hearkened silently. Allow me to say that as soon as God's presence and authority come in, opinion goes out. Without His presence and authority, no church council will ever be successful. For men's opinions create confusion.

James Brought in God's Mind

"And after they had held their peace, James answered, saying" (v.13b). This is the last authority. As a recognized leader among the brethren, James arose and spoke briefly: "Brethren, hearken unto me; Symeon hath rehearsed how first God visited the Gentiles . . ." (vv.13c,14a). And after he had concluded the word about Peter, James quoted a passage from the Old Testament Scriptures and then declared: "Wherefore my judgement is [here he made a decision], that we trouble not them that from among the Gentiles turn to God" (v.19). Here was neither argument nor strife. The authority, the presence, and the word of God were all brought in. The deliberation brought in the mind of God. And thus the church council was brought to a successful conclusion.

Not Imitating Scriptural Method, but Having Spirit of Bible

Consequently, let the brethren learn to touch the spirit of the Bible, instead of merely imitating the method in the Bible. Method without spirit is totally useless. We must have the spirit of those people in the Scriptures as well as have their method. If we live in such a spirit, we can shut the mouths of those who love to talk. But if we are loose and careless, and the presence and authority of God is not manifested in our lives, we will not be able to accomplish any good results in such meetings. If our flesh is not under restraint, it will not be restrained in the meeting. Before we can bind the flesh in our brethren, we must have our own flesh bound. If we do not allow the presence of God to be manifested in our lives, we cannot expect His presence to be manifested in the lives of the brethren. Without submitting ourselves to the authority of God, we cannot make the brethren submit to His authority.

Hence the question lies in our spiritual condition. If our condition is correct, the result will be right. To take Acts 15 as but a method is utterly useless because no method in the Bible can be used automatically. The word in the Bible is not a formula which we can adopt technically. Even if it proves to be useful, there is nothing of the Spirit in it. It is therefore not a matter of method but a matter of Spirit—not of formula but of Spirit.

10 The Coordination of the Workers

We will now approach this subject of the coordination of the workers.

(1) RECOGNIZE AUTHORITY

There is one thing we need to recognize, that in God's Work there are many workers but that some are like foremen set up by God in a particular work. This is intimated from what Paul says concerning himself: "According to the grace of God which was given unto me, as a wise masterbuilder . . ." (1 Cor. 3.10a).

Laying a Foundation and Building on It

We can see that some are laying a foundation whereas others are building on it: "As a wise masterbuilder I laid a foundation; and another buildeth thereon" (v.10b). Everybody is at work building, but some are building the foundation and some are building upon the foundation. So that nobody is building according to his own pleasure. Some people seem to be appointed by God to build the foundation, while others seem to be appointed to build upon the foundation. Accordingly, some are set up as foremen.

I believe we all know what a foundation means. Those who

lay a foundation must seek for the rock. They need to find the place and select the proper location for the foundation to be laid. The people who build on it have no such need for locating and deciding on the place to build. They are only responsible to build on wherever the foundation has already been laid.

Paul also wrote this: "Yea, making it my aim so to preach the gospel, not where Christ was already named, that I might not build upon another man's foundation" (Rom. 15.20). Here Paul was referring especially to the work done by the brethren in and around Jerusalem. He had no wish to build upon their foundation, for he was set apart by God to be a man who lays a foundation. However, according to 1 Corinthians 3, we see that other people must build on the foundation which Paul has laid. In the future, at the judgment seat of Christ, everyone will be judged according to how each builds on it. Some build with gold, silver, and costly stones; some build with wood, hay, and stubble. Thus the judgment meted out at the judgment seat of Christ will be according to how each builds on the foundation (see 1 Cor. 3.10–15).

There are Bible passages which I personally feel are quite abused. Many brothers and sisters quote them thoughtlessly. I frequently hear young people say they will not build upon another man's foundation. This is really absurd, since God has not raised up that many to lay foundations.

God did indeed raise up some brothers in Jerusalem, and He also raised up Paul. It was right for Paul to say that he would not build upon another man's foundation. That was definitely what he ought not do, since God had called him also to be a foreman to lay a foundation. But if all God's children are thinking of laying foundations like Paul and a few others, where will be the building? It will turn out to be what is described in Hebrews 6 as men always laying a foundation without ever building upon it. Paul declared that he came to lay a foundation, and that he had laid a good one. This was what he had been appointed by God to do, and he considered himself to have been a *wise* masterbuilder. He was not assuming a hypothetical position here, since God had truly appointed him as such.

Now all who followed after Paul had to learn to build on the foundation which he had laid. In the future each will be judged not on whether the foundation was right but on how each had built upon it. At the hour of judgment, the work done upon the foundation—whether it be gold, silver, costly stones; or wood, hay, stubble—is to be judged. Not the foundation, but what was built *upon* the foundation. Consequently, we cannot thoughtlessly say that we in our day will not build upon another man's foundation. Paul could say this word in his day, but others could not.

Hence we see here that there was one who laid a foundation. Paul was a wise masterbuilder. And the other brothers who came after Paul were appointed to build on this foundation. Many had responsibility for the work above the foundation, but Paul had the responsibility for the work of laying the foundation in the first place. This is quite clear.

Leaders Among the Apostles

Paul was an apostle, and so was Barnabas. Now there is no such thing as chief apostles—that is to say, there is no such position. Nevertheless, in the Bible we can distinctly discern that some apostles are leaders among the apostles.

Andronicus and Junias

In Romans 16 we notice that Andronicus and Junias were "of note among the apostles" (v.7). Evidently, some apostles are more prominent among the apostles, and some are less known among them.

Peter

It is evident that Peter led among the original twelve apostles. On the Day of Pentecost, it was not a case of the twelve apostles standing up together; it was *Peter* who stood up, and the eleven who stood up with him. Please notice the arrangement found in God's word. During the time of Pentecost, many people came to Jerusalem. They heard the sound from heaven and wondered what was happening. They came to where the apostles gathered. The Bible records that "Peter, standing up with the eleven, lifted up his voice and spake forth unto them" (Acts 2.14a). Peter stood up first, and the eleven other apostles followed in standing up with him. Peter then lifted up his voice and spoke. Naturally, we can recognize Peter as being the leading person there.

Further on in Acts (3.1ff.), the record indicates that Peter and John went up to the temple. Again we shall see the Spirit of God putting the name of Peter first. Although the beggar saw the two of them and asked alms from both, Peter's name is again placed first. Both Peter and John fastened their eyes on the beggar, yet the one who spoke was Peter and not John. Shortly afterwards, it was Peter, not John, who took the beggar by the right hand and raised him up. Still later in Solomon's porch, it was Peter and not John who addressed the people (3.11ff.).

In the case of Ananias and Sapphira (Acts 5), Peter once again was the one who personally handled the matter. Even though all the apostles were in touch with God and worked closely together, it was Peter who was there taking the lead.

After the apostles were brought out of prison by an angel of the Lord and were subsequently brought to the council by its officers to be judged, as recorded in Acts 5, we find that Peter and the apostles answered and said, "We must obey God rather than men" (v.29). Here was Peter once more doing the speaking, even though the Bible states that Peter and the apostles together "answered and said." As we continue to read on through the first part of the book of Acts, we shall notice how it repeatedly puts Peter especially at the front.

Then there was a great persecution against the church in Jerusalem, and the disciples were all scattered abroad. They preached the gospel wherever they went. Even Samaritans heard the word of the Lord, and workers were sent out from Jerusalem: Peter and John went out again. And it was still Peter who took the lead here.

I suppose all are most familiar with what happened at the house of Cornelius as recorded in Acts chapter 10. Although there were twelve apostles, *Peter* was the one sent for. And it was to this same apostle that the vision of a vessel as of a great sheet was given. Afterwards it was Peter who brought some brothers from Joppa with him to the home of Cornelius. The Bible does not mention the names of these other brothers.

Hence up to this time, the way of God was such that among the workers at Jerusalem there was one particular worker leading the rest, and that one distinctly was Peter.

Barnabas

Now as the brethren were scattered abroad from Jerusalem due to persecution, they went out preaching the gospel. The gospel was spreading out from Jerusalem to all of Judea and to Samaria. So that many believed in the word of the Lord in various places. Barnabas was then sent out from Jerusalem to visit these places. He went as far north as Antioch. He was a good man, full of the Holy Spirit and of faith. And upon arriving at Antioch, he began to help the assembly there. After a while, he went to Tarsus to find Saul, who had in the meantime become a Christian, and brought him to Antioch. There Barnabas remained a whole year. He had no office in Jerusalem and therefore he *could* stay a year outside Jerusalem. He had no need to return as Peter and John would have had to do, since he was not an elder there. And we may surmise that during that year Saul received much help from Barnabas.

Some time later, the brethren in Judea suffered great destitution because of famine. The brethren at Antioch sent relief to the elders in the assembly at Jerusalem through the hands of Barnabas and Saul. Since the relief was for the local saints, it was delivered to the elders and not to the apostles.

Later there were in Antioch in the assembly some prophets and teachers. Barnabas and Saul were numbered among them. The Holy Spirit commanded by name that these two were to be set apart to be apostles, and were subsequently sent out to work abroad.

Keep in mind that, up to this moment, Barnabas was always standing at the front. It was he and not Saul who established the assembly at Antioch. When relief was to be sent to Jerusalem it was these two who were sent: Barnabas being mentioned first, with Saul next. And when the Holy Spirit sent out workers from among the prophets and teachers, the narrative reads that "the Holy Spirit said, Separate me Barnabas and Saul for the work whereunto I have called them" (Acts 13.2). Barnabas still came first.

God Is God of Authority and Order

Let us remember that in God's Work as well as in God's Church, there is an order. Even with but two persons, one is put ahead and one is placed next. When there are twelve together, one is at the front and the other eleven follow. For God is a God of order as well as of authority. The Bible never endorses a committee system of three or five members. Although there are a few elders, God does not set them up as members of a committee with a presiding officer. Nevertheless, when elders manage the things of the Lord, God does indeed use one among them to give the final word. Now in the Work, the same principle holds true. In Jerusalem there were twelve apostles, yet God placed Peter at the front and the rest after him. Later on we find in the local assembly there that James (not the brother of John) stood at the front. Then, too, it is not simply a matter of Barnabas and Saul, but the fact that Barnabas stood ahead of Saul. In the Work we shall see that there is always someone who is ahead. The first thing to observe in the coordination of God's Work is the coordination of God's authority. If that coordination is lost, everything coordinated is lost.

The word of the Bible is exceedingly careful: "And God hath set some in the church, first apostles, secondly prophets, thirdly teachers, then . . ." (1 Cor. 12.28). God is not a God of *dis*order. He is a God of *order*. He does not believe in confusion or chaos. He believes in order and authority. And hence this word says "first" in this passage. He is not saying that here is a system—a committee system—in which everyone has the authority to speak and to cast a vote. God never endorses such a system, or any system for that matter. For that is the human way. When God states in His word—"first . . . secondly . . . thirdly," it reveals God's arrangement. So that whether in the Work or in the management of church affairs, we need to recognize our place. We must learn to line up ourselves. We should know who is ahead of us that we may stand on the ground of submission. This is a principle of the church which is most marvelous. Yet such does not come by appointment or distribution. It comes quite naturally.

Whoever Is Ahead Is Vested with Authority

God never suggests that the authority He sets up is perfect, and that because of *that* we must hear him. No, he simply says that this one has more authority than you do, and therefore you should listen to him. It is not a matter of being more perfect but a matter of being ahead. The basis of submission is not perfection but priority (or precedence). For example, God declares that wives should be in subjection to their own husbands. Yet it is not because the husband is perfect that the wife should therefore be in subjection to him. If that were the case, then no wife in the whole world need subject herself to her husband because no husband is perfect. So that the question here is not one of perfection or imperfection in a husband. It is only one of whether he is a husband. If he is, then the wife should be in subjection to him.

Similarly, in God's Work, among the coordination of workers there is also an order. Learn to take your place and say, "Brother, what do you say?", because that brother is ahead of you. Submission is not submitting to *men's* choice, but to *God's* authority. It would be most surprising if we can find no one to whom to submit. If so, it is most likely because we have not seen God's arrangement about authority.

Now when these two brothers at Antioch came together in the Work, Barnabas just naturally stood ahead of Saul. That was the order and arrangement when they were sent out by the Holy Spirit. Beginning from Acts chapter 13, we learn that Barnabas as they traveled along was always named first in the account by Luke. For instance, just look in verse 7: "The same called unto him Barnabas and Saul."

Let us also notice in the very first verse of chapter 13 that among the several prophets and teachers, Barnabas was mentioned first and Saul was listed last. Do not imagine that Paul was most advanced spiritually soon after he began. No, not so! At the outset of his service to God, he was at the bottom of the list: "Now there were at Antioch, in the church that was there, prophets and teachers, Barnabas, and Symeon that was called Niger, and Lucius of Cyrene, and Manaen the foster-brother of Herod the tetrarch, and Saul." First Barnabas, then Symeon, next Lucius and Manaen, and last of all Saul. Even at the moment when the Holy Spirit separated them, God recognized that Barnabas was ahead of Saul: "And as they ministered to the Lord, and fasted, the Holy Spirit said, Separate me Barnabas and Saul for the work whereunto I have called them" (v 2)

Paul

But *then*, something odd happened. The Bible records that at a particular point in the Work, Paul was "filled with the Holy Spirit" (Acts 13.9). Now we know he had been filled with the Holy Spirit when he was baptized (see Acts 9.17,18). But that was different from this occasion. That had been after his repentance and salvation. On this occasion the record tells us that "Saul, who is also called Paul, filled with the Holy Spirit," was used by God to perform a miracle which caused a person to experience immediate and total blindness!

Later on, when they came to Antioch of Pisidia they went into the synagogue on the sabbath day and sat down. The rulers of the synagogue invited them to speak. Paul stood up. On the one hand Paul performed miracles, and on the other hand he preached. Now we find that from the Day of Pentecost onward, the book of Acts recorded a number of sermons or messages. Peter gave several long ones, and they were recorded. Stephen also gave a long speech, and this too was set down. This message of Paul's was the first one recorded since those earlier ones by Peter and Stephen. The Bible did not record any long sermon of Barnabas, though. Here the Holy Spirit used Paul to deliver a very strong message. The Spirit used him as a minister of God's word.

And interestingly enough, hereafter the order in the Scriptures changes with respect to these two traveling apostles: "Now when the synagogue broke up, many of the Jews and of the devout proselytes followed Paul and Barnabas" (Acts 13.43a). At this moment Paul now stands at the front. Here are further evidences of this from the record: "And Paul and Barnabas spake out boldly" (13.46a). "But the Jews . . . stirred up a persecution against Paul and Barnabas, and cast them out of their borders" (13.50). All the way, Paul now stood at the forefront. Even at Lystra, it was Paul who spoke and Paul who healed the cripple.

Yet this matter was not so conclusively ended, for later in

chapter 14 Barnabas was once again placed first as they entered Lystra: "And they called Barnabas, Jupiter; and Paul, Mercury, because he was the chief speaker" (v.12). Jupiter and Mercury were gods which the people in Lystra worshiped. They called Paul Mercury because he led in speaking. In verse 14, though, we read this: "But when the apostles, Barnabas and Paul." Barnabas' name was placed first here. This was exceptional, and there was a plausible reason for it. When the priests of Jupiter learned that their god had come that day in the form of a man, they hurriedly brought oxen and garlands to the gates and would have done sacrifice with the multitude. They thought Barnabas was Jupiter, and so they put him ahead. The priests of the temple of Mercury had *not* come, and therefore the priests of the temple of Jupiter would quite naturally sacrifice to their *own* god. Accordingly, this is why, "when the apostles, Barnabas and Paul, heard of it, they rent their garments." Barnabas had only taken the lead because they had taken him for Jupiter.

Between here and chapter 15, there was one other instance in which the name of Barnabas was placed before Paul, and that too had a very good reason. Other than these two cases, however, Paul always took the lead.

Some days later after the apostles had rejected their sacrifice, "there came Jews thither from Antioch and Iconium: and having persuaded the multitudes, they stoned Paul and dragged him out of the city, supposing that he was dead" (Acts 14.19). Earlier they had wanted to offer sacrifices, but now they nearly stoned Paul to death. "But as the disciples stood around about him, he rose up, and entered into the city: and on the morrow he went forth with Barnabas to Derbe" (v.20). Once again you see Paul in the center.

The record of chapter 15 brings the apostolic party back to Antioch. Almost immediately a problem arose in Antioch. "And when Paul and Barnabas had no small dissension and questioning with them, the brethren appointed that Paul and

Barnabas, and certain other of them, should go up to Jerusalem" (Acts 15.2). Paul's name was again listed first.

However, at the council in Jerusalem, it was Barnabas who spoke first and Paul followed afterwards. This order is firmly understandable in that Barnabas had originally come out of Jerusalem. So that quite naturally in the council meeting there he would speak first and then Paul would give his own reply. The one with more weight usually spoke last. And hence in speaking later, it was given to Paul to have a more honorable position. In this connection, did not James speak at the very last?

When in the council meeting, the decision had been made, "then it seemed good to the apostles and the elders, with the whole church, to choose men out of their company, and send them to Antioch with Paul and Barnabas" (v.22). Notice, once more, that Paul stood at the front.

Yet in the letter finally sent forth, it was written to read: "with our beloved Barnabas and Paul" (v.25). Barnabas was again named first simply because he originally was of Jerusalem.

Finally, "Paul and Barnabas tarried in Antioch, teaching and preaching the word of the Lord, with many others also" (v.35). The order resumes, with Paul at the forefront once again.

No Submission, No Coordination

Before God, there is this natural, spontaneous arrangement. In the Work, there will be the worker who leads. Among Christians there must be submission as well as fellowship. What I hope is that brothers and sisters may so well learn this that they come to the point where, when two are together, one of them will be in subjection. Remember that if there is no submission there can be no coordination. Do not come to the place where, when two or more brothers are together, no one knows to whom to submit. This indicates how little we have learned before God. If we *have* learned, we just naturally know whom to submit to as we come together. We know our place.

So that in God's Work, and as it pertains to the matter of the coordination of the workers, the first thing is to ask the Lord to open our eyes that we may recognize the authority among us. As I am together with my brethren, I will know which brother is ahead of me and thus will seek to be a man of submission. This does not come through election or promotion. It comes naturally. I am to stand in my place, recognizing as I do that authority is the first principle of coordination.

(2) HAVE FELLOWSHIP

In this matter of coordination of the Work, the first principle is authority, as we have seen. The second principle is fellowship.

Co-Workers: People to Whom You Can Open Your Heart

There is a basic need among co-workers for people who work together to be able to open their hearts to one another in real fellowship. Coordination opposes individualism. Coordination is for the sake of body ministry. I serve indeed, yet I serve according to the principle of the body. There must therefore be the kind of fellowship where heart is opened to heart and where there is mutual help given. If one member is honored, the whole body rejoices. If one member suffers, the whole body suffers with it. If one member is sorrowful, the whole body is sorrowful. This is coordination.

Not Two Persons, but As One Man

Coordination does not mean simply the being together of

two or more persons. A brother whose outside shell is so extremely hard to crack is an individual when he is alone. Even when he is among ten people, he is still an isolated individual. This is not coordination at all. Many are the people who, when they are alone, pray alone and seek the Lord alone. But if they are put among ten people, they still pray and seek the Lord alone. How can anyone call this coordination? For two persons to be co-workers, it is not simply a matter of putting two individuals together. Do not make the mistake of thinking that because you formerly worked alone, that you can still work that way when you are with somebody else and call it coordination. I assure you that there is no coordination at all. No, it cannot be two people still working individually. It must be two working as one man. Yet how can this be? The two of them must be of one mind and one heart before the Lord. This means that before God I can open myself to my brother, and vice versa.

Open Your Burden Up to Co-Workers

Many brethren cannot pray with other people. Nobody knows their affairs. They never open themselves up to their brethren. Many bear their burdens alone; they will not consult with their brethren. Their problems are many, yet when they encounter them they hold on to their individualism. Their attitude is, "I take care of my own things before God, and I will do them myself." Do understand that with such an attitude as this, you may indeed live among the brethren, but your spirit is not in their midst. Your body is with the brethren, but you do not live as a member of the body of Christ.

For this reason, coordination requires knowing fellowship as well as knowing authority. He who really desires fellowship is he who is able to open up himself. When there are one or more co-workers present, he will share his burden. He will say, "Brothers and sisters, I have something I cannot get through on by myself. What do you think I should do?" or, "Brothers and sisters, I cannot get through before God in this matter; will you please make this a matter of prayer and pray with me?" Whoever is unable to bear another's burden cannot be coordinated with anyone. But likewise, whoever cannot open his heart to another is not able to be coordinated with anybody else either.

Bear Others' Burdens

Some people are so fully occupied with their own burdens that they have no way to carry other people's burdens. From dawn to dusk they can only think of themselves. They do not pray for others even when they are requested to do so. They do not care for anything other than their own affairs. There is absolutely no concept of coordination in them. They are strong individualists. Though they are members of the body, they act independently. Yet in the physical realm, if I cut off my finger and put it elsewhere, it becomes useless. If I sever my foot from my body, there will be no unity nor fellowship between my body and my foot and therefore the latter will be without usefulness. The basic principle of the body is fellowship. And likewise, the basic principle of work is also fellowship.

Perhaps we are accustomed to following our own will, perhaps we are used to bearing our own burden and to disregarding others' business. If so, we need to learn to bear the burden of others. In so doing we shall find out how difficult it is in fact to do; we shall find that it is hard to submit and to fellowship.

Seek Fellowship

I do not suggest that some of you brothers are to cast all your burdens upon other people and consequently not bear your own burdens. What we have been saying here does not mean that we never need to go to God and wrestle with our problems nor that we never need to inquire of Him. We still must bear our own responsibility before the Lord; we still must seek to draw near to Him. We cannot push our responsibility onto others' shoulders and bear none ourselves. It is as we *are* bearing our own responsibility that we are to seek fellowship with our brothers and sisters. When I am confronted by some matter which I know could greatly affect my future, I will say: "Brethren, will you not fellowship with me, and seek with me for God's mind? Will you wait on God with me?" So that I am bearing the burden myself, but at the same time I am fellowshiping in coordination with some other brothers and sisters. We need fellowship and coordination in work as well as in life.

Let us therefore learn to be an open person. Many brothers and sisters can only be open when other people open first to them. They have to wait till others open to them. Let me say that it is of course good to have other people open first; but it is equally important for you to learn to be a person who opens up too.

I can assure you that when you really understand the principle of fellowship, you will be surprised how much help you will receive from those who are commonly labeled as weak Christians. Those members of the body who are deemed to be not very useful will strengthen your hand beyond your imagination.

Seek the Lord Together, and Power Comes

In the Work, suppose some of you go to a certain place. If everyone is an isolated individual, there can be no coordination. You may live together, but your spirits are not open to one another. Many may be working as you all go out to labor, but it will be useless if all go forth as mere individuals. If you all pray your own prayer, this is not of one mind. Physically you may be together, and you may call yourselves co-workers, yet everyone wraps himself up tightly and does his own work independently. Where can such a body be found on earth? Where can such members be found on earth? This is not members one of another, this is paralysis! No, the many of you must work as one man. After you arrive at the place, each one of you is to be an open person. Together you seek the Lord's face. And by so doing, you will see power coming from above. Because two or three are seeking with one accord, such prayer God will hear.

Forsake Individualism

We must forsake our individualism. Let us learn to be open. Open your spirit to your brethren. Open your thoughts and also frequently open your mouth. Sometimes when the mouth is shut, the spirit is shut too. Some people have never in their lives made any request. I hope some of us will at last be able to say to our brothers and sisters, "For many years I have not been able to get through on this matter; will you please help me?"

Alas, we do not know how proud a person we are. Many of us are proud without realizing it. Many of us hold ourselves tightly without being conscious of it. Many profess to have been broken before God, but when we are in touch with people we reveal the fact that we are not broken at all. Let me tell you that a person who is broken before God is broken wherever he is put. This is fellowship, stretching forth the hand to seek out fellowship with others.

I repeat, do not lay your responsibility upon the shoulders of others. The prayer of a person who does this will not be answered. But let a responsible person, one who seeks God, learn to be broken before Him. As a broken person, seek the help of the other members. And as you do so, you will find that wherever you go people will be praying and consulting with you. Otherwise, where will your co-worker be? In reality, you will have none.

A given brother may work for ten or twenty years, and yet—sad to say—I am afraid no one can bear responsibility together with him. He has never learned to work with other people nor ever learned to bear responsibility together. He may be too proud to share his burden with others. He may not wish to be concerned with the affairs of other people. When requested to do so, he will not really pray and fast and seek to know the mind of God for other people. Oh, if such a brother never learns how to seek help for his own burden as well as how to bear the burdens of others, he will never know what the body is nor will he ever truly experience any coordination in the Work.

I hope that in every region of the Work, brothers and sisters will be praying together. This is an excellent phenomenon to behold: brothers and sisters praying together without any inhibition. Naturally, there is a definite place for a person to touch God personally. However, in God's Work there are many things which can be shared in prayer through the opening up of hearts and the bearing of one another's burdens.

If, on the contrary, everyone is tight and unbroken—each taking care of his own affairs without also caring for the affairs of others—each looking after his own labors without also helping in the others' labors—then there is absolutely no coordination in the Work. It is right and good for a person to rise up before God and face any and every problem which comes, but if he never says, "I need the supply and support of my fellow workers," he does not know what body coordination is. And the result? He will never be able to bear the burden of others since he is too busily occupied with his own.

The greatest test, then, is whether or not co-workers can pray together. Can they talk over matters with one mind before God? Can they bring themselves to say, "I have this problem before God, and you have that problem before God; let us lay these matters before Him"? This is a great test. I hope hereafter there will be no more bearing burdens alone. Burdens must be borne, but let us learn to seek fellowship in the sharing and the bearing of our burdens together.

Head Gives Authority, Members Have Fellowship

The use of the body lies in fellowship. The first body principle is that of authority, the second principle is that of fellowship. The supply of coordination is based on the supply of authority and the supply of fellowship. What comes from the head is authority, what comes from the body members is fellowship. The head gives authority that we may have order in the body—that is to say, order in the church. Further, though, within the members there is mutual fellowship. These are the two fundamental principles of body life.

May we test this out before God by saying, "O Lord, am I a person whose heart is closed and who never asks for help?" If you search throughout the whole Bible, you will not find such a superior Christian. Superiority is not the path of a believer. Do not boast that you take care of everything yourself before God and that you never mind the business of your brothers and sisters. You cannot be such a Christian on earth and still serve the Lord. For as you learn to serve Him, you must learn at the beginning the necessity to coordinate with your brethren in the Work. Otherwise, you will be spiritually useless. Learn on the one hand to submit to authority, and on the other hand learn to have fellowship with others to such a degree that you can say: "Thank and praise God, we bear the same burden together with one heart and one mind. We have fellowship and authority. Everything is done step by step with order." Fellowship, you discover, is absolutely necessary.

Today if there is any failure, you will see that such failure falls either into the area of authority or the area of fellowship

(3) AUTHORITY AND FELLOWSHIP IN THE BIBLE

In the New Testament, there is evidence of many arrangements—involving both authority and fellowship in God's Work. Especially can this be seen in the life of Paul. Let us review at some length the record of the Scriptures that pertain to this matter in Paul's life and ministry as he relates to others in the Work. We shall see in many places where there were arrangements, and how the younger brethren followed these arrangements. These expressed authority, but they also indicated fellowship. In putting these arrangements before the younger ones, not only was authority used to get these brethren to work, but in addition, fellowship with them in knowledge and light was experienced. We here need to recognize that these arrangements in Scripture were not merely an expression of authority, for then the apostle could have simply said, "I, Paul, order you to do this, and so you had better do it!" Not so, for in these arrangements which Paul set forth, he received light from God, that is to say, he had knowledge before the Lord. And thereupon he shared the knowledge and light which he had received from God in fellowship with those younger brothers. Authority on the one hand and fellowship on the other—these are what I trust we all will come to see as we now review Paul's experience in some detail.

Paul Sent Tychicus and Onesimus

"All my affairs shall Tychicus make known unto you, the beloved brother and faithful minister and fellow-servant in the Lord: whom I have sent unto you for this very purpose" (Col. 4.7,8a). "Together with Onesimus, the faithful and beloved brother" (v.9a). It was Paul who sent both Tychicus and Onesimus to Colosse.

In God's Work, there is a foreman who has the authority to

send out people. Tychicus was a very good brother. This is revealed to us in a number of Paul's epistles. And Onesimus, as told to us in the Letter to the Colossians, was a very lovely person. And both of them were sent by Paul.

Sent Timothy and Epaphroditus

"But I hope in the Lord Jesus to send Timothy shortly unto you, that I also may be of good comfort, when I know your state" (Phil. 2.19).

"But I counted it necessary to send to you Epaphroditus" (v.25a).

Timothy was like a son to Paul, just as Onesimus had been. Epaphroditus was a fellow worker of Paul's, but he came to the Work later than had Paul. They were both young, and both were sent by Paul.

In the coordination of God's Work, those who act as foremen send out people. The younger must learn to listen, and the older must be certain before the Lord before they send out the younger: "I hope in the Lord Jesus to send Timothy shortly unto you." Paul was quite certain before the Lord that he should send Timothy. May we all learn this.

Tychicus Went to Ephesus

"But that ye may also know my affairs, how I do, Tychicus, the beloved brother and faithful minister in the Lord, shall make known to you all things: whom I have sent unto you for this very purpose" (Eph. 6.21,22a). Paul sent Tychicus not only to Colosse but also to Ephesus.

Exhorted Titus and Sent Other Brother

"I exhorted Titus, and I sent the brother with him" (2 Cor. 12.18a). Notice that the word used here is "exhorted." This time Paul did not *send* Titus but exhorted him to go. Though Paul had authority over Titus to send him, he in this instance would rather exhort him. Sometimes it was exhorting for Paul and not a sending. The other brother—whose name was not identified—was *sent*, however. Titus, on the other hand, went because he responded to an exhortation.

"Besought Apollos . . . Not His Will to Come . . . but He Will Come"

"But as touching Apollos the brother, I besought him much to come unto you with the brethren: and it was not at all his will to come now; but he will come when he shall have opportunity" (1 Cor. 16.12). Here we can observe something quite remarkable. Paul exhorted Titus, and Titus being a young man listened and he went. Apollos, however, was *not* a young man but was a contemporary of Paul's. In other words, he was in generally the same age bracket as Paul. Cephas, though, was senior to them both. In the assembly at Corinth, some believers there had said, I am of Cephas, some others had said, I am of Paul, and still others had said, I am of Apollos (1 Cor. 1.12). The position of Apollos in the assembly at Corinth was equal to Paul's. Hence Paul *besought* Apollos, he did not *send* him; for Paul could not have sent Apollos but could only beseech him. And he besought the latter, not once, but many times. How significant it was that Apollos would *not* go. Paul had besought him again and again to go with the brethren, but Apollos replied that he would not go now. He emphatically said he would not go. Yet Paul added a word here, saying that Apollos *would* go later, for he had the assurance of it. How very beautiful it was that when an older one was besought to go but would not go, Paul was not disturbed at all but had the confidence that Apollos would go eventually.

The exhortation given to Apollos described in 1 Corinthians 16 and the exhortation given to Titus mentioned in 2

Corinthians 12 are different. Paul could order Titus, but he would rather exhort. Nevertheless, Titus took the exhortation as an order. On the other hand, Paul exhorted Apollos a number of times, but the latter would not go. Yet Paul had the confidence that Apollos would go later on. Such is the arrangement in God's Work. There is fellowship as well as authority in the Lord's Work. And how precious that is!

Directed Timothy's Movement

"Now if Timothy come . . . set him forward on his journey in peace, that he may come unto me" (1 Cor. 16.10,11b). Paul left a word with the Corinthian believers to give to Timothy, that when the latter came into their midst they should do their best to send him forward to Paul, for, added the apostle, "I expect him with the brethren" (v.11c). Do you perceive how Paul was directing the movement of Timothy here? The word of the Scriptures is quite clear: the authority whom God has set up can control the movement of the younger worker, but with the older workers there can only be exhortation and not orders.

Look Further into Letters of Paul to Timothy: Paul Shared Revelation

"This charge I commit unto thee, my child Timothy, according to the prophecies which led the way to thee, that by them thou mayest war the good warfare" (1 Tim. 1.18). This plainly shows that Paul gave direction to Timothy. He gave the young man a charge by which the latter could wage a good warfare. "These things write I unto thee, hoping to come unto thee shortly; but if I tarry long, that thou mayest know how men ought to behave themselves in the house of God, which is the church of the living God, the pillar and ground of the truth" (1 Tim. 3.14,15).

In chapter 2 of this same letter, Paul had talked about the

things pertaining to men and women. In chapter 3, he now speaks of the things concerning elders and deacons. Why did he write these things to Timothy? He expected to be with Timothy shortly, yet he was afraid that if he were delayed in coming, Timothy might not know how to conduct himself in the Church well enough in the meantime to carry on well till Paul arrived. Hence Paul wrote ahead. In other words, Paul did not leave room for Timothy to search out his own way nor let him do what he pleased. He wrote to him specifically. When Paul was present, Timothy could ask him. When he was absent, Timothy could read his letter.

I repeat, this arrangement includes both the principle of authority and the principle of fellowship. Authority, because Paul was the older brother; fellowship, because he wrote to the younger brother. Since he knew but Timothy did not, Paul shared what he knew with Timothy. And as Timothy submitted, he received the benefit of fellowship. Keep ever in mind that submission like this will never cause you to lose your position in the Work; rather, it will help you to gain what the older brother possesses, so that you may receive in your work that particular revelation which the older brother has received.

We can find a number of other passages which are similar to what we have just quoted above. All of them point out to us the way in the Work of God.

"Give diligence to come shortly unto me" (2 Tim. 4.9). Paul was not consulting with Timothy, nor did he merely expect Timothy to come. For not long after he wrote this letter, Paul was martyred. This was his last letter. And hence he wrote in this fashion: "Give diligence to come shortly unto me."

"For Demas forsook me, having loved this present world, and went to Thessalonica"(v.10a). Here was a rebellious soul who had left.

"Crescens to Galatia, Titus to Dalmatia"(v.10b). No doubt, these two were being sent by Paul.

"Only Luke is with me" (v.11a).

Brought Mark

"Take Mark, and bring him with thee" (v.11b). This was the brother over whom Paul had contended with Barnabas. In Acts, we find that Paul would not agree with Barnabas to take Mark along on their second apostolic journey, because on their first trip—at a critical moment in the Work—Mark had left them. More than likely, Barnabas had wanted to take Mark along due to their kinsman relationship to each other. Paul and Barnabas had such strong contention over this issue that they parted from each other. The ironic twist to this whole matter was that later on Barnabas had no more chance to work with Paul, whereas Mark—as we learn from 2 Timothy—did have a further opportunity! We know that Mark later learned a great deal from Peter and was greatly helped by him spiritually. In fact, the Gospel according to Mark most probably came from the mouth of Peter himself. So that before Paul died, he wrote in his Second Letter to Timothy: "Take Mark and bring him with thee." And why? Because "he is useful to me for ministering" (v.11b). Yes, Mark was indeed useful to Paul in the ministry.

"But Tychicus I sent to Ephesus" (v.12). This implies that the Work was so arranged that Paul could ask Timothy to come to him with Mark and send Tychicus away to Ephesus.

"Erastus remained at Corinth" (v.20a). How knowledgeable was Paul about the situation of the Work.

Left Trophimus at Miletus

"Erastus remained at Corinth; but Trophimus I left at Miletus sick" (v.20). Trophimus was one of the noteworthy sick persons mentioned in the New Testament. Epaphroditus was another of these.

"Trophimus I left at Miletus." Oftentimes a patient should learn to hearken. He cannot in all circumstances insist, "I want to travel." Because of sickness, he may have to remain behind for a while. And in this instance, Paul felt he should leave Trophimus at Miletus. It was better for him.

To Timothy, however, Paul instructed: "Give diligence to come before winter" (v.21a). He gave Timothy a definite time frame instead of leaving it to *him* to decide when to come.

Can we now begin to see this way in the Work? One who walked before God as did Paul must be listened to by Mark, Timothy and Trophimus. From all this evidence we can begin to perceive that in the Church there just naturally develops not only fellowship but also authority.

Left Titus in Crete, He to Give Diligence to Come to Nicopolis

"For this cause left I thee in Crete, that thou shouldest set in order the things that were wanting, and appoint elders in every city, as I gave thee charge" (Titus 1.5). Titus was a younger brother. In Paul's letter to the Corinthians, it is recorded that the apostle exhorted Titus to go to Corinth. When Paul decided to go to Crete, Titus went along. And then Paul left him at Crete to complete whatever unfinished business remained, according to Paul's instruction. Again, there is authority as well as fellowship.

"When I shall send Artemas unto thee, or Tychicus, give diligence to come unto me to Nicopolis: for there I have determined to winter" (Titus 3.12). This is the way of the Work. Paul said he would send either Artemas or Tychicus to Crete. Although the matter in Paul's mind was not yet fully decided, at least one of these two would come to Crete. And then Titus was to hurry to Paul at Nicopolis.

An elder brother arranged many things, whereas the younger brother learned to listen to the word of the older brother.

Give Timothy Charge

Finally in this review, I wish to go back to Timothy for some concluding comments.

"I charge thee in the sight of God, who giveth life to all things, and of Christ Jesus, who before Pontius Pilate witnessed the good confession; that thou keep the commandment, without spot, without reproach, until the appearing of our Lord Jesus Christ" (1 Tim. 6.13,14). Notice how solemn this matter is. The charge was given before God who gave life to all things and before Jesus Christ who witnessed the good confession before Pontius Pilate. And the charge was to keep the commandment.

"O Timothy, guard that which is committed unto thee" (v. 20a). Whatever charge Paul had given to Timothy, the latter was to keep.

I would say here that the younger brothers should learn to keep the charge which the older brothers give. As the younger workers learn to submit to the older workers, they can proceed on the way very well.

Paul Also Needed Fellowship

I hope we may today see what the Work, as spelled out for us in the New Testament, is: how it is arranged, and how it is done with authority and how it is also done with fellowship. With respect to fellowship, let me point out that even though Timothy was a comparatively younger person, the book of Acts records something quite revealing about Paul when Timothy came to him at Corinth: "But when Silas and Timothy came down from Macedonia, Paul was constrained by the word, testifying to the Jews that Jesus was the Christ" (Acts 18.5). I consider this to be a most excellent word found in the Scriptures. Paul was one greatly used by the Lord, one who knew God very well. Yet the record acknowledges that he was constrained by the word only after Silas and Timothy had come to him from Macedonia. Paul *too* was in need of fellowship. The coming of Silas and Timothy was actually a good encouragement to Paul.

To be able to appreciate this more fully, we need to see the background. "And then immediately the brethren sent forth Paul to go as far as to the sea" (Acts 17.14a). Here Paul listened to the word of the brethren in Berea, who urged him to leave because of the Jews who had followed him there. "And Silas and Timothy abode there still" (v.14b)—that is, in Berea which was a city in the region of Macedonia. "But they that conducted Paul brought him as far as Athens: and receiving a commandment unto Silas and Timothy that they should come to him with all speed, they departed" (v.15). By means of those brethren from Berea who had accompanied the apostle to Athens and who had then returned to Berea, Paul sent a message ordering Silas and Timothy to come to him quickly. After a while, he left Athens and went on to Corinth; and only when Silas and Timothy arrived from Macedonia was he constrained by God's word to preach again. How beautiful everything was! Fellowship, as well as authority, has its part to play in the Work of God too.

11 | Co-Workers and Apostles—Who Are They?

We have before us today a very important question to be answered: Who are co-workers and apostles?

A Great Misunderstanding

I think this question has been greatly misunderstood by the children of God. Even today this misunderstanding still exists. Many people misconstrue the matter of finance as determining who co-workers are. In these people's estimation, co-workers are a class of people who lay down their professions and trust wholly in God. If this is a correct definition, then Paul could never be our co-worker today because he did not completely give up his profession.

Who are apostles? Many people mistakenly think that those who have no other income and who devote their entire time to the Work of God are apostles. If this concept be correct, then Paul was never an apostle because he did not leave his profession but continued to make tents. According to the current view of God's children, Paul was neither a co-worker nor an apostle. For he did not devote all twenty-four hours per day to the Work, because he sometimes made tents. Leaving aside any consideration as to why he made tents or what he did with the income from them, the very fact that he made tents disqualified him from being a co-worker or an apostle, in the view of modern Christianity. This, of course, is a fundamental error.

I hope that brothers and sisters will come to thoroughly understand what God says in His word as to who are apostles and who are co-workers. Being an apostle does not depend on a person quitting his job. To be a worker is not based on whether or not he has a profession. In the Church today, due to tradition and custom, men always judge apostles by their finance or profession. In the opinion of many in the Church, if this matter of finance or profession is not solved, one cannot be an apostle or a worker. In their view, an apostle must quit his job and put all his time in the Lord's Work. I trust you will see that this misconception is not altogether without some reason. It is not accurate to call it an error; but it *is* accurate to say it is a misunderstanding.

Apostles Must Abandon Profession

We know that when John and James were called, they at the time were mending nets. The Lord actually told them to forsake their nets and boats and follow Him. We also observe that when Peter was called, he was casting a net. The Lord told him to leave his boat and fish and follow Him. Matthew was working in the customs house. When the Lord called him, He asked him to quit his job and follow Him. Let us see clearly before God that an apostle is one who does indeed need to abandon his profession. What God in His word requires of a worker is to accept His call and to relinquish his profession. He is truly to put all his time in the Lord's hand.

This is a fact, because it will be very difficult for him both to be an apostle and also to have another profession on earth. An apostle will be sent abroad. He will be like the apostles in Jerusalem who were sent by God to Samaria and even as far as Caesarea. If an apostle has a job, he cannot easily leave because his work for the Lord must in that case be largely restricted to but one locality.

In view of this, an elder, who is based locally, is not required to give up his profession; whereas an apostle does seem to have such an example in Scripture of leaving his trade. Some elders may need financial supply from the church because they so give of their time (most if not all of it) to manage the church's affairs that they have no time to earn a living. Under such circumstances, these elders are worthy of double honor. Part of this honor is to be in the form of financial support. Nevertheless, it is exceptional for an elder to leave his job. The Bible does not give such a command.

With apostles, though, it is different. The Lord plainly tells them to forsake all and follow Him. To be an apostle is to accept the Lord's command to go places. Such a man should therefore lay down his profession; if not, he is not free to travel around to serve the Lord. And thus we find all twelve apostles received such a calling, responded with such a following of our Lord, demonstrated such a forsaking, and evidenced such a looking to the Lord for their physical and material needs. Obviously, therefore, this is to be the way. The Lord called all twelve of them to come out completely. And as a matter of fact, He called Paul and his companion Luke to come out completely too.

But Paul Made Tents

Yet here I wish to point out that not only did Paul make tents but Aquila and Priscilla did also. Moreover, Luke remained a physician. A careful reading of the Bible will reveal that as soon as a person leaves his profession, he is no longer identified as still being that in the rest of the Scriptures. Peter had been a fisherman. But after he left that trade he was no longer identified as Peter the fisherman. The same with Matthew, who had previously been a publican or tax-collector.* But in the case of Luke, before God called him to the Work, he had been a physician by profession; but the Scriptures still continued to call him a physician, and therefore he must have continued on with that profession. Had Luke ceased practicing medicine altogether, the Bible would no doubt subsequently have referred to him as Luke and not Luke the physician. We must see that Luke was still practicing medicine, that Paul was still making tents, and that Aquila and Pricilla were also still making tents. Hence let us be very careful in our ascertaining what the meaning of all this is.

Paul lived with Aquila and Priscilla because they were of the same trade of tentmaking as he. When he bade farewell to the elders of Ephesus at Miletus, he mentioned "these hands" (Acts 20.34). Allow me to say that this is probably one of the most woeful passages in the Bible. When these Ephesian elders and many other brethren were with him at Miletus, he put forward his hands for them to look at as he said: "Ye yourselves know that these hands ministered unto my necessities, and to them that were with me" (Acts 20.34). I must observe here that these two hands must have truly been noteworthy to look at! How different in appearance they must have been from ordinary hands! For these two hands had gone through many trials and conflicts. There must have been wounds and scars from all those trials. But then too, because of his having to make tents to meet his own necessities, his hands probably suffered many additional wounds; doubtless much skin peeled off as a result. Yet Paul here did not say how by these hands he had done many things in support of many people. He simply

*By the time of Matthew 10.3, this Gospel writer was still identifying himself as "Matthew the publican." Yet this only reflected the writer's humility (in the face of God's grace in saving such a one as he) and not the name by which he was called by others to identify the profession he pursued in life. After the Lord's call on his life, Matthew never returned to the customs office.—*Translator*

mentioned that those hands of his had ministered to the needs of many others as well as his own. How different indeed were these hands from the ordinary lazy kind!.

Paul's Occupation Is Apostle, Not Tentmaker

I hope you can perceive here what the relationship is between an apostle on the one hand and financial resources and a profession on the other. By looking at Peter and his peers together with Paul and his companions you can discover the straight path. If you only look at the Gospels, you will *not be able* to discover the straight path, because there you can only ferret out half the truth. Later on, with the establishment of the Church, Paul conducted himself very differently—or may I say it, he made an improvement. Yes indeed, an apostle must leave his occupation completely. In this respect he was no different from Peter, for Paul too was one who completely forsook his former profession. As you read these pertinent chapters in Acts about this man, who can possibly imagine that Paul remained a tentmaker by trade? I can assure you that after anyone reads the book of Acts, he will go away with the distinct impression that Paul was in very truth an apostle. I myself have absolutely no notion of him being a tentmaker after reading Luke's narrative. Perhaps the professional tentmakers might argue that Paul was a tentmaker, but I can only acknowledge him as an apostle, not a tentmaker. Only those whose hearts are focused upon tents, the profit to be had from making tents, and the advantages which living in tents provide will deem Paul a tentmaker. But I believe any simple believer, when he reads the accounts of Paul's life, will have but one impression: Saul of Tarsus who became Paul the servant of the Lord was in very fact an apostle appointed by God. He will never have the idea that Paul remained a tentmaker by trade after God's call on his life. Clearly Paul was an apostle and no longer a participant in the profession of tentmaking as an occupation.

Hence let us recognize that in apostolic ministry, one must definitely be freed from his profession, but this only refers to one's not taking fishing or tax collecting or even tentmaking as an occupation anymore. If—for one who has been called to be an apostle—making tents is an occupation, then that profession must be given up; otherwise, he cannot be an apostle. Why does God require a person to leave his profession in order to be an apostle? Because apostlic ministry is an occupation in itself, and one cannot have two occupations. Particularly in this occupation of apostleship, it is absolutely forbidden to hold down two jobs. Paul declares that we are ambassadors of Christ. How can an ambassador hold another job? No, all our time is to be devoted to being apostles. We have no time for other pursuits.

Hence after God's call to the Work, Paul's tentmaking was no longer for him an occupation, neither was tentmaking the occupation of Aquila and Priscilla, nor was practicing medicine Luke's occupation.

Conditions Were Different Then

What do we see here? We see Paul being sent out from Antioch by the Holy Spirit to do itinerant work. I trust we realize that the conditions for travel and work then were very different from what they are today, especially with respect to communication! At that time, if the brethren at Antioch had wanted to send some money or other needy items to Paul, there would not have been a post office or telegraph office or bank through which to remit the money or to deliver the goods. In the record of the New Testament, there were several occasions mentioned about gifts having been sent, but all were delivered in person. When Paul was at Antioch, he did this very thing once. On that occasion he had gone out not for the sake of preaching the gospel but for the purpose of bringing financial relief to the saints of Jerusalem. He was then a messenger of the church. Later on, when Paul himself received the gifts, they were all delivered in person by messengers sent out by the various churches. How difficult it must have been without any telegraph, automobiles, airplanes, or many good roads! And those who went out for the sake of the gospel took *nothing* from the Gentiles.

Leaving Jerusalem for a short period and covering only a short distance would create no real financial problem. For people could bring with them sufficient funds for the trip to Samaria—or even to Caesarea—without taking anything from the Gentiles. Futhermore, there were assemblies in both places. So that finance would not be a problem. But now Paul was sent out from Antioch on a different errand by God. He was to go to the Gentiles, he was to take long trips from place to place. So that anyone can readily see that supply would have been a big problem back in those days.

It needs to be pointed out here that Paul's way was quite different from the way the gospel was preached during the earthly days of Jesus. At that time the twelve apostles had gone to cities and stayed in the homes of worthy ones. They were even told by Jesus not to bring staff or purse (see Matt. 10). But as the day of our Lord's death was approaching, He declared: "But now, he that hath a purse, let him take it, and likewise a wallet; and he that hath none, let him sell his cloak, and buy a sword" (Luke 22.36). This indicates that the times would be changing. For in that new day, the gospel would be preached not only to the Jews but also, and especially, to the Gentiles. John made it very clear that "for the sake of the Name they went forth, taking nothing of the Gentiles" (3 John 7). Thus one can see how heavy must have been the burden on Paul—not only for himself but also for the brethren who were with him.

In going out from Antioch, at first there were only two men, Barnabas and Paul. On later trips others went also—those such as Titus, Timothy, Luke, Silas, and so forth. These were added to his party from time to time. The farther they traveled, the larger the group grew. Aquila and Priscilla were also added. It was in light of this that Paul mentioned how "these hands ministered unto my necessities, and to them that were with me" (Acts 20.34). We need to understand that this was not a question of occupation. Paul's profession was that of being an apostle. Where necessity arose along the way, however, he worked with his hands to supply the needs of his fellow companions as well as of himself.

How very beautiful all this was. Dean Alford has informed us that during those early days, tentmaking utilized a kind of dye with which to color the cloth. That kind of dye was fairly strong. It would stain the hands so that color was not easily washed away. Furthermore, the dye would soak one's skin and damage it. Paul could therefore say in so many words to the Ephesian elders: "Behold, my hands." This was truly a big problem then, and it still is today. I hope brethren here will recognize this financial problem for the apostles. You who are to be workers in God's Work, be thankful to the Lord if supplies come in from the various assemblies. But if it does not come in, it does not mean that we can leave our occupation as apostles and take up other jobs. Quite the contrary, in order to maintain this apostolic occupation, I—like Paul—must make tents. Today, for the sake of enabling those brothers with me to continue in fulfilling their apostolic mission, I as it were will make tents. Tentmaking was obviously no longer Paul's livelihood. Yet, for the sake of providing the needs of himself and of the younger workers with him, he did make tents. While Timothy, Titus, Silas, Luke and others were with him, he was able to supply their needs because he could make tents. Behold, these two hands!

Making Tents Helped Him to Be an Apostle

Forsaking one's own profession and having but the one occupation of being an apostle does not exclude a person from earning some money. Paul became an apostle and always remained one thereafter. In reading the book of Acts, we would never dream that Paul would ever contemplate changing his occupation. Among the Ephesians Paul made tents, yet he remained an apostle. He probably made more tents in Ephesus than anywhere else so that he might know what the church was. Whether making tents or practicing medicine or doing something else, all was done by a given worker for the sake of fulfilling his occupation as an apostle and not to disqualify himself from being an apostle. It could well be that had Paul not made tents, he would not have been able to continue being an apostle. This point we must be clear on before God. For oftentimes God permitted Paul to take up a little work in order to make him a better apostle.

I hope we see that this that Paul did is quite different from a person taking another occupation. It was not the same as having a profession as such is commonly understood. If today Matthew were to go back to being a full-time tax-collector, we would probably say that Matthew had gone back to seeking an occupation. But when Paul in his day busied himself to make a few tents, no one could legitimately say that he had found another profession. Matthew could not say today that by his being a tax-collector he could still be an apostle. Yet Paul could say, "Behold, my two hands. Without these hands, it seems as though I cannot be an apostle." This tentmaking of his enabled him, in fact, to be a better apostle. His aim, his life, his work, his living, his very all were for him to be an apostle. Those two hands, far from interfering with his being an apostle, actually helped him to *be* an apostle. Is the way now clear to all of us? I trust so.

Question of Avocation

A couple of months ago a brother asked me if it were necessary for us to completely leave our job in order to go out for the Lord to preach the gospel and to do apostolic work? Could we in the future have an avocation? This would be my answer today: Everyone who is to be an apostle must forsake his profession as it is commonly understood. But on the other hand, let us notice that while you are out working and traveling here and there for the gospel's sake, it is far better for you to do something on the side which will enable you to be an apostle rather than—as some other people are doing—blaming the church for any lack of love shown. Instead of being weak in faith yet maintaining an outward appearance of trusting God while in actuality you are expecting from men, would it not be better if you could say as Paul, "Behold, these hands!"? At such a time, it would be much better to work with your hands that you may supply your own needs and the needs of other people. I consider looking for the love of the church as being far more dishonoring to God than lacking faith in the Lord. I also believe murmuring against men and not believing in God is very disgraceful. I think what is most shameful is for a person to give the outward appearance of looking to God but in fact inwardly his eyes are not looking at heaven but are instead looking around him.

The Principle of "Behold, These Two Hands"

I must reemphasize this point: that the principle of "Behold, these two hands" is for the sake of enabling me to be more of an apostle. For many, these two hands have no need to go fishing. We must know ourselves as to what we are about on the earth. What kind of person are we before God? Let us not ever forget that you and I are called by God to be an apostle. And because we are to be such, we must forsake all our professions.

Hereafter, if you ever work again, it will not be as an occupation; it will simply be to supply the necessities for yourself and for your co-workers whoever may be in need. How come there are such necessities? Because of the very fact that you *are* an apostle. You will therefore work with your hands because you will not allow any financial lack to hinder the Work or to lead you away from your calling. You will do some outside work with the hope and intention of maintaining your co-workers as well as your own self in the apostolic work.

This is a different way. Yet it is not a change of occupation but is a way to use an avocation in support of the apostolic ministry. It is not a change from being an apostle to being a tent-maker. It merely means making tents to sustain the apostolic mission.

Fishing and Tentmaking Are Two Different Things

If some apostolic brothers find their work too difficult and their finances too inadequate, they go teach school or they go fishing. Let us be reminded that at the moment our Lord died many *did* go fishing. Yet could they at the same time say that their Lord lived forever in heaven? Only the despairing and the disappointed went fishing in that day—and they could not say this because of their unbelief. But here in Paul we find a man who did not make tents because of any despair—he *believed* in the risen and ascended Lord. These two reactions were very different.

Peter's "I go a fishing" (John 21.3) and Paul's tentmaking were not the same. Peter went fishing only because he had nowhere to go—he was finished. He went fishing because he considered the Lord dead and everything else hopeless. He himself was a failure, and his Lord was no more; and so he went fishing out of despair. But look at Paul. His making tents was not at all an occupation. He firmly acknowledged that the Lord was living and that therefore he could not help but be an apostle. Whether in comfort or in suffering, whether receiving supply from the brothers or not receiving any supply, he must still be an apostle. How different this is from Peter's reaction and going back to fishing. To live or to die, Paul would still remain an apostle. He had to give his all to fulfill his apostleship. And hence he put forth his two hands and did some work. Extra though this outside work was to his regular labors and toils, he was willing to do something more so that his apostolic work might not be crushed. That was Paul's attitude. What his two hands did supported both his co-workers as well as himself. That was the way of Paul.

Not a Changing of Occupation, but Giving One's All

Today I believe brothers and sisters are going to see this fundamental principle of which we have been speaking. All who are called by the Lord to go out and preach the gospel—all who are to serve the Lord as apostles—must forsake their professions in order to be apostolic workers. This is the correct way. Yet, in case need arises, you can work for a short period if you are able to bear the double burden, but not to go back as a tax-collector who has to work at the customs house from morning till night. If there is no such need, then you have no need to work. When there is no supply coming from the church or when the church is not able to supply, you can work. Just as when the children of Israel, whenever they ceased offering sacrifices, caused the Levites to suffer hunger, forcing them to work in the fields (Neh. 13.10). At such a time of need, you can do something involving a side job to help your co-workers as well as yourself. Nevertheless, during that time you do not automatically cease being an apostle.

Recognize that this principle of tentmaking does not dissipate your heart, but on the contrary, it actually increases your singleness of heart. It is not a hindrance, rather a help. It is not a changing of occupations, it is to fulfill your present and lifetime calling and occupation better. This means that you must give your all. You must do the work and responsibility which the Lord has given you, and you must try everything which will enable you to fulfill your calling. It is right and proper for an apostle to travel on this path that we have described

Scope of Co-workers More Inclusive Than That of Apostles

With regard to co-workers, that really includes much more than the apostles. As an example from the Bible, we have Aquila and Priscilla who were co-workers. Phoebe too was a fellow worker. All the elders and deacons of the various assemblies are fellow workers.

Let All Vocations Be Avocations

We would ask all the brothers and sisters engaged in the Work to change their vocations into avocations. It would be very good if while serving God in a certain locality you forsake your profession because you have enough means to support yourself. Or if you are serving God by either bearing local responsibility or engaging in the ministry of God's word, and you work at some job in order to supply yourself and also others, that would likewise be good. Let us see that no brother or sister lives for himself or herself. Such being the case, this matter of vocation can easily be solved. With your ministry solved, your occupation will also be solved. Without having your ministry settled, your profession is really useless before God.

Purpose Is to Serve

One day a brother asked me if it was good to carry on an extra job. On that day I replied that it was good. But the question really revolves around what your principal work is. We all must have some sort of idea or desire before God: "Wherefore also," said Paul, "we are ambitious, whether at home or absent, to be well-pleasing unto him" (2 Cor. 5.9 mg.). Hence the first question we have to answer is, Why am I engaged in business today? Is it for earning money? For getting rich? Some people want to get rich simply to be rich, and not for earning money. Our aim before God should not be to get rich but to earn money to support the Lord's Work. We therefore need to have this foundation firmly established in our hearts. We must make a decision within ourselves as to what we really want before the Lord. Paul wanted to please Him; how about you? I have only one aim before the Lord, and that is, I want to serve Him, and I want to do His Work well.

Profession Is a Small Thing

In these days as all the brothers and sisters move forward to have this matter solved of wanting to give all to serve the Lord, I can tell you that the question of profession becomes a very small matter indeed. If your heart before the Lord is weak and your service to God is weak, you cannot bear the pressure of a job because it will soon swallow you up. But if your service before the Lord is strong, you can take up an avocation and your way will remain straight before God. Some brothers may wish to go back into practicing medicine or to undertake some other trade, but these things must be as it were a sideline affair. They are done only to maintain one's living. And if what brethren engage in on the side remains small, then it will not cause any problem to their ministry because their heart will not be in that undertaking.

Suppose a brother decides to return to manufacturing lace or embroidery in order that he may use the money he receives from its sale to maintain his ministry before God. His ministry before God is so weighty and earnest that all the other things he does are but sideline activities to help support that ministry. And suppose further that there is another brother who also produces lace or embroidery for sale, but his heart is set on getting rich. In comparing himself to the first brother this brother thinks that since both of them are doing the same thing, then the first brother must without any doubt be aiming at getting rich just as he himself is. There is therefore no difference between them in the thinking of this second brother. Yet his way is not right before God, and his ministry will be bound. His aim is simply one of getting rich, whereas the other brother's aim is not. Outwardly they may appear to be the same, but only that which serves God—and not mammon—is the right way.

Whatever We Do Is to Serve God

If we want to serve, then everything we do must be done for His service. We must give our all. We need to realize that not only *not* making tents is for the sake of being an apostle, even *making* tents can be for that purpose. I therefore hope all who are working as apostles will not upset the priority, and that all who serve God locally will not miss the point. Serving God is our vocation, our basic occupation. Whatever we do is for the purpose of serving Him. Earning money is for the purpose of serving God, and likewise *not* earning money. Devoting all our time is for that purpose, and devoting part of our time can be also. Whichever way we take, we serve God. Even our very life is all given to him. This is how the problem of occupation is to be solved.

All Whose Everything Is for the Lord Are Co-Workers

All whose everything is for the Lord are our co-workers, for our principal vocation is the same. All the brothers and sisters in the Work are to serve the Lord. We can therefore say that all are our co-workers, even as Paul writing in Romans 16 said that all those whom he mentioned there were fellow workers. All who serve the Lord become our co-workers. When we really see this, then our concept of co-worker will be different from how we thought before. Many may put in twenty hours a day, but they are not our co-workers. Some may work only two hours in the evening per day, and yet we can say that they are truly our co-workers.

Let us see that the matter of co-worker is neither dependent on profession nor on finance. It depends on how big a place God's Work is in your life. A person may wash clothes or sweep floors, and he is our co-worker. Another person may weave cloth or mend clothes, and he is also our co-worker. It does not depend on what he does. One brother may work on the train, another may work in a steamer. One may labor on land, another on the sea. Yet they all can be our co-workers. As long as we serve God, our basic aim is the same. For the sake of letting God have His way in China, we must put everything into it—our time, our money, our very life. We all are therefore co-workers. We work with one another: we work with a Peter, and we also work with a Paul. We are fellow workers of all who now serve God and of all who have served Him throughout these many centuries.

Not Same Work, but Same Aim

There is an erroneous view abroad which causes people to look always at the sameness of work but neglect the sameness of aim. They tend to lay stress on how people do the same thing rather than on discovering how strong the aim is. Doing the same thing does not constitute a co-working relationship. There may be fifty physicians working in the same clinic, yet they may not be considered co-workers. Their work is the same, but they are not strictly co-workers. Only one thing determines the status of co-workers one to another, which is that we live here for the Lord, we live here for the gospel, and all our income is for the gospel.

Let me illustrate this point further as follows: Being a physician is a noble profession; and yet a washerwoman can be a co-worker to the physician. A young man who is highly educated and trained and another young man who is illiterate can likewise be fellow workers. And yet, it is also possible that another Christian who has received a similar education to that of the first young man may not at all be qualified to be a co-worker.

The principal and basic issue here is, Do you give your all? If people are really violent for the Lord, giving their everything to Him and caring nothing for the world, if they live on earth wholly for the Lord under any circumstance, then they will do everything to serve God. Notwithstanding where they are and what they do, you recognize that they truly are the light of the world.

Serve God Anyway

We do not have many co-workers, and we have never had many co-workers. May God in these last days do the work of recovery. May He raise up many people who can serve Him in any circumstance, whatever may come. I love those two hands of Paul. Ordinarily, many things are not necessary. According to rule, the church ought to be responsible for the necessities of the apostles as well as for the needs of the Work. But the church is not being responsible. The church has failed in her responsibility. The church takes care of her own needs only. When the church forgets to support and begins to criticize Paul, Paul can assert. Behold, these two hands! I trust we have now seen through all this, how Paul's ministry not only did not decrease but was actually strengthened and more firmly established. His apostolic ministry depended on his two hands. In other words, those two hands—which ought never to have had to work for a living if the church had been normal—those two hands were willing to work. As long as there is any possibility of serving, let us serve this way too!

Who are co-workers? Co-workers are people who have one mind, one purpose, one ambition before God: they will serve the Lord alone and do everything to please Him. Notwithstanding what their hands may perhaps do, if the aim is the same, these people are co-workers in the Lord.

12 The Matter of Finance

We will now deal with the matter of finance. How are the finances arranged? On the one hand, how is the income the church receives to be distributed? And on the other hand, what should be the financial relationship among the fellow workers?

ONE: DISTRIBUTION OF FUNDS BY LOCAL ASSEMBLY

(1) Current Expenses

The money a local assembly receives is first of all to cover current expenses. A local assembly should not be in debt. It incurs a good deal of expenses, such as the purchasing of bread and wine for the Lord's Supper, payments for electricity, water, and sometimes rent, and so forth.

(2) Care for the Poor

God wants His people in the church to look after the poor, especially the poor among the saints. Hence a primary responsibility of the local assembly will be to take care of the poor brothers and sisters.

However, in caring for the poor brothers and sisters, extreme caution must be exercised. Under no circumstances are they to be treated ungraciously because they *are* poor. Do not create a sense of shame on their part when they receive help from the church. In just the same humble attitude of spirit that you send money to your elderly parents for their use, so let the church give alms to its poor. Just as you never allow your parents to feel you are pitying them, so those who from the church bring relief to the poor must likewise be very sensitive. Do not let those who are dull of spirit be the bearers of the gifts, for why must these brothers and sisters who must receive financial help be hurt?

Suppose, for instance, that a brother falls and is injured. As we put him in bed, we cannot let people rough in hands and dull in minds do the job. His bones may not yet be broken, but rough handling could very well break them! I often feel that many brothers who take care of church funds are much too insensitive. When a brother or sister is in need, and you are helping him or her, you must be very careful; if not, something adverse may happen. Be very delicate in your handling of the situation. Do not create the feeling that everybody is helping him or her. When a brother or sister is in distress, you must help that one to maintain his or her self-respect, for you do not know when you yourself will fall into the same situation. Let us not hurt one another in this regard.

(3) Care for Needs of Responsible Brothers

If a local responsible brother has to spend so much of his time in managing the church affairs that his own profession suffers, the local assembly should replenish him with extreme care. This is what is meant by the phrase in 1 Timothy, "worthy of double honor" (5.17). It cannot be that the church only provides money to workers but not to responsible brothers as well. It is not right to let the local responsible brothers suffer financial loss because they have to spend more of their time in the church. A local assembly should learn to take care of the needs of its elders.

(4) Send to Other Local Assemblies

A local assembly can also extend funds to other local assemblies for their use. At times an unusual instance of financial need or hardship may arise, such as occurred when Antioch felt a burden to send relief funds to the brethren at Jerusalem who were in distress because of famine. It is important to have such fellowship in this matter of finance among the local assemblies. You will recall how at the beginning, many brothers and sisters in Jerusalem had sold their houses and fields. But during the time of famine, Antioch now sent relief to them by the hands of Barnabas and Paul. I love the fact that the elders at Antioch did not ask if the assembly at Jerusalem had already spent the vast amount of money it had received at the beginning or whether there was still some of it left over. That was surely none of their business. No, the saints at Antioch simply sent relief to the saints in Jerusalem to supply the latter's need, just as in an earlier time Barnabas had come from Jerusalem to provide help to Antioch. Now, Barnabas along with Paul were chosen to bear the funds forward. How fitting! And how beautiful to behold!

(5) Gifts to Individual Workers

A local assembly should send gifts to individual workers. This was what the church at Philippi had done towards Paul. After the apostles had labored in Macedonia (including the city of Philippi), he left for Thessalonica; and the church at Philippi thereafter sent gifts to him repeatedly. As we read the letter to the Philippians, we know that while Paul was in Macedonia and Thessalonica, all his supplies came from Philippi; otherwise, he would not have been able to work in those places. Today the brethren in various localities need to learn to send gifts to those who labor for the Lord. The church at Corinth was a backward assembly; their spiritual condition was not good at all before God; for although they knew how to criticize Paul they did not support him in anything in this matter of supply. Let local assemblies be aware of the needs of those who serve the Lord and send gifts to them.

(6) Gifts to Regional Work

There is another need. If our interpretation is correct, a local assembly not only can send gifts to individual workers but also to a regional Work. Paul advised the Corinthian believers to have their money ready to be sent to Jerusalem. At that time, the churches in Macedonia had already collected money to be sent to Jerusalem. Macedonia was a province in which there were a number of local assemblies. Paul exhorted the church at Corinth to do what the churches in Macedonia had done. For there was now famine not only in Jerusalem but also in the whole of Judea. So that when the relief was sent, it was not just earmarked for the local assembly there, it was also to be used to support the regional Work then occurring in the region of Judea as represented by the Work center—Jerusalem. In other words, the funds were sent to Jerusalem that from there relief could be sent out to all Judea. Hence we have a principle here: money can be sent to a local assembly for its own use, but it can also be sent to a local assembly for that church to distribute it to the brothers and sisters throughout the entire pertinent region.

I trust you are now clear as to what a local assembly should do with its money. The contributions it receives are to be used for local current expenses, for taking care of the poor among the saints, for caring for the responsible brothers, for the workers abroad, for the needs of the assemblies abroad, and for regional Work.

TWO: RELATIONSHIP AMONG CO-WORKERS

Leaders Should Care for Co-Workers

I want to mention here that besides the local assembly having responsibility in this matter of finance, people like Paul have also a responsibility. Timothy, Titus, Silas, and Luke were known by the Church in the latter days. But at the beginning of their ministry they were not known. Consequently, all who are like Paul must learn this principle: "These hands ministered unto my necessities and to them that were with me" (Acts 20.34). No brother can be a leader in the Work and be extremely tight on money. I have known two or three brothers in China who at the start of their ministry were probably quite useful in God's hand, yet they could not be leaders among the brethren because of this issue of finance. They could live by faith but they could not give by faith. Hence they were not able to lead other servants of the Lord on. I have also known a sister in the past who really knew God, was godly, and capable of helping people, yet she did not have the faith to supply others. All who are well known by the churches must learn to be like Paul, who cared for those whose names were little known. Be mindful of the fact that your income is not for your own self, it is for both you *and* your fellow workers. If you keep all your income for yourself, at a certain point it will become manifest that you are not fit to lead your fellow workers.

Leaders among co-workers who are recognized everywhere must cultivate the habit of giving—especially giving to fellow workers. Those of you who fall into this category need to see that what the Lord has given you is for others' use as well as your own. If you hold the money tightly in your hand, sooner or later you will be taken away from the Work. If you are foolish, you may think you are serving the church by spending on yourself alone what God has given you, yet without realizing that only by giving to others as well can you *really* say that you are serving the church. Hence I hope all may do as Paul did, and learn to give to their co-workers so that they too may live. Older brothers in every place should use what they have received to care for their fellow workers. They should not only remember their own needs, they must also remember the needs of their co-workers.

Distribute According to Each Need

How should the leader distribute funds to his fellow workers? Let us suppose you have ten co-workers. How will you give to them? I believe the Biblical principle is to give according to each one's need and not according to each one's spiritual gift. Oftentimes brethren in the church will give only according to the spiritual gift of a brother in the Work. Yet to those who are useful in the Work, you must give not according to their spiritual gift but according to their personal needs. Some co-brethren in the Work may in fact act wrongly, but you cannot afford to do wrong towards them in the matter of finance, for you are a leading brother in the Work. You ought to know better.

For this reason, in ordinary times, the brother who is responsible for the Work should prepare a list of all the brethren who are involved in the regional Work. I do not mean to say that you should have a formal document. All I mean is that you simply need to know. You need to have their names and the number of children, if any, they have; for the need of a single person will be very different from the need of a family with children. Further, you should note how many of these children are of school age. You ought to know which brothers have little family responsibility and which brothers have more such responsibility. By having such information at hand, you will know how to distribute according to their respective needs whenever such funds come your way.

All Must Look to God, None Can Take Full Responsibility

In case the Lord does not bring in funds, all must continue to look to God for meeting their own needs. No one can take on the full responsibility, nor can anyone take on complete responsibility for other people. Only when there are funds can they be distributed—and then, not according to ministry but according to need. By doing so, there will be equity. A leader cannot assure any co-worker by means of any formal commitment. All the co-workers must learn to look to the Lord. I hope we may all do well in this matter of finance so that God will be glorified.

QUESTIONS

(1) How to Distribute in Practice

Question: In a local assembly where there is a Work center, how should funds be distributed? There are both workers and elders, and therefore some elders should be included in the distribution. How in practice is this to be done?

Answer: This is why there needs to be some arrangement. Though there is to be nothing formal, it requires a definite disposition nonetheless. In case of extra need, each must look directly to God.

In distributing funds, a local assembly must first of all take care of its current expenses. In a certain assembly, for example, the monthly income is a thousand dollars. Its first responsibility is to cover current bills and to take care of the poor among them. The need of the elders may often be included in the needs of the co-workers. According to principle, the church should send out whatever is left over.

A local assembly keeping its funds within itself will soon cause some unpleasant things to appear. If, for example, Rome is the place where money is, all the apostles will go to Rome. No Roman apostle will go to the place where there is no money. And in England, if ever a pastor feels called to go to a place, he will more than likely say "I am called to Rome" (where, coincidentally, there is money). How strange that many are called to places where money is plentiful, but no one is called to a poor place! I must say that the world has invaded the Church. It is something very ugly and totally unspiritual. The worldly concept of money has encroached on the Church.

I have meditated much before God on this entire matter. I look at Paul (and Barnabas for that matter) and see that at the beginning of his time in Antioch he on the one hand was one of the messengers who carried money to Jerusalem, but that on the other hand he never once mentioned the need of Antioch nor of the need for the Work at Antioch. He simply delivered the financial relief to Jerusalem. Later both Achaia (including Corinth) and Macedonia—with Paul's encouragement—all sent contributions to Jerusalem and its region. There might have arisen at that time a serious misunderstanding to the effect that Paul probably had no need of support since evidently his tentmaking company was apparently very prosperous. Hence I think the best way is for a local assembly that is also a Work center to send extra funds abroad instead of expending all such funds on only the co-workers in the local region who will doubtless also receive gifts from other assemblies that are elsewhere. This will thus place the church there on spiritual ground.

Let the brethren in one region think of the Work in other regions. How commendable was the way Paul did it. He came out of Antioch to deliver relief to Jerusalem. He exhorted the saints in the regions of Macedonia and Achaia to send help to

Jerusalem. Without drawing their attention to himself and his co-workers' needs he made these people feel that there was great need in Jerusalem and its surrounding environs; but those same people thought that he himself had no need at all, when actually his hands never ceased working when it was required. For listen again to what he said to the Ephesian elders at Miletus: "Behold, these hands!" It is common for a man to think of his own needs first. But not Paul. I hope you will learn to take care of the needs in other places first and let God take care of your own needs. As to individual need, God will lead the brethren to care for you. For we believe in the control of the Holy Spirit, and therefore we do not need to be anxious about ourselves. If, for example, I have a special need today, I look to God for a special miracle: suddenly some brother sends me a gift, and my problem is solved. God is in truth a *living* God.

On the other hand, we should not stick to a dead method. I am fearful of having a formal way. I believe the brethren who have been with us for these years know how much we are afraid of anything formal or fixed. Because the moment something becomes fixed, it immediately becomes unspiritual. Yet I hope you can still maintain this principle about caring for others' needs. If as the funds arrive in a certain region, you decide to retain at most only a part of it—say, perhaps one third or one fifth—and send the larger portion to other places, I think that would be excellent. By so doing, God can easily maintain the supplies in His Church.

Recall again how when the children of Israel failed to give, the Levites suffered hunger. The problem the Levites encountered was solely created by the unfaithfulness of the children of Israel. They would have had no hardship had the Israelites stood on the Lord's side (see Neh. 13.10). We must therefore learn to send funds abroad that we may help to take care of the Work elsewhere. And on our side, we will naturally trust God to maintain His Work in our own region. And the benefit to be derived by generally following such a principle will be that those places which have much will not have too much and those places which have little will not be lacking.

With respect to the need of the local responsible brothers and not just the need of co-workers, you ought to have some appropriate arrangement. It will avoid a great inconvenience and embarrassment if a percentage were agreed upon for the need of each. Otherwise, how will you feel in distributing the money yourself? For in being a responsible brother, it will be highly inconvenient for you to take any funds for yourself. Your Christian sensitivity will not allow you to do this. Consequently, you who are responsible brothers must devise suitable arrangements to save one another from any such embarrassment.

Two Persons in Charge of Money

One other thing needs to be considered. I think it is best to have two persons in charge of money in a region. The principle of the Bible is always "two." Barnabas and Paul were sent by the church at Antioch to Jerusalem to deliver the relief. And later on, we find that there was always at least two in every other such situation.

(2) Accounts Must Be Open

Question: Some local assemblies give a public report on church accounts, some do not. What is the principle which should govern this?

Answer: I think the accounts of a local assembly should be made public. As to the Work, the co-workers in a region should know the income and expenditure of the Work accounts.

(3) Current Expenditure First, Apostles Next

Question: Is it necessary to have separate slots in the offering box for local use and for the Work since many believers do not know how to give?

Answer: Even if the givers do not distinguish their gifts, you should divide them. In a local assembly, the first item to take care of is current expenses such as electricity, water, rent, and so forth; the second item is the poor among the saints; and the responsible brothers and workers must be listed as the third item. This is a basic principle. The church at Jerusalem gave first to the poor among the saints, not first to the co-workers. Do not make the mistake of putting the apostles first. It should be the poor among the saints first, the widows first, the orphans first. These people need to be helped first, and then the apostles. And it is obvious in the case of Jerusalem that distribution was done according to each one's need.

It is also in accordance with spiritual principle for the local church to always send money out, but let money be sent in as well. The local assembly may retain a third, a fifth, a tenth, or whatever. But the less you keep the better, and then send the rest to other places.

When money is available, distribute it according to need—according to the agreed upon percentage. If there are special personal needs, you must look to God in a special way. This matter of money is a very difficult task. Nevertheless, I believe you will be close to scriptural teaching if you follow the principles we have just enunciated.

(4) Concerning Distribution of Personal Trusts

Question: Someone entrusts me as a worker with funds to distribute. What should I do?

Answer: If there is not a list giving distribution by percentage, I will not take anything for myself if I myself am entrusted with the distribution. For if I take anything from the fund for myself, I will not appear to be faithful. No matter how clean one's conscience is, he will not feel peaceful. Conscience will never yield to reasoning. If I am to distribute the funds and I take but one dollar of it, my conscience will not be at peace. If, however, money is definitely designated for *me*, I can use it as I wish. But if it is for me to distribute, I will distribute all of it to *other* people—with none kept back for myself. And in case there is already a percentage list worked out in the region, I can distribute the funds accordingly without my having any misgiving. In short, *without* such a list, every penny goes out to others; *with* such a list, oneself may be included with a clear conscience.

(5) Sending Circular Letter about Building Meeting Place

Question: Formerly, several localities sent out circular letters to notify others of their intention to build a meeting place. Is this a good practice?

Answer: It is not a very good one. It is all right for individuals to pass on such news because this will be less formal. I am afraid of formalizing such information.

(6) Regarding Double Honor towards Responsible Brothers

Question: We know it is right for the responsible brothers to receive double honor. But it is difficult to make this known. Would it be advisable for an apostle to mention this matter when he visits various localities?

Answer: This arrangement is applicable only to a Work center, not to a local assembly where there is no such center.

Timothy Should Speak

Concerning the distribution of funds in a local assembly, in his letter to Timothy Paul explicitly charged the latter to pass on his instructions to various local assemblies. As a worker visits different localities, he should gather the saints in each place and instruct them to give double honor to the elders. This was to be Timothy's responsibility; it was not to be the responsibility of the elders. For Paul charged Timothy, saying: "Let the elders that rule well be counted worthy of double honor" (1 Tim. 5.17). When workers like a Timothy go to local assemblies and discover that some elders spend so much of their time in the church that their personal income suffers, they should instruct the local brethren to show double honor to these elders in the matter of finance.

(7) Deacons Should Bear More Responsibility

Question: Why, in your priority as to the distribution of church funds, are the elders mentioned as the third item?

Answer: Without a doubt, the distribution of church funds according to Scripture was in the hands of the elders. But the actual *use* of church funds was not in the hands of the elders but in the hands of the deacons. In other words, the use of church funds in the Jerusalem assembly was not in the hands of the twelve apostles but in the hands of the seven deacons. For in due time, we know, the apostles would no longer be serving the tables, which meant that they themselves would not be using the money for that purpose any more. The principle of distribution—that is to say, how the funds are going to be distributed—was probably still left in the hands of the apostles. Yet the actual *use* of it was indeed in the hands of the deacons. Therefore, it is true that in the practical arrangement of distribution, the deacons and not the elders will know the needs of the poor among the saints as well as the needs of current expenditures. In other words, *using* the money will be the work of the deacons and not the work of the elders. The deacons will take care of local expenses and relief to the poor.

And hence, in this matter of supply of finance to the elders, the deacons should bear even more responsibility. (This is just my personal opinion.) For it is embarrassing for the elders to decide on such a matter themselves. It is well for the church to take good care of the responsible brothers. The church needs to know its responsibility.

Here the flesh must be cast aside. When the brothers and sisters give, no personal relationship should exist. When the funds are managed, only the command of God counts. There ought not to be any personal feeling whatsoever. As the money is given to God, it must be distributed according to God's way. The first consideration, therefore, is to "owe no man anything" (Rom. 13.8), and hence all current expenses must be paid. Second, the poor among the saints must be taken care of next. And third, the needs of the responsible brothers must also be met.

The responsible brothers cannot take anything themselves; accordingly, the deacons should say, Let us give them double honor. For remember that the deacons represent the church in serving, and giving honor is not something which one does to oneself; it is given to him only by others. The deacons can therefore represent the church in this matter of showing honor. They cannot make any decision on *other* items, but in *this* regard they may.

I think this matter should be in the hands of the deacons. If the whole church must assemble to decide on this issue, it will become Laodicean in character. Consequently, it is best to entrust this matter to the deacons.

In our past history, church money was in the hands of the elders. Now, though, it should be transferred into the hands of the deacons. The elders make the decisions on the distribution of funds, but the deacons undertake the actual distribution. In other words, the deacons should be the treasurers

Let Us Talk

(1) CONCERNING ELDERS HAVING CHILDREN WHO BELIEVE

Question: The Bible mentions elders as having children who believe (Titus 1.6). Today there are several elders in the church whose children have not yet believed in the Lord. The children are young, in their early teens. They have been coming to hear the gospel, but they are not yet clearly saved. What should be done in such a situation?

Answer: I think this matter of believing children is to be stressed especially in connection with the phrase, "ruleth well his own house" (1 Tim. 3.4). If the children are small, this should not be a problem. But if the children are so disobedient, even to the extent of being defiant towards faith, then this is a sure indication that the brother is not fit to rule the church. He may be able to be an apostle, but he is not able to be an elder. When the children are young, and are not rebellious or opposing the faith but still come to hear God's word, this should not pose a problem with respect to the question asked. Naturally, when they are so young, it is difficult to tell if they have truly believed or not. As they grow older, however, they should receive the Lord as their Savior. Hence I think the emphasis here should be more on "ruling his own home well" rather than on Titus 1.6.

(2) AS ASSEMBLY GROWS AND ORIGINAL ELDERS ARE UNABLE TO BEAR RESPONSIBILITY: WHAT TO BE DONE

Question: In the past, when an assembly began, some brothers seemed to be able to take responsibility. But later on as more were added to the local church, the spiritual condition of these brothers became such that they did not appear to be able to take responsibility as before. What should be done in this kind of situation?

Answer: Judging from the arrangement which God makes in the church, I believe that as better men are raised up in the local assembly, we must learn to let them take responsibility and allow ourselves to step back into the position of listening.

Paul wrote this: "We have no such custom, neither the churches of God" (1 Cor. 11.16). Now we do not wish to keep man's tradition, yet we would like to follow godly custom. A godly thing done in one assembly may quite naturally be taken up by other assemblies. And if so, it will be very beautiful. In the early days of any assembly being developed, you might become responsible. Later, however, when other brothers come in, it would be well for you to learn to prefer the others who may be more mature: "Brothers, why not come and take responsibility? I am willing to be one who listens." Such a stance would not at all be passive. Yes, some people do stop doing everything when they cease bearing responsibility. But you should be able to add: "I will be glad to help. But you take the responsibility, because you are ahead of me." If various assemblies end up practicing this in the same way, you may think that a custom has developed in the Church. Well, if it is a godly practice, why not? When younger brothers encounter more mature brothers coming in or developing in a local assembly, they should be able to invite the latter into responsibility. God's children ought to learn to recognize higher authority as soon as they touch it.

When a few brothers are together talking, naturally there will be one taking the lead and the others following. For in everything, whether large or small, God establishes an order. This is especially true in the local church. If some brother is taking responsibility and another brother comes in, the first one ought naturally to know who is ahead of him. It will be disastrous if you do not recognize authority. You should introduce the latecomer to the brethren, and you yourself should gradually stand aside. If such a custom is practiced in the local assemblies, how gracious that will appear. For that is the church of God. Hence he who has the authority of God should obviously stand at the front.

Question: Suppose a brother does not recognize more spiritual maturity in another, then what?

Answer: I think sometimes the brother who works in the region should take a little more responsibility. In objectively judging a local situation, he is more likely to be in a position to see who should be responsible and who should not. It is evident in 3 John that there was a man who held a different view than John. John saw one way, and this man saw another: "Diotrephes, who loveth to have the preeminence among them, receiveth us not" (3 John 9). The saints there were not clear about Diotrephes, for they thought he really had the authority. Actually, he loved to have the first place. He himself did not receive the brethren, and he forbade others to receive them. So John wrote: "If I come, I will bring to remembrance his works which he doeth" (v.10a). From this we can infer that, according to custom, whether or not a person can bear responsibility in a local assembly should be the responsibility of the trustworthy worker of the Lord.

(3) PETER AND PHILIP MOVING INDEPENDENTLY?

Question: Philip went to Samaria alone and Peter went to Caesarea alone. Would they be considered as having made independent moves?

Answer: I think we need to be careful about this term "independent move." A brother may stay with several other brothers continuously and yet he can be guilty of taking independent moves. Not making an independent move does not necessarily mean you must eat with somebody else or travel with someone else. If a person has never seen the body of Christ, he will still be moving independently in any case. Even though he may move together with other people, such a person *will* be moving alone because he has neither learned how to submit to authority nor how to fellowship. Hence Philip may go out by himself, yet he was not reckoned as having made an independent move; whereas many others may indeed go out with other brethren, but they will be viewed as being highly independent.

Independent moves are to be judged by two basic principles: first, is the person under authority? Second, is he in fellowship? If he is neither under authority nor in fellowship, he may be with fifty people, yet he will be moving independently.

Touching Authority

Concerning this subject of authority, it is a most amazing thing in the Church that when a few workers of God or a few believers are together, they will just naturally touch authority. God always does things in order. Even with two persons, God sets up one to represent authority.

Name Order

You will notice that the names listed in the Bible always

follow an order. And whenever the order is later changed, there will be a special reason for it. In the Old Testament period, for instance, God had obviously set up Moses as an authority. And so, the Bible always mentioned Moses and Aaron in that order. You will not see the order reversed to read Aaron and Moses. When they were together, one represented authority while the other represented submission. Even when the Lord sent out his disciples or apostles two by two, all the people mentioned by name followed an order, one being ahead of the other. If this be true with two persons, how much more true it will be with a greater number of people.

Trusting in the Presence of the Holy Spirit

Whenever God's children are together, there will be a lining up. Not a lining up according to the flesh but a lining up because you see the brother before you. Whenever the Lord is working, there is a mouthpiece. Accordingly, let us believe in God's presence. Let us declare: "I believe in the presence of the Lord, I trust in the presence of the Holy Spirit." With the presence of God's Spirit, the next step will naturally follow by our acknowledging: "I believe the Lord has a mouthpiece here."

Not Submitting to a Perfect Man

Do you realize why the authority of God cannot be established among His children? It is because the children of God are always criticizing and demanding perfection: "I only admire a person who is a perfect man! And since this man has never existed before, is not in view now, and will never come to be in the future, I will not submit. I want to submit to a perfect man; and since this man is not present, I cannot submit." But God does not give authority to a perfect man; He only gives authority to that person who goes forward, to that one who goes ahead of you. This is a basic principle to be found in the Bible. God gives authority to the brother who is ahead of another.

Hence it is quite natural for God's children to line up in such fashion when they are together. This is not a matter of organization. This is not done by electing a captain. This is something natural. Let us therefore learn to be submissive. Whereve we are, in whatever circumstances, we have our submission.

As long as a person stands on such a ground as this, he will not commit any independent moves. But for that one who is not subject to authority, he will act independently even if he should be with *many* people. What is individualism? It means that a person cannot submit to authority. For once anyone submits to authority, his individualism vanishes.

Choose Not to Whom to Submit

I hope the brethren will see this to be not a matter of accepting one or more authorities; it is simply a problem of accepting authority in the first place.

Let me illustrate this point. I once employed two servants, one *in advance* of the other. On the very first day when they arrived at my house, I told them that they came to be *servants*, and that therefore the one basic condition was for them to listen. No matter how clever they were, they must do what they were told to do. I especially told the latecomer that he must also listen to the first servant. It turned out that this latecomer was really good in listening to *me*, but he would not listen to the *first* servant. Do you think this servant was being obedient to authority? I do not think so, for he always sought opportunity to accuse the first one of being wrong.

What is obeying authority? Let me say that it is certainly not in choosing whom to obey. If you choose whom you will obey, you do not know what authority is. The one who knows authority will recognize it wherever he goes. As soon as he meets authority, he knows to whom to submit. And if he cannot submit, it is proof that he never knew authority. He will be obeying man and not obeying authority. At most he is fearful of but one person, whom he will obey when he meets him. Authority is not a matter of location, nor of many locations, for there is authority everywhere. He who knows authority knows it wherever he goes.

When a person is under authority, he can readily see that individualism cannot exist. On the contrary, if he stands on individualism, he has no way to submit to authority. I believe this is a very important principle for us to grasp hold of. For the Christian, it is not a matter of *who*, it is a matter of *where* authority is.

Seek Fellowship

A person who seeks for fellowship will also know that individualism cannot exist. An individualist always maintains his spiritual life before God by himself. He keeps what he personally sees, and he does his individual work. He is always alone. It is hard for him to seek for fellowship. Actually, this is a problem we have in our midst. People cannot seek fellowship. They always do things by themselves. Although in words they may say they cannot do without other brethren and cannot live without the church, in practice, they *can* and *do* live without either the church or fellowship. This proves they are still individualists. If you see someone who has accepted the concept of the fellowship of the body and yet he can still live his spiritual life and carry on his work for the Lord without fellowship, then you will know he has not been broken before God and that he is therefore totally immersed in individualism—for fellowship and individualism are opposites. Today it is not what you may *say* about fellowship but whether or not fellowship is *life* to you, whether or not you can live and live without fellowship. If one day God can bring you to such a place of not being able to live without it, then I feel that this could be a big step.

Not a Failure in Faithfulness and Faith

Many when they come to an impasse think this is due to their failure in faith or in faithfulness. They do not see it is because of their failure in fellowship. For their past education teaches them of faith and faithfulness and of direct obedience to God. So that whenever they cannot get through a crisis, they naturally blame it on their weakness in faith or faithfulness. Now, of course, there is some truth to this. But they fail to see that there is another factor called fellowship in the Bible. And if they fail in fellowship, they can easily find themselves in such predicaments.

The Lord must often let a Christian wander through faith, faithfulness, and obedience until he finds out for himself that however he may believe, be faithful and obedient, he still cannot get through. At that juncture, he may perhaps begin to see that he cannot get through as a single member. Though his union with Christ is basic and elementary, he still needs the union with the body in order to get through. Perhaps at this time he begins to realize his need of help from other Christians. Nevertheless, many Christians have yet to be brought to this road, because they are still traveling on the path of individualism.

Let me tell you, though, that the day God's children are brought to this dead end it will be a great revelation. Prior to that day, even such a big thing like faith does not help. Now faith is *not* a small thing. Let us not despise it in any way. Faithfulness is also a big thing, and so is obedience. But the day will come when these big things which we think we had will fail to get us through. Then our eyes will be opened to see that fellowship too is a mighty big thing. That without fellowship, we cannot get through. Only those people who have walked on this road can forsake the principle of individualism. Merely hearing the teachings on fellowship and on the body of Christ will not deliver anyone from individualism. He may keep right on believing in fellowship and still live quite individualistically.

Peter Sought Fellowship under Authority

I believe when Peter went to Caesarea, he did not act according to the principle of individualism. For when he started out from Joppa, he took some local brothers with him. He was a man who always was under authority and who was seeking fellowship continually. That was why he returned to Jerusalem to report to the brethren there. Although the work was done, he still sought fellowship as usual.

Philip Met the Holy Spirit

When Philip went to Samaria, he was under authority; otherwise the Holy Spirit would not have called him into the desert. Whoever is met by the Holy Spirit is on the road of God's choice because everything in the Church is ordered and governed by the Holy Spirit. Christ is the Head of the Church and the movement of the Head is through the Holy Spirit. We see that the Spirit led Philip to the desert; therefore he was under authority.

Not a Question of Number of People

Hence individualism is not a question which is to be judged by the number of people involved. It is judged by whether or not one is under authority, whether or not one seeks the fellowship of the body. Today some brother may go out with several people each time, but he may still be individualistic. Let us learn to serve God on the ground of the body. We are a total failure if five people are still five persons, or ten still remain ten individuals. That cannot be fellowship. Fellowship has nothing to do with how many are in the room, how many sit by your side, or how many go out with you. Even though the Scriptures do advocate the principle of two by two so that there may be someone to fellowship with when crises arise, nevertheless, we need to understand that it is not because there are many that there is fellowship, or that if there are few, there is no fellowship.

The basic need today is for God's children to know these two principal lessons: they must recognize and submit to authority, and they must treasure the fellowship of the saints. We seek fellowship with the brethren in life so that we may receive strength to go on. And once we learn these two lessons, we shall be delivered from individualism. But without these two lessons, individualism will undoubtedly prevail.

Basic Principle: Two or More

According to the biblical principle, the sending out is usually with two or more people together. Paul in his latter days usually traveled with more than two people. Yet we must grant the occasional exception. If a person lives under authority and is in fellowship, an occasional exception will not hurt the principle.

It is not sufficient, however, merely to have more people. Unless we are one, and though we may go out together, we are still individuals. We need to see that it is the body which goes out, and then there will be no individualism. Otherwise, one person will be one individualism expressed, ten persons will be ten individualisms. The more the people, the more individualists we will simply have. It is either personal individualism or multiple individualism. That is not the body of Christ.

We must learn to know what the body of Christ is. It is a union in life and is to be under authority. This authority will be manifested wherever God's children are together. If each learns to stand in his proper place, then there will be no difficulty. And in such circumstance, there is no place for false humility or self-defense. Everyone learns to accept the opinion of the other people with whom he is associated, and learns to submit to authority. This is the straight path.

(4) APPOINTMENT OF ELDERS AND APPOINTMENT OF APOSTLES AS ELDERS

Question: According to what Paul's First Letter to Timothy says, elders must be appointed by somebody else, such as by a Paul, a Timothy, or a Titus. Did James appoint Peter and John to be elders at Jerusalem? Or in time of need, did they appoint themselves?

Answer: I believe elders need to be appointed. When the workers are at the various localities, they can appoint elders. However, we ought to pay special attention to the words of Paul spoken to the elders from Ephesus. This is different from the church where the Work center is, though the principle remains the same. "The Holy Spirit hath made you overseers, to feed the church of the Lord" (Acts 20.28 mg.). So that whenever the workers appoint elders, they must seek earnestly with prayer until they have the assurance that those whom they appointed are the very same ones established by the Holy Spirit. If not, a serious problem will develop. If the Holy Spirit has set apart one person, but you appoint a different person, the difficulty you give to the church will be enormous!

Let no one appoint elders carelessly. Paul dared to say that "the Holy Spirit has made you elders." He did not say, "I have made you elders." Let us do this with fear and trembling. Realizing what a tremendous responsibility it is, we cannot use our mind and judge people by ourselves. We must consider carefully before God and pray much. We need to find out whom the Holy Spirit has made elders. Otherwise, the appointment is not only useless but sooner or later great difficulty will arise.

The position of Peter and John in Jerusalem is fairly clear. They were apostles, and because elders were to be appointed by apostles, so Peter the apostle appointed Peter the elder, and John the apostle appointed John the elder. Since this responsibility had to be in the hands of the Jerusalem apostles, and since there arose a definite need in the locality, more than likely all among the apostles there felt that these two from among their number—or even more—should also bear local responsibility. And thus these two apostles became elders at Jerusalem. Later on, after James the brother of John was martyred, another James (most likely the half-brother of Jesus) came into the circle of local leadership. And this James probably became the leading brother in the church at Jerusalem.

(5) MAJOR FACTOR IN SENDING IS FELLOWSHIP

Question: When Peter and John went to Samaria, the Bible tells us that the apostles who were in Jerusalem sent them out (Acts 8.14). When Barnabas and Paul went out, the Bible notes that the prophets and teachers in the church at Antioch sent them out (Acts 13.3). Can you explain this in terms of authority?

Answer: In the sending out of workers, there is obviously fellowship involved. One *dare not say* there is authority involved, but at least one can say there is fellowship involved.

*Concerning Peter and John**

There were twelve apostles at Jerusalem. When the news from Samaria came to their attention (Acts 8.14), the apostles

*For concerning Barnabas and Saul, see sub-head below entitled, "Holy Spirit Spoke through Prophets."—*Translator*

realized that the Samaritan believers had not yet received the Holy Spirit. Philip only accomplished a part of the Work. So those in Jerusalem ultimately felt that Peter and John should go to Samaria. It could very well have been that the Twelve, or perhaps even others, were waiting together in prayer, and that Peter and John felt they should go—which feeling the other brothers present confirmed. And then they were sent to Samaria. Can we not see a very beautiful picture here? Although I dare not say the question of authority was totally absent, I nevertheless feel that authority was not very evident, whereas the principle of fellowship must have loomed very large in the situation. It was more a matter of fellowship than of authority.

Paul and Silas

The same was true with Paul and Silas (Acts 17.1-12). When they were at Thessalonica, they encountered danger. The brethren there sent them off to Berea. Most likely when the brethren in Thessalonica met for prayer—in Jason's house or in other houses there—to seek the Lord's mind about the way ahead, they felt Paul and Silas could not stay on if it would only create more trouble. Hence they sent the two off to Berea. Again, the flavor of fellowship, rather than authority, was predominant.

We have mentioned before how Paul often sent Timothy out into the Work. There must have been fellowship more than authority when the way was not too clear. Paul would not say that he sent Timothy out by his own authority; most likely he simply communicated the Lord's heart-desire to Timothy so that the latter might walk better in the will of God. Oftentimes, therefore, it is not preeminently a question of authority but is more than likely a question of fellowship.

In the case of Paul's leaving Thessalonica, perhaps it was the decision of the brethren, perhaps it was Paul's own decision. Whosever decision this might have been, it was in the context of fellowship. The brethren were all together with the two of them, knowing that Paul and Silas were obviously in danger since the Jews wanted to seize them. What then should be done? The brethren felt it was better for them to go forward to another place. So, they went forward to Berea. They as it were left after consultation with the brethren. True, the record says that the brethren sent them to Berea, but it was only after fellowship in the Lord. And what was the result? The result was excellent, in that the Bereans were nobler than the Thessalonicans because they were willing to search the Scriptures daily to see if those things which Paul preached to them were so! And many of them believed (vv.11–12).

I will not dogmatically say here that there was *no* authority involved, yet the principal factor was unquestionably one of fellowship. Furthermore, it could very well be that there *was* actually no authority involved in this case. From this instance, we may conclude that on many occasions when Paul sent people out—and even though he was a senior brother—he nonetheless did it in the context of fellowship. So that in the coordination of God's Work, the two fundamental principles present will be authority and fellowship. And when both principles are at work, one can obtain the highest guidance and witness the most perfect coordination.

Holy Spirit Spoke through Prophets

Question: Concerning the sending forth in Acts 13 ("the Holy Spirit said"), was it a case of fellowship or was it something else?

Answer: At the time of the early apostles, the word of the Holy Spirit probably came forth through the mouth of the prophets. The Holy Spirit would speak through some prophets among them, saying, for example, "Separate out Barnabas and Saul for the Work to which I have called them." And this most likely came not through the mouth of just one person but was confirmed as being of the Holy Spirit through the witness of *two* or *three* persons.

(6) HOLY SPIRIT MENTIONS ONLY TWO CENTERS IN ACTS

Question: Within ten years, there seemed to have already been two beginnings in the book of Acts—that is to say, two Work centers: one in Jerusalem and one in Antioch. Was there any other new start?

Answer: True, the Bible indicates that in one ten-year period there were only two such beginnings with respect to the Work. Please note, however, that Paul's Letter to the Philippians mentions that "most of the brethren in the Lord . . . are more abundantly bold to speak the word of God without fear" (Phil. 1.14). Although admittedly some of them preached Christ out of envy and strife, they were plainly not in Jerusalem nor in Antioch when they all went forth. They were obviously another group, another beginning. We may thus deduce from this that at that time there must have been several new starts taking place.

I believe the record given in Acts was written from the same perspective as was the record in Revelation chapters 2 and 3 of the seven letters sent to the seven local churches. In the province of Asia there were many local assemblies, but only seven were chosen by the Holy Spirit to receive letters. Colosse, for example, was also in Asia even as Ephesus was, yet the latter church was mentioned but the former was left out. Possibly the spiritual condition of the church at Colosse was better than that of Ephesus, since the latter, we are told, had fallen from its first love (Rev. 2.4); and consequently, for the sake of proper instruction, the Lord selected Ephesus. The particular seven churches were so chosen in order that by means of history an appropriate teaching might be given.

I likewise believe that the history recorded in Acts was for the purpose of teaching too. And hence Luke's narrative skipped over many many things. Yet in so doing it does give us a clear understanding as to Peter's relationship with Jerusalem and Paul's relationship with Antioch. There *must* have been many other new starts, there must have been many other new Work centers established. History tells us, for example, that some of the apostles went to Africa. According to Church tradition, Thomas even went to India. So that understandably the gospel was spread all over the world. We cannot say that in the period covered by the book of Acts there were only two centers. We can only say that the Holy Spirit saw fit to mention but two of them to serve His teaching purposes. Similarly, the Holy Spirit caused to be mentioned only Adam, Eve, Abel and Cain. Does this meager record mean to imply that there were only these four persons in the world at that time? Hardly. Let us see that what is useful for teaching has been recorded in the Scriptures, but that what is not useful for teaching has been omitted.

OTHER TITLES AVAILABLE

By Watchman Nee

<u>The Basic Lesson Series</u>
Vol. 1 - A Living Sacrifice
Vol. 2 - The Good Confession
Vol. 3 - Assembling Together
Vol. 4 - Not I, But Christ
Vol. 5 - Do All to the Glory of God
Vol. 6 - Love One Another

Aids to "Revelation"
Amazing Grace
Back to the Cross
A Balanced Christian Life
The Better Covenant
The Body of Christ: A Reality
The Character of God's Workman
Christ the Sum of All Spiritual Things
The Church and the Work – 3 Vols
"Come, Lord Jesus"
The Communion of the Holy Spirit
The Finest of the Wheat – Vol. 1
The Finest of the Wheat – Vol. 2
From Faith to Faith
From Glory to Glory
Full of Grace and Truth – Vol. 1
Full of Grace and Truth – Vol. 2
Gleanings in the Fields of Boaz
The Glory of His Life
God's Plan and the Overcomers
God's Work
Gospel Dialogue
Grace for Grace
Heart to Heart Talks
Interpreting Matthew
Journeying towards the Spiritual
The King and the Kingdom of Heaven
The Latent Power of the Soul
Let Us Pray
The Life That Wins
The Lord My Portion
The Messenger of the Cross
The Ministry of God's Word
My Spiritual Journey
The Mystery of Creation
Powerful According to God
Practical Issues of This Life
The Prayer Ministry of the Church
The Release of the Spirit
Revive Thy Work
The Salvation of the Soul
The Secret of Christian Living
Serve in Spirit
The Spirit of Judgment
The Spirit of the Gospel
The Spirit of Wisdom and Revelation
Spiritual Authority
Spiritual Discernment
Spiritual Exercise
Spiritual Knowledge
The Spiritual Man
Spiritual Reality or Obsession
Take Heed
The Testimony of God
Whom Shall I Send?
The Word of the Cross
Worship God
Ye Search the Scriptures

By Stephen Kaung

Discipled to Christ
In the Footsteps of Christ

<u>The "God Has Spoken" Series</u>
Seeing Christ in the Old Testament, Part One
Seeing Christ in the Old Testament, Part Two
Seeing Christ in the New Testament

God's Purpose for the Family
The Gymnasium of Christ
Shepherding
The Songs of Degrees
The Splendor of His Ways
New Covenant Living & Ministry